AMERICA REFORMED

Progressives and Progressivisms
1890s–1920s

Maureen A. Flanagan
Michigan State University

New York   Oxford
OXFORD UNIVERSITY PRESS
2007

Oxford University Press, Inc., publishes works that further Oxford University's
objective of excellence in research, scholarship, and education.

Oxford   New York
Auckland   Cape Town   Dar es Salaam   Hong Kong   Karachi
Kuala Lumpur   Madrid   Melbourne   Mexico City   Nairobi
New Delhi   Shanghai   Taipei   Toronto

With offices in
Argentina   Austria   Brazil   Chile   Czech Republic   France   Greece
Guatemala   Hungary   Italy   Japan   Poland   Portugal   Singapore
South Korea   Switzerland   Thailand   Turkey   Ukraine   Vietnam

Copyright © 2007 by Oxford University Press, Inc.

Published by Oxford University Press, Inc.
198 Madison Avenue, New York, New York 10016
http://www.oup.com

Oxford is a registered trademark of Oxford University Press

All rights reserved. No part of this publication may be reproduced,
stored in a retrieval system, or transmitted, in any form or by any means,
electronic, mechanical, photocopying, recording, or otherwise,
without the prior permission of Oxford University Press.

Library of Congress Cataloging-in-Publication Data

Flanagan, Maureen A., 1948–
   America reformed : Progressives and progressivisms, 1890s–1920s / Maureen A. Flanagan.
      p. cm.
   Includes bibliographical references and index.
   ISBN 0-19-517219-1 — ISBN 0-19-517220-5 (pbk.)   1. Progressivism (United States politics)—
History.   2. United States—History—1865–1921.   3. United States—Politics and
government—1865–1933.   I. Title.
   E661.F58 2006
   973.8—dc22   2006040048

Printing number: 9 8 7 6 5 4 3 2 1

Printed in the United States of America
on acid-free paper

For my family, Chip, Jonah, Sarah, Eddie, and Madeline June

CONTENTS

PREFACE

━━✦◈✦━━

The Destination Was "Progressive" Society: The Roads and the Travelers Were Diverse

HISTORIANS HAVE WRITTEN extensively trying to identify who were the progressives and what was progressivism. They have argued variously that the progressives were upper class, middle class, working class, or urban ethnic immigrants. They have considered whether women and African Americans were progressives. They have identified progressivism on the national, state, and local—even international—levels. They have asked whether it was democratic or undemocratic; whether it was about social control or social welfare; whether it was reform from the top down or the bottom up. Some historians have even argued that there was no such thing as the progressive era and that the changes that took place in those decades should not be viewed as "progress."

Whether one wishes to see the reform movements that convulsed U.S. society from the 1890s through the 1920s as progress, it is clear that these movements produced fundamental changes to American society that altered both government and citizenship. First, this was a period in which all American institutions—political, economic, social—moved decisively away from the laissez-faire ideal that underlay earlier institutional development. By the 1920s, government on all levels had assumed responsibility for at least minimal regulation of the economy both to foster more secure economic development and to protect the public. The institutions of government thereby accrued more power over daily life than they had previously exercised. Second, the Progressive Era altered the relationship of the citizens to their government and to each other. Progressives fought for and achieved new laws that gave social protections to Americans. Americans in turn began to look to government to protect them from impersonal forces over which they had little control. At stake in all proposed reforms was the definition of American democracy.

Yet, Americans did not agree about the precise ends, means, and reasons for Progressive-Era reforms, nor about the meaning of democracy. The Progressive Era, thus, provoked much public discussion about the country's problems and their solutions and gave rise to myriad new organizations and institutions through which millions of Americans participated in reform movements. For historians, this means that we have mountains of evidence to sift through that in turn challenges how we organize our analysis of the era.

One hundred years beyond the Progressive Era, American voters and politicians are considering whether, or how much, to roll back some of the earlier era's reforms. Deregulation of industries is taking place. Politicians are seeking to devolve powers from the national to state governments. The value and extent of social welfare programs is again open to question. Americans thus once more are confronting the question of what makes a good democratic society. They are similarly again being asked to consider the pressing question of what is this nation's role in, and responsibility toward, the rest of the world. A democratic society demands an electorate informed not just about current events but about its past history. Past history reveals how and why a society developed in specific ways and reached certain points. Examining the full range of progressives and progressivisms as historical phenomena provides the opportunity to understand both what happened in the early twentieth century and what its historical legacy is for the early twenty-first century.

This book is organized around four major ideas of progressivism: social justice, political, economic, and foreign policy, each of which will be explained individually and in relation to each other. At times, these broad categories of progressivism obviously overlapped. Americans who thought of themselves as promoting social justice, for example, were not thereby opposed to political reforms, and vice versa. All social justice progressives, for example, did not agree about the nature and resolution of different issues. Foreign policy developments and international events challenged progressives' ability to develop an approach to those events consistent with their ideas about domestic issues. The social constructions of race, gender, ethnicity, and class sometimes blinded progressives to their own inconsistencies within their reform proposals. But using these categories about how people perceived the nature of society's problems and offering particular types of solutions based on these ideas makes it possible to see the consistencies, contradictions, and differing philosophical positions adopted by a broad range of Americans. In order to focus on progressives and progressivisms in this way, this book does not present its information in a strictly chronological fashion. Rather it moves back and forth across the time period to demonstrate how ideas, issues, events, and people were connected to one another. That said, there is an overarching chronology as the book begins with events in the 1890s and ends with those of the 1920s. Each chapter also includes explanations of specific historical events, many of which will then appear in other chapters to show how progressivism was a fluid, complicated ideal.

Focusing on the ideas behind progressivism also illuminates why and how different groups of Americans agreed or disagreed on progressive reform, what kinds of reforms were actually enacted, as well as why other reform proposals were rejected. Within these themes, the book will often focus on specific individuals or groups throughout. Such individuals and groups have been chosen as representative examples of the various threads of progressivism. They are not intended to be identified as *the* progressives and should not be viewed in that way. Nor should they be seen as defining progressivism; rather they are individuals who often articulated ideas and programs that other Americans could adopt, reject, or refine to meet their own needs and ideas. Jane Addams, for example, appears often in this text. She was indeed a leading figure in the Progressive Era, but she was not *the* female progressive as too many investigators of this era tend to portray. Presidents Theodore Roosevelt and Woodrow Wilson had the power to promote and enact new progressive legislation, but behind them were legions of ordinary people demanding these reforms. One final objective of this book, thus, is to give as many Americans as possible their due recognition for working to reform their society.

Introduction
The "White City" and Dark City of 1893

I would not want to live there for anything. I did not see
anything in Chicago but darkness: smoke, clouds, dirt and
an extraordinary number of sad and grieved persons.
—GIUSEPPE GIACOSA, 1893

THE UNITED STATES marked the 100th anniversary of the signing of the
Declaration of Independence with an exposition in Philadelphia in 1876.
Rather than celebrating the country's democratic political development, the
buildings and displays at this Centennial Exposition all emphasized the nation's economic and cultural progress. The main exhibition building contained
over twenty acres of exhibits of mining and metallurgy, manufactures, education, and science. Next to it, Machinery Hall displayed the centerpiece of technological developments: the massive 1,400 horsepower Corliss Steam Engine
that stood 40 feet tall, weighed over 200 tons, and supplied the power to run 13
acres of machinery in the hall. Agriculture Hall, which resembled a connected
series of rustic barn-shaped buildings, was filled with mounds of the domestic
agricultural products that were feeding the nation. The Art Gallery Building
featured the paintings of the American artist Thomas Eakins. The entire exposition covered 450 acres, lasted for six months, and drew ten million visitors.
This was above all a domestic celebration. The exposition's architecture and
displays were meant to show Americans their country's progress over the past
years and how American ingenuity was driving this progress. The city of
Philadelphia as locale was symbolic. It was the city of the Declaration and the
Liberty Bell after all, and in 1876 it was still the center of much American culture and economic prowess.

For many Americans in 1876, their world seemed a wonderful place. The
country was finally emerging from the shadow of the Civil War. The transcontinental railroad now connected the entire country. The future, it seemed, held
nothing but promise of ongoing progress. Seventeen years later, another

1

world's fair, this one intended to mark the 400th anniversary of Colombus' arrival in North America, opened in Chicago.

The 1893 World's Columbian Exposition celebrated the fulfillment of the promise of 1876. Held on the south side of Chicago, this Fair sprawled across 633 acres of gleaming white buildings that earned it the nickname the "White City." The buildings and outdoor exhibits displayed the latest in technological and cultural wonders. Forty-three steam engines and 127 dynamos powered this Fair, making the Corliss Steam Engine, currently used at George Pullman's railroad car works just south of the Fair, seem a quaint reminder of bygone days. Machinery and Agriculture buildings still held places of honor, but the center of attention now shifted to the enormous Manufactures Building. Here visitors could marvel at a soaring clock tower, an electric elevator, and exhibits of household necessities and luxuries from textiles, to cut glass, to Vaseline, to stoves, and to Tiffany silver. Next to it, the Electricity Building, with its enormous statue of Benjamin Franklin greeting all who entered, prominently displayed the inventions of the current genius of electricity, Thomas Alva Edison, and the telephone lines of Alexander Graham Bell. Over 5,000 arc and 90,000 incandescent lamps bathed the Fair in the glow of electric lighting.[1] For Hilda Satt, recent immigrant to Chicago, the electric lighting was celestial. "As the light was fading in the sky," she wrote, "millions of lights were suddenly flashed on, all at one time . . . this was like getting a sudden vision of Heaven." When told by her father that they had not been lit by matches but turned on through switches, she exclaimed "just like the stars." "The wonders of America," her father replied, "are as wonderful as the stars."[2]

As at Philadelphia, products and cultural artifacts from around the world were represented at Chicago. This was a world's fair, after all. But no visitor to the Fair could miss the clear emphasis on American industrial production and ingenuity. The Transportation Building featured American genius in railroad travel, from a replica of the New York Central Railroad's first train—the DeWitt Clinton engine and cars named for the New York governor—to the newest means of luxury travel—the Pullman sleeping and parlor cars. Everywhere, the names of the American manufacturers, inventors, and patrons were prominently attached to the exhibits: the Westinghouse engines, the Crane elevators, the Edison dynamos, the Bell telephones, the Yerkes telescope (the largest in the world). This emphasis did not go unnoted by "certain foreign critics" who complained that "the exhibits of the United States compare[d] unfavorably with their own."[3]

---

1. William Cronon, *Nature's Metropolis: Chicago and the Great West* (New York: W. W. Norton, 1991), 341–42, and Harold L. Platt, *The Electric City: Energy and the Growth of the Chicago Area, 1880–1930* (Chicago: University of Chicago Press, 1991), 60–62. Other descriptions of the Columbian Exposition are Robert W. Rydell, *All the World's a Fair: Visions of Empire at American International Expositions, 1876-1916* (Chicago: University of Chicago Press, 1987) and Alan Trachtenberg, *The Incorporation of America: Culture and Society in the Gilded Age* (New York: Hill and Wang, 1982).

2. Hilda Satt Polacheck, *I Came a Stranger: The Story of a Hull-House Girl*, Dena J. Polacheck Epstein, ed. (Urbana: University of Illinois Press, 1989), 40.

3. "Manufactures of the United States," *The Book of the Fair* (Chicago: The Bancroft Company, 1893), ch. 8; reproduced at http://columbus.gl.iit.edu.

The very buildings of the 1893 exposition, furthermore, were intended to depict the United States as the newest stage in the progression of western civilization. The architecture deliberately linked United States' culture at the end of the nineteenth century with the glories of the European past. Columns, domes, building façades, sculptures, and fountains all imitated the architectural and sculptural achievements of ancient Greece and Rome and of Renaissance Italy. The Administration Building, for example, which was strategically placed in the center of the other important buildings, was built on three levels. Each level was an elaborate recollection of the past. Level one was decorated with Doric columns. Level two displayed Ionic columns. Level three topped the building with an enormous dome resembling Brunelleschi's soaring dome over the cathedral of Santa Maria del Fiore in Florence, Italy. Visitors entering the main portal of the Manufactures Building, for another example, passed through a Roman-like triumphal arch, whereas those arriving at the Fair from Lake Michigan docked before a renaissance arcade in the middle of which stood an arch recalling the Arc de Triomphe in Paris.

Yet, the true message of the Fair was that the future of civilization lay not in the architecture of the past, which had been produced by the oligarchies and monarchies of Europe, but in capitalist production. It was to be a future, in the words of one historian, of endless progress driven by "a corporate alliance of business, culture, and the state." The Administration Building explicitly connected the past and present in this regard also. Its main entryway was flanked with two renaissance-style sculptures of water. One side showed water untamed wreaking destruction on the world. The other showed water tamed, thus signifying the triumph of business and technology over nature. The renowned contemporary skeptic of capitalism, Henry Adams, declared the Fair "the first expression of American thought as a unity" that cancelled all other ideas about progress. Other visitors could not help but agree. An awestruck Scottish writer recalled the Fair as an "ethereal emanation of pure and uneconomic beauty." For an Indian visitor, it "exercise[d] over the mind such a charm, that its defects, like the dark spots of the sun, are invisible to the naked eye, owing to the great halo of lustre that pervades throughout."[4]

To ensure that no one failed to make the appropriate connections that the United States meant progress, the 1893 Fair included a mile-long midway with exhibits from cultures around the world that looked either quaint or primitive by comparison. Here, the emphasis was on people as spectacle and handcrafts as the old means of production. There were the Turkish Bazaar with handmade rugs and the Cairo street scene with camel drivers, donkey boys, and dancing girls; the Bedouin woman, the men from Dahomey, and the Hindu juggler; the "cottage industries" of Ireland where young girls made lace or milked cows; Javanese basket weavers; and Bavarian "beer maids." In retrospect, the arrogance and smug sense of superiority that underlay these

---

4. Trachtenberg, *Incorporation of America*, 217 and 220; for visitors' recollections, see Paul M. Angle, ed., *Prairie State: Impressions of Illinois, 1673–1967* (Chicago: University of Chicago Press, 1968) and Bessie L. Pierce, *As Others See Chicago: Impressions of Visitors, 1673–1933* (Chicago: University of Chicago Press, 1933).

exhibits is obvious. In fairness, however, they were also an effort to break down the isolation of Americans, who, aside from recent immigrants, knew relatively little about the rest of the world. Yet, even on the midway American production and technology loomed over all, dramatically in the case of the Ferris Wheel, again named after its American inventor, George Ferris, and situated at the midway's center. The wheel was dubbed the "mechanical wonder of the Fair, one that is to the Columbian Exposition what the Eiffel [T]ower, yet standing in the Champs de Mars, was to the Paris Exposition of 1889."[5] Its axle alone weighed 70 tons, the "largest piece of steel ever forged." Ferris' wheel transported riders 250 feet above the ground from where they had a panoramic view of the entire Fair.

Holding the 1893 Columbian Exposition in Chicago also symbolized the geographical and demographic shifts that had taken place in the United States since 1876. The East Coast was no longer the heart of the country. It was at the Columbian Exposition that the historian Frederick Jackson Turner declared that the frontier, the original site of democratic "opportunity," was closed. Settlement of the continuous territory of the United States by Europeans and their descendants was finished. The future of the country would henceforth be determined by its cities. Progress would be measured now in industrial production, rather than land settlement, and the locale of such production was the cities of the country's new heartland. Chicago was the biggest and the boldest of these cities. Here the sprawling Union Stockyards and the Armour and Swift meat packing plants employed 25,000 men, women, and children. By 1890 the McCormick works were churning out 150,000 of the latest products in agricultural machinery. By 1891, the mills of the Illinois Steel Company, which were strung out along the shore of Lake Michigan, had the largest steel-producing capacity in the world and were capitalized at $50 million. The Pullman railroad car works, the Crane elevator and steel manufactures, and the mail-order retailer Montgomery Ward and Company all led the country in their areas of production. Every important national and regional railroad line converged in the city, bringing raw materials into its factories and shipping out its finished products around the country.[6]

Chicago was also on the verge of becoming the nation's second largest city. Tens of thousands of new immigrants headed into the city and its promise of jobs. Between 1870 and 1890 Chicago's population grew from just under 300,000 to 1.1 million; a little under half of it was foreign born. But migrants also came from rural areas around Chicago as manufacturing was overtaking agriculture as the focus of the national economy. Chicago, Theodore Dreiser wrote in perhaps his most well-known and prophetic novel about the industrial city, *Sister Carrie*, was "a giant magnet, drawing to itself, from all quarters, the hopeful and

---

5. "The Midway Plaisance," *The Book of the Fair*, ch. 24.

6. For various statistics, see Harold M. Mayer and Richard C. Wade, *Chicago: Growth of a Metropolis* (Chicago: University of Chicago Press, 1969); Donald Miller, *City of the Century: The Epic of Chicago and the Making of America* (New York: Simon and Schuster, 1996); and Donald. F. Tingley, *The Structuring of a State: The History of Illinois, 1899–1928* (Urbana: University of Illinois Press, 1980).

the hopeless."[7] By 1893, opportunity no longer lay in acquiring land in the west. It lay in the jobs in the factories and plants of Chicago and other industrial cities such as Cleveland, Detroit, Pittsburgh, or Milwaukee. It lay in jobs in port cities such as San Francisco and Baltimore, or mining and new western commercial cities and towns such as Butte, Montana, and Denver.

If the Fair's architectural beauty was meant to signify civilization, and if cities were the new "frontier" of opportunity, industry, and civilization, then it mattered to Chicago's leaders and the Fair's directors that visitors see the city as well as the Fair, and acknowledge its beauty as well as its progress. So the city was spruced up. Over 1,000 miles of streets were resurfaced. The number of city sidewalks laid doubled to more than 4,000 miles. Of course, these improvements were undertaken only in certain areas of the city. Nevertheless, the city indeed captivated foreign and American visitors. A French diplomat predicted that "the most beautiful exhibition will be Chicago itself." Eighteen-year-old Mable Treseder from a small town in Wisconsin admired the views from the newly built downtown skyscrapers, the majesty of the Potter Palmer mansion, the abundance of goods in the department stores. Yet, even young Mable recognized that the city had a darker side to it. "Our eyes witnessed some of the contrasting sights of the great city where want, misery, and crime hold sway and where poverty deals out a full measure to all. It would fairly make one's heart sick to see the distress manifested on some of those wretched alleys and lanes."[8]

Foreign visitors were even more critical of the city. The darkness and poverty described by Italian fair-goer Giuseppe Giacosa was a pretty astute description of Chicago away from the "White City." Many streets were unpaved and ill-lit; they were strewn with garbage that went uncollected, including the bodies of dead animals. Tens of thousands of Chicago residents crowded into badly constructed tenements without clean air, clean water, or indoor plumbing. Disease stalked their neighborhoods with outbreaks of cholera and typhoid from unclean water; tuberculosis and pneumonia added to the death tolls. The infant mortality rate was high. The air and water were badly polluted from the black smoke from coal-fired furnaces and the waste dumped by factories and industrial plants into every available body of water. Coming to Chicago a few years later, a British journalist, George Steevens, saw little improvement. "There is another side to Chicago," he wrote,

> away from the towering offices, lying off from the smiling parks, is a vast wilderness of shabby houses. . . . Street stretches beyond street of little houses, mostly wooden, begrimed with soot, rotting, falling to pieces. The pathways are of rickety and worm-eaten planks. . . . The streets are quagmires of black mud, and no attempt is made to repair them. They are miserably lighted, and nobody thinks of illuminating them.[9]

---

7. Theodore Dreiser, *Sister Carrie* (New York: Modern Library, 1990), ch. 2.

8. François Bruwaert quoted in Maureen A. Flanagan, *Charter Reform in Chicago* (Carbondale: Southern Illinois University Press, 1987), 11; Treseder quoted in Cronon, *Nature's Metropolis*, 350–51.

9. Pierce, *As Others See Chicago*, 399–400.

This darkness was the other side of the "White City." Even as the Fair was closing on October 31, 1893, the darkness threatened to overwhelm the light. Chicago's mayor, Carter Harrison, was assassinated on the Fair's last day by an Irish immigrant whose delusions led him to imagine that Harrison had reneged on a promised job. The city went into mourning and substituted the planned gala closing ceremonies with a much smaller and subdued affair. At the same time, a massive economic depression was sweeping across the country. One factor that had helped account for the country's rapid economic growth was that industrial capitalism of the late nineteenth century operated almost free of any government regulation or oversight. Businessmen and industrialists had a free hand in deciding how to run their businesses, without regard to future problems. By the 1890s, many businesses were stretched thin from overborrowing and cutthroat competition. So, when the National Cordage Company went bankrupt in May, a cascade of business and banking failures and a stock market collapse quickly followed. There were no regulatory mechanisms in place to stop the economy from crashing. By the Fair's closing, 8,000 businesses and more than 350 banks had failed and farm prices had plummeted across the country. Twenty-five percent of the nation's industrial workforce was unemployed and those still working found their wages reduced.

The depression hit Chicago hard in the bitter winter of 1893–94. An estimated 100,000 workers were unemployed. Between July and November 1893, the Pullman railroad car works had reduced its workforce from 4,500 to 1,000. The massive Illinois Steel Company shut down completely. Those without work and unable to pay their rent were thrown out into the streets. Those lucky enough to still have shelter roamed the streets seeking coal or wood to burn and food to feed their families. Many without homes took shelter in the now-empty Fair buildings. In January 1894 the "White City" began to meet its inglorious end. A fire that month burned down several of the buildings. Six months later the destruction was completed by another fire that lit the night sky one last time from the site.

The dramatic rise and fall of the "White City," its reduction to a heap of burned and blackened ruins and ashes, might have symbolized the fallen hopes of many Americans by the mid-1890s. They were beginning to fear that their "land of opportunity" might experience as precipitous a rise and fall as the Fair if conditions were not changed. The "White City" itself had been a façade, the gleaming white outsides were not stone or brick or any other enduring material but plaster, behind which lay a wooden frame. Perhaps, too, American progress was a façade behind which lay a shoddy structure ready to fall. The "White City" of light and air and progress had indeed contrasted badly with the "Dark City" that seemed to surround it. At the center of that light were the city's leading families whose wealth, often accumulated from the toil of poorly paid laborers, allowed them to live at a safe remove from the darkness. After the fire of 1871 had destroyed his original mansion, for example, the real estate magnate Potter Palmer spent $3.5 million building a new mansion as a wedding present for his bride Bertha Honoré. The Palmers, especially Bertha, were not oblivious to the conditions of the city and of its working class. They contributed tens of thousands of dollars to charity, but did so without having to get too close to poverty. Nor did their awareness of these things stop them from enjoying an extravagant lifestyle of gala parties and travel, of Paris gowns and expensive jewelry such as a $200,000 pearl and diamond Tiffany necklace that Palmer had gifted upon his wife. When George Pullman died in 1897, his estate was estimated at $7.6 million. But when his workers had struck in 1894 over layoffs and wage reductions, he had refused to budge an inch on their demands.

Life for many of the tens of thousands of immigrants who lived in Chicago could not have been more different. In good economic times, jobs were plentiful and easy to find. Immigrants worked in steel mills, textile mills, coal mines, and railroad car plants. They slaughtered cows and pigs in the nation's stockyards and turned out meat for the country in its packing plants. In garment factories and in basement sweatshops they produced ready-made clothing to be sold in new department stores and in retail catalogs. But even in the best of times, the conditions of labor were grim. Among the working class, whole families, including young children, often had to work in order to live. The work was arduous, the days were long—often ten to twelve hours a day, six or seven days a week. There were few protections against injury and death at work. Job or wage security was nonexistent. Any worker could be fired, have his or her wages cut, and the work output speeded up at the whim of the employer. Sweatshop workers were generally paid by the piece so that some toiled daily for sixteen or more hours to earn enough to keep starvation and the landlord at bay.

The contrast between wealth and poverty was not just a Chicago phenomenon. Every industrial city across the country, and even in smaller towns and cities without heavy industry, resembled Chicago. By 1900, a dangerous gap existed between the rich and the rest of the population. That year, 1 percent of the U.S. population owned 87 percent of the wealth, while at the other extreme ten million people (1/8 the population) lived in abject poverty. The steel magnate Andrew Carnegie earned $23 million a year, whereas the average worker earned $500—a figure below the established poverty level. In the years around the turn of the century, between 20 and 30 percent of the workforce was unemployed for some time every year.[10] This enormous gap between the few wealthy and the many poor challenged any illusions that Americans might have maintained about theirs being a classless society of endless opportunity.

The potential risks of this situation were dramatized for all to see by a series of violent labor conflicts as laborers turned to union organizing and, in some cases, to socialist or anarchist philosophies that demanded the complete overthrow of capitalism. Chicago was the site of one of these frightening conflicts in 1886 when leaders of the city's anarchist movement called an outdoor meeting to protest police brutality toward workers striking against the McCormick reaper works. The meeting itself, in Haymarket Square, passed peacefully. But there was a heavy police presence, and as the meeting finished a bomb was thrown in their midst. Several police and bystanders were killed or injured,

---

10. Nell Irvin Painter, *Standing at Armageddon: The United States, 1877–1919* (New York: W. W. Norton, 1987), xix–xxii.

and in the antiradical hysteria that followed, the men who had organized the meeting were sentenced to death even though there was no evidence linking them to the bomb. Six years later, a strike against Andrew Carnegie's Homestead Steel Works outside of Pittsburgh ended in violence as Carnegie and his manager Henry Clay Frick deployed Pinkertons—a private security firm skilled at strikebreaking—local police, and the state militia against the workers breaking the strike, blacklisting its leaders, and destroying the Amalgamated Association of Iron, Steel, and Tin Workers. Then with the onset of the depression of 1893, industrial "armies" of the unemployed began marching across the country. Labor violence, the threat of radicalism, and the appalling conditions in which millions were working and living were signs to many Americans that something was very wrong in their country. The questions they confronted by the mid-1890s were what had produced these problems and how should they be resolved.

AMERICA AT A CROSSROADS

The Fair, its destruction, and the visible contrast of the "White City" and "Dark City" found the United States at a crossroads in its history. The United States had been built around the ideal of individual freedom and opportunity to get ahead free from government interference. This laissez-faire liberalism dictated that government exercise relatively little control over economic development, not redistribute wealth in any fashion, and not provide for social welfare. During the rise of capitalist industrialization, business thus had been left free to do pretty much as it wanted. Labor was left at the mercy of business and the marketplace. Although the law theoretically was to be equal for all, in fact the legal system protected the rights of businessmen over workers. As in the Homestead strike, the police power of the state was always brought in to protect business in the event of labor demonstrations and the courts denied that workers had a right to organize. Taxation was minimal so cities provided very little in the way of public services beyond those necessary to attract business and industry. The poor, the sick, the hungry, and the homeless were left to themselves or the care of private charity.[11]

The Fair and critiques of Chicago did not alone, of course, cause people to think differently. Individuals such as Jane Addams, who had founded Chicago's Hull House—one of the country's first social settlements in 1889—

---

11. For broad overviews of the late nineteenth century in these regards, see Mark W. Summers, *The Gilded Age: Or, the Hazard of New Functions* (Englewood Cliffs, NJ: Prentice-Hall, 1997) and Kathleen McCarthy, *Noblesse Oblige: Charity and Cultural Philanthropy in Chicago, 1849–1929* (Chicago: University of Chicago Press, 1982). See also, Ballard Campbell, *The Growth of American Government: Governance from the Cleveland Era to the Present* (Bloomington: Indiana University Press, 1995) and the essays in *The Gilded Age: Essays on the Origins of Modern America*, Charles W. Calhoun, ed. (Wilmington, DE: Scholarly Resources, 1996). For an extended consideration of the ideal of individualism, see Michael G. McGerr, *A Fierce Discontent: The Rise and Fall of the Progressive Movement in America, 1870–1920* (New York: The Free Press, 2003) and for more discussion of laissez-faire liberalism, see Alan Dawley, *Struggles for Justice: Social Responsibility and the Liberal State* (Cambridge, MA: Harvard University Press, 1991).

had already begun to speak out against rampant individualism, uninvolved government, the lack of protection against social and economic dislocation, and about the threat of radicalism if the country did not begin to move in a new direction. A growing number of Americans across the country shared this sentiment. The settlement house movement was perhaps the first organized manifestation of this call for a new America. It expanded quickly in cities everywhere across the next decade. Vida Scudder founded the Rivington Street Settlement in New York City in 1889 and the Dennison House in Boston in 1892, the same year the first settlement opened in Philadelphia. Locust Point Settlement opened in Baltimore in 1896. By the end of the century there were more than one hundred settlements in place.[12]

Chicago in 1893, however, does make a place to start exploring why Americans began to change their ideas of what constituted a good society and government. The caustic comments of foreign visitors both before and during the Fair had penetrated the consciousness of the city's middle class. Their discomfort was magnified at a public meeting in early November in Central Music Hall in the middle of downtown. The meeting had been organized by visiting Englishman William T. Stead, who harangued the well-to-do audience about the evils of the city. "If Christ came to Chicago," he asked, would he want to change it? Stead's answer was a resounding "yes!" And if Stead's charges were not enough to shame some in the audience, socialist labor leader Thomas Morgan's threat helped shake them out of their complacency. "May someone blow you out with dynamite" if you do not begin to change things, Morgan thundered.[13] By the following year, a group of Chicago businessmen, ministers, and a few women had formed the Civic Federation to investigate problems in the city and work to solve them. Similar reform organizations were organized in other cities.

From this point, Americans settled down to the business of reforming the country and "modernizing" their society. "Modern" in this context means moving ahead, rather than looking backwards; deciding what the future should look like based not on past ideas such as laissez-faire liberalism but on new ideas about democratic government and its purposes. But the big questions were still to be faced. What exactly was wrong with the United States? How should it be reformed and why? And whose ideas about reform should be followed? There was no common agreement on how to answer these questions.

What would differentiate the decades from the 1890s into the1920s, however, from earlier nineteenth-century reform episodes were the variety of reform groups, reform proposals, and numbers of people involved. The 1880s, for example, had seen a number of reform initiatives. One group of elite

12. For general information on the settlement house movement in the United States, see Allen Davis, *Spearheads for Reform: The Settlement House Movement and the Progressive Era, 1890–1914* (New York: Oxford University Press, 1967); Elisabeth Lasch-Quinn, *Black Neighbors and the Limits of Reform in the American Settlement House Movement, 1890–1945* (Chapel Hill: University of North Carolina Press, 1993); and Daphne Spain, *How Women Saved the City* (Minneapolis: University of Minnesota Press, 2001).

13. See Miller, *City of the Century*, 536, for a brief account of this meeting that includes Morgan's comments.

liberal Republicans, the so-called "Mugwumps,"[14] had railed against party politicians and new immigrant groups, whom they thought did not understand democracy, as responsible for corrupting the political system. They sought to replace party appointees to offices in government with the "Best Men"—honest, educated men such as themselves—and to institute property and educational requirements for voting. The Greenback Labor Party, which ran candidates for positions that included the presidency in 1880, had focused on monetary reform as the path to a more democratic society. A labor organization, the Knights of Labor (1878–1888) had attacked competitive, market-based industrialization as destroying democracy, proposing instead to form "producer" cooperatives using the slogan "An Injury to One Is the Concern of All."[15] Beginning in 1877, Farmers' Alliances, based mainly in the South and Midwest (including the plains area) of the country, similarly sought to slow down market-based capitalism by instituting farmers' cooperatives, eventually organizing a People's, or Populist, Party to defend the "people" against the "interests" of politicians and businessmen. The party's guiding principle was the first systematic articulation of the idea that "powers of government—in other words, of the people—should be expanded." Although the Populists are not generally considered "progressives," some of their ideas about increased government responsibility for social and economic welfare contributed to the reform era, especially once the Populists were absorbed into the Democratic Party in 1896.

What also distinguishes the progressives from the Mugwumps, Greenback Laborers, Knights of Labor, Farmers' Alliances, and Populists is that the latter groups tended to identify one particular group or issue as the problem to be corrected. Their solutions tended also toward trying to recapture a past predicated on liberal republican ideals that they believed had produced a more cooperative society rather than the competitive one they saw being fostered by capitalist industrialism. This is not to say that those earlier reform impulses had not played a role in beginning to shift Americans' thinking about their society. The progressives, however, worked to develop a comprehensive reform program that would save liberal capitalism by eliminating, or regulating, its worst excesses. To do so, they realized, required reforming the country by instituting major changes in how government and the economy functioned and for whom these structures worked. Progressives wanted to change some of liberal capitalism's premises so that it would work better and produce more good for all Americans. Even various elements of socialist movements at times supported progressive reform proposals, so they too will be discussed for the crucial role they played in this era's reform initiatives. But socialists cannot just be

---

14. This was a derogatory term for party members sitting on the fence unable to decide to which side they belonged. The term was depicted in cartoons with someone sitting on a fence with his "mug" (his face) on one side and his "wump" (his bottom) hanging over the other side.

15. See Leon Fink, *Workingmen's Democracy: The Knights of Labor and American Politics* (Urbana: University of Illinois Press, 1983); Gretchen Ritter, *Goldbugs and Greenbacks: The Anti-Monopoly Tradition and the Politics of Finance in America* (Cambridge, UK: Cambridge University Press, 1997); and John Sproat, *The Best Men: Liberal Reformers in the Gilded Age* (New York: Oxford University Press, 1968).

lumped in with progressives because elements of socialism wished to eradicate capitalism. Therefore, distinctions between socialism and progressivism must continue to be acknowledged.

No matter which road progressives took toward reform, they were all looking for ways to meet the challenges of a new America. It was an increasingly urban, industrial, and immigrant society—a new society that required new ways to meet the challenges of maintaining a good democratic society. The following three chapters will examine those progressives who emphasized the need for social justice progressivism.

Hilda Satt arrived in Chicago as an immigrant from Poland. Her arrival and first years in Chicago were marked by marvel at her new home and its opportunities (well beyond what she had faced in Poland), but she also developed a keen sense of its shortcomings.

We arrived in Chicago a few minutes after midnight, on June 16, 1892. It was raining as we stepped off the train. The station was dark and gloomy. But it became light and sunny when we caught sight of my Father. He was standing near a lamppost. I could see his eyes shining. . . . My first home in Chicago was on South Halsted Street, four blocks south of Hull-House. I did not realize that my future as an American would be measured by that distance. . . . The only play space was the street in front of the house. The small yard in the back of the house had been rented to a junk man and it was used to store junk. Compared with some of the homes of children I played with, our home was luxurious. We had a toilet with running water in a narrow hall just outside of the kitchen. . . . Most of the houses had privies in the yards. In many cases the owner of the front house would build a shanty in the rear to bring in additional income. Very little attention was paid as to how near the privy was to the shanty. On hot days the people living in these shanties had to keep their windows closed to keep out the stench.[*]

---

[*]Hilda Satt Polacheck, *I Came A Stranger: The Story of a Hull-House Girl*, Dena J. Polacheck Epstein, ed. (Urbana: University of Illinois Press, 1989), 27–30.

CHAPTER 1

The City

The Crossroads of Social Justice

> Man has entered on an urban age. He has become a commu-
> nal being . . . and society has developed into an organism, like
> the human body, of which the city is the head, heart, and cen-
> tre of the nervous system.
>
> —FREDERIC C. HOWE, *THE CITY:*
> *THE HOPE OF DEMOCRACY*, 1905

HILDA SATT WAS just one of millions of people crossing into new places in the Progressive Era. The industrial city was indeed a difficult place for those who were unskilled labor and without sufficient income to provide a decent place for their families to live. Yet, the city offered opportunity, which immigrants by the hundreds of thousands seized upon. It also offered excitement and new lifestyles for both immigrants and rural migrants. By the late nineteenth century, despite all its problems, the city was the place to be. So, like Hilda Satt, most people on the move ended up in cities.[1]

The effect of such large-scale migration was especially dramatic in the industrial areas of the Northeast and Middle West. These were also the areas where new waves of foreign immigrants landed. The population of New York City in 1900 was 3.437 million. Thirty-seven percent were foreign born. In Chicago, 34.6 percent of the city's 1.698 million residents were foreign born. Respective figures for Cleveland were 32.6 percent out of 381,768; for Boston, 35.1 percent out of 560,892; for Newark, New Jersey, 29 percent out of 246,070. No city south of Baltimore exceeded that city's 13.5 percent foreign born of a population of 508,957. In the West, San Francisco had 34.1 percent foreign born out of 342,782 and Portland had 28.6 percent of its 90,426 residents foreign born.

---

1. In the 1920 census, the United States officially became an "urban" country. More than 50 percent of the population now lived in cities, almost double the percentage of 1880. Sixty-eight cities had populations over 100,000 as opposed to the twenty of that size forty years before. Not all cities were large ones. The official marker of "urban" is a population of more than 2,500, but even here the United States had grown dramatically. There were 2,728 urban areas now, where there had been 939 in 1880.

1880 Cities with Populations over 100,000

1900 Cities with Populations over 100,000

Although the highest percentages of foreign born in these cities and other cities were still German and Irish in 1900—Portland was an anomaly with its highest percentage being Chinese—new immigrants from Poland, Russia, Italy, and various parts of the Austro-Hungarian Empire were swelling urban populations. The 1860 census had shown the foreign-born population of Detroit, for example, as primarily British, Irish, and German (excluding Canadian). Each decade from 1890 to 1920 saw the foreign-born population of the city shift decisively to Polish, Russian, Italian, and other east European groups. These new immigrants generally were culturally different from the older ones. They were Catholic or Jewish, rather than Protestant; they were often landless, relatively poor, sometimes uneducated, peasants; most did not speak English.[2]

LIVING AND WORKING IN THE CITY

Hilda Satt's description of the streets, housing, and privies of Halsted Street captures some of the crowding, dirt, danger, and basic poverty that characterized the daily lives of many of these immigrants. Her description of her surroundings also agrees with the impressions recorded by foreign visitors such as Giuseppe Giacosa and George Steevens. According to Satt:

> The sidewalks were wooden planks, which became slimy and slippery after a rain. The streets were paved with wooden blocks and after a heavy rainfall the blocks would become loose and float about in the street. During the drying process the stench was nauseating. There were many places where the blocks did not return to their mooring and the smelly water would remain for days. If this happened at an intersection, it was impossible to cross the street.

"I remember a sign," Polacheck recalled, "that some pranksters put up on one such intersection after it had been raining for a week":

**The Mayor and the Aldermen
are invited
to swim here**[3]

Such a description of the streets and sidewalks reminds us that Upton Sinclair's death of a young child who drowned in such a hole was fiction only in the case of that fictional child.[4]

Death from disease and accident was often the fate of the urban poor and working class. Human waste from privy vaults (pits dug into cellars and yards) leached into the ground and when it rained it was carried into the water supply. At the turn of the last century typhoid outbreaks from such contaminated water

---

2. Olivier Zunz, *The Changing Face of Inequality: Urbanization, Industrial Development, and Immigrants in Detroit, 1880–1920* (Chicago: University of Chicago Press, 1982); tables 5.3–5.6 give population statistics for Detroit. For general discussion, see Howard P. Chudacoff, *The Evolution of American Urban Society* (Englewood Cliffs, NJ: Prentice-Hall, 2nd edition, 1981), ch. 4.

3. Polacheck, *I Came a Stranger*, 30.

4. Upton Sinclair, *The Jungle* (New York: Doubleday Page & Co., 1906).

were not uncommon. Pittsburgh was the worst large city for the disease. Between 1882 and 1907 it averaged 100 deaths per 1,000 of the population. The percentage of deaths was highest in immigrant and African American neighborhoods. Cleveland had fifty-four deaths per 1,000 in 1900 and Philadelphia, which had major outbreaks of both cholera and typhoid in the 1890s, had thirty-five typhoid deaths per 1,000. During the typhoid outbreak of 1902 in Chicago, the immigrant 19th ward—home to Jane Addams, Hull House, and Hilda Satt—had a death rate well above other areas of the city.[5] Infant mortality was high. In 1893 alone, Chicago recorded over 3,200 deaths from infant diarrhea of children under two years of age mainly caused by spoiled or adulterated cow's milk.[6] As late as 1916, there were 141 deaths of children under two years of age for every 1,000 births in Chicago. Detroit's rate was 129 and New York City's was fifty-eight. Because statistics were often not recorded among some of the very poor, and among African Americans, the actual rates of infant mortality were undoubtedly higher.[7] With so little access to running water, of course, bathing was a luxury for many urban residents.

Statistics alone cannot convey how miserable life could be for people in cities. Housing conditions in all cities for the poor and the working class ranged from adequate to abysmal. At the turn of the century, in Manhattan and the Bronx, there were 44,000 tenements. These tenement buildings followed a general pattern. They were constructed on narrow, deep lots twenty-five feet wide by 100 feet deep, with each building connected at the back and front with its neighbor, a pattern that bestowed upon them the name "dumbbell" tenements. They were generally six or seven stories high, with fourteen rooms on each story. Only the four rooms at the front and back of the building had any direct light. All the others got whatever light and air they could from a narrow air shaft that was the only opening between the connected buildings, although sunlight barely penetrated below the fifth floor.[8]

Smaller tenement types proliferated in other cities, but these provided no better living conditions for the poor. Philadelphia's pattern was to build three- to

5. Harold Platt, "Jane Addams and the Ward Boss Revisited: Class, Politics, and Public Health in Chicago, 1890–1930," *Environmental History*, 5 (April 2000): 194–222; and Joel Tarr, "The Metabolism of the Industrial City: The Case of Pittsburgh," *Journal of Urban History*, 28 (July 2002): 511–45. For outbreaks of typhoid in Dallas, see Judith McArthur, *Creating the New Woman: The Rise of Southern Women's Progressive Culture in Texas, 1893–1918* (Urbana: University of Illinois Press, 1998). For a summary of the introduction of techniques to clean water and the dropping death rates from typhoid, see Martin Melosi, *The Sanitary City: Urban Infrastructure in America from Colonial Times to the Present* (Baltimore: Johns Hopkins University Press, 2000), 143–48.

6. Jacqueline H. Wolf, *Don't Kill Your Baby: Public Health and the Decline of Breastfeeding in the Nineteenth and Twentieth Centuries* (Columbus: Ohio State University Press, 2001), Appendix A.2.

7. For more extensive discussion of infant mortality, see Lynne Curry, *Modern Mothers in the Heartland: Gender, Health, and Progress in Illinois, 1900–1930* (Columbus: Ohio State University Press, 1999).

8. Description from Lawrence Veiller, *Charities Review*, 10 (1900–1901):19–25. For more details on New York City tenements, see Chudacoff, *The Evolution of American Urban Society*.

four-story tenements that were just as crowded and deprived of any amenities as those in New York. One description conveys life in a Philadelphia tenement:

> Five families, 26 individuals were in nine living rooms. . . . The bathroom at the rear of the house was used as a kitchen. The bathtub was disused, broken, and dirty. . . . The waste water from the third story hall sink discharged into the sink on the second floor. One privy compartment in the yard was the sole toilet accommodation for the five families living in the house.[9]

Overcrowding and lack of sanitation were the norm in many Chicago neighborhoods. When Jane Addams and other Hull House residents surveyed their immediate neighborhood they counted 19,654 people living in one-third of a square mile. Crammed in with them were warehouses and small factories. Of these people, only 26 percent of families had access to a water closet (the rest had only privy vaults) and fewer than 3 percent lived in buildings with a bath.[10]

Even in smaller industrial cities such conditions existed. An inquiry into Jersey City, New Jersey, tenements in 1903 revealed that 75 percent of those investigated had only privy vaults. In Milwaukee, where the working class could sometimes afford to buy small frame houses in outlying areas, the living conditions were almost as precarious. Property owners had to pay for connections to sewer and water pipes, so these areas were often built up without such amenities. In order to pay for their mortgages, however, working-class families often rented out rooms, leading to overcrowding and poor sanitation. As a result, mortality rates were significantly higher in these areas of Milwaukee than in those of the middle class.[11]

If the poorer residents of a city survived their living conditions, they were still at tremendous risk at work from industrial accidents. In the Pittsburgh steel mills, for example, between 1899 and 1915, the county coroner reported 2,313 accidental deaths in steel mills, an average of 136 deaths per year. It takes more than statistics of fatalities to comprehend the working situation of so many Americans. Thousands more, for example, were injured in the Pittsburgh steel mills during those years. Death and injury in the steel mills could be particularly gruesome. Workers were hit by falling machinery and pieces of equipment, caught between machines, crushed between pieces of steel, or burned by hot metals. Those who weren't killed had limbs so severely injured that they could not work again.

---

9. Emily Wayland Dinwiddie, "Housing Conditions in Philadelphia," pamphlet of Octavia Hill Association (Philadelphia, 1904) [found in Harvard University Library Open Collections Program].

10. *Hull-House Maps and Papers, a Presentation of Nationalities and Wages in a Congested District of Chicago, Together with Comments and Essays on Problems Growing out of the Social Conditions, by Residents of Hull-House, a Social Settlement at 235 South Halsted Street, Chicago, Ill* (New York: T. Y. Crowell, 1895).

11. See Mary Buell Sayles, "Housing Conditions in Jersey City," *Annals of the American Academy of Political and Social Science* (January 1903) and Roger Simon, *The City-Building Process: Housing and Services in New Milwaukee Neighborhoods, 1880–1910* (Philadelphia: Temple University Press, 1996).

Andrew Antonik worked in the Homestead Steel Works at a "skull-cracker"—a heavy iron weight which is allowed to drop from a height to break up pieces of scrap. When it falls big chunks of scrap fly in every direction, and one must be quick to dodge them. On the night of April 29, 1907, "Andy" failed to dodge in time. . . . His leg was crushed and had to be taken off below the knee.

The report went on to say that Mr. Antonik's compensation from the company was $150.[12] The Homestead Works were the property of Andrew Carnegie, who fifteen years earlier had broken the union there.

Other jobs may not have been quite as dangerous as those in steel, but workers were killed and maimed in every area of industry. By the turn of the century, most factories were mechanized so workers were always in danger of having their limbs caught in machinery that generally had no safety protections. Workers fell down unguarded elevator shafts, packinghouse workers cut themselves badly with their knives, explosions and cave-ins killed miners. Railway workers were crushed while coupling and uncoupling cars. Construction workers tumbled off buildings that had no protective scaffolding.

Women and children generally worked at less dangerous jobs. By 1900, about five million women worked for wages and one-fourth of them were in manufacturing. They were concentrated in canning factories, garment making, commercial laundries, and in the South and New England, in textile mills. Their work, too, was generally long and arduous. At the turn of the twentieth century in New York City, shirtwaist makers (the general term for those sewing women's clothing) labored sixty-five hours a week. These women often had to provide their own materials, such as needles and thread, or scissors. Female laundry workers in Boston's South End earned an average of $3.50 per week in 1903. In 1912, laundry workers in New York City were working ninety hours per week for $4.50. Pittsburgh's cigar factories ran on the labor of women. In 1907 they were employing 2,211 women and only 463 men. The men had the higher-paying, skilled jobs in the trade, whereas the women often worked in factory basements stripping the tobacco plants.[13]

Poor pay and the loss of adult wage earners through injury, death, and illness meant that the children of the working class often went to work at a young age. Children were less likely to be employed in factories in cities where heavy industry dominated. Yet, in those cities you would see young newspaper, shoeshine (bootblack), and Western Union delivery boys out on the streets well into the night. Boys and girls as young as fourteen were employed in the garment industries in various parts of the country. Children formed a significant part of the workforce in textile and cotton mills of New England or the

---

12. Quoted in Edward S. Slavishak, "Artificial Limbs and Industrial Workers' Bodies in Turn-of-the-Century Pittsburgh," *Journal of Social History*, 37 (Winter 2003): 365; statistics from ibid., 365–67.

13. Roswell F. Phelps, "South End Factory Operatives: Employment and Residence" (1903) and Ruth Delzell, *The Early History of Women Trade Unionists of America*, pamphlet reprint of articles from *Life and Labor* (1912 and 1914) [1914]. See also, *The Pittsburgh Survey*, 6 vols. (New York: Charities Publication Committee, 1909–1914).

South, or in the carpet mills of Philadelphia. In the South, textile workers were often rural migrants who came to the mill towns when they could no longer support themselves on small patches of land. Some of them were displaced tenant farmers. But, to earn enough to support themselves in the mill towns, whole families often went to work, so children as young as seven or eight worked long days and into the night in the mills where their small and nimble fingers could quickly untangle threads or repair broken ones. For such work, they earned no more than thirty cents a day. Across the decades from 1870 to 1900, an estimated one million children moved into the labor force throughout the country.[14]

In some types of light manufacturing such as garment making, pieces of the work were often "farmed out" to people working at home or in small establishments known as sweatshops. The system worked by the manufacturer employing a middleman, commonly called a "sweater," who contracted with the manufacturer to produce a certain amount of clothing and be paid a certain price for it. The "sweater" then took the pieces of garments and paid people working in their homes or sweatshops to produce the product. Because both the manufacturer and "sweater" wanted to make money, the workers were paid as little as possible. Because they were also paid by the piece, some "sweated" workers labored as many as eighteen hours a day. Here, too, the nimble fingers of children could be put to work and often were in order to support the family. The urban sweating system resembled in many respects the mill town textile factory system. Whole families were put to work, and these were generally the newest and poorest arrivals to the city or town.

Beyond the exploitation of the poor, immigrants, and migrants, the sweating system was a potential health threat to the broader society. Doing the work at home, and employing the whole family, often meant that clothing was made in the midst of the diseases circulating through the poor neighborhoods. In Boston, Chicago, and New York, investigations uncovered clothing being made in the presence of scarlet fever, typhus, measles, and typhoid. Florence Kelley, who was appointed the first factory inspector in Illinois in 1893 and maintained that she had visited 900 to 1,000 sweatshops in Chicago, reported on the connections of disease and sweated work:

> I found a case . . . where four children were just recovering from scarlet fever, and cloak making had been carried on continuously throughout the illness. I found a case of measles, with women finishing cloaks in the same room with the patient. . . . I found two children . . . finishing knee pants in their mother's bedroom, while suffering from a most aggravated case of scabies—the itch.

---

14. Irene M. Ashby, "Child-Labor in Southern Cotton Mills," *World's Work*, 2 (October 1901); reprinted in William A. Link, ed., *The Rebuilding of Old Commonwealths and Other Documents of Social Reform in the Progressive Era South* (Boston: Bedford Books of St. Martin's Press, 1996), 90. See also, Eric Rauchway, *Murdering McKinley: The Making of Theodore Roosevelt's America* (New York: Hill and Wang, 2003), 125. For work in the South during this time period, see Edward L. Ayers, *The Promise of the New South* (New York: Oxford University Press, 1992).

Conditions were not much better for those working in the so-called sweat-shops where the sewing machine workers were constantly forced to produce more at higher speeds in order to earn a living. Again according to Kelley:

> I found one girl for one week in the height of the season to be working 15 hours a day for seven consecutive days at seam binding, which is the heaviest work in the trade, and is usually done by strong men, she earned $18. I found an able-bodied girl speeding a machine making knee pants for nothing, and she told me, and the man beside her corroborated her statement, that she had been working three weeks for nothing; and three men in the shop told me that they had earned their places by working six weeks for nothing.[15]

All too often this was the situation. "Sweaters" would not pay workers until they had labored for several weeks. Even worse, "sweaters" sometimes delivered the garments to the manufacturer and then disappeared, not paying the workers at all.

THE CONDITION OF THE CITY

Advances in technology made urban living both more convenient and dangerous. Streetcar lines began to crisscross cities in the 1890s, making it easier to get to work or go shopping. But the street-level crossings were often unguarded and fatal accidents grew in number every year. Crashes and other accidents on these lines caused by inexperienced drivers and conductors added to the toll of injured and dead. In a five-month period in 1906, over 1,300 Chicagoans were injured in transit accidents; in New York City the following year, forty-two people died in a single month. Once the automobile became a feature of urban life early in the first decade of the twentieth century, it too was a nuisance as well as a convenience. Electricity lit up the indoors, but it also caused electrocutions when overhead electrical wires fell or started fires in poorly wired buildings. The development of steel frame construction made it possible to construct taller buildings for accommodating growing numbers of office workers and factory operatives. But the taller the building, the more perilous it was for those inside to flee in case of fire. The abundance of coal deposits in the United States and the development of newer types of building furnaces increased the number of heating units in cities and added to people's daily comfort in the winter. It also increased the industrial capacity of the United States as coal was one of the dominant fuels for running plants and factories. But coal was a terrible air pollutant and industrial cities were overhung with heavy clouds of ashy smoke. Smoke pollution obscured buildings, dropped soot onto people's clothing and food, blackened buildings, and air

---

15. See "Report of Inspection by Committee," *Report of the Committee on Manufactures on the Sweating System* (Washington: GPO, 1893), xi; Testimony of Mrs. T. J. Morgan, in ibid., 71–74; and "Florence Kelley's Testimony on the Sweating System," *Report and Findings of the Joint Committee to Investigate the "Sweat Shop" System* (Springfield, IL: H. W. Rokker, 1893), 135–39.

Smoke Pollution: Anaconda Copper Mines and Smelters, Butte, Montana
Source: Library of Congress, Print & Photographs Division, LC-USZ62-113600

inversions could make it difficult to see in front of oneself in really smoky cities such as Pittsburgh.[16]

A mining city such as Butte, Montana, was, if anything, worse for the public health. By 1890 its Anaconda copper mines were the largest copper producers in the country. But the mining, and especially the smelting of copper, was a severe health hazard. The process produced sulfur and arsenic fumes and when air inversions trapped the smoke, residents sickened and died from numerous breathing-related diseases. In December 1890, smoke completely covered the city twenty-eight times; the following month it happened forty times. In 1902, the smelters were discharging 59,000 pounds of toxic substances into the air every day.[17]

When both parents had to work, children left home alone often took to the streets all day—the only places where they could play. Most cities did not have playgrounds or any kind of organized recreation in poor neighborhoods. New York had its grand Central Park, Chicago its large parks such as Washington, Jackson, and Lincoln park, and Boston its Commons. But these were generally the preserve of the well-to-do and the middle classes. Poor immigrant children were not encouraged there. African American city neighborhoods had even fewer possibilities for children's play. So children spent their days and evenings, often unsupervised, in the streets among the garbage, dead animals, and water holes. Street railways and automobiles made the streets even more perilous for them, but they had nowhere else to play and their homes were too

---

16. See Paul Barrett, *The Automobile and Urban Transit: The Formation of Public Policy in Chicago, 1900–1930* (Philadelphia: Temple University Press, 1983), 18 and 242 n. 26, for transit accidents, and 132 for auto fatalities.

17. Donald MacMillan, *Smoke Wars: Anaconda Copper, Montana Air Pollution, and the Courts, 1890–1924* (Helena: Montana Historical Society, 2000), 32, 48, and 87.

"Newsies," White and Black, Indianapolis, Indiana
Source: Library of Congress, Print & Photographs Division, National Child Labor Committee Collection, LC-DIG_nclc-03221

cramped for them to play indoors. Children also spent their days scrounging through garbage dumps for usable items, or in industrial or rail yards looking for coal and wood to heat stoves at home. Although most states had some form of compulsory education laws, these often set a low age limit of ten or twelve. Even these limits were rarely systematically enforced, so truancy rates were high. Besides, most cities had not invested in building enough schools to hold the growing numbers of immigrant children.

New inventions in electricity, transportation, and machinery also brought more entertainment, and night life, to the city. Restaurants, theaters, and other places of entertainment stayed open later much to the delight of the growing numbers of middle-class city dwellers. Children were also drawn into this new night life. Newspapers took advantage of the increasing night life to print almost around the clock. Rafts of newsboys sold these papers on the streets well into the night, especially in the entertainment districts, and bootblack boys stayed out to shine the shoes of "swells" coming out of theaters and restaurants. Most of these boys were under sixteen and some were as young as ten. As increasing numbers of prosperous people appeared on the streets day and night, many of these streetwise boys also worked as pickpockets lured by "the diamond-studded stickpins, gold pocket watches, and hard cash pedestrians conspicuously exhibited while traversing the streets." Not too many young girls could work the streets in the same way, but cities had their share of female pickpockets, one of whom remembered targeting passing women and using small knives "to slit open the bags so that I could get my fingers in."[18] There were also the new entertainments that attracted children, such as the nickelodeon, the first of which was opened by Edison in New York City in 1893. But it cost money to enter the nickelodeon, which poor children could only earn by selling in the streets or by stealing. So these new amusements increased the temptations for children.

The city streets were not filled just with children or the more well-off city residents. Theodore Dreiser's observation that Chicago was a magnet for the hopeful and the hopeless applied everywhere. Young men and women, like Dreiser's *Carrie*, gave up on rural and small-town life and headed for the cities by the thousands every year. Cities had jobs, amusements, and fine clothes. They were exciting and offered the possibility of independence. Recreation such as the new dance halls, jobs that weren't heavy farm work, new friends, and freedom from family and from small community supervision and gossip drew rural women especially to cities. Sometimes entire families migrated off the land, but a huge number of migrants came alone. The city became filled with single men and women, unloosed from family ties and strictures but also without family members to fall back on for support in case they lost their jobs. During the depression of 1893, as many as 80,000 to 90,000 women, and probably more, were thought to be earning their own living in New York City.[19] Young women without jobs and families to fall back on often ended up turning to prostitution. The 1893 exposition had drawn many single men to Chicago seeking work at the Fair. Once the Fair closed, thousands of them were unemployed and roaming the streets looking for work that was not to be found in the midst of a depression in Chicago or any other city. The urban "vagrant" was seemingly becoming a permanent part of city life.

Along with vagrancy, the late nineteenth century brought more drinking and saloon life to cities. Many of the new, and older immigrant groups such as the Germans and the Irish, came from cultures where public drinking was a part of daily life. The workingman's saloon was a source of conviviality and often of food: some saloons provided free food as long as you paid for the alcohol. Saloons could be rough-and-tumble places when too much liquor resulted in fights that spilled over into the streets. Although saloons and bars were distinctly male, by the 1890s these venues were adding "ladies entrances" and attracting working-class women. Saloons also sold beer in pails or tins—called growlers—that were brought into the saloons, filled up, and then carried home. This practice was dubbed "rushing the growler," and often children were sent on this errand. So children too ended up in the saloons and

---

18. Peter C. Baldwin, "'Nocturnal Habits and Dark Wisdom': The American Response to Children in the Streets at Night, 1880–1930," *Journal of Social History*, 35 (Spring 2002): 595–96, and Timothy J. Gilfoyle, "Street-Rats and Gutter-Snipes: Child Pickpockets and Street Culture in New York City, 1850–1900," *Journal of Social History*, 37 (Summer 2004): 853–62; quotes from 867 and 865. For the growth of urban amusements and night life in general, see David Nasaw, *Going Out: The Rise and Fall of Public Amusements* (New York: Basic Books, 1993).

19. Joan M. Jensen, "'I'd Rather Be Dancing': Wisconsin Women Moving On," *Frontiers: A Journal of Women Studies*, 22:1 (2001): 1–20. *Harper's Weekly* (January 13, 1894).

could be seen day and night on the streets of some neighborhoods carrying pails of beer.

African American migrants from rural areas were also moving to cities. Although it was not until the World War I era that African Americans come in great numbers to the big northern cities, southern cities experienced African American migration well before that. Young black men and women saw cities as the site of jobs, entertainment, education, and independence much the same way as did young whites. Their desires for equal access in cities competed with white southern desires to keep "control" over blacks, including segregating public places by race. Technology made this more difficult. Street railways, for example, were supposedly for everyone to ride. Electricity, new forms of public entertainment, even elevators opened further possibilities for racial mixing on the streets and in all places that were public or served the public. The South secured a major victory when the Supreme Court ruling of 1896, *Plessy v. Ferguson*, legitimated segregation in public areas and accommodations. Segregation laws were enacted all across the South but when these were not enough for urban white southerners racial riots erupted in cities such as Wilmington, North Carolina, in 1898 and Atlanta, Georgia, in 1906 as white southerners attacked black southerners. Outside the South, the *Plessy v. Ferguson* ruling emboldened smaller cities to pursue racial segregation. In the small city of Alton, Illinois, the African American population was 943—7 percent of the total population. The school system had been integrated for twenty years, but the city's leaders took advantage of the ruling to segregate the schools. Black Altonians fought back, but despite rulings in the Illinois courts against the city on this issue, the city leaders refused to change their position.[20]

Technology also made it possible for urban residents of even moderate income to remove themselves from the poorer parts of the city and live a more comfortable existence away from the noise, dirt, poverty, disease, and the unemployed. They could use street railway lines to commute into the center for work and shopping. They could afford to pay for sewer and water main extensions, or to have their streets and sidewalks paved, so that they could live in cleaner and healthier neighborhoods. As cities expanded their networks of electric and telephone lines, the middle class could afford to light their homes and use telephones to keep in touch with family living in other parts of the city. They were aided in making this move by real estate speculators who often worked in tandem with street railway owners to extend mass transit into newer areas of the city where the developers wanted to build. People were thus lured out of the crowded city centers with the promise of new homes with access to convenient transportation. By the late 1890s, the contrasts between parts of cities was so stark that a visiting Scotsman, James Fullarton Muirhead, concluded that Chicago deserved the name "'City of Contrasts'. . . In the one,

---

20. Shirley J. Portwood, "'We Lift Our Voices in Thunder Tones': African American Race Men and Race Women and Community Agency in Southern Illinois, 1895–1910," *Journal of Urban History*, 26 (September 2000): 740–58. See ahead, pp. 30, 51–52, and 120 for *P v. F.*

height, narrowness, noise, monotony, dirt, sordid squalor, pretentiousness; in the other—light, space, moderation, homelikeness."[21]

The contrasts were not just about physical differences. More Americans were becoming concerned about social problems developing from these conditions. Boston's South End in 1898 was described as composed of "dreary and depressing" streets, and "dark squalid courts and alleys." But the concern for some reformers was as much what the area might produce as what it looked like. Robert Woods declared Boston's South End "a fit haunt for the depraved and vicious," an area where "evils of all kind find congenial soil and produce a rank growth." That same year Julia Farrington described a Philadelphia neighborhood as a "badly lighted overcrowded quarter with the most frightful sanitary conditions, the people ignorant and lawless." New York's tenement areas were "the nurseries of pauperism and crime," the haunt of "a standing army of ten thousand tramps," the places where "all the influences make for evil."[22]

Words such as evil, ignorant, lawless, and vicious were freely used by many Americans to describe cities at the turn of the twentieth century. Another word was corruption. American cities did not govern so much as they dispensed favors. If homeowners could afford to pay for sewer connections, water pipes, sidewalk and street repairs—a process called special assessment—then they might have these provided. Other services that are commonly called public utilities today, such as transit systems and garbage collection, were provided then by private companies through the franchise system, rather like cable television service today. Under this system, companies submitted proposals to the city government to provide a service. In return for providing the infrastructure—for example, building the tracks for streetcars—the company was awarded a franchise (a monopoly), normally for twenty years. Under the terms of the franchise, during those years the company generally retained the right to determine how and where the service was provided and what it would charge customers. This meant that the city government did not take responsibility for these services, making for inequitable provision across the city. In the case of garbage collection, because tenement building owners rarely wanted to pay for the service, they failed to provide the required garbage bins and much garbage went uncollected in many poor neighborhoods. Many other features of urban life were also left strictly to private enterprise as cities were reluctant to get into the business of enacting building codes, mandating sanitary provisions, or curtailing business practices by regulating allowable chimney smoke or outlawing the dumping of wastes into rivers and ponds.

Such miserable conditions prevailed for several reasons. First, city governments had neither the money nor the legal right to exercise much power. The

---

21. Quoted in Bessie L. Pierce, ed., *As Others See Chicago* (Chicago: University of Chicago Press, 1933), 354.

22. Woods and Farrington quoted in Daphne Spain, *How Women Saved the City* (Minneapolis: University of Minnesota Press, 2001), 189 and 171. On New York, Jacob A. Riis, *How the Other Half Lives* (New York: Charles Scribner's Sons, 1890), 3.

specific situation differed according to state law, but generally a city could only raise revenue by levying property taxes or issuing bonds for specific infrastructure purposes. Thus, through the end of the nineteenth century cities had very little money to spend on services. The second reason was that prevailing state laws strictly limited municipal government power to passive rather than active functions.[23] Third, there was the prevailing view that the city was a business arena within which provision of services should be open to the possibility of making money. Finally, many Americans still valued the concept of private property much more than any sense of social responsibility. What resulted from these legal and ideological conditions came to be called the "corrupt bargain."

THE CORRUPT BARGAIN

Included in the franchise agreement was usually a sum of money that would be paid to the city. Because it was always hoped that a franchise could be a lucrative enterprise, payment often included bribes to the officials awarding the franchise. In other cases, if city governments considered regulating business practices, or tried implementing housing codes, many municipal officials were openly bribed to vote against such legislation or to ignore any infractions if laws were passed. As Americans became more concerned about the problems of their cities, they began to view this situation as a "corrupt bargain" between government and business. Business bribed its way toward riches and those in power, seemingly in a position to do something about it, instead were complicit in constructing a society where the divide between the few rich and the many poor was growing worse every year. Here, then, the word evil also appears in a different context. According to Cleveland "reform" Mayor Tom Johnson: "The kind of big business that deals in the profits from public service grants and taxation injustices that is the real evil of our cities."[24]

This corrupt bargain was made possible not just by cities' lack of power and revenue but by the lack of power exercised by national government, and by the political party system of the time. Later chapters will discuss the national picture of American society in the late 1890s and the growth of understanding of how the "corrupt bargain" functioned on every level of government. Because the "corrupt bargain" seemed so obvious and flagrant within cities, the urban response to it helps explain how social justice developed out of these conditions.

---

23. See Eric Monkkonen, *American Becomes Urban: The Development of U.S. Cities and Towns, 1780–1980* (Berkeley: University of California Press, 1988) for the distinction between passive and active cities and Stanley K. Schultz, *Constructing Urban Culture: American Cities and City Planning, 1800–1920* (Philadelphia: Temple University Press, 1989) for an overview of the legal situation of American cities.

24. Tom Johnson, *My Story*, Elizabeth Hauser, ed. (New York, 1911; reprint, Kent, OH: Kent State University Press, 1993), 125.

The City as the Hope of Democracy

It may be hard to imagine after the descriptions of cities earlier in this chapter that many Americans saw the city as the best place to begin reforming their society. One might be tempted to think that they would just throw up their hands in disgust and move as far away from the problems as possible. But this actually was quite a reasonable idea. Beyond the fact that the United States was becoming an urban country, the city was the place where you could be confronted almost daily with the immediate problems. You could see the conditions in which others lived and worked. Even if you were able to move up to a better neighborhood, you could not totally isolate yourself anymore in industrial cities. The smoke and water pollution produced by industry did not miraculously stop at neighborhood boundaries. Polluted rivers and streams fed into other bodies of water, including sources of drinking water. Expensive garments manufactured in sweatshops might carry disease into your home. Diseased animals could be turned into meat that would end up on your family's dinner table. If you went "downtown" for work, recreation, or shopping you could see the young children on the streets. They were often barefoot and dressed in raggedy clothing. They were selling newspapers, picking pockets, or carrying home pails of beer, from which they were presumably also drinking. You could witness young women and men trudging to work early in the morning and leaving it late in the evening. You could hear the babel of languages and know the presence of immigrants. You could read about industrial and street accidents, outbreaks of typhoid, fatal fires in factories and tenements, or infant mortality statistics in your morning, afternoon, and evening newspapers. In short, the city was the visible experience of how large, complicated, and unequal American society had become. Escape, even for the middle class, was not a particularly viable option.

It was also at the local level where you could see and experience the corruption of your government. Newspapers were filled with reports of the latest "deals" between city officials and businessmen. Accounts of favorable contracts given to certain businesses, the failures of franchise holders to provide the promised services, the refusal of business to pay their property taxes, and the favors given to the businesses and property holdings of government officials struck an immediate chord with urban residents. For anyone concerned about these practices, it would have seemed easier to attack problems on the local level than on the national.

But such practical reasons do not sufficiently explain why the period from the late 1890s into the 1920s became one of massive reform of all institutions in the country. The appalling conditions of living and working as well as the corruption of government also betrayed the democratic ideals for which the country supposedly stood. The belief that minimal government would secure the most freedom for every individual to thrive could simply no longer be sustained by Americans' daily experiences. Moreover, the "corrupt bargain" between government and business, including the use of the police power of the state always to support one side in industrial conflict, contributed to convincing

Americans that, in fact, government was actively working to favor some groups over others.

Yet, the United States had grown so socially diverse, and so economically powerful, that there would be no going back to an "imagined" better past. To go forward meant to decide how and why society should be reformed in certain ways. It also meant explaining how to reconceptualize what constituted a good society. This is where the quote from Frederic Howe that began this chapter comes into context. Intellectuals such as Howe, settlement house residents such as Jane Addams, Lillian Wald, and Victoria Earle Matthews, the women of Seattle who in 1891 organized the Century Club, Mayors Tom Johnson of Cleveland and Samuel ("Golden Rule") Jones of Toledo, the Women's Public School Association of Memphis were all seeing the city as "an enormous collectivity . . . a vast network of mutually dependent relations" in which private interests had to give way to the creation of a public good.[25] No one aspect of that collectivity could be allowed to become diseased or the whole would become sick. For progressives this meant first accepting that the causes of societal problems were social or structural rather than individual personal failure. Disease, poverty, crime, corruption, etc., prevailed because some individuals took advantage of other people's needs and the institutions of government were inadequate to the task of creating a better society. Second, progressives believed that reforms would cure the sickness without destroying the whole.

Every individual or group that can be spoken of as "progressive" agreed with the first premise. They were eager to discard old ideas about limited government and rejected the concept that every individual bore personal responsibility for her or his lot in life. Progressives, thus, called for "a new civic engagement" whereby citizens would acknowledge their responsibility for one another and come together to tackle the problems. For many progressives, this new civic engagement could best begin in cities where residents could have direct experience of one another and meet face-to-face to discuss and implement solutions. The process of reforming the entire society could then flow outward and upward, from the city to the country and eventually to reform the entire world.

On the second premise, however, there was far less agreement. There were many directions that this new civic engagement could take and here is where we speak about many "progressivisms." One may start with a broad definition that to be progressive was to support "a politics of social justice and civic engagement over a politics of patronage and power." But what exactly those ideas meant to various groups of Americans is a complicated question. For in the end, what was at stake during the Progressive Era was a struggle over the meaning of American democracy. It was this struggle that allowed the different "progressivisms" to emerge to challenge one another as much as they challenged the existing institutions.[26]

---

25. Daniel Rodgers, *Atlantic Crossings: Social Politics in a Progressive Age* (Cambridge, MA: Harvard University Press, 1998), 114–15.

26. Quote from Alan Dawley, *Changing the World: American Progressives in War and Revolution* (Princeton, NJ: Princeton University Press, 2003), 15. See Robert Johnston, "Re-Democratizing the Progressive Era: The Politics of Progressive Era Political Historiography," *The Journal of the Gilded Age and Progressive Era*, 1 (January 2002): 68–92, for discussion about democracy.

Although much of the pressure for reform began at the local level, it could not be confined there. National government, indeed, suffered from the same kinds of problems as did cities and states. It had limited sources of revenue—mainly from tariffs levied on specific imported goods, sale of government-owned lands, and control of the money supply. The American sense of individualism and a fear of too much government were legacies of the revolutionary period. Such ideals had bred both laissez-faire capitalism and limited government. A key word used to describe nineteenth-century American government was "distributive." This was understood to mean government that, ideally, favored no group or section of the country because it did not tax and "redistribute" the wealth. It was supposed to neither help nor harm anyone but merely administer foreign policy and make laws that governed the whole. According to laissez-faire capitalism, the market was to determine production, and government should not interfere with economic developments. Powerful, activist government, many Americans believed, was a threat to freedom.[27]

After the Civil War, this thinking had produced two political parties that closely resembled each other ideologically. On the big issues of the time, such as the tariff and the dispersal of western lands, for example, or on the idea that government should not regulate the economy nor pass social legislation, the Republican and Democratic parties often displayed little difference. Without grand plans to distinguish themselves, parties had to gain voter allegiance either from enduring Civil War sectional rivalries or by appealing to voters on the basis of favors they might dispense to loyal supporters should the party win the election. Both voters and financial supporters expected rewards for their allegiance if the party won, and the winning party indeed dispersed jobs and favorable economic decisions to its partisans as the Mugwumps charged in the 1880s.

Underlying this system, however, were two assumptions that many Americans were finding false and undemocratic. The first assumption was that there was a competitive marketplace of "rough equality of opportunity" that afforded everyone "formal equality before the law, liberty of contract, and the ever-expanding frontier." The second assumption was that equality of opportunity did not mean total equality. Many Americans had accepted a hierarchy of social inequality that elevated property rights, men, and white Americans and subordinated laborers, women, and nonwhites to a secondary position in society.[28] The first assumption was showing itself to be absolutely false. The second assumption was being challenged as undemocratic favoritism. Industrialists and businessmen claimed that rights of property gave them supremacy over labor, politicians and courts passed favorable legislation and legal rulings, tariff legislation

---

27. Just how much the political party system adhered to distributive government is a matter of debate among historians. For my purposes, the distinction is between the earlier ideas of non-interventionist and later ideas about interventionist, socially responsible, government. See Ballard Campbell, *The Growth of American Government: Governance from the Cleveland Era to the Present* (Bloomington: Indiana University Press, 1995) and Ronald Formisano, "The 'Party Period' Revisited," *Journal of American History*, 86 (June 1999): 93–120.

28. Alan Dawley, *Struggles for Justice: Social Responsibility and the Liberal State* (Cambridge, MA: Harvard University Press, 1991), 64.

helped industry and hurt farmers, and court rulings denied workers the right to strike or organize while sanctioning the use of the police power of the state by industry against workers, as had occurred at Andrew Carnegie's Homestead Steel Works in 1892. When the governor of Illinois refused to break the 1894 strike at George Pullman's car works in Chicago, President Cleveland used the army to do this. At the request of business, judges constantly issued "labor injunctions" forbidding worker actions. When around 500–600 protestors, dubbed Coxey's Army after the group's leader Jacob Coxey, reached Washington, D.C., in May 1894 to request government relief from the economic depression, their gathering was forcibly broken up and Coxey was arrested for trespassing on the steps of Congress. The "army" was decidedly not a radical group. Coxey himself was a small businessman, and he was accompanied by his wife and children.

The "corrupt bargain" was also a regional one. Northern industrialists and their congressional supporters (largely Republican) turned a blind eye to southern Democrats' repression of African Americans in return for getting favorable business legislation through Congress. Through the 1890s, thus, Congress refused to stop southern states from passing discriminatory legislation or violating the voting rights of African Americans, despite federal legislation passed during Reconstruction to guarantee political, social, and legal equality for African Americans.[29] By the end of the decade, Congress had officially abandoned any role in protecting the rights of African Americans. Southern states systematically disfranchised African Americans and racially segregated all public accommodations. When the Supreme Court ruling in *Plessy v. Ferguson* (1896) ceded to states the right to determine access to public accommodations, under the specious "separate but equal" concept, legalized racial segregation and whites-only voting became the rule in the South. The last African American member of Congress, George H. White of South Carolina, was defeated in 1900. At that time, 12.5 percent of the population was African American, with the vast majority living in the southern states. Thus a sizeable portion of the population was deprived of any representation in Congress. In his farewell speech, Rep. White listed all the accomplishments of African Americans since the end of slavery:

We have nearly 300 newspapers. . . . We have now in practice over 2,000 lawyers and a corresponding number of doctors. We have over $12,000,000 worth of school property and about $40,000,000 in church property. We have about 140,000 farms and homes, valued at in the neighborhood of $750,000,000, and personal property valued at about $170,000,000. We have raised about $11,000,000 for educational purposes, and the property per capita of every colored man, woman, and child in the United States is estimated at $75. . . . We are operating successfully several banks [and] commercial enterprises . . .[30]

---

29. The Reconstruction Act of 1867, the Enforcement Act of 1870, and Civil Rights Acts of 1874 and 1875 had guaranteed full political participation, forbade the denial of the right to vote on the basis of race, allowed federal supervision of elections to stop illegal voter registration practices, and guaranteed full and equal access for African Americans to all public accommodations.

30. White quoted in Michael Perman, *Struggle for Mastery: Disfranchisement in the South, 1888–1908* (Chapel Hill: University of North Carolina Press, 2001), 33–34.

Ideas about white supremacy clearly trumped property rights and any pretenses to democratic equality for black Americans. As more African Americans moved north, and into cities, progressives would have to confront racial injustice as an American, not just a southern, problem. In the same way, as more women began to assert themselves into public life—a process that will be considered more fully in the following chapter—the gender inequalities of American society could not withstand the movements for women's rights, including the suffrage movement and demands made by working women.

The two national woman suffrage organizations had merged into the National American Woman Suffrage Association (NAWSA) in 1890 to secure the vote on a state-by-state basis and to work for a national suffrage amendment that had been introduced in Congress in 1878. By the end of the nineteenth century, however, only Wyoming, Utah, Colorado, and Idaho had passed woman suffrage amendments or laws. Neither political party supported woman suffrage and the suffrage amendment languished in Congress. Various states still had laws denying women rights to property and to their children in case of divorce. Working women were paid less while often working just as long and as hard as working men. The American Federation of Labor (AFL) did not want to organize women, preferring to move women out of the workplace to create more jobs for men.

By the end of the nineteenth century, thus, more and more Americans believed that political corruption was trampling on the democratic ideals of equality and opportunity. The entire political system appeared corrupted by capitalist elites and property owners in league with the politicians to secure their own fortunes while exploiting other members of society. The premises about equality of opportunity were not only false in such a system, accepting such premises without question had led many Americans to accept disparities of wealth, massive social and labor inequality, and exploitation that negated any possible opportunity for millions of people to live a decent existence. These circumstances, in turn, were producing a thoroughly undemocratic society that could no longer be tolerated.

Jane Edna Hunter (1882–1971) arrived in Cleveland, Ohio, in 1905 from the South. She had just received her nursing degree from the Hampton Institute, one of the most prestigious institutions of higher education attended by African Americans. Her immediate priorities were to find a job and a place to live. Despite her "respectable" demeanor and her nursing degree, she found neither easily. In her recollections she described trudging "up one dingy street and down another" and having finally to settle on taking "the least disreputable room." Trained nurses were not numerous and desperately needed in industrial, immigrant cities such as Cleveland, but Hunter had to work as a domestic cleaning offices. Hunter's "problem" was that she was African American. More reputable housing was closed to African Americans. Even the YWCA, which provided rooms for single working women, would not allow her to stay. White physicians and hospitals would not take on a black nurse. Black nurses, in fact, could only work in segregated wards in public hospitals in the city. And, of course, as a woman she could not vote or hold public office, although Cleveland's African American men could.

Hunter was not defeated by this unpromising start to her professional life. Within a few years, Hunter had used her personal experiences to become part of progressivism. She was determined not to allow other African American young women to face the same trials as she had. In 1913, Hunter established the Working Girls' Home Association, which eventually changed its name to the Phillis Wheatley Association. The home was to be a safe residence for homeless African American working women and girls. By 1927 it was the largest independent residence facility in the country for African American women and one that also provided an employment service for these women. Hunter remained its executive director until 1946.

CHAPTER 2

꩜

Democracy Must
Have a Social Dimension

The cure for the ills of Democracy is more Democracy. . . .
—JANE ADDAMS, *DEMOCRACY AND SOCIAL ETHICS*, 1902

THE SOCIAL, ECONOMIC, and political inequality that Hunter faced was a common condition of life in the United States at the turn of the last century, and not just for African Americans. Because American democracy had been built around the ideal of individual responsibility, as progressives began to reject the earlier assumption that the poor, the unemployed, or certain ethnic groups were to blame for their own conditions, they had simultaneously to redefine what democracy meant. They needed to explain that democracy had to possess a social dimension. Jane Addams expressed it simply as the need for democracy to become more democratic. For social justice progressives, this meant a recognition of *social* rights as well as individual political rights. But because this was a relatively new concept in American democracy, progressives had to work out exactly what this meant, how it could be justified, and what needed to change so that a social dimension could be part of democracy.

In a series of lectures later reprinted as *Democracy and Social Ethics*, Jane Addams explained that real democracy could be achieved only if Americans developed a sense of social morality. Concern for individual rights of property, and individual "righteousness," as she put it, had to be balanced against a concern to secure the good of the whole society. All individuals must assume responsibility for the structure of society and for the welfare of all people, especially those they did not know or understand. Americans, according to Addams, had to realize that they had social, as well as political and individual, obligations.

33

All social justice progressives agreed with Addams on the broad point of social responsibility. For some of them, this meant applying Christian religious
values to social problems. For others, it required rearranging the public sphere
of political life to eliminate political corruption, poverty, and economic exploitation. Rather than leaving decisions to the political parties or seeking individual favors from elected officials, citizens, these progressives argued, had to
participate in more direct democratic debate and action. They had to demand
that public officials address social problems. For these progressives, only a new
sense of civic democracy would bring about social justice. Still other progressives believed that having more control over their labor, and having the rights
of labor acknowledged, would produce a more socially just society. Others
focused on creating a better society by protecting women and children and families. For African Americans, social justice could only be attained if racial discrimination was eliminated and they were recognized as equal citizens.

The movements and the people involved in reevaluating the meaning of
justice in a democratic society, thus, were numerous and their efforts oftentimes overlapped. Wherever one looks, for example, one finds Jane Addams.
The progressives engaged in the social justice crusades came to their view of
how and why to reform society from a variety of different settings and experiences. What they had in common, however, was a belief that all people and
politicians had to incorporate a sense of social responsibility into their actions
and decisions. If this were done, these progressives believed, the guiding principle of these actions and decisions would be promotion of a common welfare.
The result would be a socially just society.

THE SOCIAL GOSPEL

Beginning in the 1880s, a number of Protestant ministers, among them men
such as Washington Gladden and Josiah Strong, urged Christians to focus on
reforming society. These advocates of the new social gospel preached that it
was no longer sufficient to aspire to personal moral righteousness. There had
to be a collective social morality as well. If Americans undertook a great reform "crusade," according to the social gospelites, they could attain a "social" salvation that would produce God's kingdom on earth. The religious
motivation was quite important for some progressives, and recognizing this
helps explain the enduring influence of religion—especially Protestantism—
in American society.[1] The vast majority of progressives who were influenced
by the social gospel took from it a more worldly and sympathetic vision than
perhaps Gladden, Strong, and ministers had in mind. For Mary McDowell,
founder of the University of Chicago Settlement, and Celia Parker Woolley
and Caroline Bartlett Crane (both of whom were ministers), the social gospel

---

1. Unfortunately, Josiah Strong's call for a social gospel was tied to a vision of Anglo-Saxon superiority that cast anyone belonging to another group as in need of being reformed by their betters.
One outcome of this aspect of the social gospel has been a negative interpretation of progressive social gospelers as racists and ultimately as imperialists. An opposite outcome is to overstress the role
of the social gospel, and Protestantism generally, in progressive reform.

led them to identify with the conditions of other people and to call for reforms that would promote the everyday welfare of all Americans. The Kingdom of God on earth may have been a nice idea, but a daily common welfare was the more readily obtainable goal for these women. The tenets of a social morality embedded in the social gospel opened a doorway to public action for many women. It gave them courage, and reason, for demanding new public roles for women. If it were the duty of all Christians to work toward a better society, then women certainly ought to play a role in this work. Jewish and Catholic women did not follow the religious vision of the Protestant social gospel, of course. But for some of them, religious principles also provided a foundation for their reform activities.[2]

Other groups of progressives expressed their ideas about democracy in more secular terms. They called upon Americans to accept responsibility for the conditions of others and to work actively to change these conditions. As part of this change, they began demanding that government pass new laws and establish mechanisms to ensure that all Americans had a decent standard of living. One element that characterized a difference between the social gospel advocates and the more secular advocates of a new sense of social responsibility is how they overlapped with those progressives who were demanding more democratic social rights and civic action as the pathway to social responsibility.

The Social Settlement and Urban Missions

Urban settlement houses are one obvious site for exploring this new sense of social and civic responsibility and democracy. Settlements had two principal aims. The first aim was to replace private charity as a means of aiding the poor and unemployed in cities. The vast majority of social settlement residents and workers saw themselves as "helping" others. They were primarily middle-class women—far fewer men ever became settlement workers—who were educated and often professionally trained. They believed that they had something to bring to the people of the settlement neighborhoods. The Henry Street Settlement on New York's Lower East Side, headed by Lillian Wald, was originally named the Nurses' Settlement because it provided home health care and visiting nurses. Like Wald, Harriet Vittum, who headed the Northwestern

---

2. For a range of interpretations on the role of religion in progressivism, see Victoria Bissell Brown, *The Education of Jane Addams* (Philadelphia: University of Pennsylvania Press, 2004); Robert Crunden, *Ministers of Reform: The Progressives' Achievements in American Civilization* (New York: Basic Books, 1982); Susan Curtis, *A Consuming Faith: The Social Gospel and American Culture* (Baltimore: Johns Hopkins University Press, 1991); Marjorie N. Feld, "'An Actual Working Out of Internationalism': Russian Politics, Zionism, and Lillian Wald's Ethnic Progressivism," *The Journal of the Gilded Age and Progressive Era*, 2 (April 2003): 119–49; and Deborah Skok, "Catholic Ladies Bountiful: Chicago's Catholic Settlement Houses and Day Nurseries, 1892–1930" (Ph.D. diss., University of Chicago, 2001). For writings of social gospelers, see, for example, Washington Gladden, *Social Salvation* (Boston: Houghton Mifflin, 1902); Walter Rauschenbusch, *Christianity and the Social Crisis* (New York: Macmillan, 1907); and Josiah Strong, *Our Country: Its Possible Future and Its Present Crisis* (New York: American Home Missionary Society, 1885; 1891).

University Settlement on Chicago's immigrant Near West Side, was also a trained nurse. The Neighborhood Union, founded by Lugenia Burns Hope in Atlanta in 1908, provided playground facilities and a health clinic for its African American neighborhood. Providing such services in poorer neighborhoods sprang from the belief that everyone in the community had to assume responsibility for the conditions of everyone else. Jane Addams called this the *objective* necessity for the social settlement. For her, settlements were to occupy a new position between the city's neediest residents and the traditional charity organizations. She believed that charity workers were too focused on ameliorating immediate need rather than seeing how social conditions, and not personal failures, caused such need, and then working to change the conditions, not the people.[3]

The second aim was what Jane Addams, in a 1892 lecture, called the *subjective* necessity for settlements. Addams believed that many young Americans wanted to change society. They were experiencing, in her words,

> the desire to make the entire social organism democratic, to extend democracy beyond its political expression . . . the impulse to share the race life, and to bring as much as possible of social energy and accumulation of civilization to those portions of the [human] race which have little . . . a certain renaissance of Christianity, a movement toward its early humanitarian aspects.[4]

The three elements of this statement provide a concise look at the ideas and actions that motivated many settlement workers. First, there was the idea that Americans had "to extend democracy beyond its political expression" of universal (white) male suffrage to a guarantee of citizen participation in all facets of life because all elements and classes of society were interdependent. Second was the idea that no one in society could ignore its other members. The settlement aimed to turn this idea into everyday experience and practice. By living in proximity with the poor and sharing all the problems of their neighborhoods, the more privileged members of society would "grow into a sense of relationship and mutual interests." This ideal extended the work of settlements well beyond "helping" to sharing, working with, and learning from their neighbors. In her memoirs, Lillian Wald expressed this ideal as a process of

---

3. See Brown, *The Education of Jane Addams*, 267–68, for her explanation of Addams' first attempts to explain the difference between charity work and settlement work in 1892, and Daphne Spain, *How Women Saved the City* (Minneapolis: University of Minnesota Press, 2001), 66–67. Jane Addams, "Charitable Effort," in *Democracy and Social Ethics* (New York: Macmillan, 1902; reprint edition, Urbana: University of Illinois Press, 2002), explains this in more detail. See also, Joan Waugh, "'Give This Man Work'! Josephine Shaw Lowell, the Charity Organization Society of the City of New York, and the Depression of 1893," *Social Science History*, 25 (Summer 2001): 217–46, for her assessment of how the depression caused the New York Charity Organization to begin thinking about attacking the structures that were causing poverty.

4. Addams, "The Subjective Necessity for Social Settlements," lecture subsequently published in Addams, *Philanthropy and Social Progress* (New York: Crowell, 1893): 1–26. Addams was referring to the human race.

mutual learning that would create a good democratic society: "the good in their old-world traditions and culture shall be mingled with the best that lies within our new-world ideals." Third was the belief in religion as a worldly humanitarian idea as much as a spiritual one.[5]

It is undeniably true that the relationship between settlement workers and neighborhood residents, while mutual, was never precisely equal. The class and cultural divides between the middle-class native born and the immigrant working class and poor always gave the settlement house workers the upper hand in all their dealings. And because one of the goals of the settlement was to "Americanize" immigrants into the norms of their new society, settlement workers had their own ideas of what they wanted to accomplish. Mutuality never meant complete equality, but settlement house workers did learn from their neighbors. Addams, for example, gently chided Chicago matron Louise DeKoven Bowen for thinking that the women of the Hull House neighborhood should be grateful to her. Bowen, to her credit, was chagrined to have thought in that way.[6] Nor were settlement workers ever able to dictate to their neighbors how they should behave or what they should do in their neighborhood. After discussing the sanitary conditions of their neighborhood at a meeting of the Hull House Women's Club, the neighborhood women undertook to investigate their neighborhood and bring their findings back to Hull House. The settlement residents prepared a document of complaint to the city council, based on the work and findings of the neighborhood women. Addams recognized that the work had been initiated and carried out by the neighborhood, not by the settlement:

> For the club woman who had finished a long day's work of washing or ironing followed by the cooking of a hot supper, it would have been much easier to sit on her doorstep during a summer evening than to go up and down ill-kept alleys and get into trouble with her neighbors over the condition of their garbage boxes. It required both civic enterprise and moral conviction to be willing to do this three evenings a week during the hottest and most uncomfortable months of the year.[7]

The mutuality of which Addams spoke was that of a mutual recognition of interests in which all residents would learn "to regard the entire life of their city as organic, to make an effort to unify it, and to protest against its over-differentiation."[8] The women residents of Hull House knew how to make complaints to city government, but the neighborhood women were the ones who wanted to reform their living conditions. Initiatives that lacked neighborhood support quickly died, as happened to Addams' attempt to run a neighborhood kitchen serving a "nutritious" diet. Her idea of a "nutritious" diet, however,

---

5. See Brown, *The Education of Jane Addams*, 265–66, for an assessment of Addams' ideas in this regard. See also, Lillian Wald, *The House on Henry Street* (New York: Henry Holt, 1915), 66.

6. Louise DeKoven Bowen, *Growing Up with a City* (New York: Macmillan, 1926; reprint, Urbana: University of Illinois Press, 2002), 87–88.

7. Addams, *Twenty Years at Hull House* (New York: Macmillan, 1910), 102.

8. Ibid., "Subjective Necessity."

the so-called New England, or Boston, kitchen consisting of overcooked stews, vegetables, and cornmeal mush proved too bland to interest the diverse immigrant residents of the neighborhood, and they simply stayed away.

The role in the settlement movement of religion, the third element of Addams' subjective necessity, is similarly complicated. Addams herself thought less about religion as faith and more about the principles of human behavior—its "humanitarian aspects"—from which people could learn how to treat one another and how to tell right from wrong. Thus, Hull House never had a religious affiliation and even the nondenominational Protestant services that it held in its early years were later eliminated. Addams' most recent biographer, Victoria Bissell Brown, contends that Addams "did not simply refuse to impose Christian beliefs on her neighbors, she declined to identify with organized Christianity." In a neighborhood that was growing more heavily Catholic and Jewish every year, the settlement would not have met Addams' vision of mutuality if it had a religious affiliation. When the official handbook on settlements was published in 1911, it stated that a typical settlement was one that was neutral on religion. Many settlement house residents followed this thinking, although others—Vida Scudder of Boston's Dennison House and even Hull House's cofounder Ellen Gates Starr, for example—declared themselves to be personally motivated by religion.[9] Whether grounded in some religious principle or not, social morality for social justice progressives meant developing a new code of behavior for how individuals acted socially, rather than personally.

Because so many of the earliest settlements took specifically Protestant Christianity as a guiding force, Catholics and Jews also founded their own settlements, sometimes with overt religious orientations, as a protection against what they feared were attempts to convert people to Protestantism. The Madonna Center in Chicago, the St. Rose Settlement in New York, the Brownson House Settlement in Los Angeles, and the St. Elizabeth Center in St. Louis were distinctly Catholic. The Hebrew Industrial School (later renamed Hecht House) in Boston and the Irene Kaufmann Settlement in Pittsburgh were likewise distinctly Jewish.

On the other hand, Lillian Wald and other more secular Jews of the Henry Street Settlement fought against calls to "Judaize" the settlement. As Wald herself expressed it:

> Our experience in one small East Side section, a block perhaps, has led to a next contact, and a next, in widening circles, until our community relationships have come to include the city, the state, the national government, and the world at large. It is rare indeed to find an experienced settlement worker who does not feel kinship with all peoples.

Because Wald's understanding of mutuality was very similar to that of Addams, making Henry Street a "Jewish" settlement would have violated this ideal.[10]

---

9. Brown, *The Education of Jane Addams*, 273. Robert A. Woods and Albert Kennedy, eds., *Handbook of Settlements* (New York: Charities Publication Committee, 1911), noted in Spain, *How Women Saved the City*, 69–70

10. Feld, "An Actual Working Out of Internationalism," 124–35; quote from Lillian Wald, *Windows on Henry Street* (Boston: Little, Brown, 1934), 10.

The influence of religion in social action for African Americans, the vast majority of whom were Protestant, was different still. Women of the National Baptist Convention, for example, used religion as a way to justify their active public engagement. In 1900, they formed a Woman's Convention auxiliary and used this organization to promote women's work in social justice reform. For African American women especially, church work had given them the training and organizational skills they would bring to new public activities. Whether African American settlements (or missions, as some were called) were overtly religious depended on their founders. The Institutional Church and Social Settlement in Chicago was directed by a male minister of the African Methodist Episcopal denomination. The White Rose Mission and Industrial Association founded by Victoria Earle Matthews in New York City was secular, but prayer was an integral part of the mission, whose purpose was to "train boys and girls and make a social center for them where the only influences would be good and true and pure."[11]

THE PUBLIC FORUMS MOVEMENT

Although settlement house workers often spoke in the intimate terms of creating social kinship and neighborhood ties, other progressives sought more democracy in the public sphere through the creation of a participatory civic life. This movement took many forms and its ideals spread to many different groups and aspects of American life. Foremost among these was the public forums movement.

Americans prided themselves on their political democracy. By the start of the twentieth century, universal white male suffrage, which did not exist in Europe, was a reality. Eligible voters turned out for elections in higher percentages at the time than they would subsequently. The parties held spectacular public rallies for candidates that were well attended by the party faithful. But progressives argued that there was more to democracy than voting and party membership. A truer democracy required places where ordinary people could gather together and discuss the problems of society and such places were in short supply. The settlement houses provided some such venues, but these were private spaces with limited capacity for an audience. The late-nineteenth-century Chautauqua Movement, begun in upstate New York, was also deemed insufficient. The Chautauqua often required paid admission, it had a religious foundation, and other than its upstate New York locale, it held primarily sporadic traveling lectures.[12] The proponents of a more vibrant democratic life, or a more democratic public as it has also been called, wanted to establish permanent public community forums where anyone who wanted could come and

11. Matthews quoted in Spain, *How Women Saved the City*, 151. For the Woman's Convention, see Evelyn Brooks Higginbotham, *Righteous Discontent: The Women's Movement in the Black Baptist Church, 1880–1920* (Cambridge, MA: Harvard University Press, 1993). In Texas cities, Methodist women organized Wesley Houses in Mexican-American neighborhoods where there was not yet a tradition of female social involvement. See Judith N. McArthur, *Creating the New Woman: The Rise of Southern Women's Progressive Culture in Texas, 1893–1918* (Urbana: University of Illinois Press, 1998), 82–83.

12. For more on this movement, see Andrew Rieser, *The Chautauqua Moment: Protestants, Progressives, and the Culture of Modern Liberalism* (New York: Columbia University Press, 2003).

debate the pressing issues of the day.[13] These open forum advocates also believed that the most effective public gatherings had to be in cities where the masses of the population lived and where some of the worst problems of society were manifested.

The People's Institute, founded by university professor Charles Sprague Smith in New York City in 1897, was a pioneer in this movement. It organized a People's Forum with free admission. Often as many as 1,000 people at a time came to listen to speakers and debate pressing issues of the day. At the end of the evening everyone voted on whether to forward protests to the city government. In Cleveland, newly elected Mayor Tom Johnson began holding public tent meetings in 1901, claiming they were the best way for the people of the city to educate themselves about municipal problems. The structure of his tent meetings was particularly conducive to engaging a large audience. Speakers were invited to present opposing views, working-class residents felt comfortable in attending, and plenty of time was given over for questions from the audience. For Johnson and other progressives, public forums were the means to educate a democratic public in how to fight political and economic corruption.[14]

Frederic Howe was an enthusiastic champion of the forum movement. He was living in Cleveland when Johnson was mayor and his experiences with the tent meetings convinced him the city was the place where a democratic society would be formed. He subsequently left Cleveland to become director of the People's Institute. As director, he broadened the reach of the People's Forum by organizing local equivalents throughout the city. People's forums were also founded in Boston and other cities, mainly, but not exclusively, in the Northeast. For a time, these forums were drawn together into a Cooperative Forum Bureau that recruited and sent out speakers across the country. Public intellectuals as diverse as the feminist Charlotte Perkins Gilman, African American leader W.E.B. DuBois, and social gospeler Walter Rauschenbusch participated in the forums. The advocates of the people's forums were convinced that this was the best way to educate a democratic public because, as one of its admirers put it, here "the rank and file of the people participate."[15] There was, of course, an element of paternalism in this movement. The intellectuals assumed that they would teach the "rank and file" how to be a democratic public. The public did not direct or decide upon these forums; they were mainly to listen and learn.

Because one of the movement's aims was to educate average citizens away from following the lead of the political parties and toward putting more educated and expert men into political office, public forums were a favorite target for professional politicians. These men derided the intellectuals as being out of touch with the people and what they wanted from their society. As New York City democratic politician George Washington Plunkitt put it,

13. The best history of this movement is Kevin Mattson, *Creating a Democratic Public: The Struggle for Urban Participatory Democracy During the Progressive Era* (University Park: Pennsylvania State University Press, 1998).

14. See Tom Johnson's autobiography, *My Story* (New York: B. W. Heusch, 1913).

15. Quoted in Mattson, *Creating a Democratic Public*, 45.

College professors and philosophers who go up in a balloon to think are always discussin' the question: "Why Reform Administrations Never Succeed Themselves!" The reason is plain to anybody who has learned the a, b, c of politics. . . . The fact is that a reformer can't last in politics. He can make a show for a while, but he always comes down like a rocket. Politics is as much a regular business as the grocery or the dry-goods or the drug business.

Or, as a popular fictional satirist of the time quipped of the reformers' failures in politics: "Politics Ain't Beanbag."[16]

Yet, it would not be fair to dismiss the public forum movement as the patronizing attempt of the intellectuals to tell the "rank and file" how to behave in a democracy.[17] There was genuine concern then, as there is in the present day, about the role and the voice of the individual in a complex democratic society. Nor was the public forum movement as advocated by intellectuals such as Smith and Howe the only progressive idea about changing the relationship of the American people to one another and to their government. In Boston, Mary Parker Follett proposed to design a new public democracy through social centers in neighborhood schools that, unlike the public forums, were to be organized and run by the people of the neighborhood. The idea was that such social centers would be a place where neighbors could get together, decide what the pressing problems of their neighborhoods were, and act upon them. Follett believed that such a group process would lead to "continuous, collective self-education" that was rooted in everyday life. Her concept of a public democracy was one that flowed from the bottom up. Social centers located in the familiar setting of the neighborhood school would bring together heterogeneous urban residents to debate, argue, and resolve their differences and learn to live together. But for Follett, democracy was not to stop in the neighborhood. As she expressed it "Every neighborhood must be organized; the neighborhood groups must then be integrated, through larger intermediary groups, into a true state." Follett's progressivism, thus, fell somewhere between that of men such as Frederic Howe and that of many of the female settlement workers. Why Follett developed her particular idea, however, is an example of Jane Addams' belief that experience helped fashion ideas and actions. Follett had trained for an academic career but had abandoned this in favor of doing social work in one of Boston's poorest neighborhoods from 1900 to 1908.[18] Follett's progressivism, like that of many settlement and other social workers, was shaped by her personal experiences and direct contact with the enormous problems of American society.

---

16. William L. Riordon, *Plunkitt of Tammany Hall* (New York: McClure, Phillips, 1905), essay on "Morning Glories." A beanbag was a child's toy of the time. Both quotes were intended to show that democratic politics had to be left in the hands of professional politicians.

17. Leon Fink, *Progressive Intellectuals and the Dilemmas of Democratic Commitment* (Cambridge, MA: Harvard University Press, 1997), assesses the genuine belief that intellectuals had in democracy but presents a compelling case for how difficult it has been for intellectuals in the twentieth century to connect with the majority of people.

18. Mattson, *Creating a Democratic Public*, ch. 5, examines Follett's ideas and work. Quote from 97. Unfortunately, the best book on Follett is only available in Italian. Raffaella Baritono, *La democrazia vissuta: individualismo e pluralismo nel pensiero di Mary Parker Follett* (Torino: LaRosa, Italia, 2001).

WOMEN'S VOLUNTARY ORGANIZATIONS

The objectives of advocates of the public forums and social centers were part of the social justice progressives' design to construct a wider democratic public. Other progressive groups agreed with the idea of creating a more democratic public from the bottom up but turned to individual responsibility backed by group action as the means to it.

In fact, the ideal of a more vibrant public life with a call for social action to reform American society had originated well before the public forum movement in the voluntary organizations that urban women formed across the nineteenth century. In their early decades, such organizations tended to limit their focus to literary, cultural, or charitable purposes. But many such women's groups quickly discovered that even with a limited scope, whatever they did drew them into contact with other groups in their cities, especially with poor women and children. Thus, even before the Civil War, women's voluntary groups had begun to turn their work outward into the larger society. The Civil War enhanced women's public work in the Sanitary Commission, after which ever larger numbers of women refused to move back into the private world of home and family.[19] Instead, they built upon their earlier foundations to form new organizations specifically intended to be agencies of urban reform. One of the first of these was the Woman's Christian Temperance Union (WCTU, 1874), whose first national leader was Frances Willard, who had also been the first Dean of Women at Northwestern University. As the name implied, the women of this organization wanted to eliminate, or at least moderate, alcohol consumption, believing it to be an evil moral influence. Although the organization is often derided by pointing to the spectacle of "WCTUer" Carrie Nation marching into saloons and chopping them up with an ax, the organization articulated a broad understanding of the social and economic problems that alcohol use was causing for many women and children. The WCTU argued that in the prevailing societal structures women and children were left unprotected if husbands and fathers spent too much of the family's earnings on liquor. Before long, in addition to advocating temperance, the WCTU began to support an array of other social reforms: woman suffrage, the eight-hour workday, and women's equal legal rights all were part of a WCTU vision of bringing about more social justice.[20]

---

19. Barbara Berg, *The Remembered Gate: Origins of American Feminism, the Woman and the City, 1800–1860* (New York: Oxford University Press, 1978); Nancy Hewitt, *Women's Activism and Social Change: Rochester, New York, 1822–1872* (Ithaca, NY: Cornell University Press, 1984); Lori Ginzburg, *Women and the Work of Benevolence: Morality, Politics, and Class in the Nineteenth-Century United States* (New Haven, CT: Yale University Press, 1990); and Judith Giesberg, *Civil War Sisterhood: The U.S. Sanitary Commission and Women's Politics in Transition* (Boston: Northeastern University Press, 2000).

20. Ruth Bordin, *Woman and Temperance: The Quest for Power and Liberty, 1873–1900* (Philadelphia: Temple University Press, 1981).

Activist Women and Women's Organizations

Most women's voluntary organizations began on the local level. Caroline Brown organized the Chicago Woman's Club (CWC, 1876) to have a means for women "to take up the live issues of this world we live in." In less than a decade the CWC moved from discussing these issues to doing "practical work" to change existing conditions. The Philadelphia New Century Club (1877) created a Woman's Health Protective Association (1893) to examine how the city's government dealt with public health issues and to study better methods of water filtration and protection against contagious diseases. Women's Educational and Industrial Unions appeared in other cities, such as in Boston (1877) and Los Angeles (1888), to connect middle-class and working-class women in efforts to better the conditions of the latter. Women in smaller towns and cities organized Women's Town Improvement Associations and enlisted women to plant trees, clean the streets, and even keep farm animals from invading those streets. There were so many women's clubs by 1890 that women formed the General Federation of Women's Clubs (GFWC) to help coordinate their public activities throughout the country. African American women formed their own voluntary organizations. In 1896, they gathered them together in a parallel national organization, the National Association of Colored Women (NACW).[21]

Women's voluntary organizations had a variety of names, but all of them signaled women's preoccupation with urban conditions and with the condition of women, children, and families. There were citywide or neighborhood women's clubs, women's city clubs, and women's civic federations, associations, or leagues. There were juvenile protective leagues, public school associations, health protective associations, consumers' leagues, and women's trade union leagues. Unlike settlement house or social workers, these middle-class women did not directly experience poverty, want, and social injustice. Instead, what they saw around them led them to believe that only through personal and public action could they, first, understand the situation of other people in their city, and second, work for reform. An example of this can be seen with the middle-class Chicago women of the Protective Agency for Women and Children. They knew, for instance, that poor women were disadvantaged in the legal system but not how the system functioned. In order to learn more about how justice was meted out, they went into the city's Justice of the Peace courts. Here they found poor women accused of prostitution and fined, whether there was proof of it or not, simply on the word of the male police officer. Prosecutions for this "crime" were entirely directed against women, as men involved in soliciting prostitutes were never even required to appear in court. When men tried to keep the middle-class women out of the court, saying that court was no place for respectable women, the leader of the organization retorted that the women were seeking justice. They wanted the public to learn that "the virtue of poor women" was "as well worthy of the protection of the law as the purse of a rich man."[22]

African American women in the NACW did similar work in their cities. The Texas Association of Colored Women's Clubs entered social welfare work by founding an institution for "unfortunate" black boys. The Emanuel Settlement in Chicago provided day care and other services for African American children. The Tampa Women's Improvement Club focused on education in their community. The Women's League of Newport, Rhode Island, ran a day nursery.[23]

---

21. Chicago Woman's Club quoted in Maureen A. Flanagan, *Seeing with Their Hearts: Chicago Women and the Vision of the Good City, 1871–1933* (Princeton, NJ: Princeton University Press, 2002), 31–32. For more on the pre-progressive women's clubs, see Sarah Deutsch, *Women and the City: Gender, Space and Power in Boston, 1870–1940* (New York: Oxford University Press, 2000); Gayle Gullett, *Becoming Citizens: The Emergence and Development of the California Women's Movement, 1880–1911* (Urbana: University of Illinois Press, 2000); Spain, *How Women Saved the City*; Bonj Szczygiel, "'City Beautiful' Revisited: An Analysis of Nineteenth-Century Civic Improvement Efforts," *Journal of Urban History*, 29 (December 2003): 107–32; and Anne Firor Scott, *Natural Allies: Women's Associations in American History* (Urbana: University of Illinois Press, 1992), for an excellent general overview.

22. Quoted in Flanagan, *Seeing with Their Hearts*, 35.

23. McArthur, *Creating the New Woman*, 88–89, for Texas; Anne Meis Knupfer, *Toward a Tenderer Humanity and a Nobler Womanhood: African-American Women's Clubs in Turn-of-the-Century Chicago* (New York: New York University Press, 1996), 98–107, for Chicago; and Nancy Hewitt, *Southern Discomfort: Women's Activism in Tampa, Florida, 1880s–1920s* (Urbana: University of Illinois Press, 2001), 155–56, for Tampa.

Day Nursery Founded and Run by the African American Women's League of Newport, Rhode Island
Source: Library of Congress, Prints & Photographs Division, LC-USZ62-51556

Women's organizations worked hard to establish the juvenile court. Until this reform, children who were arrested—even for petty thievery or truancy—could be put into the adult justice system, sometimes even held in jails with adult offenders and tried in the same courts. Juvenile court advocates pointed out that this was a fine way to turn children into adult criminals. But these progressives wanted a separate juvenile justice system because they believed it would produce a better society. Children, they argued, needed justice, not punishment. Justice meant identifying the causes of a child's behavior and then finding ways to help her or him change it. By such means, not only would a child's welfare be protected, the child's family would also be helped. With less juvenile crime, society as a whole would benefit. Once established, the juvenile court investigated a child's family circumstances to try to understand how to prevent future delinquency. Although the juvenile court advocates obviously wanted children of the working class and poor to behave according to the norms of middle-class society, they cannot be dismissed only as maternalist social-control advocates. Urban industrial society used and abused children of the poor. Those progressives who wanted to establish this separate legal system were genuinely concerned to make life better for children and their families.[24]

Changes to the legal system were examples of how women's organizations across the country were turning toward government to provide for the common welfare of all people. They saw justice and welfare for women, children, and families as fundamental to producing a socially just democratic society. In Dallas, for example, the Federation of Women demanded that the city immediately build a new water filtration plant to eliminate recurring typhoid epidemics that killed children every summer. In Galveston, Texas, the Women's Health Protective Association demanded new municipal ordinances for enforcing sanitary conditions in grocery stores and bakeries. Women from Seattle, to Memphis, to Chicago, to Boston were outraged at the conditions of the public school system, which everywhere was overcrowded, underfunded, and ill-equipped in immigrant and working-class neighborhoods. One of women's aims was to put women on their local board of education. They were convinced that a democratic society absolutely required equal access to a good education for every child and that women's engagement with decision making on schools was essential for achieving this goal. These same women's groups demanded passage of compulsory-age legislation so that children would remain in school longer and become better prepared for life after school. They also called on cities to build and maintain public baths, eliminate air and water pollution, and foster the overall health and sanitation conditions within their cities. They argued that cities had a social obligation to prevent illness, disease, and death, especially for the most vulnerable in society—young children.

Many female progressives believed that reform of such conditions could best be accomplished through women's participation in public affairs—especially because businessmen often seemed more interested in their personal profits than in the public good. Chicagoan Anna Nicholes was appalled when a banker told her that he loved the smell of the noxious odors coming from the stockyards because it meant "Dollars!" Chicago settlement resident and woman's club member Mary McDowell accused the businessmen of the city of favoring a particular means for garbage disposal because they wanted to

---

24. The first juvenile court was formed in Chicago in 1899. Other cities instituted theirs immediately after: Cleveland and New York (1902); Pittsburgh, Denver, and Los Angeles (1903); Detroit (1907). Although recent research is demonstrating that the treatment of child offenders before the institution of the juvenile court varied from state to state, the fact that they were established everywhere leads to the conclusion that they were deemed a valuable and necessary reform. See David Wolcott, "Juvenile Justice Before Juvenile Court: Cops, Courts, and Kids in Turn-of-the-Century Detroit," *Social Science History*, 27 (Spring 2003): 109–36. The juvenile court is now called family court. See also, Victoria Getis, *The Juvenile Court and the Progressives* (Urbana: University of Illinois Press, 2000).

"extract money out of the garbage."[25] In the struggle over pure milk, social justice progressives confronted this same attitude. As cities had grown larger, more numerous, and more industrial, rural and farm areas were pushed geographically further away from urban consumers. At the same time, for a number of reasons, including having to go out to work whether they wanted to or not, women had turned largely to bottled milk for feeding babies. Lacking nearby sources of fresh milk, families depended on shipments from the countryside and distribution through dairies, which were becoming big businesses. Few cities had regulations to guarantee the safety of this milk and less than scrupulous producers and suppliers took advantage. Much milk came from tuberculin cows or those fed on the byproducts from breweries, which were considerably cheaper than grain. Milk was shipped in open, unrefrigerated containers; it was often diluted with water, or worse, with "milk expander," a mix of soda, ammonia, salt, and water. Milk "colorings" such as chalk were often added to cover up such "dirty" milk. Women's groups across the country attacked these practices and demanded that government test cows, regulate the production and distribution of milk, and investigate the possibilities of pasteurization. Women charged that the country's high rate of infant mortality—by 1910 it was 124 deaths per 1,000 live births compared with 106 in Great Britain—was directly attributable to unscrupulous business practices and lack of government regulation to ensure milk safety. They demanded that government make it a priority to secure the health and safety of babies and young children. In this and other health and sanitation crusades, progressive women were determined to make it the duty of government to protect the health and safety of the most vulnerable members of society. They were not content to let justice trickle down from economic prosperity but demanded that social justice be actively fostered by government. When both government and business resisted regulation, women's organizations opened pure milk distribution centers as they kept up the fight for regulation. Yet women could not feel satisfied even if they achieved regulation in their own locale because of the ripple effect in an interconnected industrial society. When Milwaukee passed an ordinance to prevent milk from tuberculin cows being sold in that city, Wisconsin farmers simply sold their sick cows to Illinois farmers where there was no such regulation. Infant and childhood mortality began to descend as women succeeded in their quest for government regulation of food, milk, and drugs. Even so, the time that it took to secure such legislation throughout the country resulted in a rather grim surprise for Americans as they prepared to go to war in 1917. A high percentage of young men were found medically unfit to serve in the military. In time of emergency, such findings spurred government and business

---

25. For Dallas and Galveston, see McArthur, *Creating the New Woman*, 34. Banker quoted in Anna Nicholes, "How Women Can Help in the Administration of a City," *The Woman Citizen's Library*, vol. 9 (Chicago: Civics Society, 1913), 2150. McDowell quoted in Flanagan, *Seeing with Their Hearts*, 97.

into action. Once the emergency was over, however, public health matters would again be relegated to a low priority.[26]

Women's organizations produced a sea-tide change in women's public visibility from their neighborhoods up through the national level. The millions of women involved struggled to make a more socially and economically just society, which they believed would be a more democratic one. Indeed, without the ideas and initiatives of women, social justice progressivism would have been a pale shadow of the other forms of progressivism. Moreover, women's participation in progressivism undoubtedly struck many people at the time as truly "the rising of the women"—the title of a book about one of these organizations. There were always tensions between the middle-class women who formed the bulk of the membership of these voluntary organizations and working-class women who often had other priorities—for instance, cheap milk that they could afford. Yet women were learning to work together on health and sanitation issues because they wanted all children protected. According to Jane Addams, mothers' clubs from settlement houses demanded pure milk and groups of ethnic women sought the right to vote so that they could "get rid of the shocking Chicago grime on all their food." The *Rising of the Women* recounts the work of the cross-class Illinois Women's Alliance to force municipal government to undertake social measures such as building public bathhouses to give all urban residents access to clean water for bathing.[27]

Women had some tremendous successes in promoting social justice progressivism. Cities built public baths, began regulating food and milk production, passed new ordinances to improve housing conditions, and accepted responsibility for picking up garbage, cleaning the city, and lessening smoke and water pollution. The reforms and new regulations women managed to enact, however, did not change the overall priority of the country to constructing a democracy in which social justice was the first priority. Social justice progressives were not able to make the motto of the women's Memphis Public School Association—"To the Public Good Private Respects Must Yield"—become the motto of the country.[28] Without this ideological change, social justice progressives would continue to confront competing visions of progressivism whose agendas seemed more palatable. Nonetheless, as later chapters will explore, these women kept working for their reform agenda.

---

26. Jacqueline H. Wolf, *Don't Kill Your Baby: Public Health and the Decline of Breastfeeding in the Nineteenth and Twentieth Centuries* (Columbus: Ohio State University Press, 2001); Jennifer Koslow, "Putting It to a Vote: The Provision of Pure Milk in Progressive Era Los Angeles, *The Journal of the Gilded Age and Progressive Era*, 3 (April 2004): 111–44; Judith Walzer Leavitt, *The Healthiest City: Milwaukee and the Politics of Health Reform* (Madison: University of Wisconsin Press, 1982); and Scott, *Natural Allies*, 151–52.

27. See also, Addams, *Twenty Years at Hull House*, 237–38. Meredith Tax, *The Rising of the Women: Feminist Solidarity and Class Conflict, 1880–1917* (New York: Monthly Review Press, 1980). For the public bath movement generally, see Marilyn Thornton Williams, *Washing "The Great Unwashed": Public Baths in Urban America, 1840–1920* (Columbus: Ohio State University Press, 1991). See Spain, *How Women Saved the City* for extensive discussion on public baths in Boston, Chicago, and New York City.

28. Marsha Wedell, *Elite Women and the Reform Impulse in Memphis, 1875–1915* (Knoxville: University of Tennessee Press, 1991), 114.

JUSTICE FOR LABOR/LABOR FOR JUSTICE

In the last decades of the nineteenth century, court rulings and state laws had gravely hampered labor's right to organize unions and to strike. Courts issued injunctions to stop strikes and management had a free hand in determining wages, hours and conditions of labor, and hiring and firing practices. Nevertheless, by the mid-1890s labor organizations had been leading large strikes throughout the country for several decades. One of the enduring questions of U.S. history is why socialism seemed to have succeeded far less than in Europe. Looking at certain actions undertaken by labor in this era, we see the appeal of social justice progressivism among the working class as a factor that suggests some reasons for the relatively muted impact of socialism.

Urban labor in the United States was quite active in this period. For one thing, technology increased the number of workers in the so-called public-service sector. Municipal utilities were privately owned and operated, but by striking, their workers were able to shut down vital services that urban residents were coming to depend on for everyday life. Cleveland, St. Louis, Seattle, New York City, San Francisco, and Milwaukee, for example, experienced transit strikes accompanied by street violence. These actions alerted other urban residents to the plight of workers, but also to how the utility owners were exploiting their workers, providing miserable service to users, and pursuing business practices that were dangerous to the populace. In many cities, residents supported striking transit workers and demanded municipal ownership of utilities. In Cleveland, the city's residents were furious with the Big Consolidated streetcar company for fatal accidents caused by running the streetcars at rapid speeds through crowded neighborhoods. When the Big Consolidated's workers struck in 1899, the people of the city stood behind them and boycotted the cars run by replacement workers—scabs, in the vernacular of laborers. One direct outcome of this situation was the election of reform mayor Tom Johnson in 1901. In his campaign, Johnson promised to lower streetcar fares and advocated municipal ownership of transit lines. The *Cleveland Plain Dealer* reported that there was a "tidal wave" of support for Johnson because of "his focused attacks on the streetcar companies." Of course, this was not always the situation. Although San Franciscans had supported the streetcar strike of 1902, they did not support the strike of 1907. In that year, the political situation worked against the strikers. The labor-backed mayor was indicted for extortion and one result was that the strikers received very little support from either the public at large or the politicians.[29]

Municipal ownership (which will be discussed in detail in Chapter 5) was not just a tactic to rein in business practices. It meant more democracy in cities and for their workers. If municipal governments owned and operated utilities, voters could hold local officials accountable for bad service. Male transit workers also

---

29. See Shelton Stromquist, "The Crucible of Class: Cleveland Politics and the Origins of Municipal Reform in the Progressive Era," *The Journal of Urban History,* 23 (January 1997): 192–220, 221, for Johnson. Events in San Francisco can be followed in the city's newspapers and a Web essay: Robert Emery Bionaz, "Death of a Union: The 1907 San Francisco Streetcar Strike," http://user-www.sfsu.edu/~epf/1996/street.html#48.

believed that because they were voters, municipal ownership would give them more control over their labor. Universal white male suffrage, thus, influenced segments of the working class to reject socialism in favor of reforming the state into a more democratic one that protected workers and labor interests. But so too did a deep-seated faith in democratic possibilities of reform shape the perspective of workers toward reform. In 1894, Thomas Morgan, who headed the radical Chicago Central Labor Union and had a short time earlier threatened the audience listening to William Stead, appealed to the government for depression relief for workers. He did not threaten violence or revolution, but demanded this aid on the basis of the "declaration of independence . . . [and] the fundamental principles upon which our government rests."[30]

Women workers could not vote, and male worker organizations were largely opposed to organizing women. The AFL, which had organized most of the country's craft unions, was hostile to women workers. Women formed their own unions, many of which came under an umbrella organization founded in 1903, the National Women's Trade Union League (NWTUL). Unlike most male trades organizations, the NWTUL was composed of both working- and middle-class women. Its stated purpose was to "assist in the organization of women wage workers into trade unions and thereby to help them secure conditions necessary for healthful and efficient work and to obtain a just reward for such work." The motto of the organization, "The eight-hour day, a living wage, to guard the home," very explicitly connected conditions of labor with conditions of life. Its official publication was titled *Life and Labor*. For the women of the NWTUL, social justice demanded a complete revisioning of all conditions in American society, not just of labor. So across the Progressive Era, the organization and its local affiliates led movements for higher wages, limited hours of work, and abolition of child labor, but also fought for housing, sanitation, and public safety reforms such as fire prevention in cities, better educational opportunities for children, and funding for infant and maternal health care. The NWTUL actively supported woman suffrage, declaring that only with political power could women protect both their economic power and their families.[31]

---

30. See Georg Leidenberger, "Working-Class Progressivism and the Politics of Transportation in Chicago, 1895–1907" (Ph.D. diss., University of North Carolina, 1995) and "'The Public Is the Labor Union': Working-class Progressivism in Turn-of-the-Century Chicago," *Labor History*, 36 (Spring 1995): 187–210. See also, Alan Dawley, *Struggles for Justice: Social Responsibility and the Liberal State* (Cambridge, MA: Harvard University Press, 1991). For Morgan, see newspaper clipping, January 16, 1894, in Thomas and Elizabeth Morgan Collection, Book 2, in Illinois Historical Survey, University of Illinois Library, Urbana, Illinois. See also, Richard Schneirov, *Labor and Urban Politics: Class Conflict and the Origins of Modern Liberalism in Chicago, 1864–97* (Urbana: University of Illinois Press, 1998).

31. Elizabeth Anne Payne, *Reform, Labor, and Feminism: Margaret Dreier Robins and the Women's Trade Union League* (Urbana: University of Illinois Press, 1988) and Nancy Schrom Dye, *As Equals and As Sisters: Feminism, the Labor Movement and the Women's Trade Union League of New York* (Columbia: University of Missouri Press, 1980).

Streetcar Derailed and Damaged During Strike, Cincinnati, Ohio (1913)
Source: Library of Congress, Prints & Photographs Division, LC-USZ62-76633

RACIAL JUSTICE

Justice may be blind, but during the Progressive Era unfortunately, if social justice reformers were blind, it was to racial justice. This means white social justice progressives, of course, because black social justice progressives were there in plain view and in large numbers. Theirs was a terrible uphill battle, however, as the simmering racial resentments of white southerners erupted into a full-blown racist assault under the guise of progressivism. Between 1898 and 1918, the vast majority of African American men in the southern states were disfranchised through enactment of poll taxes, literacy tests, and the "white" primary. When Congressman George H. White of North Carolina was defeated in 1900, the House of Representatives returned to being an all-white body and would remain so until 1928, when Oscar DePriest was elected from Chicago.[32] Moreover, in 1896 the notorious Supreme Court ruling *Plessy v. Ferguson* had legitimized state laws on segregation in public accommodations. Although these accommodations, which included everything from schools to public drinking fountains,

---

32. Michael Perman, *Struggle for Mastery: Disfranchisement in the South, 1892–1908* (Chapel Hill: University of North Carolina Press, 2001). Poll taxes and literacy taxes also technically disfranchised poor white men, but the laws often had loopholes for them and various other means were used to allow these men to vote if they wanted to.

were supposed to be "separate but equal," they of course never were. The most insidious aspect of the majority decision was its supposition that "culture" should decide social arrangements. As social justice progressivism was trying to bring people together, the Supreme Court was ruling that people could not be forced to live together if they did not want to do so. These events were accompanied by virtually unrestrained lynching and urban racial riots to keep African Americans "in line." The African American Tuskegee Institute estimated that a black man was lynched every three days. Between 1889 and 1918, fifty black women were lynched.[33]

Racial justice and democratic equality for blacks in the South were virtually nonexistent, but southerners often used the language of progressivism to support this situation. At their best, white southern progressives advocated biracial social progress. They practiced segregation but urged black southern leaders to improve their communities so that the South as a whole would seem more progressive. This "new paternalism" contributed, on the one hand, to certain successes in southern black communities as literacy rates increased in some cities to resemble those of white literacy rates. On the other hand, careful examination of these communities reveals how financial and other resources were systematically put into the white schools, for example, and not into black schools. Black southerners were supposed to "progress" with far fewer resources. Other southern white progressives argued that they were reforming society by eliminating the influence of its baser elements. Lynching was a way to keep African Americans from pursuing equality. But it also had a gender dimension to it as the excuse for it was often to protect white women from the supposedly predatory black men. Here too progressivism was given a strange twist as articulated by Rebecca Latimer Felton, a southern white woman identified as a progressive. She defended lynching as a way to protect white women from rape but equated the "crime" of lynching with the "crime" of election fraud as practiced by black men. As she explained it, black men raped white women because they believed they could get away with it, just as, she asserted, they rigged elections because they lacked democratic principles. Reforming southern society then, meant instituting new progressive policies that kept black men in their place. Thus white southerners claimed that disfranchisement was a way to foster a more democratic society.[34]

Unfortunately, southerners received support for their racist attitudes from the national government. President Theodore Roosevelt himself was develop-

---

33. See *Southern Horrors and Other Writings: The Anti-Lynching Campaign of Ida B. Wells, 1892–1900*, Jacqueline Jones Royster, ed. (Boston: Bedford Books of St. Martin's Press, 1987), 10, and the relevant essays in *Democracy Betrayed: The Wilmington Race Riot of 1898 and Its Legacy*), David S. Cecelski and Timothy B. Tyron, eds. (Chapel Hill: University of North Carolina Press, 1998).

34. Don Doyle, *New Men, New Cities, New South: Atlanta, Nashville, Charleston, Mobile, 1860–1910* (Chapel Hill: University of North Carolina Press, 1990), 260–61 and 274. For Felton, see LeeAnn Whites, "Love, Hate, Rape, and Lynching: Rebecca Latimer Felton and the Gender Politics of Racial Violence," in Cecelski and Tyson, *Democracy Betrayed*, 148–49. For more extensive analysis of white/black and gender relations and southern white use of the ideas of progressivism to pursue an agenda of racial discrimination, see Glenda E. Gilmore, *Gender and Jim Crow: Women and the Politics of White Supremacy in North Carolina, 1896–1920* (Chapel Hill: University of North Carolina Press, 1996).

ing an idea of racial hierarchy. According to his idea, those "races" that were hybrids had the most vigor. These hybrids were primarily Europeans who had mixed over the centuries. Nonwhite, unmixed "races" were viewed as having inbred weaknesses, so they had not yet developed the necessary "intellectual and moral competence" for equal democratic citizenship. Both the president and Congress were content to leave the South to deal with its racial problems on its own. The way the South intended to do so was clearly and horrifically expressed in 1908 by a Florida representative in a speech before Congress: "this is our country, as it was the country of our fathers. The country of the white man, not the home of the mongrel. It will always be the white man's country."[35]

Conditions were always better for African Americans outside of the South. It is important to remember that disfranchisement was not national. In other areas of the country, African American men could and did vote and hold office. African American women voted in states with woman suffrage. But better did not mean equal or just, as Jane Edna Hunter's experience in Cleveland shows. African American women formed the NACW both because they believed that they had particular "race" problems to solve and because the GFWC did not welcome the membership of black women. Cooperation between white and black women's clubs that were often working on the same issues varied from nonexistent in the South to sporadic in northern and western cities and towns. Ida B. Wells-Barnett lived and worked freely in Chicago after being driven out of her hometown of Memphis by death threats for her racial justice activism. She held membership in some Chicago white women's organizations and received money and cooperation from these same organizations for activities aimed at bettering the situation of Chicago's African American community. In 1909, she and a group of black and white social activists, among them W.E.B. DuBois and Jane Addams, organized the National Association for the Advancement of Colored People.

Interracial cooperation was generally not an equal partnership, however. Wells-Barnett and Celia Parker Woolley cofounded the interracial Frederick Douglass Center in Chicago. Wells-Barnett ultimately broke with Woolley when the latter supported a white woman to preside over the settlement's Woman's Club rather than Wells-Barnett. To support the Working Girls' Home Association that she founded in 1911, Jane Hunter had to appeal for financial support from white philanthropists and organizations. The condition for this support was white control of the association's governing board. In both cases, these women refused to take a back seat to white activists, with Hunter ultimately freeing her association from white control and raising money from the black community.

Whether through interracial cooperation or in their own organizations, African American women promoted social justice progressivism. One of their

---

35. Gary Gerstle, *American Crucible: Race and Nation in the Twentieth Century* (Princeton, NJ: Princeton University Press, 2001), 45–46, for Roosevelt and hybridity, including short quote. See also, Eric Rauchway, *Murdering McKinley: The Making of Theodore Roosevelt's America* (New York: Hill and Wang, 2003), for how these ideas affected Roosevelt's progressivism. For Clark's speech, see *Congressional Record* (1908).

major aims was to protect and teach young black women so that they would
be able to assert their rights to justice and equality. They founded working
girls' homes to provide them with decent places to live, fought for their rights
to employment, and worked for all African American women to be treated
with dignity by American society. As with the white women's club movement, there were often tensions between middle- and working-class black
women. Black women faced a double-bind. They were struggling for equality
as women and for respectability as black women. Many of the middle-class
organizations, particularly those in the NACW whose motto was "Lifting As
We Climb," saw their mission as setting standards of respectable middle-class
behavior that all black women should adopt. Yet, the working girls and old-
age homes, schools, settlements, and missions, mothers' clubs, playgrounds,
and health clinics established by these women in the face of a racist society
were a testament to their belief in social justice very similar to that being pursued by many white women.[36]

African American men faced different obstacles in trying to promote social
justice. Disfranchisement, lynching, and public segregation made it extremely
difficult during the Progressive Era for them to act in the South. In the face of
these obstacles, many middle-class black southern men pursued what justice
they could by establishing black colleges and training schools. Outside of the
South, black men tried to work through politics and the political parties. Because almost all African Americans voted Republican, activist black men, with
the support of black women, tried to use the Republican Party to advance
racial justice. On the local level in cities such as Chicago, they had some success. The national-level Republican Party, on the other hand, moved steadily
away from its Civil War-era commitment to racial justice.

With all the very real desire of many progressives to create a more socially
just democratic society, one of the era's true failures was not to overcome racial
prejudice and establish racial justice. This was a lost opportunity that left a
tragic legacy for the rest of the twentieth century. It also resulted, as we shall
see later, in the growing sense among many black Americans that they would
never be accorded true equality by white Americans. Nevertheless, any analysis of progressivism that regards creating a racially segregated society as a specific aim of progressivism dramatically overstates the situation.[37] Some progressives, certainly in the South, aimed for this. But for others, it was a failure
to see how they looked through another person's eyes. Celia Parker Woolley in
Chicago, for example, was a tireless campaigner for equal employment opportunities for black women in white establishments. Yet, she apparently could
not see that favoring a white woman over a black woman to lead the Douglass
Center Woman's Club looked like racial prejudice to Ida B. Wells-Barnett, or

36. See Gilmore, *Gender and Jim Crow*; Spain, *How Women Saved the City*; Deborah Gray White,
"The Cost of Club Work, the Price of Black Feminism," in *Visible Women: New Essays on American
Activism*, Nancy Hewitt and Suzanne Lebsock, eds. (Urbana: University of Illinois Press, 1993):
249–69; and Ida B. Wells-Barnett, *Crusade for Justice: The Autobiography of Ida B. Wells*, Alfreda M.
Duster, ed. (Chicago: University of Chicago Press, 1970).

37. See Michael McGerr, *A Fierce Discontent: The Rise and Fall of the Progressive Movement in America, 1870–1920* (New York: The Free Press, 2003), esp. ch. 6, for this argument.

perhaps a white woman not wanting to put herself on an equal plane with a black woman. At other times, it may have been a lack of courage or an eye to the "larger" issues that led some progressives not to confront directly their movement's failure to support racial equality. Despite being a founding member of the National Association for the Advancement of Colored People in 1909, along with W.E.B. DuBois, Jane Addams stayed with the Progressive Party in 1912 after it rejected DuBois' plea that the party make immediate racial equality part of its program. She acknowledged that this would be just and she did try to change the decision of the party leaders. But in this case, and in others, Addams and other white women put their priorities ahead of a strong call for racial equality—as, indeed, African American men had done years earlier in regard to woman suffrage. How much the white progressives' decisions owed to their own racial thinking is impossible to gauge. But it was certainly a deep flaw in their social justice progressivism.

THE TRIANGLE FIRE
A Labor Crossroads

Young Women Pickets, 1910 Garment Workers' Strike, New York City
Source: Library of Congress, Prints & Photographs Division, LC-USZ62-49516

141 Men and Girls Die in Waist Factory Fire
Trapped High Up in Washington Place Building
Street Strewn with Bodies
Piles of Dead Inside

These were the blaring headlines of the *New York Times* on Sunday morning March 26, 1911. Late the previous afternoon a fire had erupted on the top floors of a ten-story building on New York's Lower East Side. The garment workers at the Triangle Waist Company, most of whom were young Italian and east European immigrant girls and women, were still at work on these top floors. As they tried to escape the flames, they found their way blocked by locked doors. The only fire escape on the ninth floor did not even reach to the street and was so flimsy that it bent under the weight of the few who tried to use it. Tragedy was the result. Unable to escape their blazing workshop, the workers either burned to death or threw themselves out of the windows. The newspapers gave pitiless descriptions of the horrible sight:

> The girls rushed to the windows and looked down at Greene Street, 100 feet below them. Then one poor, little creature jumped. There was a plate glass protection over part of the sidewalk, but she crashed through it, wrecking it and breaking her body into a thousand pieces. . . . Then they all began to drop. The crowd yelled "Don't jump!" but it was jump or be burned, the proof of which is found in the fact that fifty burned bodies were taken from the ninth floor alone. . . . They jumped, they crashed through broken glass, they crushed themselves to death on the sidewalk.

When all the bodies were finally taken to the city morgue, the final death count stood at 146. The vast majority of the victims were young women.

The irony of the tragedy? The building was one of the newer fireproof ones. The structure itself suffered hardly any damage.[*] Newspaper readers across the country could see the results for themselves and draw their own conclusions. Pictures of shrouded bodies lined up in rows to be identified by grieving relatives appeared next to photos of the still-standing Asch Building.

---

[*] *New York Times*, March 26, 1911. Accounts from the newspaper and other information can be found on a Cornell University website, http://www.ilr.cornell.edu/trianglefire/.

CHAPTER 3

The Rights of Individuals in a Democratic Society

The alternative is to work or to starve. To refuse means to be dismissed.

—JOSEPHINE GOLDMARK, 1912

HORRIBLE AS IT was, the Triangle fire was just one of numerous work-related tragedies in the Progressive Era. It caught the attention of many Americans, however, when other events did not because it combined into one episode many problems that the social justice progressives were addressing. The victims were young women, mainly between the ages of sixteen and twenty-three. They were working long hours—the fire broke out at 4:40 on Saturday afternoon—under exploitative working conditions. The owners of the Triangle Company had employed subcontractors to hire and pay the workers. They apparently paid no attention to what these workers were paid, how many were employed, or under what conditions they labored. Supposedly, doors were locked from the outside to prevent the workers from stealing any materials. The owners and the subcontractors made the money; the workers were little more than commodities to be shuffled in and out of the factory. Almost all were immigrants, many of whom could barely speak any English, and many of them were reported to be the main support of their families. They all knew that to complain about any of their conditions would get them fired, for they could be easily replaced by other hungry immigrants desperate for work. The Triangle factory was a "nonunion shop." Workers could be immediately dismissed if they were found to have joined a union or engaged in any type of union activity.

In the winter of 1909–10, the factory's workers, inspired by the nascent International Ladies' Garment Workers' Union (ILGWU, 1900), had joined other garment workers to protest working conditions and wages in the city. They had also asked that fire escapes and open doors be mandated for places of work. Some women were fired; those who returned to work did so without having any of their demands met. But at least they had succeeded in raising public consciousness. Prominent New York City women, including Alva Vanderbilt Belmont and future Secretary of Labor Frances Perkins, had supported the strikers with money, joined the picket lines, and interceded for them in court after they were arrested. In that same period, the city council had refused the pleas of New York City middle-class women's organizations to institute mandatory fire drills in factories. In the face of this tragedy, social justice progressives could now point to the inhumanity of designing buildings to withstand fire but providing no protections for their workers.[1]

The Asch Building was a modern structure that had been declared fireproof. Despite the city fire department's notice that it lacked a sufficient number of exits in case of fire, nothing had been done to force the building's owners to rectify the situation. The Asch was also a ten-story building and no fire department ladders or hoses reached that high.[2] At the beginning of the century, scientific study had concluded that better construction materials and techniques were the best means to ensure fire safety. Scientific study had also produced the New York City law that calculated the number and type of exits needed for a multistory building based on number of stories, number of apartments, and number of square feet of a building. The law was also predicated on how "easy [regulations were] for owners to understand and for building inspectors to administer." Even the deaths of 600 people in the "fireproof" Iroquois Theater in Chicago in 1903 had not turned emphasis away from techniques, technology, and property ownership toward the human element in fire safety. Fire escapes in taller buildings were few in number and often not scaled to the number of people who might need to use them. Narrow, winding, interior staircases, such as were judged adequate for the Asch Building, quickly filled with smoke and flames, making egress impossible.[3]

The tragedy of Triangle exposed four problems that sorely troubled social justice progressives. First, it demonstrated how decisions made on the basis of economics and technology failed to consider the human lives involved. Second, it highlighted the divide between progressives who wanted a more socially just democracy and other Americans who clung to the idea that a democratic society was best fostered by protecting individual rights, especially those of property. Third, it illuminated the difference between social justice progressives who believed in personal action and personal responsibility for reforming society and those progressives (who will be examined more fully in the following chapters) who relied heavily on "expertise" to decide on how to

---

1. *New York Times*, March 26, 1911. Accounts from the newspaper and other information can be found on a Cornell University website, http://www.ilr.cornell.edu/trianglefire/. See also, Sara Wermiel, *The Fireproof Building: Technology and Public Safety in the Nineteenth-Century American City* (Baltimore: Johns Hopkins University Press), 206–08.

2. Wermiel, *The Fireproof Building,* 206–08.

3. Ibid., 193–203, has an extensive discussion of this issue.

reorder society, economics, and politics. Finally, it showed that the police power of the state was still being used to protect property, and businessmen rather than to protect workers. All four problems, social justice progressives believed, were creating a society in which the majority of people could not live a decent life.

The Triangle fire and its aftermath, thus, brought together all the elements of "indecent" living and working conditions. According to Addams, these conditions existed because Americans had not yet developed a new "social ethos." Addams attacked the idea that it was sufficient to have a set of personal ethics. Americans had to accept that they also had social obligations that in turn compelled them to act differently than in the past. People could not accept situations as simply the way things were because daily experience was proving that the conditions in which too many people lived and worked was inhuman.[4] A social ethos, or social conscience as it might also be called, had to be practiced by individuals in everyday life, by those who owned the factories and industries, and by government on all levels. But before the arduous task of convincing people to see their society in this way could be accomplished, the obstacles presented by existing laws and the Constitution had to be eliminated.

FREEDOM TO CONTRACT

The 14th Amendment to the U.S. Constitution, ratified in 1868 to protect the rights of African Americans, defined the rights of American citizenship for the first time. This amendment decreed that no state was to "deprive any person of life, liberty, or property, without due process of law; nor deny to any person within its jurisdiction the equal protection of the laws." In 1873 and 1874, a series of court cases in Louisiana altered the scope of the amendment. In a ruling known as the *Slaughterhouse* cases, the Supreme Court interpreted the amendment to apply to corporations as well as individuals. Business was then able to argue that the state could not deprive it of its property, nor deprive the worker of his or her right to property in labor. Businessmen argued there existed the "freedom to contract" so the state could not interfere in the right of employer and employee to negotiate issues such as wages, hours, and working conditions. Subsequent judicial rulings upheld this right without considering that in real life this was an unequal bargaining situation.

When Congress passed the Sherman Anti-Trust Act in 1890 to prevent and to break up economic monopolies, workers were further restricted. Unions were regarded as monopolies so court rulings legitimized the use of police power against union organizing and strike activities. Businessmen called upon local police forces, private police such as the Pinkertons, state militia, and even federal troops to put down strikes. In an era of massive

---

4. Jane Addams, *Democracy and Social Ethics* (New York: Macmillan, 1902; reprint Urbana: University of Illinois Press, 2002), 6–9.

immigration into the country and rural to urban migration, with people
begging for any kind of employment, the law gave workers no protection of
any kind against prevailing economic practices.

Almost twenty years before Triangle, Florence Kelley, who was a lawyer
and Hull House resident, had led the first sustained progressive assault
against the exploitation of workers. After undertaking intensive investigations of sweatshop and factory labor in Illinois, she persuaded that state's
legislature in 1893 to pass a law mandating the eight-hour day for women
and teenagers and outlawing child labor in factories. Two years later the
state Supreme Court ruled that the sections of the law pertaining to women
were unconstitutional because they violated due process—by applying only
to one type of work—and "freedom of contract," because they were not directly related to promoting public health and safety. This ruling, *Ritchie v.
People*, presented progressives with two stumbling blocks to labor reform.
The first was that it construed quite narrowly the police power of the state to
protect health and safety. Second, it declared that since men and women
were equal citizens (notwithstanding lack of suffrage and other legal inequalities) they had equal rights to freedom of contract and it would be ille-
gitimate to distinguish between male and female laborers. Progressives had
been hoping to use protective labor legislation for women as an "entering
wedge" to secure such legislation for all workers. Now they had to refine
their strategy and find new arguments to counter the individualistic "freedom to contract" ethos.

Concerned female reformers in New York City, led by Josephine Shaw Lowell, opened a new direction by organizing a consumers' league. The league's
immediate target was the poor working conditions of female store clerks, who
worked long hours for low wages, and in rush seasons were forced to work
overtime without extra pay. Boycotts, or blacklists, were illegal so the league
compiled "white lists" of department stores that treated employees more justly
and urged women shoppers to frequent only those stores. The idea spread
across the country and in 1898 local leagues formed into the National Consumers' League (NCL). Florence Kelley left Hull House to become executive
director of the NCL. Under her untiring leadership—Josephine Goldmark
described her as "a guerrilla warrior . . . in the wilderness of industrial
wrongs"—the organization developed into a formidable lobbying group, compiling and distributing its white lists, investigating working conditions, and ap-
pearing at state and national legislative hearings. By 1904 there were sixty-four
leagues in twenty states and the NCL agenda had expanded beyond store
clerks to working to outlaw child labor, sweatshops, low wages, and long
hours. If the police power of the state was off-limits to protect workers, the NCL
turned to the power of the consumer.[5] The NCL's call for both personal action

---

5. Nancy Woloch, *Muller v. Oregon: A Brief History with Documents* (Boston: Bedford Books of St.
Martin's Press, 1996), 23, including quote of Goldmark. Landon R.Y. Storrs, *Civilizing Capitalism:
The National Consumers' League, Women's Activism, and Labor Standards in the New Deal Era* (Chapel
Hill: University of North Carolina Press, 2000) gives a brief overview of the NCL's early years.

and personal responsibility reflected its belief that no one could pretend that the conditions of labor were not her or his responsibility. As Florence Kelley put it: "To live means to buy, to buy means to have power, to have power means to have responsibility." Having resided at Hull House, Kelley surely developed some of her ideas about consumer-worker cooperation and collective social responsibility working with Jane Addams.[6]

The NCL depended on grass roots woman power to advance its agenda, although it craftily named influential men to its national and local boards. Without suffrage, the NCL knew that it needed male allies to pass new laws essential to these women's vision of social justice that demanded state responsibility for ensuring a common welfare. In general, however, male reformers interested in similar social justice causes proceeded differently from women's organizations. A comparable male organization at the time was the American Association for Labor Legislation (AALL, 1905). Its active members were primarily lawyers, university professors, and other professionals whose principal goal was to work through the political system to secure new labor legislation. The AALL "exercised power through the prestige of their position and expertise not through numbers." It did not view the state as "a democratic extension of the popular will." Although the men of the AALL wanted to better the conditions of labor for all workers, they believed that legislation to protect workers was also necessary to secure a better economic climate for the country. The men of the AALL were appalled at the conditions of labor and the group worked tirelessly for new laws for worker compensation, minimum wages, and universal health care, for example. They wanted a more socially just society, but their chief focus was to reform the overall economic structure, not to recognize the rights of labor, or to foster citizen participation in decision making.[7] One consequence of the AALL position was that it could never fully ally itself with labor organizations. The AFL wanted recognition that workers had a right to better conditions, better pay, and a voice in the economic system. Given labor's experiences, it reasonably did not trust the courts to uphold any new labor legislation. AFL leader Samuel Gompers also turned toward working to elect congressmen sympathetic to labor, a dip into direct political action that was not favored by the AALL.[8]

On the other hand, similar means and ends made tight allies of the women of the NCL and NWTUL. Female social justice reformers worked with the AALL; rarely did these men work with the NCL. NCL's emphasis on personal responsibility led it to organize groups composed of employers, workers,

6. Kathryn Kish Sklar, *Florence Kelley and the Nation's Work: The Rise of Women's Political Culture, 1830–1900* (New Haven, CT: Yale University Press, 1995) for Kelley at Hull House. Kelley's labor activism must also be attributed to her socialist beliefs.

7. Kathryn Kish Sklar, "Two Political Cultures in the Progressive Era: The National Consumers' League and the American Association for Labor Legislation," in *U.S. History As Women's History: New Feminist Essays*, Alice Kessler-Harris, Linda Kerber, and Sklar, eds. (Chapel Hill: University of North Carolina Press, 1995), 51, 57, and 60.

8. For the AFL, see Julie Greene, *Pure and Simple Politics: The American Federation of Labor and Political Activism, 1881–1917* (Cambridge, UK: Cambridge University Press, 1998).

and representatives of the consuming public to work together to set wages. The AALL and the AFL preferred either new laws, as will be explained later, or collective bargaining between business and labor unions to such broad citizen activism. Thus, a common desire to achieve justice for workers split progressives into three different groups pursuing different strategies and means to their ends. Nonetheless, all three groups recognized that the legal theory of freedom of contract had to be undermined in order to end worker exploitation.

THE ATTACK ON FREEDOM OF CONTRACT

After the Illinois Supreme Court overturned protective legislation for the state's female factory workers in 1895, activists sought to expand the scope of the legitimate use of the police power of the state to protect the health and safety of all the people. This traditional, but amorphous, concept was always subject to a judicial "reasonableness" test. Because the courts were currently construing reasonable in a narrow fashion, new reasoning would be needed to secure a broadening of court decisions on this issue. Social justice progressives proposed a dual argument: individuals had a right to be protected by the state; and that health and safety needed to be construed broadly in order to foster this right and simultaneously protect society. These arguments were then played out in a series of Supreme Court decisions.

In 1898, in *Holden v. Hardy*, the Court upheld a Utah state law limiting miners to eight-hour workdays. Mining was a dangerous occupation, the Court ruled, so protecting the health of its workers was good for the public health generally. Social justice progressives celebrated the ruling as the break they needed to pursue more protective legislation. But seven years later the Court rejected a New York state law limiting the daily hours of male bakers. In *Lochner v. New York*, the judges decided that there was no health concern at stake, so the state had no right to break freedom of contract. In the meantime, several states had enacted hours limitations for women workers that had been upheld by state supreme courts. Once *Lochner* showed how difficult it was going to be to secure hours limitations for all workers, progressives returned to their "entering wedge" strategy and began preparing new arguments for hours limitations for women workers. Adopting the scientific methods of the new disciplines in the social sciences, they gathered both statistical and anecdotal evidence to show that long hours of work harmed women's health.

The opportunity to use the information came in 1908 when Curt Muller, an obscure laundry owner in Portland, Oregon, challenged that state's law limiting women's work in laundries to ten hours per day. Muller could be seen as an avaricious, exploitative employer, wanting to work his employees until they dropped from exhaustion. Laundries were hot, damp workplaces and the work itself required a fair amount of heavy labor. Lawyers for Muller argued that the law was an arbitrary exercise of state power that deprived women as individuals of their equal rights to contract their labor in a work situation where no serious risk to health could be proven. Such arguments revealed how tenaciously some Americans clung to nineteenth-century ideas that a good democracy protected individual rights against the heavy hand of government.[9]

Louis Brandeis presented the case to uphold the Oregon law. Florence Kelley and Josephine Goldmark of the NCL's New York office gathered evidence to demonstrate that long hours of work, not just in laundries, harmed women's health. Rather than try to overturn *Lochner*, Brandeis argued, in what became known as the "Brandeis Brief," that the Oregon law was not a breach of freedom to contract because it only affected women. Women's "special physical organization" needed protection by the state, he argued, because harming their health would harm that of the public health generally. This was an ingenious argument and the Court agreed unanimously with it. But the judges' opinion in *Muller v. Oregon* went perhaps further than its advocates had anticipated. Not content to concede the principle of women's different physical structure—by which everyone meant biological—the Court placed women categorically in a legal and social position inferior to men. Writing the decision, Justice Brewer declared that women's reproductive capacities were of interest to the state:

> . . . and as healthy mothers are essential to vigorous offspring, the physical well-being of woman becomes an object of public interest and care in order to preserve the strength and vigor of the race. . . . The limitations which this statute places upon her contractual powers, upon her right to agree with her employer as to the time she shall labor, are not imposed solely for her benefit, but also largely for the benefit of all.

Moreover, he equated the position of women in society to that of children: "woman has always been dependent upon man. . . . As minors, though not to the same extent, she has been looked upon in the courts as needing especial care."[10] What on the one hand could be celebrated as a victory for protecting women workers led to decades of discrimination against women's economic opportunities. Furthermore, because it only applied to women, some employers responded by eliminating women workers from their employ. Muller, for his part, replaced his women workers with Chinese men. The AFL supported the ruling frankly because the almost-all-male organization wanted to eliminate women as competition in labor. The *Muller v. Oregon*, opinion, moreover, supported organized labor's previous declaration that work outside the home "unsexed" women and stripped them "of that modest demeanor that lends a charm to their kind."[11]

---

9. Robert D. Johnston, *The Radical Middle Class: Populist Democracy and the Question of Capitalism in Progressive Era Portland, Oregon* (Princeton, NJ: Princeton University Press, 2003).

10. See the Brandeis Brief and Justice Brewer's opinion in Woloch, *Muller v. Oregon*, 109–32 and 148–49.

11. Edward O'Donnell, "Women as Bread Winners—the Error of the Age," *American Federationist*, 4 (October 1897).

Most social justice progressives hailed the ruling. Very few of them at the time realized how it would embed gender inequality into constitutional law for decades to come. To a certain extent they celebrated because they realized how difficult it was to redefine democratic rights in the direction of social rights. They optimistically continued to see this ruling as an "entering wedge" that before too much longer would allow them to secure protective legislation for all workers. But social justice progressives also were not much dismayed by the gendered implications of the ruling because most of them believed that women had a special responsibility in both the bearing and raising of children and needed the state's protection in order to do this. They were justifiably hor-rified at how long work hours at minimal wages were harming the health of women and the well-being of children and families. To give them credit, these same reformers were also working to secure laws that would allow women to stay at home and raise their children without having to work.[12] Many working women agreed with this strategy. The NWTUL and its various affiliated women's unions, for example, celebrated this ruling. They optimistically, prob-ably myopically, believed that they were on the road to defining social rights as a marker of democracy. As significant as this ruling was for women work-ers, it also marked a change in American law, the import of which will be con-sidered in Chapter 6.

NEW IDEAS ABOUT SOCIAL RIGHTS

1. The Right to Leisure

This early fight for protective labor legislation raised into public discussion ad-ditional ideas about rights in a democratic society. Florence Kelley was again at the forefront of this rethinking. She challenged the legal right to contract, which had been invoked to justify every kind of labor exploitation, by positing that all individuals had a right to leisure. Kelley was profoundly influenced not just by Jane Addams but by the ideas of socialism that she had studied in Europe. Kelley's idea that all individuals were entitled to leisure time as a just reward for creating a more productive and affluent society might seem to re-semble the argument of the labor theory of value—that is, work gave a com-modity its value, not the employer, and therefore the workers were entitled to a just reward for creating value. Yet, Kelley feared labor organizations such as the AFL were only concerned to protect male workers and their wages and would be most concerned to "make favorable terms for themselves." If leisure were to become a recognizable right first applied to women workers—and Kelley believed that women would always work—then sooner or later it would be applied to all Americans, whether workers or not, and especially to children.[13]

---

12. Joanne Goodwin, *Gender and the Politics of Welfare Reform: Mothers' Pensions in Chicago, 1911–1929* (Chicago: University of Chicago Press, 1997) and Molly Ladd–Taylor, *Mother-Work: Women, Child Welfare and the State* (Urbana: University of Illinois Press, 1994).

13. Florence Kelley, *Some Ethical Gains in Legislation* (New York: Macmillan, 1905). See also, Woloch, *Muller v. Oregon*, 24–25.

Mill Hands, Newberry, South Carolina
Source: Library of Congress, Prints & Photographs Division, National Child Labor Committee Collection, LC-DIG-nclc-01469

2. The Rights of Children

In the Progressive Era, many social justice progressives argued that in a democracy children also had rights. In 1907, they formed the National Child Labor Committee to promote the abolition of child labor on both the state and national levels. They took advantage of new technology and hired the superb photographer Lewis Hine to document the conditions of child labor. Hine traveled across the country taking pictures of children at work. He found children as young as five working in canneries, glassworks, textile mills, mines, and out in the streets selling newspapers. In pictures and words he documented their stories. He showed children who had lost limbs in machinery. He detailed young children working into the night and some who started work before the sun was up. He spoke to children who were illiterate because they had never been to school.[14] The opponents of child labor argued that it was shameful that any democratic nation would allow these conditions to exist. But the anti–child labor movement went beyond trying to protect children to argue that all children had rights to education and recreation. This idea led

---

14. Many of Hine's photographs with their original captions can be seen on the website http://www.historyplace.com/unitedstates/childlabor.

social justice progressives to agitate for reforms to the public school system and demand that cities and towns build parks and playgrounds specifically for children.

The women of the Memphis Women's Public School Association (WPSA), formed in 1905 mainly by middle-class women of the city, believed that education was a key to increasing democracy. Because at one time or another most people had children in school, making education a social responsibility would give all Americans a "much needed voice in public affairs." These women also thought that the public schools themselves were undemocratic. It was not only child labor that kept poorer children out of school but also the high cost of books and supplies charged by school suppliers, the cost of transportation to school, and the lack of public health provisions. The WPSA organized a school book exchange, successfully lobbied for half-fares for school children on public transportation, and brought public health into the schools. The Texas Congress of Mothers persuaded that state's legislature to pass an amendment raising the legal limit on school taxes and successfully guided the amendment through ratification. The African American Tampa Women's Improvement Club raised money to buy supplies and pay teachers in their segregated schools. Such movements were shared by women's organizations across the country that assailed their local school systems for poorly paying teachers— and paying the female teachers less than male teachers—for failing to provide enough money for books and supplies, for not providing sufficient fire escapes on school buildings, for failing to finance kindergartens, and for attacking teachers' efforts to organize unions. Wherever women investigated the school system, they found evidence of school board budgeting and resource allocation that benefited business more than children. As early as 1889, the middle-class and working-class women's coalition, the Illinois Women's Alliance (IWA), had castigated the Chicago school board for its "business" attitude: "Are there not enough money making industries without using the education needs of the children as one?" the women asked. They labeled it a disgrace that children went without a proper education while the city financed the Columbian Exposition and spent "hundred[s] of thousands of dollars for a Grand Opera."[15]

---

15. Marsha Wedell, *Elite Women and the Reform Impulse in Memphis, 1875–1915* (Knoxville: University of Tennessee Press, 1991), 115–18; Judith McArthur, *Creating the New Woman: The Rise of Southern Women's Progressive Culture in Texas, 1893–1918* (Urbana: University of Illinois Press, 1998), 61; Nancy Hewitt, *Southern Discomfort: Women's Activism in Tampa, Florida, 1880s–1920s* (Urbana: University of Illinois Press, 2001), 156 and 237; Sandra Haarsager, *Bertha Knight Landes of Seattle: Big-City Mayor* (Norman: University of Oklahoma Press, 1994), 32–34; and Maureen A. Flanagan, *Seeing with Their Hearts: Chicago Women and the Vision of the Good City, 1871–1933* (Princeton: Princeton University Press, 2002), 59–70. In Chicago, for example, the businessmen on the Board of Education were tied to the business community and although they cut teacher pay and the instructional fund, they never touched the building fund and they increased tax exemptions for buildings constructed on school property. One of the board's presidents was the corporation counsel for Armour and Co., one of the city's largest meatpackers and the plaintiff in a suit filed by the teachers' union against the city's major corporations for failing to pay property taxes. Flanagan, 114–15. IWA quoted in ibid., 45.

Social justice progressives disagreed with the idea, fostered by business-men, that schools for the working class should train children to be good and docile industrial workers. Women's organizations, on the contrary, declared that all children had a right to a good education in order to have equal oppor-tunity in life and to learn to be good democratic citizens. This concept of the rights of children held by progressives sometimes ran counter to what parents and ethnic communities wanted. The movement for education reform sought to mandate only English-language teaching in the schools. As a nation of im-migrants, the issue of language in schools has always been a difficult one for Americans, and many immigrants in the Progressive Era justifiably saw this movement as targeted against them. On the other hand, social justice progres-sives argued that because English was the national language, children who were not taught properly in English would be severely handicapped once they left school.[16]

Progressives also demanded that cities build public parks and playgrounds for children. In 1900, only 11 of the 100 largest cities in the country provided public playgrounds. Working either in local organizations, or with the Play-ground Association of America (PAA, 1906), they challenged the idea that a park should be a carefully sculpted site of middle-class leisure such as New York's Central Park, Chicago's Jackson Park, or Boston's Commons. Vigorous lobbying by playground activists resulted in the residents of cities and towns in Massachusetts voting for more playgrounds and parks. In Chicago, progres-sives prodded Mayor Carter Harrison II to appoint a special parks commission to investigate park conditions in the city's poor neighborhoods in 1899. That same year, Boston's Mayor Josiah Quincy authorized public schools to finance schoolyard playgrounds. Even before such official steps were taken, settlement houses were providing playground spaces and boys and girls clubs for neigh-borhood children. Hull House is well known for doing this, but less well known were the recreational activities provided by small African American settlements such as the Locust Street Settlement run by Janie Porter Barrett in Hampton, Virginia, and the Neighborhood Union presided over by Lugenia Burns Hope in Atlanta. The Tampa Civic Association, founded in 1911 by Kate Jackson, fought for playgrounds in that city to be built in African American and Latino neighborhoods as well as in white neighborhoods. The playground movement was an immediate success. By 1909, a combination of municipal and private financing had built playgrounds in 77 of the 100 largest cities, with smaller communities following suit.[17]

Historians have not been especially kind in their assessment of the parks and playgrounds, movement. They have viewed these progressives as being

---

16. Flanagan, *Seeing with Their Hearts,* 45–46.

17. Sarah Jo Peterson, "Voting for Play: The Democratic Potential of Progressive Era Play-grounds," *The Journal of the Gilded Age and Progressive Era,* 3 (April 2004): 145–75; Robin Bachin, *Building the South Side: Urban Space and Civic Culture in Chicago, 1890–1919* (Chicago: University of Chicago Press, 2004); and Daphne Spain, *How Women Saved the City* (Minneapolis: University of Minnesota Press, 2001). Playground figures from Peterson, 145–46 and 165. See also, Hewitt, *South-ern Discomfort,* 190–93.

elites who wanted to build these areas to remove children from the streets and thereby control them better. Parks and playgrounds, whether overseen by cities or by settlements, were to be places of recreation supervised by "trained" adults.[18] Progressives *were* concerned about what they perceived as growing problems with juvenile crime and delinquency and with the unsupervised play of children in the streets and alleys, especially those children whose parents worked and were unable to watch over them. Reformers were also concerned that other new sites of leisure, such as the nickelodeon and dance halls, might be damaging the morals of young people. So, there is no denying the "moralistic" values that some progressives placed on parks and playgrounds.[19] But, the urban industrial world of the Progressive Era was a difficult and often chaotic one for children as well as adults. Park reformers realized this and were genuinely concerned for children's welfare. Moreover, when given a chance to vote on financing playgrounds, the working-class voters of Massachusetts cities showed how much they wanted these playgrounds for their children. In the factory city of Lynn, the referendum on this issue drew a record number of voters who overwhelmingly approved the measure. Nor were the ideas of how to build and arrange such areas readily controlled by elite reformers. Residents of working-class and immigrant neighborhoods demanded that these areas be constructed in specific ways that they wanted and then they used their neighborhood parks much as Follett had envisioned them doing in school social centers. Neighborhood parks and playgrounds did not just get children off the streets, they brought urban residents together.[20]

The parks and playground movement owed its growth also to optimistic new theories about the crucial role that environment played in developing human beings. In what today we might call the "nature versus nurture" argument, many progressives believed that the surrounding environment rather than innate characteristics was the significant factor for human growth. Parks, playgrounds, as well as a juvenile justice system, were viewed as ways to nurture children and help them to become productive citizens who would contribute to the continuing development of a democratic society. One of the PAA's first presidents, Joseph Lee, saw similar instincts for competition and cooperation in play as in politics. He believed that if children learned these lessons early in life, they would be able then to apply them to democratic decision making. Organized recreational facilities for children, therefore, were to

---

18. For the social control thesis as applied to parks and other progressive reforms, see Paul Boyer, *Urban Masses and Moral Order in America, 1820–1920* (Cambridge, MA: Harvard University Press, 1978) and Peter C. Baldwin, *Domesticating the Street: The Reform of Public Space in Hartford, 1850–1930* (Columbus: Ohio State University Press, 1999).

19. Elisabeth Israels Perry, "Men Are from the Gilded Age, Women Are from the Progressive Era," *The Journal of the Gilded Age and Progressive Era*, 1 (January 2002): 25–48, makes a compelling case that we not forget the moral element of progressive reforms.

20. Bachin, *Building the South Side*, 159–64. See also, Roy Rosenzweig, *Eight Hours for What We Will: Work and Leisure in an Industrial City, 1870–1920* (Cambridge, UK: Cambridge University Press, 1983).

serve a preventive purpose but were also being defined as a democratic "right" for children.[21]

3. The Right to a Decent Life

The term "decent life" is vague and subject to differing definitions. Social justice progressives assembled a list of problems that needed correcting if the United States were to provide this for all its people, yet listing problems and demanding specific remedies to them was not the same as articulating what a decent life meant and why a society should provide it. If one picks apart the various elements of Triangle and then reassembles them into a picture of how millions of Americans lived and worked, a clearer picture of what social justice progressives were trying to achieve begins to emerge.

One first looks at the majority of workers and the conditions of their labor at Triangle. They were girls and young women who worked six days a week, often twelve hours a day. Most of them had little education. They were totally at the mercy of the employer and the factory boss. A girl could spend hours at a task, for example, and if the boss decided it was not done well enough, he could refuse to pay her for the time worked. The workers were immigrants, many of whom barely spoke English, so they had little idea of whether they had any rights in their labor. When they tried to join unions, they were fired. Without their income their families, or themselves if they were alone, would go hungry or be evicted from whatever miserable tenement they lived in, so they worked in constant terror of being thrown out of work.

Next, one looks at the Asch Building and the role of the city in providing for public safety. Despite the building being certified as fireproof, the fire department had noted the absence of exits, and yet nothing was done to compel the owners to rectify this, nor had anyone listened to women's pleas for fire drills. The city also pretty much ignored conditions inside the factory. Doors were often locked from the outside so that workers could not leave their posts until official quitting time, a practice that was apparently very common. There were no real safety or sanitary standards inside the Triangle factory. It burned so quickly because the floors were strewn with fabric scraps and the finished clothing hung on wires dangling over the heads of the workers. The workers were locked inside, could not use the one fire escape, and were surrounded by flammable clothing.

Finally, one looks at the aftermath of the fire. An investigation of the conditions and causes was prodded into motion largely by the NWTUL. The Triangle owners were acquitted of criminal charges against them because it could not be proved that they knew the doors were locked. They settled the civil cases brought against them for $75 per victim. The governor of New York quickly appointed a commission to investigate factory conditions, but it took five years before new legislation was passed on factory safety.

---

21. See Peterson, "Voting for Play," 158–59 for extensive discussion of Lee and 150 for discussion of children's freedom as part of this movement.

Everything about Triangle violated the ideal of social responsibility that social justice progressives had been promoting. The city, supported by the law,
saw the factory as private property. Female progressives countered this concept by arguing that society had to be seen as a larger home rather than as a locale of private business enterprise. This was an apt analogy drawn from so
many women's experiences. Without suffrage, women in the United States
had been consigned to "private citizenship." Their role was to stay in the home
and raise good democratic children in a healthy family environment. Even
though this ideal was always more myth than reality for most families,
women's daily experiences differed from most men's—even for working-class
women who still bore the primary burdens for children and home. In the Progressive Era, many women translated this experience into a concern for the
larger society. As Chicago reformer Anna Nicholes put it, the city could no
longer afford to be seen as a business corporation but had to be viewed as "a
city of homes, as a place in which to rear children." In Atlanta, Lugenia Burns
Hope expressed it in almost exactly the same way. She founded the Neighborhood Union in 1908, "to make the West Side of Atlanta a better place to rear
our children." Neither woman was speaking of her children; each was speaking about all children.[22]

Once progressives began to speak about the rights and needs of children
and comparing the city to a home, they could argue more effectively what a
decent life meant and why it was the right of all Americans to enjoy it. For
the city to be a home, everyone in it had to have a home. To achieve this goal,
there had to be decent, affordable, and available homes, guaranteed by a regulated housing market, not left to private initiative alone. University of
Chicago Professor and social advocate Sophonisba Breckinridge called for
public standards of housing "below which no living in the community will
be allowed to continue." Juvenile court worker Sadie T. Wald told a meeting
of the National Council of Jewish women that we "are tampering with the
fundamental principles of the nation when we deny the child the privilege of
a home—not a shelter, if you please, but a home." After investigating housing in Chicago's African American neighborhoods, despite being told by the
Health Department not to do so because it was not worth looking into, an appalled Breckinridge concluded that "a decent home . . . in a respectable
neighborhood and at a reasonable rental" was one of "three indisputable
rights" to which citizens were entitled—the other two were employment and
education. Health, safety, a clean physical environment, pure food and milk

22. Nicholes quoted in Flanagan, *Seeing with Their Hearts*, 1; Hope quoted in Elisabeth Lasch-
Quinn, *Black Neighbors: Race and the Limits of Reform in the American Settlement Movement, 1890–1945*
(Chapel Hill: University of North Carolina Press, 1993), 122. For extensive explanations of the idea
of separating men and women in democracy into public and private citizenship, see Linda Kerber,
No Constitutional Right to Be Ladies: Women and the Obligations of Citizenship (New York: Hill and
Wang, 1998); Carol Pateman, *The Disorder of Women: Democracy, Feminism, and Political Theory* (Cambridge, UK: Cambridge University Press, 1989); and Anne Phillips, *Engendering Democracy* (University Park: Pennsylvania State University Press, 1991).

at reasonable prices, clean water, infant and child welfare measures, and a police force that operated in the public interest, not that of business, became defined as other elements necessary for a decent life in both the individual and the collective home.[23]

The concept of a shared social responsibility challenged deeply embedded American values of individualism, unimpeded economic growth, and property rights above all else. American ideals about limited government, and laws in place upholding this principle, would also have to change before this "decent life" for all might be fostered. The social justice progressives did succeed slowly in bringing some of this change about, though often only after tragedy. In Dallas, where every year babies and small children died during the summer from typhoid, women begged the city to build a new water reservoir to stop water-borne diseases that were being carried by the old water sources. Only after another deadly outbreak did the city comply; it had stalled spending the money by mixing water from various sources, hoping that would prevent an epidemic. The crusade to provide pure milk for all children encountered the same reluctance to interfere with private enterprise and to spend for public improvements. Thousands of infants and small children died annually in cities across the country from diseased milk before government enacted sufficient safety regulations to ensure that the product would arrive in homes untainted by bacteria. Enacting strict housing codes and actually enforcing them often took calamities such as fires and disease to prod governments into action. Many people died in cities before governments passed new public safety measures such as fire codes or speed regulations for street-level railway cars—both public transit and major railroads—or new safety measures at street-level crossings.[24] Still, by the 1920s, government had accepted responsibility for enacting many such progressive reforms. Government officials could not, and would not, have done so if the social justice campaigns had not convinced the majority of Americans that this was the correct and just solution to so many of the country's problems.

Social justice progressives had less success in the struggle to regulate air and water pollution. Even when it was acknowledged that the air particles caused by burning fossil fuels, especially smoky soft bituminous coal, "blocked the sunlight, irritated lungs, discolored clothing . . . and threatened the public health," cities and businesses resisted smoke-pollution laws. Pittsburgh and surrounding communities dumped untreated sewage into their rivers until 1959 despite the fact that as early as 1910 the head of the city's

---

23. Wald and Breckinridge quoted in Flanagan, *Seeing with Their Hearts*, 91, 92–93, 96.

24. McArthur, *Creating the New Woman*, 34; Harold L. Platt, "Jane Addams and the Ward Boss Revisited: Class, Politics, and Public Health in Chicago, 1890–1930," *Environmental History*, 5 (April 2000): 194–222; Jacqueline Wolf, *Don't Kill Your Baby: Public Health and the Decline of Breastfeeding in the Nineteenth and Twentieth Centuries* (Columbus: Ohio State University Press, 2001); Lynne Curry, *Modern Mothers in the Heartland: Gender, Health, and Progress in Illinois, 1900–1930* (Columbus: Ohio State University Press, 1999); and Paul Barrett, *The Automobile and Urban Transit: The Formation of Public Policy in Chicago, 1900–1930* (Philadelphia: Temple University Press, 1983).

health department had demanded that the city enact a comprehensive sewage treatment plan that included separating the city's water and sewer systems.[25]

Controlling air and water pollution also pitted social justice progressives against other powerful groups. To accept the primacy of social responsibility, individuals had to surrender certain things for the good of the whole. Homeowners resisted switching to different methods of heating, or to burning smokeless anthracite coal rather than smoky bituminous variety, because it would cost them more money. Businessmen and railroads, one of the leading producers of smoke pollution, resisted pollution controls for similar monetary reasons. The noxious odors coming from the Chicago slaughterhouses that signified "dollars" to the Chicago banker were judged by many like him to be more beneficial to society than clean air. Sometimes this became a multi-faceted struggle, as in Salt Lake City, where middle-class homeowners, businessmen, and the state itself resisted smoke controls. Between 1890 and 1919, six different plans to control the burning of soft coal within the city were advanced, but none succeeded. Smoke-control efforts were hampered in Salt Lake City, as they were in Pittsburgh and St. Louis, because their states' large deposits of bituminous coal were an economic boon. Everywhere, social justice progressives were pitted against groups who elevated a cost-benefit analysis to pollution control over health and cleanliness concerns. Here progressives ran up against an aspect of democracy that they could not always counter. Democracy theoretically represents the voice of the people. If enough people resisted pollution controls, politicians were afraid of not being elected if they implemented them.[26]

The working class had a different stake in this issue. In most areas of the country, people used coal-burning stoves—one of the reasons why in industrial cities young children were often seen digging in coal heaps at industrial sites in order to cadge free coal for their houses. Factories such as the Triangle were generally heated by coal—when heated at all. Since in the overcrowded areas of cities the working class was likely to breathe in more pollution than residents who could remove themselves to cleaner areas, the poor were assaulted by polluted air both at work and at home. Yet, to change to a more expensive fuel or to regulate what industries could burn or where they could dump their waste products was likely to threaten the jobs of those same people. The working class was often trapped between wanting better health conditions for their families and desperately needing what work they could get

25. Joel A. Tarr, "The Metabolism of the Industrial City: The Case of Pittsburgh," *The Journal of Urban History*, 28 (July 2002): 519–20, quote from 523. For earlier problems with water control issues that help to explain the deeply held resistance to paying for improvements that might benefit the entire city, see Maureen Ogle, "Water Supply, Waste Disposal, and the Culture of Privatism in the Mid-Nineteenth-Century American City," *Journal of Urban History*, 25 (March 1999): 321–47.

26. For Salt Lake City, see Theodore H. Moore, "Capital Cities: Planning, Politics, and Environmental Protest in Lansing, Michigan and Salt Lake City, Utah, 1920-1945" (Ph.D. diss., Michigan State University, 2004), chs. 4, 5, and 6. For an overview of competing interests on smoke pollution, see David Stradling, *Smokestacks and Progressives: Environmentalists, Engineers, and Air Quality in America, 1881–1951* (Baltimore: Johns Hopkins University Press, 1999).

and paying as little as possible for rent. They were left balancing their right to live against a right to a cleaner environment. Without any guarantees that the former would be protected, and not entirely trusting middle-class reformers to protect their jobs, it was hard for the working class to surrender to a greater social good on this issue.[27]

So the struggle for more social justice in daily life was always an uphill battle. Progressives were caught in a bind. They knew what they wanted to accomplish and why, and generally were reluctant to compromise. They also believed that it would be dangerous for all Americans if they could not work across class if they hoped to reform society without overturning capitalism. In the days after Triangle, at a memorial service for the dead, the socialist labor organizer Rose Schneiderman warned the middle-class reformers of how near they might be to disastrous class warfare:

> I would be a traitor to those poor burned bodies, if I were to come here to talk good fellowship. We have tried you good people of the public—and we have found you wanting. . . . The life of men and women is so cheap and property is so sacred! There are so many of us for one job, it matters little if 140-odd are burned to death. . . . I can't talk fellowship to you who are gathered here. Too much blood has been spilled. I know from experience it is up to the working people to save themselves. And the only way is through a strong working-class movement.[28]

The tragedy of Triangle and the ensuing anger it generated did help social justice progressives to convince more people of the need to surrender individual privilege and to think about achieving a better balance between the rights of property and the rights of individuals. In this regard, in what is actually a very short historical time period, American society indeed became more democratic as new regulations were enacted across the country to provide for public health and safety. The rights of property, while never done away with of course, were no longer held to be sacred above all else. New laws and regulation in the Progressive Era legitimized that property could be made to give way to the need to provide a more common welfare.

4. The Rights of (Wo)Man[29]

Progressivism helped ensure that woman suffrage was inevitable. The National American Woman Suffrage Association (NAWSA) was a powerful force for the rights of woman, but now the ideals of democratic rights that had driven the movement for decades received a tremendous boost from the social

---

27. David Stradling, "Dirty Work and Clean Air: Locomotive Firemen, Environmental Activists, and Stories of Conflict," *Journal of Urban History*, 28 (November 2001): 35–54.

28. Schneiderman quoted in Leon Stein, *The Triangle Fire* (Philadelphia: Lippincott, 1962), 144–45.

29. The "Declaration of the Rights of Man" was the document passed by the French National Assembly in 1789 on the verge of the French Revolution. The "Rights of Man" was written as a letter from Thomas Paine to George Washington after the latter had become the country's first president.

justice movement. Middle-class women's voluntary organizations formed political equality leagues; the NWTUL was firmly committed to suffrage; working women founded equality leagues of self-supporting women and wage-
earners' suffrage leagues.[30] Even socialist women elevated suffrage to a top
priority, convincing the 1908 National Convention to replace its tepid call for
equal suffrage with a stronger resolution for "unrestricted and equal suffrage
for men and women." Josephine Kaneko, editor of socialist women's journals,
declared that her work had made her realize

> that women are a part of our social order, that they help to bear its burdens and
> that they should share its privileges with the rest of mankind. I learned that I was
> not a consistent Socialist unless I was an active advocate of woman suffrage. So, I
> joined a suffrage club. And thus, I became, through Socialism, a suffragist.

Yet, relatively few women in the country had the vote. By 1913 twelve states
west of the Mississippi had adopted complete woman suffrage; Illinois law
gave women the vote in local and national, but not state, elections.[31]

What all these women wanted was power—to achieve social justice reforms, to enable all women to protect themselves and their families, and to
eliminate conditions of labor such as those at the Triangle factory. Nannie Helen Burroughs, a founder of the Woman's Convention of the National Baptist
Convention, challenged her African American sisters to mobilize for suffrage,
saying "if women cannot vote, they should make it very uncomfortable for the
men who have the ballot but do not know its value." When they had the vote,
women tried to use it for change. In 1911, organized Seattle women spear-
headed a campaign to recall the current mayor, charging that his administration was spreading gambling, corruption, prostitution, and vice. As a result,
23,000 Seattle women registered and the estimates are that 20,000 of them
voted for the successful recall. At other times, the fear of women's votes drove
change. In Chicago, the women's campaign to municipalize garbage collection
and disposal intimidated the city council into doing so. Even without suffrage,
poor Jewish women in Boston organized to fight for fairer food prices, charging that the "beef trust"—the monopoly of the country's handful of major
packing houses—were keeping prices artificially high. Immigrant Chicago
women were demanding the vote to secure safer, healthier, and more affordable food and drink for their families.[32]

Full suffrage came only in 1920, as many men were not eager to surrender
either political or social power. Even as progressives convinced more Ameri-

---

30. Ellen Carol DuBois, "Working Women, Class Relations, and Suffrage Militance: Harriot
Stanton Blatch and the New York Woman Suffrage Movement, 1894–1909," *Journal of American History*, 74 (June 1987): 34–58.

31. First quote from Sally Miller, ed., *Race, Ethnicity, and Gender in Early Twentieth Century Socialism* (New York: Garland, 1996), 272; second quote from *The Coming Nation* (March 1914): 10.

32. Evelyn Brooks Higginbotham, *Righteous Discontent: The Women's Movement in the Black Bap-
tist Church* (Cambridge, MA: Harvard University Press, 1993), quote, 203; Haarsager, *Bertha Knight
Landes*, 49; Maureen A. Flanagan, "Gender and Urban Political Reform: The City Club and the
Woman's City Club of Chicago in the Progressive Era," *American Historical Review*, 95 (October
1990): 1032–50; and James Connolly, *The Triumph of Ethnic Progressivism: Urban Political Culture in
Boston, 1900–1925* (Cambridge, MA: Harvard University Press, 1998), 65.

cans of the righteousness of social responsibility, existing laws, old ideals, and different ideas about how to reform society muted the ultimate impact of social justice progressivism. Competing notions of progressivism played out across the same years and those men holding power were often the victors. The following chapters, then, turn to looking at the advocates and ideas of political progressivism.

At the turn of the twentieth century, "muckraking" journalist Lincoln Steffens regaled the country with his findings of pervasive political corruption. In St. Louis, he recounted, "Bribery was a joke." Steffens said that a newspaper reporter had overheard this conversation one evening in a corridor of City Hall:

> Ah there, my boodler, said Mr. Delegate.
> Stay there, my grafter, replied Mr. Councilman. Can you lend me a hundred for a day or two?
> Not at present. But I can spare it if the Z—bill goes through tonight. Meet me at F——S later.
> All right, my jailbird; I'll be there. . . .

Of that city's mayor, he wrote, "Mayor Ziegenhein, called 'Uncle Henry,' was a 'good "fellow,"' 'one of the boys, ' and though it was during his administration that the city grew ripe and went to rot, his opponents talked only of incompetence and neglect, and repeated such stories as that of his famous reply to some citizens who complained because certain street lights were put out: 'You have the moon yet—ain't it? '"

In Minneapolis, when "Doc" Ames fell out of favor with the Democrats, he ran for mayor as a Republican and won. According to Steffens, "Immediately upon his election before he took office (on January 7, 1901) he organized a cabinet and laid plans to turn the city over to outlaws who were to work under police direction for the profit of his administration."*

---

*Lincoln Steffens, *The Shame of the Cities* (New York: McClure's, 1904), 24, 25–26, and 47.

CHAPTER 4

The Corrupt Bargain

I seen my opportunities and I took 'em.
—GEORGE WASHINGTON PLUNKITT, 1905

THE JOKES, ANECDOTES, and witticisms about government corruption in the Progressive Era were infinite. "Boodling" and "grafting" were the common means for doing business, as the muckraking journalist Lincoln Steffens recounted in his famous exposé of urban corruption, *The Shame of the Cities*. Businessmen bribed municipal officials for business favors and the politicians delivered these favors for a price. In some cities it seemed as if every official was "on the take." George Washington Plunkitt of New York's Tammany Hall preferred to see it simply as opportunity, or "honest graft" as he called it. When a city needed a street paved, for instance, the work could be steered to a politician's family business. The people got a paved street; the politician made money. What was wrong with that, he asked? As the original Mayor Daley of Chicago put it many years later: What kind of world would it be if a father could not do something for his son? "Dishonest graft," on the other hand, was "sandbagging," as when Chicago's 1890s' notorious "Grey Wolves" alderman created a fictitious gas company in order to run up the supposed costs of a franchise and then pocketed the extra money. Tammany Hall and most of the "Grey Wolves" were Democrats, but Republicans were also boodlers. In Philadelphia, Republicans controlled elections. The party drew up fictitious voter lists, appointed all election officials, and "repeat" voting was endemic.[1]

1. William L. Riordon, ed., *Plunkitt of Tammany Hall: A Series of Very Plain Talks on Very Practical Politics, Delivered by Ex-Senator George Washington Plunkitt, the Tammany Philosopher from His Rostrum, the New York County Court House Bootblack Stand* (New York: McClure, Phillips, 1905). Lincoln Steffens, *The Shame of the Cities* (New York: McClure's, 1904), chapters on Chicago and Philadelphia.

Steffens had published his city exposés first in *McClure's Magazine*, one of a raft of new popular publications making their way into homes everywhere in the country. Tales of city officials selling off pieces of their city to the highest bidder—with bribery built into the bids—who then provided miserable public service were daily reading. What cities had to sell were mainly the services made possible by new technology. Public services at this time meant providing something for the public, not that the city itself provided them. Instead, American cities functioned through the franchise system wherein private businesses bid for the contracts to supply new services such as transit, electricity, telephones, and gas. The marketplace, according to customary values of capitalism, should determine urban development. But the rampant corruption ignored the marketplace in favor of manipulation. Progressives began to assail this "corrupt bargain" between business and government and set out to reform urban politics and to redefine its values.

Progressives had no single explanation for the cause and effect of the corrupt bargain. Some progressives organized new municipal groups to investigate political conditions and recommend solutions. Many of these groups immediately focused their efforts toward reforming the mechanisms of local government in hopes of electing "better" men to municipal office. Other progressives focused on changing the powers of city governments by making "public" those services that had been considered "private." Still others, mostly women, demanded the municipal suffrage so that women could have a voice in city affairs. What they all had in common, however, was a sense that the city could no longer be seen primarily as an arena for economics but rather as "an enormous collectivity . . . a vast network of mutually dependent relations.[2]

THE PROBLEMS OF URBAN POLITICS

Industrialization, mass migration into cities, and technological development changed cities of western Europe as well as in the United States and Canada. In comparison with Europe, American cities and their "progressives" were late in viewing the city as a collective enterprise. Despite similar thinking among Europeans and Americans about problems and reforms for cities, their differing urban political structures would affect choices of reform. European cities were part of a national governing system, not independent governing bodies. This meant that municipal reforms could be decided on and financed from the top down and applied to many cities at once. By the 1890s, England, Scotland, and Germany had moved decisively toward turning street railways, electricity, and housing into municipal, rather than private, enterprises. In France, a 1912 provision made municipal housing subject to national legislation. In England, the 1890 Housing of the Working Class Act gave local authorities power to

---

2. Daniel Rodgers, *Atlantic Crossings: Social Politics in a Progressive Age* (Cambridge, MA: Harvard University Press, 1998), 114–15.

1920 Cities with Populations over 100,000

borrow money from their Public Works Board in order to build housing. German progressives failed to secure a national housing act, but their cities exercised strong power to buy up undeveloped land on which to build housing.[3]

Progressive reforms in the United States, thus, were part of a transnational progressive movement, but the particular characteristics of American government and society dictated how progressive political reforms were carried out and by whom. U.S. cities are also legal creatures of their individual states, which give cities their governing powers—either through a specific municipal charter or through a statewide general incorporation act. Whichever method is used, the state determines both the types and limits of power that any city can exercise as well as its allowable taxation policies. This situation had prevailed in law since 1868 when Judge John F. Dillon, a justice on the Iowa State Supreme Court, ruled that a municipality could exercise only the powers given it by the state. Dillon's ruling was somewhat softened by subsequent judgments, but it effectively defined a city as a "corporate entity." A city was "not so much a miniature state as it is a business corporation—its business

---

3. Ibid., 121, 176–77, and 188, for England, Scotland, and Germany. For France, see Susanna Magri, "La réforme du logement populaire: la Société française des habitations à bon marché, 1889–1914," in *Laboratoires du Nouveau Siécle: La nébuleuse réformatrice et ses réseaux en France, 1880–1914*, Christian Topalov, ed. (Paris: Ecole des Hautes Études en Sciences Sociales, 1999), 239–68.

being wisely to administer the local affairs and economically to spend the revenues of the incorporated community."[4] As a result, by the turn of the last century most American cities had limited governing and taxing powers. Cities had few sources for raising revenue beyond general property taxation. The courts also held that the police power of the city was negative—for example, to prevent violence—and could not function positively to ensure a general welfare. In this state-centered context, and in the absence of any national urban policy, cities could expect very little monies either from the state or national governments. Cities often came up with creative financing schemes to build their infrastructures, but direct municipal financing of services would have required raising property taxes, something that many property owners resisted. Because most Americans still believed in limited, de-centralized government, they feared giving their city governments too much power. These conditions combined to make American cities what historian Eric Monkkonen has called "passive" cities. They regulated certain situations but did not actively provide services for their residents. Becoming an "active" city that provided a broad range of services for its residents required changing laws and perceptions of the proper role and powers of municipal government.[5]

American cities differed from European cities in two other crucial aspects. First, unlike their European counterparts, American cities were new and were not faced with rebuilding the city to accommodate change. They were not to be "Haussmannized"[6] but to be built and expanded. Local businessmen viewed this city building as an economic opportunity for themselves. Because cities owned the property on which transit lines were to be laid, streets laid out and paved, schools built, railroad terminals erected, electricity and telephone lines put up, etc., either the city had to finance these projects from its limited funds or give private enterprise the rights to do so. The franchise system had been the answer to this problem. It absolved the city from direct financing, gave businessmen the opportunity to make money from the city's needs, and put extra money into the pockets of city officials. What more could anyone want, except maybe the bulk of urban residents who were discovering just how corrupt the system was and how little city residents received from it.

The second important difference between European and American cities extended the problem beyond the "corrupt bargain." American universal white male suffrage left a city balancing its decisions among competing groups of male voters. Businessmen wanted franchises; labor wanted the city

---

4. Stanley K. Schultz, *Constructing Urban Culture: American Cities and City Planning, 1800–1920* (Philadelphia: Temple University Press, 1989), 67–74, quote from 74.

5. Eric Monkkonen, *America Becomes Urban: The Development of U.S. Cities and Towns, 1780–1980* (Berkeley: University of California Press, 1988). As always, there are caveats to generalizations. U.S. cities were never totally passive, as Monkkonen documents. The distinction is more about a basic passivity that by the Progressive Era had been changing into a notion that a city must actively promote the growth of the city, finance and supply services, and safeguard the welfare of its residents.

6. This refers to the grand plans of Baron Georges Haussmann to transform the center of Paris along the lines that had originally been proposed by Emperor Napoleon III. Much of the funding for this transformation came from the national government. The main idea of Haussmann's plan was to "modernize" Paris by destroying what remained of the medieval city.

to protect workers; and various immigrant communities wanted things for their members. Because most cities functioned under some type of decentralized council system—council members elected by wards or districts—every council member wanted to "deliver" something for his ward and to avoid doing something that would benefit others at the expense of his voters. Bribes bought franchises; favors to voters determined local elections; municipal services went to those who could pay for them or had the strongest political "clout."[7]

By the turn of the century, city residents were suffering from the lack of any sense of the city as a collective entity or as a network of mutual relations. Not only the poor were suffering. In Chicago between 1884 and 1895 the city council had issued street railway franchises to ninety-eight different companies. The resulting chaos made travel difficult across the city as each company controlled its piece of territory and riders could not move freely from one line to the next. Many of these companies failed, of course, resulting in a spate of consolidations in the late nineteenth and early twentieth centuries that produced transit conglomerates such as Cleveland's Big Consolidated, the Seattle Electric Company, or the United Railroads Company of San Francisco. Service was no better under consolidation. The new companies' objective was the same as that of the old ones: to make money. Fares were unregulated, workers were subject to the whims of the company, and streetcar accidents and streetcar strikes were chronic problems. As Chicago's infamous traction magnate Charles Yerkes put it when he refused requests to run more cars to lessen serious overcrowding: "It's the straphangers who pay the dividends!" The moon provided the light in St. Louis and the squashed, swaying urban masses financed the transit system in Chicago.

THE PROPOSED SOLUTIONS

1. Experts and Mechanisms

Progressive businessmen and professionals believed the answer to better governed cities was to remove politics from control of party politicians and to change the mechanisms of government. They argued that government by "experts," more home rule powers for cities, and less popular democracy would lead to better governed cities, and to a more democratic city. These political progressives were modernizers. The chaotic urban growth produced by rapid industrialization had to be made orderly through application of expert, scientific

---

7. For how this system functioned in different cities, see, among others, William Issel and Robert Cherny, *San Francisco, 1865–1932: Politics, Power, and Urban Development* (Berkeley: University of California Press, 1986); James J. Connolly, *The Triumph of Ethnic Progressivism: Urban Political Culture in Boston, 1900–1925* (Cambridge, MA: Harvard University Press, 1998); Maureen A. Flanagan, *Charter Reform in Chicago* (Carbondale: Southern Illinois University Press, 1987); Harold L. Platt, *City Building in the New South: The Growth of Public Services in Houston, 1830–1915* (Philadelphia: Temple University Press, 1983); and Georg Leidenberger, "Working-Class Progressivism and the Politics of Transportation in Chicago, 1895–1907" (Ph.D. diss., University of North Carolina, 1995).

techniques. New professional experts trained in political science, economics, the law, and business methods had to be put into office.[8]

To accomplish these objectives, political progressives formed "good government" organizations—leading to the derisive epithet "goo-goos" pinned on them by their opponents—in virtually every city. By the beginning of the twentieth century, there were enough such groups that they founded national organizations such as the National Municipal League and the National Civic Federation to coordinate their work. In municipal elections they organized reform coalitions to elect "experts" to offices. A New York City "fusion" ticket backed by "goo-goos" from both main parties defeated Tammany Hall in 1901, electing as mayor Seth Low, a successful businessman and president of Columbia University. Between 1898 and 1913, with one exception, the good government reform candidates captured the mayor's office in Los Angeles. The one exception was recalled for encouraging vice and corruption. Chicago political science Professor Charles Merriam—backed by the Municipal Voters' League (MVL)—lost his two bids to become Chicago's mayor, but he and other "good government" reformers were elected to the city council. The sentiment for cleaning up government even pushed regular Democrat Mayor Carter Harrison II to confront franchise fraud and other corrupt practices in that city.[9]

For these political progressives democratic government was *instrumental*. If businesslike expertise were applied to government, and experts put into office, then democratic opportunity would be available to all. As Frederic Howe expressed it, "the great problem now before the American people is, how can opportunity be kept open." His solution was instrumental:

> With home rule secured, with popular control attained, with the city free to determine what activities it will undertake, and what shall be its sources of revenue, then the city will be consciously allied to definite ideals, and the new civilization, which is the hope as well as the problem of democracy, will be open to realization.

Howe's vision of democracy, like that of many professional men, was also one wherein intellectuals, "experts" such as himself, were best equipped to lead. Home rule and increased municipal resources would bring democracy only if experts controlled the mechanisms of such newly empowered government.[10]

Political progressives were applying social science methodology to government, just as social justice progressives were putting social science to use for

---

8. The best analysis of the modernization ideas of political progressives is Robert Wiebe, *The Search for Order, 1877–1920* (New York: Hill and Wang, 1967).

9. Kenneth Finegold, *Experts and Politicians: Reform Challenges to Machine Politics in New York, Cleveland, and Chicago* (Princeton: Princeton University Press, 1995) and Martin J. Schiesl, *The Politics of Efficiency: Municipal Administration and Reform in America, 1880–1920* (Berkeley: University of California Press, 1997).

10. Frederic Howe, *The City: The Hope of Democracy* (New York: Charles Scribner's Sons, 1905), 311–13; Kevin Mattson, *Creating a Democratic Republic: The Struggle for Urban Participatory Democracy During the Progressive Era* (University Park: Pennsylvania State University Press, 1998), 46, is sympathetic to Howe but points out his "undemocratic" tendencies when he led the People's Institute.

reforming society. For political progressives it was largely the science of economics, not sociology, that was appropriate. Frederic Howe declared that it was "economic environment" that caused all the city's problems: "The worst of the distressing poverty, as well as the irresponsible wealth is traceable to economic institutions, to franchise privileges and unwise taxation." For these political progressives, government was a machine to be run and administered by those who understood how best to use the machinery. Only in this way would the city's ongoing progress be assured.[11]

Home rule power for cities was the perfect vehicle through which to apply economic science. Home rule could give cities control of their finances and prevent the state legislature from interfering in municipal affairs. State legislators had played their part in the "corrupt bargain." When businessmen failed to get what they wanted from a city, they had often persuaded state lawmakers to pass a new law, or rescind an existing one, that would give businessmen what they wanted. Legislative approval of new home rule power was forthcoming in many states where legislators had tired of the parade of special pleaders coming from their cities. Moreover, the needs of large industrial cities were overtaxing the state's ability to administer them from afar.[12] The National Municipal League drafted a model home rule charter. The centerpieces of the model were a strong mayor and a small city council elected at-large, not by districts. This model appealed to progressives because it promised an "expert" mayor holding much municipal power and fewer councilmen elected by all the city's voters, a method these progressives believed would replace party politicians with "experts." Not incidentally, this electoral reform was aimed at reducing the influence in municipal government of the lower classes and immigrants, whom some progressives believed were largely responsible for electing corruptible council members.

The model charter was a business vision of government. It had a strong CEO (mayor) at the top, advised by a board of directors (a small council), that would administer the city. The fact that it promised to diminish the power of party politicians and the immigrant working-class voters made it an unpopular reform in older large cities where it was rarely adopted. When cities did adopt this form, the results were not always what the progressives had predicted. In 1910, Seattle changed to an at-large system that reduced its

---

11. Robert Wiebe, *Businessmen and Reform: A Study of the Progressive Movement* (Cambridge, MA: Harvard University Press, 1962). Some important standard works in this interpretive vein are Samuel L. Hays, *The Response to Industrialism* (Chicago: University of Chicago Press, 1957) and "The Politics of Reform in Municipal Government in the Progressive Era," *Pacific Northwest Quarterly*, 55 (1964): 157-69; Richard L. McCormick, "The Discovery that Business Corrupts Politics: A Reappraisal of the Origins of Progressivism," *American Historical Review*, 85 (April 1981): 247–74; and Schiesl, *The Politics of Efficiency*. Howe quote, *The City: The Hope of Democracy*, ix. See also, Finegold, *Experts and Politicians*, and Issel and Cherny, *San Francisco, 1865–1932*.

12. For examples of home rule charter movements, see Flanagan, *Charter Reform in Chicago*; Amy Bridges, *Morning Glories: Municipal Reform in the Southwest* (Princeton: Princeton University Press, 1997); Connolly, *The Triumph of Ethnic Progressivism*; Finegold, *Experts and Politicians*; and David Hammack, *Power and Society: Greater New York at the Turn of the Century* (New York: Columbia University Press, 1987).

council from fourteen to nine. But it had a weak mayor who actually served only a two-year term, while council members served for three years. Boston voted for a reduced, elected-at-large council, but its well-organized ethnic politicians and subsequent mayor, Michael Curley, adapted the language of businesslike efficiency for their own purposes. Even small shop owners running for city council in Boston proclaimed themselves as business experts. When the reformers did win some battles, such as Seth Low's election, they often found themselves losing the next election as party politicians reasserted their control. Chicago voters rejected a new charter in 1907 and the city did not even redistrict the wards from seventy with two aldermen each to fifty with one each until the 1920s. As Chicago's leading ethnic politician Anton Cermak later summed it up: running government was a business and it should be left in the hands of politicians who knew how to run this particular type of business.[13]

Progressives also proposed to eliminate politicians almost entirely from municipal government through commission or city manager types of governments, in which experts would be hired to make municipal decisions. The men of the National Municipal League introduced a model charter explaining these new forms in 1915. It called for a council manager plan under which voters would elect a small city council, which in turn would hire "from anywhere in the country, a city manager who is their sole agent, and the chief executive of the city, with appointive power over the rest of the city's administration, except the clerk, auditor, and civil service commission, whom the council chooses." Only some smaller cities, or newer cities in the west and southwest, adopted this plan. Seattle voters rejected a city-manager plan as not being responsible enough to the voters. With the exception of a few council members, the municipal government under this proposed system would be appointed, not elected, and quite possibly put in the hands of people who had not even lived in the city before appointment. The National Municipal League argued that such changes to the mechanism of government would forge good "tools for democracy to work with."[14]

New forms of government were adopted in cities where middle-class professionals faced little competition for control. The Los Angeles municipal charter was adopted in 1889 when the city had barely 50,000 residents. It gave the city a mayor/council form, but appointed commissioners administered the various city departments. A new charter written in 1925 conferred more power on the mayor and reduced further the number of elected officials. Phoenix, which was just beginning to grow during the Progressive Era, was firmly con-

---

13. Sandra Haarsager, *Bertha Knight Landes of Seattle: Big-City Mayor* (Norman: Oklahoma University Press, 1994); Connolly, *The Triumph of Ethnic Progressivism*; Flanagan, *Charter Reform in Chicago*; Finegold, *Experts and Politicians*; and Anton Cermak, "Why Business Men Fall Down in Politics," *Nation's Business* (January 1933): 24–27.

14. Quotes from National Municipal League, "National Municipal League and Structural Changes in City Government: 1894–1916," *The Survey*, 36 (May 27, 1916): 225.

trolled by the professional classes. In 1913, Phoenix voters ratified a home rule charter giving the city a council-manager government desired by these men.[15]

Some historians have argued that these reformers and their proposals were "undemocratic" because they envisioned removing power from the people. Yet these same progressives proposed other reforms to bring government closer to the people. They advocated popular power to initiate legislation—the *initiative*—, the right to a popular vote on proposed legislation—the *referendum*—, and the power to remove elected officials from office—the *recall*. Wherever they were adopted, voters have exercised these powers over the past century. Seattle voters recalled their mayor in 1912. California voters recalled their governor in 2003. Chicago women put municipal suffrage to an advisory referendum vote in 1912—not surprisingly, it failed to pass, as the voters were all male. Cleveland voters rejected municipal ownership of streetcars in a referendum, much to the dismay of Mayor Tom Johnson. California is famous, or infamous as some would have it, for exercising the power to initiate legislation. Beginning in 1912 with a successful campaign to abolish the poll tax, going on to Proposition 13, passed in 1978 to limit property taxation, and Proposition 187, passed in 1994 to refuse public services to illegal immigrants, California voters have exercised this form of popular democracy with alacrity.

Other successful reforms to electoral mechanisms had mixed democratic possibilities. Before the Progressive Era, the parties controlled election procedures. In some places, for instance, voters had to ask for ballots by party. Oftentimes these were printed on different colored paper so that everyone could see for whom one was voting. The illiterate could vote easily with this system, but party politicians could watch how people voted. Party caucuses, not voters, chose candidates in a primary race. Progressives attacked these processes as "undemocratic" and successfully introduced the secret ballot and the direct primary into the political system. On the one hand, these seem perfectly reasonable reforms. Who would want to return to the nonsecret ballot or be deprived of a voice in candidate selection? On the other hand, both reforms were used to disfranchise some voters. White southerners were particularly effective in using the primary to disfranchise black voters even further by instituting the "whites-only" primary.[16] Removal of party control of voting, historians have also suggested, lowered the incentive of politicians to recruit voters because they could not be sure of knowing how they would actually vote. Conversely, voters were said to be less interested in voting because they were not being promised favors in return for votes nor were they interested in the "experts" running for office. Commission and city manager

---

15. Bridges, *Morning Glories*.

16. Philip J. Ethington, *The Public City: The Political Construction of Urban Life in San Francisco, 1850–1900* (Cambridge, UK: Cambridge University Press, 1994), 74–77, gives a particularly nice account of how these voting manipulations worked in that city. For the whites-only primary, see Darlene Clark Hine, *Black Victory: The Rise and Fall of the White Primary in Texas* (Millwood, NY: KTO Press, 1979) and Michael Perman, *Struggle for Mastery: Disfranchisement in the South, 1888–1908* (Chapel Hill: University of North Carolina Press, 2001).

governments obviously diluted the power of voters in those cities. Progressive reforms that tightened rules on residency and voter registration undoubtedly also contributed to keeping some voters away from the polls.[17]

An interpretive middle ground probably best captures the democratic ideas of political progressives such as Howe, the founders of the National Municipal League—among whom were Louis Brandeis and future president Theodore Roosevelt—, and politicians such as Hiram Johnson of California and Seth Low of New York. These men were seeking a *via media*, as historian James Kloppenberg has defined it: a middle way between the destructive results of laissez-faire capitalism and ineffectual government and the potentially destructive impulses of socialism or complete popular democracy. Their education, their middle-class status, their gender, and their experiences both inside and outside of government led them to believe that their preferred reforms would preserve sufficient individual freedom while putting the United States back on the path to a "progressive" democratic future.[18]

2. The Wisconsin Idea

California and Wisconsin were considered the most "progressive" states. Hiram Johnson, elected governor of California in 1911 and then U.S. senator, and Robert LaFollette, three-term governor from Wisconsin and then U.S. senator, were two of the era's most progressive politicians. LaFollette's reform agenda as governor, dubbed the *Wisconsin Idea*, epitomized the political progressive agenda. The *Idea* included overhauling election procedures, ousting corrupt officials from office, and reforming tax structures. Wisconsin was the first state to require the direct primary for choosing all candidates for public office. Sixty-two percent of Wisconsin voters had voted in favor of this reform. LaFollette promoted what his most recent biographer called a "commonwealth conception of society." He believed that government should be a cooperative venture shared among political officials, university professors, and the private sector (business). Such cooperation, he believed, would serve the public interest over all else. LaFollette had been educated at the University of Wisconsin and its faculty included some of the most original thinkers on political progressivism, such as the economist Richard Ely. In a state with only one big city—Milwaukee—the *Idea* was also aimed to pull together small farmers, industrial labors, and middle-class consumers into this "commonwealth" by convincing them

---

17. For these reforms as "undemocratic," see Alexander Keyssar, *The Right to Vote: The Contested History of Democracy in the United States* (New York: Basic Books, 2000).

18. James Kloppenberg, *Uncertain Victory: Social Democracy and Progressivism in European and American Thought, 1870–1920* (New York: Oxford University Press, 1986); Leon Fink, *Progressive Intellectuals and the Dilemmas of Democratic Commitment* (Cambridge, MA: Harvard University Press, 1997); Mattson, *Creating a Democratic Public*; Rodgers, *Atlantic Crossings*; and Robert Johnston, "Re-Democratizing the Progressive Era: The Politics of Progressive-Era Historiography," *Journal of the Gilded Age and Progressive Era*, 1 (January 2002): 68–92. The issue of gender and political progressivism will be discussed specifically in later chapters.

that despite their differences they shared a common interest in a well-ordered government. LaFollette's was the concept of collectivity applied at the state level.[19]

When LaFollette left Wisconsin for Washington, D.C., the state still followed his reform spirit. Across 1909–11 voters adopted the referendum, initiative, and recall, and new constitutional amendments gave municipalities more home rule powers and forbade the state to "alienate"—sell or give away—any of its natural resources. Other legislation gave municipal governments powers to regulate air quality, ensure the health and safety of residents in specific instances, and require employers to install specific safety measures for their workers. Many of these new laws reflected progressives' great faith that applying professional expertise to controlling such problems as smoke and pollution, or improving health and safety conditions at work and in daily life, could all be accomplished by "unbiased" professional men using their scientific and technical expertise.[20]

3. Rethinking Government Responsibility

Other progressives disputed the efficacy of relying solely on this approach. The tragic deaths at the Triangle fire could have been prevented, they would argue, if experts had not assumed that fire safety simply rested on new techniques and mathematical calculations about how many staircases should be sufficient for "x" number of people. Well before the Triangle fire Jane Addams had rejected reliance on this type of political progressivism. Businessmen and "the better element," she contended,

> are almost wholly occupied in the correction of political machinery and with a concern for the better method of administration, rather than with the ultimate purpose of securing the welfare of the people. They fix their attention so exclusively on methods that they fail to consider the final aims of city government.[21]

What were those final aims that Addams had in mind? The answer is deceptively simple: that government take responsibility for the welfare of all residents. What exactly this meant and how to accomplish it is decidedly more complicated. Historians have tended to speak of social and political progressivism as two distinct movements. Women were said to want social reform and

19. Nancy Unger, *Fighting Bob LaFollette: The Righteous Reformer* (Chapel Hill: University of North Carolina Press, 2000), 121–22, 129, 133, and 137–38, and Alan Dawley, *Changing the World: American Progressives in War and Revolution* (Princeton: Princeton University Press, 2003), 59–60. Oregon was the first state to adopt the referendum and initiative in 1902. See also, Frederic Howe, *Wisconsin: An Experiment in Democracy* (New York: Charles Scribner's Sons, 1912) and Ballard Campbell, *Representative Democracy: Public Policy and Midwestern Legislatures in the Late Nineteenth Century* (Cambridge, MA: Harvard University Press, 1980).

20. Charles McCarthy, *The Wisconsin Idea* (New York: Macmillan, 1912).

21. Jane Addams, *Democracy and Social Ethics* (New York, 1902; reprint edition, Urbana: University of Illinois Press, 2002), 98–99.

to have no interest in the political system.[22] It was a safe historical analysis to
think of women as wanting to "help" people rather than wanting political reform because then historians could confine women's progressivism to women's
history. Yet, progressive women knew they could not accomplish the reforms
they wanted without attacking the political system. Evidence abounds that progressive women advocated different political reforms than did progressive
men. Why this was the case becomes a troubling question because the answer is
an "unsafe" one—it is because of gender and that in turn challenges notions of
class or race solidarity that most historians favor. To accept gender difference is
not to make an essentialist argument, although by claiming that women were
more interested in helping people because they were women, historians have
reduced women to their gendered nature. Rather, what occurred in the Progressive Era was that women, just as men, began to apply their gender experiences
to politics. Women and men both turned to government for reform solutions,
but "[I]n emphasis and values . . . they were dramatically different." As historian Paula Baker pointed out, men took the corporation with its top-down decision making as their model for political reform. Politically active women used
the model of the home and broadened it out to encompass the entire community.[23] These women progressives wanted not just social reform but a complete
overhaul of the institutions and purposes of government so that social justice
would prevail. Bringing women into political reform exposes how gender experiences shaped ideas about political reform into sometimes complementary,
but more often competing, ways. And, we can see that what these women
wanted challenged the political reform ideas of many men.

Bertha Knight Landes of Seattle, for example, was a leading progressive
clubwoman of that city: a member of the Century Club, founder of the
Women's City Club, and president of the Seattle Federation of Women's Clubs.
She was elected to the city council and then to the mayor's office in 1925. Landes' 1922 campaign for city council was filled with rhetoric about governing
the city as a home rather than as a business. According to Landes, the physical
manifestations of the city were entwined with social needs because they "most
vitally affect the well-being of the home, and in them the woman has as great,

---

22. This tendency began with the publication of Melvin Holli's book, *Reform in Detroit: Hazen S.
Pingree and Urban Politics* (New York: Oxford University Press, 1969). See also, David Stradling,
Smokestacks and Progressives: Environmentalists, Engineers and Air Quality in America, 1881–1951 (Baltimore: Johns Hopkins University Press, 1991) and Alan Dawley, *Struggles for Justice: Social Responsibility and the Liberal State* (Cambridge, MA: Harvard University Press, 1991), esp. 102, where he
analyzes women reformers as reprising "the standard nineteenth-century paired opposites of corrupt masculine commerce and virtuous feminine domesticity." For an argument countering this
this "split" and women's motives, see Maureen A. Flanagan, "Gender and Urban Political Reform:
The City Club and the Woman's City Club of Chicago in the Progressive Era," *American Historical
Review*, 95 (October 1990): 1032–50.

23. Quote from William Chafe, "Women's History and Political History," in *Visible Women: New
Essays in American Activism*, Nancy Hewitt and Suzanne Lebsock, eds. (Urbana: University of Illi-
nois Press, 1993), 105. See also, Paula Baker, "The Domestication of Politics: Women and American
Political Society, 1780–1920," *American Historical Review*, 89 (June 1984): 620–47, esp. 641, and Mau-
reen A. Flanagan, *Seeing with Their Hearts: Chicago Women and the Vision of the Good City, 1871–1933*
(Princeton, NJ: Princeton University Press, 2002).

if not greater interest than the men." Food inspection, public safety, street grading and pavements, garbage removal, and building inspections, for example, all had to be done by municipal government in order to foster the public welfare. But it did not take professional "experts" in office to do this. In her 1925 campaign, and in a 1926 speech to the Illinois League of Women Voters (ILWV), she made it clear that her vision of city government and of a good democracy did not accord with those of most male progressives.

> The city of Seattle represents a great big family consisting of men, women and children each with their own peculiar needs and desires which must be attended to. . . . City governments exist largely because of the family. There is nothing sentimental or womanish in this philosophy. . . . It is hard common sense. No city is greater than its homes. . . . City government looks after the welfare of the people, or should. It concerns itself with sanitation, public health, clean and safe streets, protection of the home, education, care of the poor and the sick.

Hers was a personalized vision of the city as a home and of democracy wherein women had as much knowledge and rights as men to govern the city. City government, she argued, was *obliged* to provide protection, transportation, education, recreation, and a moral and clean environment. These were not merely things to do if the economics were right or the right people were in office.[24]

Women across the country had adopted this idea, calling it "municipal housekeeping." This term was another reason why historians have downplayed women as interested in politics. They looked at the term and claimed that women were merely interested in tidying up the city as they would their homes. But, municipal housekeeping was a metaphor behind which there was a definite political strategy. It enabled women to circumvent opponents who wanted to keep women confined to private life, and not in the public arena of politics. The president of the Dallas Federation of Women's Clubs responded to complaints that Dallas women were stepping out of their proper place when they concerned themselves with the "male arena" of public policy, cleverly writing to the *Morning Times* that it was "for love of home and children" that women were doing this. She and her sister clubwomen then went right ahead challenging male decisions on sanitation, health, safety, etc. Under this guise women were demanding actual power in the public arena. They wanted not just the vote but a voice in all municipal decisions. As the women of the Chicago Woman's City Club put it in 1913 when they demanded municipal ownership of garbage collection and disposal:

Any number of departments
Caring for our waste;
Woman's City Club wants one,
and wants that one in haste.

---

24. Haarsager, *Bertha Knight Landes*, 29–30, 71, 85, 95, and 142. Text of her speech to the ILWV in *Chicago Tribune*, November 10, 1926.

Or, as the citizens of Seattle found when women voted in 1911, they wanted the power to recall the mayor, whose policies did not reflect their desires.[25]

Landes also reemphasized the need to keep government close to the people and that the city was the best place to do this.

> The farther away we get from the people in government, the less democratic it becomes, the less responsive to the voice and will of the people. Therefore the cities become the battleground of democracy and in them must be fought out the question of its preservation or its destruction for all future time.[26]

It is true that some men progressives talked about the city as a home, yet theirs was generally an instrumental idea rather than a personalized one. This instrumental sense underpinned Frederic Howe's idea of the city as the "hope of democracy." By eliminating the franchise system, he wrote, "the city would become in effect an enlarged home, offering to its members many of the comforts and conveniences that are now denied to any save a few." He believed that municipal ownership would create a new "civic sense" among city residents. "Under municipal ownership there will be no readily organized class wanting bad government. . . . Moreover, with the franchise question removed, the so-called respectable element would be free to enter politics." Municipal ownership, he concluded, "is the struggle of democracy seeking to divorce itself from a privileged class."[27]

Although Howe yearned for a new "civic sense," Jane Addams wanted a "civic virtue" that would not come through new mechanisms alone but by a realization of public needs.

> It is only necessary to make it clear to the voter that his individual needs are common needs, that is, public needs, and that they can only be legitimately supplied for him when they are supplied for all. . . . surely the demand of an individual for decency and comfort, for a chance to work and obtain the fulness of life may be widened until it gradually embraces all the members of the community, and rises into a sense of the common weal.[28]

University Professor Sophonisba Breckinridge worked to bring about this ideal when appointed a tenement inspector for the Chicago Department of

---

25. For Dallas, see Elizabeth Enstam, *Women and the Creation of Urban Life: Dallas, Texas, 1843–1920* (College Station: Texas A & M University Press, 1998), 136–37. For Chicago women, see Anna Nicholes, "How Women Can Help in the Administration of a City," *The Woman Citizen's Library*, vol. 9 (1913), 2194, and Woman's City Club of Chicago, *Its Book* (Chicago: Civics Society, 1915), 55, and Bulletin, 4 (September 1915). For Seattle, see Haarsager, *Bertha Knight Landes*, 49.

26. Haarsager, 150–51. For the political agenda of municipal housekeeping, see Maureen A. Flanagan, "The City Profitable, the City Livable: Environmental Policy, Gender, and Power in Chicago in the 1910s," *Journal of Urban History*, 22 (January 1996): 163–90; and Philip J. Ethington, "Recasting Urban Political History: Gender, the Public, the Household, and Political Participation in Boston and San Francisco during the Progressive Era," *Social Science History*, 16 (Summer 1992): 301–33.

27. Howe, *The City*, 312, and Howe, "The Case for Municipal Ownership," *Publications of the American Economic Association*, 7 (February 1906): 126, 127, 132.

28. Addams, *Democracy and Social Ethics*, 117.

Health—an unpaid position. When she found black Chicagoans living in the most appalling conditions, she could not imagine that once white Chicagoans were informed about such wretched living, they would tolerate its continuance. Given both her progressive idealism and her social science training, this just seemed logical to Breckinridge. But she failed to reckon with the deep-seated racial prejudice that kept African Americans physically segregated and without public resources. Her findings, alas, did not lead to any significant changes for Chicago's African American residents.[29]

Not all female progressives thought exactly like Landes, Addams, and Breckinridge. In their quest for suffrage, elite white Los Angeles women aligned themselves with the male good government faction that sought to restrict popular democracy in that city. Yet, many of these same clubwomen had sought to convince men that they were "city mothers" who would "create a civic home that provided services . . . for its members" if they could vote rather than stressing that they would support what men wanted. The Women's Municipal League in Boston appears to have been more interested in good government than in government for the common welfare. On the other hand, Mary Parker Follett's social center movement was far more democratic than Howe's idea of the People's Institute, which he believed was a "tool" to lead the people to the right decisions.[30]

A comparison of many middle-class men's and women's urban reform organizations, however, does reveal that the majority of female progressive organizations functioned along the democratic lines suggested by Addams, whereas many male organizations operated in a fashion even less "democratic" than Howe's. The women were "doers" who specifically set out to investigate urban conditions, connect with other women across the city, and through these means pressure government to enact reforms. The founding principles of the Woman's City Club of Chicago (1910) were to "aid in improving civic conditions and to assist in arousing an increased sense of social responsibility for the safeguarding of the home, the maintenance of good government, and the ennobling of that larger home of all—the city." The Cincinnati Woman's City Club (1915) said that it wanted to be a center "for active work in the public welfare." The Women's City Club of Seattle sought to involve women across class lines in municipal affairs. The women's Tampa Civic Association (1911) collected data and circulated petitions to have playgrounds and parks built and public health concerns addressed. The committees of the Women's Municipal League of Boston directly inspected the conditions of markets, playgrounds, and waste

---

29. Sophonisba Breckinridge, "The Color Line in the Housing Problem," *The Survey*, 29 (February 1, 1913): 575–76, and Ellen F. Fitzpatrick, *Endless Crusade: Women Social Scientists and Progressive Reform* (New York: Oxford University Press, 1990), 180–82.

30. Gayle Gullett, *Becoming Citizens: The Emergence and Development of the California Women's Movement, 1880–1911* (Urbana: University of Illinois Press, 2000), 46, 108, 151–53, and 161–63 for San Francisco women and good government men; Connolly, *The Triumph of Ethnic Progressivism*, 47–48; and Mattson, *Creating a Democratic Public*, 46.

disposal and went into city hall demanding new health and sanitation regulations for the city.[31]

Men tended to be "talkers." They hired "experts" to investigate conditions
and to report back to the club members who would then discuss the issue.
The Chicago City Club (1904) said its purpose was to bring together men
"who are genuinely interested in the improvement, by non-partisan and disinterested methods, of the political, social, and economic conditions of the
community in which we live." The Cleveland City Club (1912) decided that
its purpose was to gather information, not to try to effect reforms. The Boston
City Club described itself as "an impartial club for discussion by men of all
walks of life." The New York City and Philadelphia City Clubs expressed
their purposes in exactly the same terms.[32]

Because most male reformers believed that government as currently constituted was corrupt, the discussions in most of their clubs were about changing
the mechanisms of government before enacting any other reforms. Female
civic organizations wanted better government too. But they were willing to
work with what was in place in order to secure reforms immediately for the
general welfare. Sophonisba Breckinridge, for example, believed that any government could be forced by its people to, first, enforce its own laws. "Can we
not," she asked

> take hold of this outworn and awkward tool, the city government, and extract all
> the service possible. . . . Can we not here and now notify the Council that we will
> have no more improper exemptions [from the housing code]; let the Building
> Committee of the Council know that the eyes of influential men are upon them to
> resist exemptions, not to seek them; make known to the corporation counsel that
> we are not children to play a game of make-believe; and [obtain] from [city gov-
> ernment] not in a remote future but here and now, in the year 1914, all the benefit
> it has for the dwellers in the poorer quarters of our city?

Similarly, New York City settlement house founder Mary Kingsbury
Simkhovitch tried to convince the new urban planning professionals to make social needs of each neighborhood their first priority. "Parks, playgrounds,
schools, churches, shopping centers, residences, and good transit facilities," she
argued, "all hang together." She wanted these professionals first to find out from
people what they wanted and then determine how to bring it to them. But men
such as Frederic Howe and Benjamin Marsh, executive secretary of the Committee on Congestion of Population in New York, believed that housing was an
"economic" problem. Proper planning for the "orderly development of a city by

---

31. Flanagan, "Gender and Urban Political Reform," 1032; Andrea T. Kornbluh, *Lighting the Way
. . . The Women's City Club of Cincinnati, 1915–1965* (Cincinnati: Young and Klein, 1986), 2; Haarsager,
Bertha Knight Landes, 95–96; Nancy Hewitt, *Southern Discomfort: Women's Activism in Tampa, Florida,
1880s–1920s* (Urbana: University of Illinois Press, 2001), 188–91; and Connolly, *The Triumph of Ethnic
Progressivism*, 49–50.

32. For the Chicago City Club, *Yearbook* (Chicago, 1904); for Boston and Cleveland, www
.cityclub.org/content/aboutus/index/history.asp; for New York and Philadelphia, see Scheisl, *The
Politics of Efficiency*, 42.

which each section is arranged for the purpose for which it is best and most economically adapted," Marsh declared, could help cure the housing crisis. This was the progressive concept of zoning laws, which originated in Europe and the progressives managed to implement in many U. S. cities. But in Germany zoning was a method to save land for building working-class housing. In the United States, it became a "realtor's asset," a way to promote property. Marsh also believed that population congestion resulted primarily from "protected privilege and exploitation, and must be dealt with largely as an economic problem and the result mainly of economic conditions." For Marsh the solution was to enact new land taxation schemes, not to consult the people.[33]

Certainly there were men who agreed with women and vice versa on issues of political progressivism and all were truly appalled by the terrible housing conditions of so many Americans. But the preponderance of evidence shows female and male reformers assessing the problem from a different perspective and arriving at different conclusions about causes and solutions. Women almost always spoke about the social responsibility of all citizens and the municipal government to do something about housing immediately. Florence Kelley, now in New York heading the NCL, urged municipal governments immediately to begin buying vacant land and building housing, a practice that German cities had initiated. By 1920, Chicago reformers Mary McDowell and Harriet Vittum had become so discouraged by the failure of planning solutions that they believed that only the police power of the state to acquire land and build housing could solve the problem. Men continued to focus on mechanisms and instruments, and always on private enterprise. Howe and Marsh called for lowering property taxes and finding ways to encourage private enterprise to build more homes. The Chicago City Club wanted the city council to provide financial incentives for private builders.[34]

When Florence Kelley and Mary Simkhovitch planned the first National Conference on City Planning in 1909, they chose the theme "using planning to deal with social problems." Yet, Simkhovitch was the only woman who spoke and the only one who addressed the assembly along these lines. The other speeches focused on mechanisms and economics, such as John Nolen's when he declared that "a more honest, economical, and wiser expenditure is indeed sorely needed, and ultimately the change of policy proposed would lead here, as it has elsewhere, to a decided reduction in taxes." The difference was aptly summed up by Simkhovitch when she pleaded instead to "let life, not theory,

---

33. Breckinridge quoted in Flanagan, *Seeing with Their Hearts*, 93–94. For Simkhovitch, see Susan Marie Wirka, "The City Social Movement: Progressive Women Reformers and Early Social Planning," in *Planning the Twentieth–Century American City*, Mary Corbin Sies and Christopher Silver, eds. (Baltimore: Johns Hopkins University Press, 1996), 55–75, quote from 73. Howe, *The City*, viii–xi and *The Modern City and Its Problems* (New York: Charles Scribner's Sons, 1915), 287. Marsh, "Economic Aspects of City Planning," *Proceedings*, Municipal Engineers of the City of New York, paper 57 (1910): 73–87 and Marsh, "Causes of Congestion in Population," *Proceedings of the Second National Conference on City Planning and Congestion* (May 1910): 35–39. For zoning, see Rodgers, *Atlantic Crossings*, 177, 184–87.

34. For Kelley and municipal land purchase, see Rodgers, *Atlantic Crossings*, 183 and 176; for Vittum, McDowell, and the City Club, see Flanagan, *Seeing with Their Hearts*, 166–67.

lead the way." Finding the mainstream planning movement so unreceptive to her ideas, Simkhovitch withdrew and helped form the National Housing Association in 1911. By 1912, the Planning Conference had dropped housing altogether from its agenda. Streets, traffic, transportation, and aesthetics were the focus of planning into which housing could be inserted. The annual conferences of the male-dominated National Conference on Housing were also skewed toward listening to male professionals while barely making time for any female presentations. In Cincinnati, women objected when that city's Better Housing League (BHL) appointed a board of ten men, contending that "the city boosters [i.e., businessmen] and its social workers might have an entirely different viewpoint about the nature and goals of the housing organization." Writing later in life, Simkhovitch summed up her differences with most planners: "no matter how good a plan looks from the point of view of a sound economy, it is not a good plan unless the people like it."[35]

4. The View from Labor

No consideration of political progressivism and the "corrupt bargain" can ignore the role of the workers. Despite admittedly strong class solidarity among the working class regarding the problems they faced at work and in daily life, solidarity remained a problem for women workers in the area of organizing. Organized male labor did not welcome the presence of women in the workforce, resented what it considered women's "economic competition," and was so reluctant to organize women workers that the National Women's Trade Union League (NWTUL), which formed at an AFL convention, pursued its separate path organizing middle-class and working-class women together. Among the organizers of the new NWTUL was Mary Kenney O'Sullivan, who had worked for five months in the 1890s as the AFL's first national organizer of women. The NWTUL insisted that social and economic reforms had to proceed together; the AFL insisted that if the rights of labor to organize and have a voice in production were recognized, then social reform would follow. The animosity AFL leader Samuel Gompers felt toward the NWTUL came to a head in 1917, when he forced NWTUL president Margaret Dreier Robins off the executive board of the Chicago Federation of Labor (CFL) despite the strong support for her by CFL head John Fitzpatrick. The AFL's motto, "a fair day's wages for a fair day's work," and the NWTUL's motto, "the eight-hour

---

35. See John Nolen, speech to First National Conference on Town Planning and the Congestion of Population, May 1909, in Washington, D.C. For Simkhovitch and Kelley, see Spain, *How Women Saved the City*, 71, and Wirka, "The City Social Movement," 73–75, quote, 73. For National Conference on City Planning in 1912, see Rodgers, *Atlantic Crossings*, 196. For National Conferences on Housing, see Breckinridge's description of the 1913 Cincinnati conference in City Club of Chicago, *Bulletin* (January 1914). See also, Robert B. Fairbanks, *Making Better Citizens: Housing Reform and the Community Development Strategy in Cincinnati, 1890–1960* (Urbana: University of Illinois Press, 1988), 186, n. 22 and 29–30, for the prominent role of the Women's City Club in organizing the BHL. For the most current literature on gender and planning, see the essays in *Gender and Planning*, Susan Fainstein and Lisa Servon, eds. (New Brunswick, NJ: Rutgers University Press, 2005).

day, a living wage, to guard the home," encapsulated the different perspectives of the two groups.[36] The former emphasized the wages to be earned for working; the latter emphasized family life.

Yet there was a distinct labor progressivism in local-level politics wherein class sometimes brought the genders together, even though at other times gender experiences pushed them apart. Laboring men knew that the "corrupt bargain" worked to exclude them from political power. Municipal governments allowed business to use the police to break up strikes. Franchises contained no restrictions on how franchise holders paid or treated their workers. Workers understood how some good government reforms would work to take democracy further away from people such as themselves. Clearly, laborers wanted to realign municipal government away from the bargain as it existed, but they also believed that government had to be more responsive to the needs of more people. In its way, the working class was developing its own new "civic sense," as Frederic Howe was calling for. As much as they were labor actions, the Cleveland streetcar strikes of 1899 were aimed at the municipal government's lack of concern for the conditions of life in the city. The People's Institute drew large crowds of workers to its weekly gatherings on political and social issues. There is abundant evidence of the new civic sense developing among the working class.[37] But this labor vision of political progressivism was different from other visions. Labor wanted to construct a workingmen's democracy. Unlike the earlier vision of the Knights of Labor, which wanted to construct a cooperative of all producers, Progressive Era workers turned to political reforms to bring them democracy. For Chicago transit workers municipal ownership meant that they could better protect their labor if elected officials controlled this public service. Samuel L. Jones, mayor of Toledo, drew over 70 percent of the votes in the working class and immigrant wards of Cleveland when he ran for Ohio governor in 1899 on a platform promising to end private exploitation of the city. The same groups and issues resulted in Tom Johnson's election as Cleveland's mayor in 1901.[38]

In some cities labor joined with socialist groups to try to implement municipal socialism. In Milwaukee, socialists gained control of the city in 1910, lost it in 1912, regained it in 1916, and held it under Mayor Daniel Hoan until 1940. Hoan and the socialists appealed to the city's working class with a strategy to improve municipal services through municipal ownership in ways that promised not to raise property taxes. Not increasing property taxes was considered essential in this city, where a considerable portion of the working class owned small homes. Such a strategy ultimately meant that the socialist administration

---

36. Payne, *Reform, Labor, and Feminism*, 95–107, for Gompers and Robins and the relationship between the AFL and the NWTUL.

37. See Flanagan, *Charter Reform in Chicago*; Kevin Mattson, *Creating a Democratic Public*; and Shelton Stromquist, "The Crucible of Class: Cleveland Politics and the Origins of Municipal Reform in the Progressive Era," *Journal of Urban History*, 23 (January 1997): 192–220.

38. Leon Fink, *Workingmen's Democracy: The Knights of Labor and American Politics* (Urbana: University of Illinois Press, 1983); Georg Leidenberger, "Working-Class Progressivism"; and Stromquist, "The Crucible of Class."

could not succeed with some of its more radical reform proposals, so what resulted in Milwaukee was in fact a system that looked much like that advocated by many female progressives. When socialist Josephine Kaneko ran for city council in Chicago in 1914 she also sounded as much like the women of the Woman's City Club as she did a socialist. In fact, she declared she could not see much difference:

> When I began to look into the woman movement of this country I found that the women were also looking out for the interests of the people, rather than the interests of the private corporations. The women did not got [sic] as far as the Socialists, and yet their demands were almost identical with what we call the immediate demands of the Socialist party. . . . committees for the abolition of child labor; for the eight-hour day for working women; . . . for sanitation; for good housing ordinances . . . for many things that are essential to the welfare of the whole people.

Not that it was always the case that municipal socialism could sound more progressively democratic than socialist. In Los Angeles in 1911, for instance, where the middle class firmly controlled the political system, the city's working class was furious with the business-led city government. They put together a fusion labor/socialist ticket headed by socialist Job Harriman for mayor. The hope was that as mayor he would wholeheartedly pursue municipal ownership and shift government decisions toward workers rather than business. This was a bitter and very close campaign that Harriman barely lost. The rhetoric of the Los Angeles campaign was much more about class struggle than about municipal democracy.[39]

By the 1920s, the political progressives, with rare exceptions, had accomplished enough reform in cities throughout the country to rupture the "corrupt bargain" in most urban politics. There would never again be business as usual of underhanded trading of municipal favors for bribes. And cities were gradually accepting responsibility for providing many public services. Yet as with many things, reform "is in the eye of the beholder." Mainstream male political progressives had wanted more reform, but new charters and changes to the mechanisms of city government went a long way toward satisfying them. For many female progressives, the results were highly unsatisfying. Protecting property and private enterprise, and creating a good economic climate, remained among the highest priorities of even reformed city government. Entering the 1920s, urban government was definitely more humane; it did more for the poor than ever before and had replaced private enterprise with municipal control of some public services. But government that functioned from a sense of social responsibility had not been attained. Whether reformed or unre-

---

    39. Douglas E. Booth, "Municipal Socialism and City Government Reform: The Milwaukee Experience, 1910–1940," *Journal of Urban History*, 12 (November 1985): 51–71; Kaneko, "What a Socialist Alderman Would Do," *The Coming Nation* (March 1914); and Daniel J. Johnson, "'No Make-Believe Class Struggle': The Socialist Municipal Campaign in Los Angeles, 1911," *Labor History*, 41 (February 2000): 25–45. For a broad overview, see Richard W. Judd, *Socialist Cities: Municipal Politics and the Grassroots of American Socialism* (Albany: State University of New York Press, 1989).

formed, the business of government remained business; it just shifted its perspective some. The concept of "social politics" (which will be taken up in Chapter 6) had made it into the collective consciousness of Americans but never became the driving force of politics and government in the United States.

> Treason is a strong word, but not too strong to characterize
> the situation in which the Senate is the eager, resourceful, and
> indefatigable agent of private interests as hostile to the Amer-
> ican people as any invading army could be.

These startling words were written in 1906 by David Graham Phillips. They were part of a series of nine articles titled "Treason of the Senate" that he would publish in *Cosmopolitan Magazine*, owned by William Randolph Hearst. Phillips accused the U.S. Senate of being bought and sold by private interests. No piece of legislation, he contended, was passed by that body "that was not either helpful to or harmless against 'the interest.'" The result was that

> property is concentrating in the hands of the few and the little children of the masses are being sent to toil in the darkness of mines in the dreariness and un-healthfulness of factories instead of being sent to school; and why the great mid-dle class . . . is being swiftly crushed into dependence and the repulsive miseries of "genteel poverty."

For Phillips, both political parties were culpable, but the Republican leadership of the Senate was the worst offender. He accused them of colluding openly with big business to destroy American democracy. Republican President Theodore Roosevelt was so offended by this series that he coined the term "muckraker" to describe this type of sensationalist journalism. Yet, Roosevelt and progressives in both parties knew that there was truth in the charges. And Phillips was not alone in making such charges and publicizing them in the popular magazines and newspapers of the day. Laissez-faire capitalism, according to many progressives, was undermining the "opportunity" to advance that democracy supposedly offered its ordinary citizens.

CHAPTER 5

Reforming the State

Our whole political machinery in all its parts must be adapted
to all the changing purposes of government.
—WALTER WEYL, 1912

AMERICANS AT THE turn of the century were discovering that on every level of government "business corrupts politics."[1] The "corrupt bargain" was the modus operandi of national government and the Republicans had become particularly adept at it. They had become the leading party of the country in great measure from the money pouring into it from big business. The 1896 election had solidified Republican control of the political system. The Democrats were already suspect in the eyes of much of the middle class as the party of the "backward" South. When the Democrats incorporated the Populists into the party and chose their leader, William Jennings Bryan, as Democratic presidential candidate that year, the party was further identified with rural and lower-class urban radicalism.

A little background to this election, and national politics in general, helps to understand how political progressivism functioned in the years after 1896. On the one hand, small government ideology and lack of revenue had kept national government policymaking circumscribed through the late nineteenth century. The presidency, in particular, was still mainly confined to administering the government and not to developing policy. On the other hand, the two issues that troubled the 1896 election, as they had for the past several elections—the tariff and the monetary issue—involved policymaking. Briefly explained, the tariff protected business from foreign competition but drove up prices at home. The monetary question concerned whether to back currency with silver or to keep it backed by gold. Gold was more scarce, so using the

---

1. Richard L. McCormick, "The Discovery That Business Corrupts Politics: A Reappraisal of the Origins of Progressivism," *American Historical Review*, 86 (April 1981): 247–74.

gold standard kept the money supply tight and prices high. Populists had charged that tariffs and gold-backed currency favored business while it harmed farmers, small producers, and consumers. In 1896, Bryan delivered a dramatic, religiously symbolic, speech to the Democratic convention that clarified the issues for adherents of both parties:

> I come to speak to you in defense of a cause as holy as the cause of liberty—the cause of humanity. . . . We have begged, and they have mocked when our calamity came. We beg no longer, we entreat no more; we petition no more. We defy them! . . . you shall not press down upon the brow of labor this crown of thorns. You shall not crucify mankind upon a cross of gold!

The Republicans nominated the exact opposite candidate: the sober, upright William McKinley who promised to maintain the gold standard and bring economic recovery from the 1893 depression years. Bryan campaigned frenetically across the country prophesying economic and social doom. McKinley stayed on his front porch, the picture of serene confidence. The Republicans used the contrast to depict Bryan and the Democrats as unpatriotic, backward-looking rabble-rousers who would ruin the country's prosperity and bring on class warfare. A cartoon published in a satirical magazine during the campaign showed Bryan riding into battle on a donkey, leading a ragged army carrying swords and banners, and dressed in old-fashioned clothing. Facing them was a modern industrial army that was defending the White House, the Capitol, sound money, and the "National Honor."[2] McKinley won, the gold standard stayed in place, and the economy began to recover, although this was thanks primarily to an increase in the world's gold supply. McKinley was then easily reelected in 1900, again defeating Bryan. Everything seemed just fine—at least to many Republicans—until McKinley was assassinated in September 1901.

McKinley's assassination changed the political and social climate of the country. Americans were horrified by the act itself but even more appalled by the assassin and his motives. Leon Czolgosz (pronounced *cholgosh*) was a self-proclaimed anarchist who calmly told his captors, "I only done my duty." When questioned as to why he had killed the president, he replied, because "McKinley was going around the country shouting about prosperity when there was no prosperity for the poor man." Hard-line conservatives called for his immediate execution; radical anarchists who advocated deeds rather than talk must have secretly approved that someone had taken action. But the trial caught the mass of Americans on the proverbial "horns of a dilemma": the defense argued that Czolgosz was insane; the prosecution that he was not. If he were sane, then the fear of anarchist violence—which by then had become a

---

2. Bryan, *The First Battle: A Story of the Campaign of 1896* (Chicago: W. B. Conkey, 1898) contains the speech, which is reprinted in *William Jennings Bryan: Selections*, Ray Ginger, ed. (Indianapolis: Bobbs-Merrill, 1967); cartoon from *Puck*, 40 (September 30, 1896). In the cartoon, Kansas populist leader Mary Lease was in the front line carrying a broom—a favorite image used by cartoonists of the time for women reformers. For the monetary issue, see Ballard Campbell, *The Growth of American Government: Governance from the Cleveland Era to the Present* (Bloomington: Indiana University Press, 1995); Robert Cherny, *The Politics of the Gilded Age, 1868–1900* (Wheeling, IL: Harlan Davidson, 1997); and Gretchen Ritter, *Goldbugs and Greenbacks: The Anti-Monopoly Tradition and the Politics of Finance in America* (Cambridge, UK: Cambridge University Press, 1997).

global problem—was heightened. There would be others just like him waiting to commit similar acts. If he were insane, then did the "inhumanity" of capitalism drive him insane, as some claimed? These events unfolded as social scientists were raising the issue of environmental determinism, so the insanity question was perhaps the more upsetting for Americans to contemplate. What if their society really was inhumane? What if it really did drive some people insane enough to undertake as violent an act as assassinating the president? And if the answer were yes, then where was it at fault and how could it be rectified? These are not merely rhetorical questions, for they were exactly the questions that were forced upon Americans by the McKinley assassination.[3]

No single historical incident, no matter how grave, by itself changes history. The McKinley assassination happened as progressives were already questioning the righteousness of their society. So the assassination of the president added a spark to smoldering concerns about the nature of American society and politics. What a smoldering fire often needs is someone to fan it into a roaring blaze. Here the progressives were lucky. McKinley's vice-president was Theodore Roosevelt, who was the darling neither of the Republican Party leadership nor of businessmen. Many regular Republican leaders distrusted and avidly disliked Roosevelt because he believed that the McKinley administrations had represented the "tyranny of money over principle."[4] As police commissioner of New York City (1895–1897), Roosevelt had learned first-hand about poverty, hunger, crime, and political corruption. He was friends with Jane Addams and crusading reform journalist Jacob Riis, who had taken Roosevelt on tours of New York's tenement districts. Roosevelt was so distressed by what he saw that he credited Riis for his conversion to progressivism.

> The midnight trips that Riis and I took . . . gave me personal insight into some of the problems of city life. It is one thing to listen in a perfunctory fashion to tales of overcrowded tenements, and it is quite another actually to see what overcrowding means, some hot summer night. . . . Looking back, I made my greatest strides forward while I was police commissioner, and this largely through my intimacy with Jacob Riis, for he opened all kinds of windows into the matter [of immigrant life] for me.[5]

In this aspect, at least, Roosevelt was a progressive that Jane Addams could, and did, take to heart. Personal experience of other people's lives had begun to transform Roosevelt's ideas about government and society. For progressives who wanted to transform "the national state" into "a 'moral agent,' which should set the rules under which society conducted its affairs,"[6] Roosevelt was the right man, in the right place, at the right time.

Roosevelt represented the best hope for progressives to pursue the *via media* in national reform. They now had a president who believed that the United

---

3. Eric Rauchway, *Murdering McKinley: The Making of Theodore Roosevelt's America* (New York: Hill and Wang, 2003), 16 and 42 for Czolgosz quotes, 43–53 for the trial and questions of sanity.
4. Ibid., 13.
5. Roosevelt quoted in Rauchway, *Murdering McKinley*, 141.
6. Quote in Eric Foner, *The Story of American Freedom* (New York: W.W. Norton, 2nd edition, 1998), 152.

States was at a crossroads: if it did not reform, the alternatives were social-ism/anarchism or the continuing repression of democracy by the growing power of the wealthy industrialists. If the United States were to be reformed by constraining the power of the latter, it would remove the conditions responsi-ble for the spread of radical ideas. Almost all political progressives believed that excessive allegiance to laissez-faire ideals had damaged democracy. Thus, they preferred to reform the system by changing the mechanisms of govern-ment, reallocating the power to make policy for the country as a whole, and re-placing party politicians with better men who would assure that corrupt politi-cians and businessmen could never again control the government.[7]

Describing the myriad reforms to government during the Progressive Era can read like an early catalog of New Deal reforms without the initials. The re-forms of the Progressive Era did lay the foundation for the even more dramatic changes that took place in the 1930s. But behind the actual reforms lay an even more profound change that would make the future reforms possible, let alone thinkable. The Progressive Era changed the relationship of citizens to their government and to each other. By the 1920s, Americans had moved decisively away from a firm belief in small government as an article of faith. The national government had become the focus of political power; the role of the presi-dency in policymaking had been significantly enhanced; and the institutions of government had accrued more power over daily life. Progressive Era re-forms also redrew the boundaries between private and public life. New laws and regulations gave social protections to Americans, who in turn began to look toward government to protect them from the impersonal forces of the marketplace. A sense of national citizenship was superceding local citizenship. The federal government, like cities, was to become an "activist state."

For progressive intellectuals these changes were necessary to preserve democracy. They believed that the prevailing negative concept of liberty em-bodied in laissez-faire was actually depriving people of their freedom. In order to maintain democracy in the complicated world of the twentieth century, they sought to replace negative liberty with positive liberty: citizens and govern-ment had to accept that democracy required duties toward society as well as protection of liberties.[8] The critical problem for progressivism was balancing the freedom of the individual with social responsibility as they restructured government.

NEW DIMENSIONS OF POLITICAL DEMOCRACY

Creating a more powerful, activist state would require assurances of good and honest government. The figures identified here as "mainstream" political pro-gressives sought three broad changes to assure this. They wanted good men

---

7. Rauchway, *Murdering McKinley*, is a thoughtful and provocative assessment of the impact of the McKinley assassination and of Roosevelt's role in progressivism. See especially, xii–xiii, 13, and 89–90.

8. James Kloppenberg, *Uncertain Victory: Progressivism and Social Democracy in American and European Thought, 1870–1920* (New York: Oxford University Press, 1986), 7.

elected and appointed to important offices. They wanted government to take sound measures to regulate the economy. They wanted the court system to accept that government had to regulate the economy and take a broader responsibility for society in general.

1. National Voting Reforms

Progressive measures of the secret ballot and the direct primary had been initial steps toward breaking the stranglehold of party politicians on elections. On the national level, progressives proposed another major electoral reform. Under Article I, section 3 of the U.S. Constitution, U.S. senators were chosen by state legislators, not by popular election. This system had been one of the major targets of "The Treason of the Senate." Phillips specifically attacked the leaders of both parties—Republican Senator Nelson Aldrich and Democrat Arthur Gorman—as working together to manipulate the tariff and all legislation to give corporate interests "full and free license to loot" the country.[9] Whether he was exaggerating or not, the fact that two other senators were in the process of being convicted of corruption for interceding on behalf of "private interests" gave credence to his general charges. In fact, sufficient outrage over collusion of state legislators and U.S. senators had already surfaced to push some states into giving their voters more voice in selecting senators. The problem on the national level was that the mainly Democratic southern senators had been blocking a constitutional amendment to mandate popular election for all states, fearing the possibility that black voters could shift the balance in the South to the Republican Party. Now that southern whites had disfranchised most black voters, their senators no longer opposed the measure. Congress ratified the 17th Amendment in 1913 and shortly thereafter so too did the necessary three-fourths of state legislatures. This was clearly a popular electoral reform.

2. Trustbusting

In the popular lore of the Progressive Era, Theodore Roosevelt is the fabled trustbuster. In this fable, corrupt, money-grubbing industrialists and bankers who had grabbed power through mergers and trusts—economic monopolies or consolidations that strangled competition and controlled prices—met their match in a Roosevelt determined to break their power. Monopolies were indeed growing throughout the industrial economy. Between 1897 and 1904 one-third of American companies disappeared as fewer, bigger entities were created. U.S. Steel produced 60 percent of all steel; coal mines became the property of railroads, many of which were controlled by banker J.P. Morgan; six meat-packing companies merged into the National Packing Company, with a controlling interest in every major stockyard in the country.[10] But Roosevelt

---

9. Full texts of all essays in *Cosmopolitan* (1906); also in David Graham Phillips, *The Treason of the Senate*, George E. Mowry and Judson A. Grenier, eds. (Chicago: University of Chicago Press, 1964).

10. Nell Irvin Painter, *Standing at Armageddon: The United States, 1877–1919* (New York: W.W. Norton, 1987), 177–80.

attacked monopolies not because he disliked big business, which he recognized as the source of American economic prowess. Rather, he disliked the way it was operating. Unrestricted consolidations, he believed, threatened democracy because they gave a few industrialists too much power over politics and over labor. This system had corrupted the political parties, who now competed for monetary contributions from these businessmen. He also feared that the virtually unrestrained power of business over workers was leading the country toward class warfare.

As a politician, Roosevelt was also jealous of his own power. He did not like the industrialists' arrogant behavior. Nothing could have irritated Roosevelt more than Morgan's reply to Roosevelt's expressed concerns about the size and power of Morgan's consolidated railroad holding company, Northern Securities: "send your man to my man and they can fix it up," wrote Morgan. Roosevelt responded by pursuing Morgan using the 1890 Sherman Antitrust Act, and in 1904 the Supreme Court dissolved Northern Securities as violating this act. Morgan was a bête noire for Roosevelt, but Roosevelt was up to the challenge. When anthracite miners in the West Virginia and Pennsylvania coal fields struck in 1902 for higher wages and the eight-hour day, the mine owners' syndicate, headed by Morgan, refused to negotiate. One of the mine owners declared that "the rights of the labouring man will be protected and cared for—not by the labour agitators but by the Christian men to whom God in his infinite wisdom has given the control of the property interests of this country." Fearing the potential for class warfare, again angered by business arrogance, and like a good progressive who had absorbed well his lessons from Jacob Riis, Roosevelt turned to investigation to resolve the issue. He appointed a Coal Commission to look into worker demands and recommend how to settle the strike. Roosevelt's actions were aimed at taming the power of business over labor and the American people generally. The strike had become a national issue, not necessarily for the coal miners' cause but because of the rising cost of coal—the primary fuel for heating homes and running business. Before long that cost had quadrupled from $5 to $20 a ton.[11]

The coal strike clarified Roosevelt's thinking that business could no longer be allowed a totally free hand to dictate how Americans lived and worked. Using the power given to Congress in the Constitution to regulate interstate commerce, Roosevelt and his progressive allies in Congress passed new legislation to regulate railroad rates (1906 Hepburn Act); to oversee food and drug production (1906 Meat Inspection Act and Pure Food and Drug Act); and to outlaw predatory business practices (1903 Elkins Act). Under his presidency, he strengthened the power of the administrative branch of government, creating the Department of Commerce and Labor in 1903 to oversee the practices of corporations engaged in interstate commerce. In 1906, the Department of Agriculture was empowered to inspect and set standards in meat packing, using

---

11. Accounts of Roosevelt and the coal strike can be found in any standard work on the Progressive Era or his presidency. See Rauchway, *Murdering McKinley*, 172–74, quote, 173, for an astute account of this event, especially of Roosevelt's personality in dealing with businessmen. See also, Painter, *Standing at Armageddon*, 180–86, for more on the effects of the strike.

increased powers given to the Bureau of Chemistry (whose name was subsequently changed to the Food and Drug Administration). Because cabinet positions and the bureaucracies they manage are in the administrative branch of government, new and more powerful departments increased the power of the presidency.

In 1913, the Department of Labor and Commerce separated into two departments. The AFL, led by Gompers, wanted a separate cabinet-level post to oversee the conditions of labor and the welfare of workers. Separating commerce and labor did not just fulfill this demand. It shattered the decades-long ideal that there was a community of interests between commerce and labor. Many Americans had clung to this idea even as industrialization was proving it did not exist. Moreover, creating a separate cabinet-level department for labor gave labor a separate voice in government. The political progressives' idea that democracy could be guaranteed by efficient government run by experts was steadily being accompanied by the rise of "special interest," or pluralist, democracy.

3. Interest-group Politics

It became the fashion later in the twentieth century to rail against the influence of special interests in government. It is important to understand the genesis of this aspect of American democracy. In the first place, this was a means to counter the business control of politics. David Graham Phillips and other progressives were correct that money ran the two-party system. Parties and their candidates were now beholden to their large contributors—often big business—to finance national campaigns. To counter the influence of "big money" and dilute favoritism toward big business, new groups organized to promote their interests on the national level. Samuel Gompers moved the AFL into politics in the first decade of the twentieth century, making organized labor into a political interest group as well as a union organization. A new Farmers' Union rose from the ashes of populism in the South, Southwest, and Midwest, and a Country Life Movement formed to represent rural Americans. The National Association of Manufacturers, the National Association for the Advancement of Colored People, the National Women's Trade Union League, and the National Consumers' League are all examples of the new trend toward interest-group politics.[12]

Obviously, all these organizations intended to lobby for legislation from government. But with the shifting center of power in government toward the administrative branch, they also quickly realized the potential of new federal

---

12. Phillips, "The Treason of the Senate"; Julie Greene, *Pure and Simple Politics: The American Federation of Labor and Political Activism, 1881–1917* (Cambridge, UK: Cambridge University Press, 1998); Elizabeth Sanders, *Roots of Reform: Farmers, Workers, and the American State, 1877–1917* (Chicago: University of Chicago Press, 1999); and Robert Wiebe, *The Search for Order: 1877–1920* (New York: Hill and Wang, 1967). James Connolly, *The Triumph of Ethnic Progressivism: Urban Political Culture in Boston, 1900–1925* (Cambridge, MA: Harvard University Press, 1998) argues persuasively that the rise of interest-group ethnic politics characterized one important element of political progressivism in that city, and that this was the element of progressivism that survived.

agencies and regulatory commissions to advance specific agendas. Groups of citizens could now appeal directly to these bodies for particular rulings, services, and protections. The AFL began serious politicking once the Department of Labor was in place. The increased powers of the Department of Agriculture spurred farmers into new organization. Interest-group politics helped limit the power of the old "corrupt bargain" by expanding the popular voice in government. Interest groups also simultaneously accepted government by expertise, while turning it to their advantage. The country was so large and its population and diversity so great that individuals could not expect to have a direct voice beyond voting. Through organized groups, they could appeal directly to government for their special needs. Illinois farm women used the Children's Bureau in the Department of Labor to secure health funds for their families. Rural women used a 1913 Department of Agriculture survey to demand that it allocate funds for modern technology, such as indoor plumbing and electricity, inside their homes rather than just outside where the money was currently going. Theodore Roosevelt was even persuaded to appoint a Committee on Country Life in 1908 to examine rural problems. Moreover, interest-group politics allowed people to circumvent the political party leadership, something that was vital for those groups of Americans who did not have a central role in the parties.[13]

Interest-group politics was a work in progress during its early years. Progressives secured the Pure Food and Drug Act and the Food and Drug Administration (FDA), but the actions and outcomes of such new regulation were uncertain as groups then competed for a voice in designing the regulation. Food and drug producers fought for loose regulations coming from the FDA, whereas progressive activists demanded tight controls and enforcement. When William Howard Taft succeeded Roosevelt in 1908, business interests had a friend in the administration. Businessmen quickly learned how to "politick" the new Federal Trade Commission (FTC, 1914), once it was in place, despite evidence that farmers were most responsible for the creation of this new agency. Long-term congressmen did not give up their power or their patronage easily and as the courts continued to be leery about government "interference" in business, business continued to find protections from new regulations. The National Consumers' League had to struggle for many years before it obtained more of what it wanted in the way of consumer and worker protections.[14]

The creation of these new mechanisms in the national government did open a new door in democracy. Americans of all kinds rushed through it to compete for influence within the new administrative agencies of national government. Even if newspaper columnist H.L. Mencken's quip that Theodore Roosevelt "didn't believe in democracy; he believed simply in government" was accu-

---

13. Lynne Curry, *Modern Mothers in the Heartland: Gender, Health, and Progress in Illinois, 1900–1930* (Columbus: Ohio State University Press, 1999), 77–80 and 70. See also, Arthur S. Link and Richard L. McCormick, *Progressivism* (Arlington Heights, IL: Harlan Davidson, 1983), 56–57.

14. Lorine Swainston Goodwin, *The Pure Food, Drink, and Drug Crusaders, 1879–1914* (Jefferson, NC: McFarland, 1999) and Landon R.Y. Storrs, *Civilizing Capitalism: The National Consumers' League, Women's Activism, and Labor Standards in the New Deal Era* (Chapel Hill: University of North Carolina Press, 2000). For farmers and FTC, see Sanders, *Roots of Reform*.

rate, Roosevelt had opened that door. Roosevelt may have been an "avid aggrandizer . . . who encouraged those aggrandizing executive officials who sought to construct small empires out of the growing demand for public management," yet his aggrandizing started a new era of politics. He placed the United States on the road to developing a powerful administrative state that its citizens were learning to use for democratic purposes.[15]

4. Progressive Citizenship

If interest-group politics brought light into the political process, progressivism also had its dark underside to refashioning political democracy. The immediate aftermath of the McKinley assassination exposed one of progressivism's less fine moments. Czolgosz was not an immigrant, but he had a "strange" name and came from eastern Europe, the home of anarchism. His action played into the anti-immigration sentiment that had been building in the United States for at least two decades before the event. In 1882, Congress had passed the Chinese Exclusion Act and renewed it ten years later to eliminate immigration from China. Then a group of Boston professional men founded the Immigration Restriction League in 1894 seeking legislation to restrict all future immigration. In 1896, one of its members, Senator Henry Cabot Lodge of Massachusetts, introduced a bill in Congress to restrict immigration to those who could pass a literacy test.[16] To a great extent this anti-immigrant sentiment arose from the nature of the new immigration. In massively increasingly waves, new people were pouring into the United States and many native-born-Americans considered them a threat to the "American" race and to democracy. The new immigrants were coming from southern and eastern Europe. Their complexions were darker. They were heavily Catholic and Jewish, not Protestant. They were considered to be largely illiterate. Although Jane Addams and others were working to bring people together to create a new kind of democracy, the Immigration Restriction League and organizations such as the rabidly anti-Catholic American Protective Association targeted new immigrants as the cause of the country's problems. To Addams' call for a new civic virtue, and Frederic Howe's call for a new civic sense, was added another call: that for civic racialism.

The concept of a civic racialism, no matter how justified, is in the end undemocratic. But as an element of the rethinking of democracy, it must be acknowledged as part of the American heritage. Andrew Carnegie had written in 1885 that the United States was great because of its British Protestant origins. Elements of progressivism picked up on this idea and began to wonder aloud whether everyone could be an American. Some progressives asked whether new immigrants were "fit" to contribute to a functioning popular democracy. If they were somehow "unfit" and could be eliminated from voting—or kept out

---

15. Menken quoted in Foner, *The Story of American Freedom*, 154–55; and Wiebe, *The Search for Order*, 190–91.

16. Jeanne Petit, "Breeders, Workers, and Mothers: Gender and the Congressional Literacy Test Debate, 1896–1897," *The Journal of the Gilded Age and Progressive Era*, 3 (January 2004): 35–58.

of the country altogether—then democracy would be improved. The question of fitness had both racial and gender overtones. Restrictionists worried that illiterate male immigrants coming from southeastern Europe would lower the quality of American manhood. Lodge called Anglo-Saxons a "vigorous body of men" who were responsible for the "upbuilding of the United States" and passing on those genes to their male children. Advocates of literacy testing even debated whether this should be extended to female immigrants even though they could not vote. For some, the answer was yes. Lodge worried that illiterate immigrant women would breed more illiterate unfit children.[17]

These virulent forms of anti-immigration sentiment percolated through progressivism. Proponents of restriction convinced the Senate to appoint the Dillingham Commission in 1907 to investigate the impact of new immigrants on the country. The commission's forty-two-volume report concluded that they were indeed largely responsible for the country's problems and recommended implementing literacy requirements in order to protect democracy. From 1897, successive presidents vetoed the congressional attempts to pass restrictive legislation. Congress finally succeeded in passing a literacy bill in 1917 over the veto of President Wilson, who opposed this legislation for denying opportunity to people who wanted to come to the United States.[18]

Many progressives concerned about what made a good democratic citizen chose to stand on the middle ground, rejecting the boldest protectionist approach but also not falling in line with those who believed that education and assimilation would incorporate all immigrants into American society. As president, Theodore Roosevelt's theorizing about an "American" race led him to ponder the possibility of "race" suicide if too many of the wrong sorts were allowed full participation in democracy. Unlike Carnegie, he did not narrowly define American as Anglo-Saxon and, unlike Lodge, he did not consider all men and women from south and eastern Europe as racially undesirable. Rather, from his theory of European hybridity, he concluded that weaker minds still existed among certain groups, and those were the ones susceptible to anarchism. The McKinley assassination convinced him that all Europeans could be incorporated into the nation—could become "American"—by enacting reforms giving them more political and economic opportunity and eliminating the conditions that made the weaker ones succumb to radical ideologies. As an additional safeguard, however, Roosevelt and Congress in 1903 approved new naturalization requirements. Five consecutive years of residence, English-language skills, proof that one was not an anarchist or polygamist, and two sponsors swearing to one's "moral principles" and "attachment to the principles of the Constitution" there-

---

17. Petit, "Breeders, Workers, and Mothers," 45 and 52–56. For more discussion of immigrant women and reproduction vis-a-vis citizenship, see Katrina Irving, *Immigrant Mothers: Narratives of Race and Maternity, 1890–1925* (Urbana: University of Illinois Press, 2002) and Wendy Kline, *Building a Better Race: Gender, Sexuality, and Eugenics from the Turn of the Century to the Baby Boom* (Berkeley: University of California Press, 2001).

18. Reports of the Immigration Commission (Washington, D. C., 1911); Robert F. Zeidel, *Immigrants, Exclusion, and Progressive Politics: The Dillingham Commission, 1900–1927* (DeKalb: Northern Illinois University Press, 2004); and Roger Daniels, *Coming to America: A History of Immigration and Ethnicity in American Life* (New York: Perennial, 2nd edition, 2002).

after became the standard for acquiring citizenship. This was the first time that "eligibility for Americanness [was defined] in terms of a belief."[19] Not only did this set the standard for naturalization, it opened the way for people and ideas to be labeled as "un-American," a concept that has been deeply embedded in American consciousness ever since. Some historians have claimed that such measures, along with new voting requirements, disfranchised millions of lower-class and immigrant voters. Whether such a claim can be absolutely substantiated or not, the fact remains that some progressives intended to make it more difficult for those deemed "unfit" to come into the country and to be able to vote.[20]

If European hybridity was Roosevelt's standard for an "American" race, then "non-whites" were not hybrids and would need more time to achieve the right "intellectual and moral competencies" for full democratic participation. Believing this allowed Roosevelt to reject the pleas of African American leaders such as W.E.B. DuBois and Ida B. Wells-Barnett to take a forthright stand for racial equality. He preferred to go along with the more accommodationist approach of Booker T. Washington and not confront southerners about disfranchisement or lynching. To a certain extent his lack of concern about southern African Americans' disfranchisement was political. The Republican Party had virtually written off the South as solidly Democratic. Black votes would not change this situation. Roosevelt was such a political animal that one can readily believe him making this calculation. Yet, he also professed to be a moral being and Jane Addams always tried to appeal to the "more generous side of his nature." Addams and Roosevelt both believed in the efficacy of social science for gathering the evidence to promote political actions, but this common belief did not always lead to the same uses or reach the same conclusions. Unfortunately in this case, Roosevelt's ideas about European hybridity were bolstered by prevailing pseudosocial scientific theories that took scientific Darwinism and turned it into social Darwinism. The mistake here, the philosopher William James had earlier observed, was to think that observation of human behavior could be turned into theory of innate characteristics—race or class, for example—"as if they had the power to cause the patterns" of behavior. Nonetheless, such thinking allowed Roosevelt to turn his back on African Americans and Asians. In 1908, he signed the "Gentlemen's Agreement" with Japan in which that country agreed to stop issuing passports to laborers in return for the United States not discriminating against

---

19. Gary Gerstle, *American Crucible: Race and Nation in the Twentieth Century* (Princeton, NJ: Princeton University Press, 2001), 45–6, 71–72, and 55; and Rauchway, *Murdering McKinley*, 142–47, 146 for quote about belief. Former Confederates had had to take such an oath to be reinstated to citizenship but never before had immigrants.

20. See Alexander Keyssar, *The Right to Vote: The Contested History of Democracy in the United States* (New York: Basic Books, 2000), 158 and 170–71, for "millions." Previously, many states had allowed alien men who had declared their intent to become citizens to vote. These laws were all repealed by the 1920s. Some states also enacted new laws on residency requirements and registration. See Liette Gidlow, *The Big Vote: Gender, Consumer Culture, and the Politics of Exclusion, 1890s–1920s* (Baltimore: Johns Hopkins University Press, 2004), 25, for a summary of these changes.

Japanese immigrants already in the country. This agreement effectively eliminated future immigration from Japan.[21]

Once theories about innate characteristics and fears of race suicide became
popular, equal citizenship became a more elusive goal for African Americans
and Asians. African American women sought to counteract this "scientific"
racism through the politics of "respectability." By changing the behavior of
lower-class African Americans, these women believed they could demonstrate
that there were no innate racial characteristics, just learned sets of behaviors
that could be changed. But racial theorizing had emboldened southerners to
pursue segregation, discrimination, and to propagate racist hatred. Successive
presidents were willing accomplices to these actions. President Taft's federal
appointments in the South went only to men "whose appointment would
commend themselves in the community where they live"—that is, white su-
premacists. Democratic "progressive" President Woodrow Wilson—a south-
erner—segregated the federal government in 1913. Belle Case LaFollette, an
antilynching and antisegregation crusader from Wisconsin, was outraged at
this decision. She tried unsuccessfully to have reinstated two female African
American federal employees who had been fired for refusing to eat at a segregated lunch table. Then she publicly excoriated Wilson. Her choice of words
indicated not just that she saw this as an injustice, but that she did not believe
in racial citizenship:

> To have the United States Government take a backward step, to have the color
> line drawn in places they have won on their merits, to be humiliated, repressed
> and degraded at the capital of the nation by their own government, which has no
> right to discriminate among its citizens, is a body blow to hope and pride and
> incentive.

Unfortunately, there were far too few other progressives willing to stand up
with her.[22]

There was one final group that made it into the considerations of progressive citizenship: American Indians. According to the Constitution, indigenous
people were not citizens. By the Progressive Era, national policy toward indigenous people had shifted several times. Once all groups had been forcibly
subdued in the 1890s, attention turned to making them into citizens. Progressives faced three problems in dealing with this issue: Indians could not be excluded from the country; indigenous peoples' cultural practices and ideas
were extremely different from European Americans'; and the government was

---

21. Gerstle, *The Crucible of Race*, 45–46; and Rauchway, *Murdering McKinley*, 147–48 for Addams,
146–47 for James, and 72–74 for Roosevelt, the South, and Washington.

22. Evelyn Brooks Higginbotham, *Righteous Discontent: The Women's Movement in the Black Bap-
tist Church, 1880–1920* (Cambridge, MA: Harvard University Press, 1993), 187, 192–94; LaFollette is
quoted in Nancy Unger, *Fighting Bob LaFollette: The Righteous Reformer* (Chapel Hill: University of
North Carolina Press, 2002), 56; Morton Keller, *Regulating a New Society: Public Policy and Social
Change in America, 1900–1933* (Cambridge, MA: Harvard University Press, 1994), 253–59, 255 for
Taft. See also, Glenda Gilmore, *Gender and Jim Crow: Women and the Politics of White Supremacy in
North Carolina, 1896–1920* (Chapel Hill: University of North Carolina Press, 1996) for a discussion of
ideas and roles of the "New White Man" in the southern states.

moving steadily away from wishing to oversee the reservation system. In this context, Progressive Era reformers never entirely agreed on what to do, but the idea that Indians could be assimilated into society gradually won out. For Indians to assimilate meant giving up "Indian" culture and behaving like "white" people in exchange for citizenship. Enmeshed in this reform was the desire of both Congress and many people to be able to dispose of Indian reservation lands—a nice way of saying take away their land and give it to white people. Two Supreme Court rulings upheld this process. In 1903 the Court agreed that the government was not bound to respect past treaties with Indian tribes. Two years later, Justice Brewer (who would write the majority opinion in *Muller v. Oregon* in 1908) concluded that the government was "under no constitutional obligation to perpetually continue the relationship of guardian and ward." Therefore, he ruled, the government was free to carry on with its policy "which looks to the breaking up of tribal relations, the establishing of the separate [I]ndians in individual homes, free from national guardianship and charged with all rights and obligations of citizens of the United States." Race continued to be an important factor in Indian citizenship. "Freedom from government restriction" was first granted to those Indians who had a "preponderance" of white blood. Those with half or more Indian blood first had to take a competency test.[23]

In its most benign form, musings about "fitness" of immigrants led to calls for educating immigrants in how to be democratic rather than resorting to exclusion. Progressive theorist John Dewey believed that the new immigrants just needed time and opportunity to learn how to be "disinterested" voters who would apply "'scientific' solutions to social problems." Dewey felt this necessary because he believed that ethics had been divorced from politics. Some groups were further ahead in bringing the two back together; other groups would need more time.[24] Jane Addams, on the other hand, chastised those progressives who blamed immigrants for undemocratic tendencies. "It is most difficult to hold to our political democracy and to make it in any sense a social expression and not mere governmental contrivance," she wrote, "unless we take pains to keep common ground in our human experience." The process of assimilation that she and other settlement house workers advocated was one to help immigrants adjust to American society and culture as a whole. Naturally there was a class element to this idea, but it was not one that feared the new immigrants as unfit. Middle-class African American women in the Woman's Convention of the Baptist Church approached lower-class African Americans in the same way, working to assimilate them into "respectable" middle-class norms of the larger society. Boarding schools, rooming houses,

---

23. Keller, *Regulating a New Society*, 283–87, looks at this from the perspective of policy formation. See, Fred Hoxie, *A Final Promise: The Campaign to Assimilate the Indians, 1880–1920* (Lincoln: University of Nebraska Press, 2nd edition, 2001) and Hoxie, ed., *Talking Back to Civilization: Indian Voices from the Progressive Era* (Boston: Bedford Books of St. Martin's Press, 2001) for a social, and Indian, perspective.

24. Dewey as quoted in Foner, *The Story of American Freedom*, 154. See also, Kloppenberg, *Uncertain Victory*, 351–52.

and club work of African American women were all dedicated to bringing together the middle and lower classes in the work of assimilation. These facilities
were shelters "that helped newcomers make the required transitions" to new
places and traditions, the same as many white women's clubs, organizations,
and settlement houses were doing with European immigrants.[25]

Proponents of the idea of environmental determinism attempted to turn
the idea of innate characteristics on its head, arguing that bad environment
was responsible for less than admirable behavior. If the evils of the new urban and industrial society were eliminated, then the natural good in people
would prevail. As one Pittsburgh reformer, Frederick C. Wilkes, declared, "It
is well established as an immutable law, that environment is what makes the
character of men. Cleanliness of a man makes a good man. Cleanliness of a
city makes a good city." Compassion and extending a "helping hand" to others—even if at times these seemed condescending attitudes—exposed a faith
in a common humanity and the innate decency of people that challenged the
exclusionists and overt racists. This idea also was a product of the Progressive Era.[26]

DIMENSIONS OF A NEW REGULATORY STATE

To reform the state, progressives believed they had to regulate the state. New
administrative agencies, regulatory legislation, and presidential commissions
and committees to study pressing problems continued to alter American national government through the presidencies of Theodore Roosevelt, William
Howard Taft, and the first term of Woodrow Wilson. In order to achieve the
scope of the regulatory state that they believed necessary, progressives needed
to persuade the courts to accept these changes. They also had to find the
money to run the new agencies, and they needed individual states to enact
regulations when the federal government could not, or would not, do so.

Regulatory reform on the national level was most likely to be upheld when
advanced under the umbrella of congressional power to control interstate
commerce. The court accepted the Clayton Anti-Trust Act of 1914 that further
restricted restraint of trade and recognized workers' rights to organize—
although the courts failed to enforce this latter provision until new legislation
in the 1930s—because the progressive rhetoric of eliminating unfair competition—trustbusting—fit nicely into older ideals of American society. By 1914,
there was broad public support for regulating the economy in the public in-

---

25. Addams, *Democracy and Social Ethics* (New York, 1902; reprint ed., Urbana: University of Illinois Press, 2002), 98; Higginbotham, *Righteous Discontent*, 198–99; and Daphne Spain, *How Women
Saved the City* (Minneapolis: University of Minnesota Press, 2001), 121–22.

26. Martin Melosi, *The Sanitary City: Urban Infrastructure in the United States from Colonial Times
to the Present* (Baltimore: Johns Hopkins University Press, 2000), 106–08, and Melosi, "Environmental Reform in Industrial Cities: The Civic Response to Pollution in the Progressive Era," in *Effluent
Cities: Cities, Industry, Energy, and the Environment* (Pittsburgh: University of Pittsburgh Press, 2001),
quote, 219. See also, Elizabeth Enstam, *Women and the Creation of Urban Life: Dallas, Texas, 1843–1920*
(College Station: Texas A & M University Press, 1998), ch. 6, and Spain, *How Women Saved the City*.

AN AWFUL BLOT.

The "Blot" of Child Labor of the American Landscape
Source: Library of Congress, Prints & Photographs Division, National Child Labor Committee Collection, LC-DIG-nclc-04992

terest. Of course, defining the public interest and passing it through the courts were the tricky parts of this new way of thinking about the relationship between government and the economy. The Supreme Court upheld Clayton, for example, but it overturned the 1916 Keating-Owen Child Labor Act that banned the interstate sale of products made with child labor. The Court ruled that Keating-Owen violated state powers to regulate local conditions of labor. In his dissenting opinion, Justice Oliver Wendell Holmes declared the inherent evils of child labor to be so great that Congress ought to be able to regulate when individual states failed to do so. But the power of states' rights prevailed here and progressives' subsequent attempts to pass a constitutional ban on child labor also failed. Federal antichild labor legislation did not come until later in the New Deal.[27]

---

27. Supreme Court ruling, *Hammer v. Dagenhart* (1918).

Regulating property in the public interest, thus, could only go so far as the courts would agree was a federal power, or that powerful politicians and groups agreed was the "right" public interest. Businessmen accepted the Federal Reserve System in 1913 because it promised to bring much needed control to the money supply and the banking system upon which they depended. Moreover, it kept the system out of the hands of government by creating an agency that would be "a regulatory-corporate complex that left the main decisions in private hands." Businessmen felt certain that member banks and the Federal Reserve Board would be controlled by bankers and businessmen such as themselves. In this way it would be impervious to interest-group politics— at least those of other interest groups—and politicians. The proposed Kessinger Housing bill to create a federal bureau of housing and living conditions, on the other hand, was unacceptable even to many progressives. This was deemed regulation of property that was not sufficiently enough in the public interest to interfere with rights of private property.[28] A statement made by the Woman's City Club of Chicago illustrates the ideological divide between the acceptance of a national banking policy and the rejection of a national housing policy. The United States, wrote the women, "has spent large sums of money on the promotion of scientific farming, the care of cattle, sheep, and bees, on the development of commerce and manufacturing . . . [but it] has taken no cognizance of the problem of housing its citizens." As housing activist Edith Elmer Wood discovered to her dismay in 1913:

> Municipal housing or municipal slum clearance, or any form of government aid (including loans at cost) were taboo and anathema. They were un-American. They were something pertaining to the effete monarchies of Europe. It was extremely bad form even to mention them.

The resistance to public housing or public housing assistance was so strong that even municipal schemes for such policies failed.[29]

Political progressives also turned to their state governments for regulation that they could not obtain on the federal level. New state laws set up regulatory agencies for public utilities, for example. State regulatory agencies appealed to many progressives because theoretically they would be staffed by experts in finance and policymaking. Progressives also believed this was a means to break the franchise system while simultaneously undercutting calls for too much municipal ownership. Every state passed different regulations and proceeded at a different pace toward the rather inevitable public ownership of some public utilities—transit systems, for example—and some critical municipal services such as garbage collection. But most entities Americans call public utilities are public in name only. They are privately owned utilities whose delivery of public goods and services is overseen by independent regu-

---

28. Alan Dawley, *Struggles for Justice: Social Responsibility and the Liberal State* (Cambridge, MA: Harvard University Press, 1991), 147. The bill failed in spring 1921.

29. Woman's City Club of Chicago, *Bulletin* (February 1920). Wood quoted in Rodgers, *Atlantic Crossings*, 198. See also, Lawrence J. Vale, *From the Puritans to the Projects: Public Housing and Public Neighbors* (Cambridge, MA: Harvard University Press, 2000), 110–14, for the dismal fate of a few housing schemes in the Boston area in the Progressive Era.

latory commissions. The utility companies are obliged to make pricing, costs, etc., transparent to the public and the commissions are obligated to take public input. One reason for the popularity of this method of controlling public services is that there were many Americans who recoiled at the thought of public ownership of what they viewed as capitalist private property. Yet, there were vibrant enough municipal socialism movements in some cities, whose state laws would have allowed municipal ownership, that one might have expected more of this to have happened in the Progressive Era. When put to referendum, many cities received voter approval, although often these were advisory and not binding referenda. Even in Milwaukee, the socialist government could not achieve municipal ownership of the electric utility. On the other hand, Seattle established Seattle City Light in 1902 as a publicly owned and operated utility to compete with private utility companies, and Los Angeles municipalized its water distribution that same year.[30]

Besides the enduring opposition to interfering with private enterprise, the nature of municipal financing constrained movements for municipal ownership of utilities and services. State laws controlled the level and type of taxation that cities could levy, and states were generally stingy in this regard. Without money, cities could neither buy up utility companies nor run them. Even so, the vast majority of political progressives who considered this issue eventually opted for regulation rather than ownership as much from an ideological stance as a financial one. The National Civic Federation had constituted a Public Ownership Commission to investigate the issue. It was described as having an "ample budget," which it used to make "extensive field comparisons" in England and Ireland and to interview "hundreds" of witnesses. The final report concluded that the marketplace did not work for public utilities so some type of regulation was necessary. It left it up to individual states, however, to decide between regulation and public ownership.[31]

On the national level, the 16th Amendment to the Constitution, passed in 1913, gave Congress the power to tax incomes. Thereafter, political progressives had a new means to secure funds for national government financing of economic regulation and provision of services. The Populists had earlier demanded an income tax, although they had viewed it as a just measure to draw money away from the rich and redistribute it somehow throughout society. The amendment's progressive proponents saw it less in that vein than as a way

30. Douglas E. Booth, "Municipal Socialism and City Government Reform: The Milwaukee Experience, 1910–1940," *The Journal of Urban History*, 12 (November 1985): 51–74, and Lee F. Pendergrass, "Urban Reform and Voluntary Association: The Municipal League of Seattle, 1910–1916," in *The Age of Urban Reform: New Perspectives on the Progressive Era*, Michael Ebner and Eugene Tobin, eds. (Port Washington, NY: Kennikat Press, 1977), 55–67, and Martin J. Schiesl, "Politicians in Disguise: The Changing Role of Public Administrators in Los Angeles, 1900–1916," in ibid., 102–16.

31. Gail Radford, "From Municipal Socialism to Public Authorities: Institutional Factors in the Shaping of American Public Enterprise," *Journal of American History*, 90 (December 2003): 863–90. See also, Eric Monkkonen, *America Becomes Urban: The Development of U.S. Cities and Towns, 1780–1980* (Berkeley: University of California Press, 1988) and *The Local State: Public Money and American Cities* (Stanford: Stanford University Press, 1995); and Mary Furner, *Advocacy and Objectivity: A Crisis in the Professionalization of American Social Science, 1865–1906* (Lexington: University of Kentucky Press, 1975), 269–70, for Public Ownership Commission.

for the federal government to raise the necessary revenue to finance the new bureaucracies responsible for carrying out progressive reforms. Originally the tax was only levied on the very rich—one reason why it received as much popular support as it did. Three years later, a new tax act raised the levy on the wealthy and introduced federal inheritance taxes. From this point, the expanding federal bureaucracy could count on having a financial base from which to function.

THE PROGRESSIVE PRESIDENCY

Theodore Roosevelt's administrations began the decisive shift in national government power toward the presidency. "The Executive," he declared, "is the steward of the public welfare." He believed that as the only position in government whose officeholder is responsible to all the people, the presidency should lead, not follow. The Supreme Court and Congress, particularly the Senate, were reluctant to cede any control to the executive. Giving the president power to make policy and the administrative branch control over economic regulation was a process that, once begun, would not be turned back. By the end of Roosevelt's second term in 1908, the questions facing future administrations were how much further the presidency would evolve in this direction and how this would be justified.

The regular Republicans breathed a sigh of relief in 1908 when Roosevelt announced that he would not run again. Their chosen candidate, William Howard Taft, was more conservative and less prone to flights of enthusiasm for change than Roosevelt. With Taft in the office, they hoped to restore somewhat the older balance of power back toward Congress. Not that they or Taft wanted to, or could, go back to laissez-faire capitalism. Taft "busted" more trusts than did Roosevelt, but always from a conservative ideology that restraint of trade was bad business. Once interest-group politics had begun to mobilize citizen organization, however, the lobbying of organizations such as the National Civic Federation, National Association of Manufacturers, American Federation of Labor, National American Women's Suffrage Association, and the National Association for the Advancement of Colored People could not be ignored by politicians. So, while Taft and the Republicans tried to slow the progressive tidal wave to a more manageable stream, they found themselves overwhelmed by the idea that the public interest was what the "people" defined it to be.[32]

Unhappy with how regular Republicans supported big business in both the Senate and on the state levels, progressive Republicans, including Wisconsin Senator Robert LaFollette and California Governor Hiram Johnson, founded the National Progressive Republican League as a countervailing force. LaFollette's stirring speech in the Senate against the power of the railroads—in which he charged that "to permit the railroads to control the commerce of this

---

32. See Rauchway, *Murdering McKinley*, 184–89.

country is, in the final analysis, to permit the railroads to control the country" —had helped Roosevelt secure passage of the Hepburn Act (1906) that strengthened federal regulation of the railroads. By the end of his first term in the Senate (1906–12), LaFollette "had shaken profoundly the conservative bastion of the Senate, forced a division within the Republican Party, and emerged as the most promising national spokesman and leader of the rapidly growing, aggressively progressive group of senators and governors."[33] The final test for political progressivism on the national level would come in the 1912 election. The Republicans would nominate Taft, although both LaFollette and Roosevelt contested for the nomination. The choice of Taft split the party, and a newly formed national Progressive Party ecstatically chose Roosevelt as its standard bearer. The Democrats, for their part, chose Woodrow Wilson, ex-governor of New Jersey and president of Princeton University, a trained political scientist about whom the party could make its own claims to expert progressivism. The Republicans stood pat and Roosevelt and Wilson squared off to decide whether the former's "New Nationalism" or the latter's "New Freedom" would lead the nation toward further reform. The story of this campaign and the Wilson presidencies will continue in the following chapters.

33. Unger, *Fighting Bob LaFollette*, 144 for Senate railroads speech, 192 for quote, and 194. See also, Rauchway, *Murdering McKinley*, 185–86 for Hepburn Act.

The transatlantic world was a marketplace of goods and ideas at the turn of the last century. As with any marketplace, its shoppers picked and chose among what was on offer. After generations of spurning Europe as the decadent continent, Americans at the end of the nineteenth century began to travel east. The extremely wealthy embarked upon the "grand tour" of Europe. They went to soak up the rediscovered culture of "old" Europe, to buy its art by the cratefull, and hoping to marry their daughters to aristocracy. The participants in this grand cultural tour chose among purchasing the art of the old masters, the impressionists, and the up-and-coming modernists. They filled their private homes with these treasures and then endowed new art museums to display them. J.P. Morgan acquired a Raphael altarpiece painting from the early 1500s, titled "Madonna and Child Enthroned with Saints," and a late 16th century work by the German painter Ludger tom Ring the Younger, titled "Christ Blessing, surrounded by a Donor and his Family." He gave both paintings to the Metropolitan Museum of Art in New York—and one might wonder about the symbolism of donating a painting about a blessing for a donor. Chicago hotel magnate Potter Palmer and his wife Bertha, they of the $3 million mansion, were fond of the impressionists. They donated works by Renoir, Corot, and Monet to the Art Institute of that city. Banker Andrew Mellon was an avid collector. He founded the National Gallery of Art in Washington, D.C., which, upon his death, received paintings from his collection, including those by Italians Raphael, Titian, Bellini, and Carpaccio, and masterpieces by Roger van der Weyden and Gerard David. Andrew Carnegie's partner Henry Clay Frick, who had ruthlessly ended the 1892 strike at their Homestead steelworks, created an entire museum out of his New York mansion to house his collection. Among his acquired paintings were works of continental painters Titian, Vermeer, Rembrandt, and British artists George Romney and Sir Joshua Reynolds. These men and their art collections are just the tip of the iceberg. Practically any museum other than those dedicated to contemporary art in the United States was built around the art bought in Europe by wealthy industrialists and businessmen in the late nineteenth and early twentieth centuries.

Along with collecting art, the industrialists collected titles for their daughters and granddaughters. Consuela Vanderbilt, of the wealthy railroad family, married—albeit unhappily—the 9th Duke of Marlborough. Jennie Jerome, daughter of a Wall Street financier, married Lord Randolph Churchill. Helen Stuyvesant Morton, daughter of banker Levi Morton, married a French count. By one estimate by 1915 almost 400 women from wealthy American families had married European aristocracy.

CHAPTER 6

The New Social Politics

The Socialists stand for progress, the women stand for
progress.
—JOSEPHINE CONGER KANEKO, 1914

WEALTHY BUSINESSMEN WERE not the only Americans touring Europe at the turn of the last century. Middle-class progressives also journeyed to Europe, although they went not to buy and enrich themselves but to soak up the new social politics that western Europe was pioneering. The driving ideal of this movement was that all politics must have a social dimension. Debates over the "problems and miseries of 'great city' life, the insecurities of wage work, the social backwardness of the countryside, or the instability of the market itself" drove a transatlantic exchange of ideas and reform agendas that all focused on the need for government to relieve these social problems.[1]

In search of new ideas, Frederic Howe, economist Richard Ely, and social gospeler Walter Rauschenbusch went to study in Germany, where professors such as Max Weber and Werner Sombart were expounding new social theories. After graduating from Cornell and being denied entrance into the University of Pennsylvania, Florence Kelley studied government and law at the University of Zurich and married a Polish socialist. Jane Addams, Ellen Gates Starr, Vida Scudder, and Robert Woods traveled to London to visit the social settlement experiment Toynbee Hall. Mary McDowell led a group of women to Germany to study its garbage disposal methods. The New York City Committee on Congestion of Population sent representatives to international housing conferences in France and England. Other American delegations went to England to study the housing management ideas of Octavia Hill or the garden cities initiative of Ebenezer Howard. Future Chicago mayor Edward Dunne toured European cities in 1900 to examine the viability of municipal ownership.

---

1. Daniel Rodgers, *Atlantic Crossings: Social Politics in a Progressive Age* (Cambridge, MA: Harvard University Press, 1998), 3.

The travelers on this new type of social circuit were choosing among innovative social science theories about how to reorganize society. Their common denominator was that they were all looking for new ways to make politics responsible for society and for curing its problems by developing and sustaining social policies. The common road that almost all of them chose to travel was the *via media* somewhere between laissez-faire capitalism and socialism.

TAMING THE COURT

This transatlantic marketplace of ideas contributed to shaping the work of American progressives.[2] But the work of American progressives toward developing a new social politics differed from that of their European counterparts in one dramatic way. The Supreme Court held the balance of power in the United States. No new legislation, no new government power, no new economic regulations or social policies could be secured unless the Court—or the state supreme courts—assented. The U.S. Supreme Court was notoriously conservative. Most of its judges held to a strict construction interpretation of the Constitution, especially in limiting the power of national government vis-a-vis the states and over economic growth. This attitude had resulted in the despicable *Plessy v. Ferguson* ruling of 1896, the Court's subsequent failure to stop southern states from disfranchising black voters, and its numerous decisions to support business prerogatives over the rights of labor. Because the entire federal court system tended to rule in the same way, it would not be too harsh to credit the legal system and those who enforced it with facilitating and rationalizing the growth of a racially, socially, and economically unjust country.

Moreover, progressives worried that court decisions were, in fact, not made simply from an abstract following of the law but that cultural and social ideals influenced the process of legal rulings. Prominent, wealthy men such as Andrew Carnegie and their lawyers were certain to impress jurists more with their legal erudition and obvious business acumen than the ragtag army led by Jacob Coxey or the demagogic skills of William Jennings Bryan, the "boy orator of the Platte" with his cross of gold rant. The plaintiff in the case resulting in the Plessy ruling was a thirty-year-old "black" shoemaker; the defendant's case was presented by the polished white lawyers representing the state of Louisiana.[3] Social gospel progressive Walter Rauschenbusch expressed his concern about legal inequality when he wrote that

> The courts are the instrument by which the organized community exercises its supremacy over the affairs of the individual, and the control of the courts is therefore of vital concern to the privileged classes of any nation. . . . In our own coun-

---

2. James Kloppenberg, *Uncertain Victory: Social Democracy and Progressivism in European and American Thought, 1870–1920* (New York: Oxford University Press, 1986); Rodgers, *Atlantic Crossings*; and Alan Dawley, *Changing the World: American Progressives in War and Revolution* (Princeton, NJ: Princeton University Press, 2003). See also, Dawley's earlier work, *Struggles for Justice: Social Responsibility and the Liberal State* (Cambridge, MA: Harvard University Press, 1991).

3. "Black" is in quotation marks because Homer Plessy was in fact only 1/8 African American and made his case based on his not being black. So, beyond legitimizing segregation, the ruling upheld the Louisiana law designating what constituted a "race."

try all are equal before the law—in theory. In practice there is the most serious inequality. The right of appeal as handled in our country gives tremendous odds to those who have financial staying power.

Farmers in Montana encountered this fact when they sued the mining companies in Butte, Montana, for poisoning the land, killing their livestock, and damaging their crops. "No one appears here [in court] for the company but wealthy or high salaried men," the farmers' association charged. A judge in one of the farmers' suits had attended an elaborate dinner along with the future president of the Anaconda Copper Company and the company's chief spokesperson. An embittered farmer remarked that the "wining and dining" of the judge involved in the case against Anaconda was "oppression by the rich."[4]

On the other hand, the English common law tradition and the American constitutional system required judges to follow precedent when ruling on issues of constitutionality. At the beginning of the Progressive Era, the judges of the Supreme Court had long followed the abstract concept of *legal formalism*. They ruled through a deductive process that followed the logic that had shaped preceding rulings. In such a system, precedent of law and not social condition was the deciding factor in their conclusions. Society was to conform to law; law was not to take account of social change. So the long-standing precedents about freedom of contract gave justices ample justification to reject any new legislation imposing restrictions on business practices.

To reconsider this concept would require more than new laws because the justices had shown that they would simply rule them unconstitutional. Change necessitated advancing new arguments that would push justices to rethink the relationship between law and society. Progressives argued that rather than law being a set of abstract principles and accumulated precedents from which jurists could not deviate, law had to take account of social conditions from which laws arose. They wanted the courts to adjudicate legislation on the basis of concrete realities. They urged that attachment to legal formalism be abandoned and replaced with *legal realism*.[5]

Legal realism was a perfect complement to social science. One of its earliest proponents, Louis Brandeis, argued that legal rulings should be made after gathering facts and presenting these facts within the social context of the problem. Lawyers, he said, "should be familiar with economics, sociology, and politics. Judges, similarly, should be trained 'to perform adequately the function of harmonizing law with life.'"[6] Philosophically then, Brandeis was the lawyer that social justice advocates were looking for to argue in defense of new labor laws; personally, he was the brother-in-law of the New York National Consumers' League leader Josephine Goldmark. The fit was perfect for a new approach to

---

4. Walter Rauschenbusch, *Christianity and the Social Crisis* (New York: Macmillan, 1907), 258, and Donald MacMillan, *Smoke Wars: Anaconda Copper, Montana Air Pollution, and the Courts, 1890–1924* (Helena: Montana Historical Society, 2000), 113 and 139.

5. For a short, succinct discussion of this idea, see Nancy Woloch, *Muller v. Oregon: A Brief History with Documents* (New York: Bedford Books, 1996), 26–27. For a more complete discussion, see Laura Kalman, *The Strange Career of Legal Realism* (New Haven, CT: Yale University Press, 1996).

6. Woloch, *Muller v. Oregon*, 27, including quote from Brandeis that originally appeared in Brandeis, "The Living Law," *Illinois Law Review*, 10 (February 1916): 469–70.

the Supreme Court. All that was needed was the opportunity. The case for limiting the hours of women's work in Oregon laundries (see Chapter 3) created the opportunity. The 113-page Brandeis Brief was crafted to argue for legal realism. Citing testimony and investigations from doctors, factory inspectors, health authorities, and academics as to the harmful effect of long work hours on women's health, it made the affirmative argument that restricting hours of labor for women was a "reasonable exception" to freedom of contract. Lawyers' opinions were conspicuously absent from the citations in the brief.

Reformers' victory in this case was, in retrospect, a good news/bad news result. The good news was that they had convinced the Court that hours restrictions were legitimate, and they had convinced the Court to take into account concrete realities—*legal realism*. The bad news was twofold. First, the ruling applied only to women. Second, the justices (as described in Chapter 3) had added their own peculiar twist to the ruling by declaring that women's reproductive capacities were the concern of the state. No one could have known for sure at the time that this case would give ongoing validity to *legal realism* or what this might mean for future cases. But it was quickly clear that protective legislation applying only to women placed one gender in an unequal economic position in relation to the other gender. The precedent having been set, women were henceforth "protected" in labor but continued to be economically unequal the remainder of the century.[7]

Progressives later discovered the inherent dangers in arguing from concrete realities. When Congress passed minimum wage legislation for women workers in Washington, D.C., in 1918, the Court overturned the law. Opponents argued that the concrete realities of men's economic situation demanded that they too be eligible for minimum wage guarantees. Because the Court had accepted the Oregon law based on protecting women's health, it could not now give women workers a wage guarantee on the basis of need without extending this to men. In the 1923 ruling, *Adkins v. Children's Hospital*, the Court returned to legal formalism.[8] As the *Muller v. Oregon* ruling in 1908 had not worked as an "entering wedge" for protective labor laws for all workers, *Adkins* now dashed progressive hopes that it could be used as an "entering wedge" for securing a general minimum wage. Laborers would have to wait until the New Deal's Fair Labor Standards Act (1938) to achieve a guaranteed minimum wage.

DETERMINING THE SOCIAL GOOD

Social Democracy

If politics were to have a social dimension that pursued a social good, then what constituted this social good and how to achieve it both had to be defined. Here was the arena in which picking and choosing from European

---

7. For women's economic situation through the twentieth century, see Alice Kessler-Harris, *In Pursuit of Equity: Women, Men and the Quest for Economic Citizenship in 20th Century America* (New York: Oxford University Press, 2001) and *Out to Work: A History of Wage-Earning Women in the United States* (New York: Oxford University Press, 1982; reprint, 2003).

8. Woloch, *Muller v. Oregon*, 27–29 and 51–55.

ideas came into play for American progressives. Circulating broadly through Europe was the new ideal of social democracy. There, new social democratic and labor parties were formed to insert social politics directly into the governing system. The emphasis in social democracy was on reform of the existing systems, not on overthrow of the systems. Pre-eminent social democrats in England, for instance, were the Fabians, led by Sidney and Beatrix Webb. The Fabians did not advocate complete popular democracy but a democracy that expanded the franchise to all citizens—here, too, Europe differed from the United States because European countries lacked universal male suffrage—through which the citizens would direct government to pursue policies desired by the people. Social democracy advocated reforming the "forms of democratic structures" in order to express the socialist purpose. Social democrats wanted society to evolve toward these ends through gradual change, "not revolutionary cataclysm." French social democrat Léon Bourgeois expressed this idea as one of a "continuous struggle toward a cooperative society." Social democrats "thought of themselves as heirs to the legacy of socialism, responsible for revitalizing rather than recreating that tradition." Nor did the newly forming Labour Party in England want radical change. Its leaders' concept of social democracy was one in which labor and the rights of labor were fostered actively by government.[9]

The Fabians, the Labour Party, and social democrats envisioned a government that wielded significant control over economic development and provided for social welfare. For them this included government ownership of industries crucial to the general well-being of all the people as well as enacting far-reaching social welfare legislation. Their "quintessential social democratic principle" was "the extension of democracy from the political to the socioeconomic realm." England began the process of enacting public health measures in the 1870s, which culminated in the National Insurance Act of 1911. France decided that public health measures were a national matter necessary to arrest national "degeneration." The United States was the only industrialized country that had no health insurance program in place before World War I. Business leaders and labor leaders alike had objected to any laws mandating compulsory health insurance on the national level, although obviously for different reasons. The AFL clung tenaciously to its fear that an activist state might interfere with it achieving collective bargaining between labor and business.[10]

Real social democracy, thus, would have brought more radical change than the majority of Americans probably were willing to accept. Moreover, many progressives believed this would be unnecessary if they could implement a more moderate version of social politics that protected some of the needs of daily life from the uncertainties of the economic marketplace. Progressives came to define such social goods to include housing, transportation, protective

---

9. See Mark Bevir, "Republicanism, Socialism, and Democracy in Britain: The Origins of the Radical Left," *Journal of Social History*, 34 (Winter 2000): 362–63, and Kloppenberg, *Uncertain Victory*, 248 and 249 for the Webbs and Bourgeois, and 298 for general assessment of the social democrats.

10. Kloppenberg, *Uncertain Victory*, 300. For comparisons of public health programs and insurance, see Morton Keller, *Regulating a New Society: Public Policy and Social Change in America, 1900–1930* (Cambridge, MA: Harvard University Press, 1994), 191–93, 196.

labor legislation and child labor laws, parks and recreation, public education, public health and sanitation, juvenile justice, and women's rights. If these issues could be protected from the "unwanted consequences of the unregulated market," progressives such as Walter Weyl believed they could fashion "a kind of democracy that would place public interest over that of the individual; use the state to harness economic means for human ends; and end the long drift toward social atomism and political fragmentation that the 19th century had witnessed." Progressives, as usual, agreed on promoting a concept of a public interest, but they differed as to how far these social goods should be removed from private property and about whether government should actively promote social legislation. This last possibility particularly troubled many American progressives because they were philosophically committed to "voluntarism." They believed that "private power [could] be brought under control without resorting to government ownership of industry," and that a welfare state would impinge too much on individual freedom.[11]

The Economic Perspective

In 1905, Frederic Howe declared "I have become convinced that it is the economic environment which creates and controls man's activities as well as his attitude of mind. This arouses his civic or his self-interest; this underlies the poverty and the social problems with which the city is confronted." Howe's idea, shared by many other progressives, was that progressivism could be achieved by "voluntarism" rather than through government imposition. If Americans could be persuaded voluntarily to surrender some individual freedoms to a social good, the problems inherent in the current system would then disappear. The country would progress forward and democracy for more people would result. For Howe and other progressives who had been trained in the new ideas of social science, certain structures of society impeded the social good and they wanted to make Americans understand that if they changed these structures, the social good would be attainable. These progressives believed that nothing could be more important than restructuring the property relations of a capitalist society that had been built on rampant individualism. "The individualism of the American city has retarded development of social activities necessary to a well-ordered municipal life," Howe declared, and people had to accept that they had an individual self-interest in creating a better social order.[12]

These progressives did not depend solely on voluntarism, of course. They worked to bring order to chaos in cities and country by stamping out the excesses of unfettered capitalism that they saw as impeding opportunity. Hiram Johnson and Robert LaFollette together targeted the railroads as a primary source of the nation's problems. Both men believed that if railroads were regulated the economy would function better. If the economy functioned better, it

---

11. See Alan Dawley, *Changing the World*, 42–43; Walter Weyl, *The New Democracy* (New York: Macmillan, 1912); Rodgers, *Atlantic Crossings*, 29–30; and Kloppenberg, *Uncertain Victory*, 358–61.

12. Howe, *The City: The Hope of Democracy* (New York: Charles Scribner's Sons, 1905), viii, and *The Modern City and Its Problems* (New York: Charles Scribner's Sons, 1915), 271–72.

followed that society would run better. Viewing certain progressives in this light gives context to LaFollette's impassioned speech to the Senate, where he declared that giving the railroads the power to control commerce was tantamount to letting them control the country. Theodore Roosevelt's later progressivism fits well into this mold. Although he left office in 1908, within two years he was formulating a new progressive agenda—his "New Nationalism"—that would include the graduated income tax and inheritance taxes, tariff reform, and public disclosure of campaign funding. Roosevelt firmly believed that enacting legal barriers to business abuses through moderate economic regulation would enhance the social good. Acceptance of a graduated income tax was a key to this thinking because it acknowledged that people owed a debt to their society based on their ability to pay.[13]

By 1912, Walter Weyl optimistically predicted that the "old laissez-faire philosophy is done for and the old absolute socialism is dying in the embrace of its dead adversary." For these progressives, economic regulation was the *via media* for advancing the social good. Drift was to be replaced by mastery over the system by experts who could remake society "by application of rational inquiry." Howe celebrated the loosening of individualism that was making it possible "to develop markets for the reduction of the cost of living, the intensive supervision of the health of the people, the protection of the public against false weights and measures, the supply of pure food and milk, and other measures of a similar sort." These progressives did not advocate a statist solution in which government made all decisions about the economy or dispensed social welfare. They wanted instead, and largely put into place, a system that would temporize the worst aspects of free market capitalism and thereby bring "a minimum standard of life below which no human being can fall." This, proclaimed progressive Walter Lippmann, "was the most elementary duty of the democratic state."[14]

This "minimum standard" was not enough reform for other Americans, as evidenced by continuing labor violence. Ironically, this violence actually helped these progressive reformers to put their ideas into action. In late 1910, the bombing of a newspaper building in Los Angeles killed twenty people. Socialists were accused—and two eventually confessed—of planting the bomb. This event was followed by a heated mayoral campaign in which the socialist candidate, Job Harriman, barely lost. The public outrage over the bombing and fear of creeping socialism was redirected into anger again with the Triangle fire a few months later. Then in early 1912, whole families working in the textile mills of Lawrence, Massachusetts, went on strike and the country was treated to the sight of police beating women and children. Two months later

---

13. Kloppenberg, *Uncertain Victory*, 300. Kloppenberg refers to the men he was examining as "philosophical" progressives. I have chosen to place them into the group of "economic" progressives who were concerned with carrying out the political reforms of the type they all generally agreed upon because it must be realized that there was more than one type of philosophical progressivism.

14. Weyl, *The New Democracy*, 188, and Eric Foner, *The Story of American Freedom* (New York: W.W. Norton, 2nd edition, 1998), 155. Howe, *The Modern City*, 271–72; and Walter Lippmann, *Drift and Mastery: An Attempt to Diagnose the Current Unrest* (New York: M. Kennerley, 1914), 254.

the West Virginia National Guard was called out to break the strike of coal miners. For many Americans it seemed as if class war had come to America. Economic progressives believed that a way had to be found to bring the two warring sides together and establish new rules for employer/worker relations. With little sympathy among them for either socialism or social democracy, they found their preferred way to end labor strife through independent investigation and mediation—through voluntarism. In late summer 1912, Congress set up the Commission on Industrial Relations, whose immediate charge was to investigate conditions of labor and the effect on labor relations of growing associations of employers and laborers who were arrayed against each other. The commission had no enforcement powers. Rather, it reflected the progressive faith that if men of expertise and good will could sit down together, they could resolve the tensions inherent in the existing economic structure. "The challenge of twentieth-century politics," John Dewey wrote, "is not one of magnifying the powers of the State against industry, but is one of making individual liberty a more extensive and equitable matter."[15]

The Social Perspective

Other progressives brought back different lessons from Europe. Unlike the economic-minded progressives, they argued less about correct property relations than about implementing policies that would make life better for all Americans. They wanted to make the United States a more democratic country socially by constructing a truly activist state. The abiding difference between their ideas and those of the economic progressives was that they wanted the state to provide directly for improving the standards of daily life for all Americans, but especially for the poor and the working class. They wanted the welfare state that the economic progressives feared. Just as men were the primary advocates of economic progressivism through regulation and "voluntarism," women were the primary movers of social progressivism through direct political action on the part of local, state, and federal governments.

Much of this agenda has already been explained as part of social justice progressivism, so only a few additional examples need to be touched upon here to make the comparison. Howe, for example, had addressed the issue of providing pure food and milk. For him, regulations mandating how milk was produced, shipped, and sold would provide pure food and milk and protect the public. From the perspective of the more socially oriented progressives, such regulation was desirable but insufficient. Poorer Americans had to be guaranteed that they could afford to purchase good milk, food, and medicines for their families. Regulating the mechanism of milk production thus had to be accompanied by other reforms such as enacting a minimum wage, building affordable housing, providing affordable and good health care, and passing laws

---

15. Dewey quoted in Kloppenberg, *Uncertain Victory*, 397. See Dewey and Tufts, *Ethics*, as collected in *The Middle Works, 1899–1924*, v. 5, JoAnn Boydston, ed. (Carbondale: Southern Illinois University Press, 1976–1983). See also, Dawley, *Struggles for Justice*, 154–55.

to protect both men and women at work and in the event that injury prevented them from resuming work.

This stream of progressivism wanted the state to be responsible for the social welfare of all the people, not just to provide economic regulation that would protect them from rapacious, or inattentive, capitalism. When Florence Kelley appeared before Congress in 1920 arguing for money for women's and children's health care, she told the men that "women deeply resented the fact that Congressmen legislated salary and pension increases for postal employees and veterans, but claimed that the government could not afford to provide health care for women and children." Julia Lathrop, head of the Children's Bureau, argued that the abolition of poverty was "a necessity of the democratic state": she demanded that the state provide mothers' pensions, a family wage for fathers, maternal health care for all women, well-baby clinics, decent public education, and, of course, a pure milk supply. By packaging all these issues together, Lathrop and women's organizations supporting this type of agenda were demanding the government actively provide all these programs to eliminate poverty. They neither wished to wait until better property relations were established or the excesses of capitalism could be controlled, nor did they believe that this would sufficiently provide for all people to experience a minimum standard of life, let alone a truly decent existence.[16]

Even those progressive men who were more socially oriented always saw the economic security of men as the first and most necessary priority for social reform. Louis Brandeis and Father John A. Ryan both believed that enacting a living wage for male workers was the principal and most ethical means for establishing democracy and the social good. Ryan's book, *A Living Wage*, argued it was a right of citizenship to have a decent wage that would permit an "American" standard of living. Brandeis and Ryan were simultaneously following a progressive agenda that would reform capitalism in ways that would "protect" women and allow men to work for wages that would raise their standard of living.[17] Most women social progressives supported the idea of the living wage, but this was only a mechanism to aid in a more thorough reform of how the state provided for its people. The difference would become painfully clear as women pursued campaigns to abolish child labor and to secure federal and state legislation to fund maternal and infant health care, housing subsidies, birth control, and mothers' pensions.

The struggle to regulate child labor illustrates how difficult it was for reformers of different perspectives to design a comprehensive program of social politics. Progressivism had too many strands that could not always be woven together. For many progressives, child labor was immoral. Statistics in 1900 revealed at least 1.75 million children between the ages of 10 and 15 were

16. Kelley quoted in Molly Ladd-Taylor, *Mother-Work: Women, Child Welfare, and the State, 1890–1930* (Urbana: University of Illinois Press, 1994), 170. For Lathrop, see Robyn Muncy, *Creating a Female Dominion in American Reform, 1890–1935* (New York: Oxford University Press, 1991), 91.

17. John A. Ryan, *A Living Wage: Its Ethical and Economic Aspects* (New York: Macmillan, 1906). This book includes an introduction by economic progressive Richard Ely. See also, Foner, *The Story of American Freedom*, 145. When progressives argued for a living wage, they did mean for men. This, they hoped, would free women from having to work outside the home.

working. Some states passed child labor laws; others, such as Pennsylvania, failed to pass any such laws and the southern states that employed hundreds of thousands of little children in their textile mills were virtually devoid of any regulation. Even the proposed Keating-Owen law would not have been far reaching, as it affected only children working at jobs that participated in interstate commerce. Best estimates at the time were that 100,000 to 150,000 of a total of 1.85 million child workers would be affected. Louis Brandeis and Father John Ryan were adamant backers of legislation to outlaw child labor. One incensed antichild labor advocate objected that other items of morality such as lottery tickets, liquor, and transportation of women across state lines for "illicit purposes" had been banned from interstate commerce. "Why not," he asked, "the products of child labor." Yet, other progressives feared that even regulating child labor would impinge upon individual freedom. In 1914, the progressive publication the *Nation* objected that "a national act [on social welfare] would strain the Constitution and create a whole new scale of federal interference." The case that eventually overturned the legislation was brought by a man who argued that the law deprived him of his property—the property in his young sons' labor. Only four states ever ratified the proposed child labor amendment; thirty-six others either rejected it or refused to consider it. In the context of the 1920s (which will be examined later), opponents of the amendment were further able to argue that banning child labor was communistic and deprived children of their right to work.[18]

Socialism

Fear of socialism ran high in the Progressive Era. The adoption of a Marxist agenda by the Socialist Labor Party (SLP) in 1890, headed by Daniel DeLeon, the formation of the Socialist Party of America (SPA) under the leadership of Eugene V. Debs in 1901, the 1910 bombing of the newspaper building in Los Angeles, the founding of the radical Industrial Workers of the World (IWW) in 1905, and the IWW participation in the 1912 Lawrence strike all provoked antisocialist hysteria. Anarchists and Marxist socialists such as Emma Goldman and Daniel DeLeon believed that capitalism and democracy were essentially one and the same, so that both had to be wiped out to achieve justice for the working class. But what socialism meant in a country with universal white male suffrage, no hereditary aristocracy to overthrow, and a labor movement that advanced working through the democratic forms to achieve workers' rights was unclear. Despite its radical elements, socialism in the Progressive Era was generally moderate in its leadership and its aims. Much of it became characterized as Debsian socialism, which was more concerned with agitating and educating Americans to the evils of capitalism than to overthrowing the government. It was this type of thinking that allowed socialists such as Daniel

---

18. Keller, *Regulating a New Society*, 205–09. See also, Kriste Lindenmeyer, *"A Right to Childhood": The U.S. Children's Bureau and Child Welfare, 1912–46* (Urbana: University of Illinois Press, 1997), 117–32, for specific discussion of both the legislation and the amendment, and for the gender dimension of this issue that became apparent when the Children's Bureau was given the power to investigate and enforce the law.

Hoan to be elected mayor of Milwaukee and Victor Berger to Congress. It also accounts for Debsian socialism concerning itself generally with bringing about socialism through electoral politics and to connecting with those rural Americans who had previously flocked to populism. "Rather than the Marxian socialism of the SLP, they [the SPA] turned to non-revolutionary, ethical forms of socialism."[19]

There was also a similarity in reform ideas between some female socialists and mainstream progressive women. Josephine Conger Kaneko was a committed socialist who edited several socialist newspapers, married a Japanese-American socialist, attended the annual national SPA conventions, and ran for alderman in Chicago in 1914. Her rhetoric in that campaign reveals one aspect of American socialism in the context of progressivism. "The Socialists stand for progress, the women stand for progress," she declared. "As a Socialist I could not do one thing that would be against the interests of the masses of the people, as a woman I would not want to do any such thing." Her platform promises of what she would do, if elected, show what she meant by the interests of the people and why she tied her socialism to her gender:

> I would insist upon municipal ownership of public utilities wherever possible, such as telephone, gas and electric light, rail traffic, etc.; upon the inauguration of municipal markets where food and clothing could be sold direct from the producer to the consumer, thus cutting out the costs of middlemen; upon the erection of municipal lodging houses for working women and girls; upon a minimum wage for workers of both sexes; upon relief of the unemployed by the extension of useful public works; upon the extension of the playgrounds system to the public parks, and the opening of the schools for social centers. I would do what I could toward the alleviation and abolition of the white slave traffic by providing employment for working girls and by paying both men and women a living wage, and opening respectable places of amusement for the city's great army of young people.

Her proposals put her closer to female socially oriented progressives than to male progressives or even many socialists, especially as she went on to strike another familiar theme of female progressives: "there is one fundamental point upon which we can agree—that is, we cannot expect much from a home in which children are hungry and ragged and dirty." Kaneko laid out her program in speeches before women's organizations, where she ended by saying "I do not believe there is a woman here who can criticize this program."[20]

---

19. Stephen Burwood, "Debsian Socialism through a Transnational Lens," *The Journal of the Gilded Age and Progressive Era*, 2 (July 2003): 253–82. Quote from Richard Schneirov, "New Perspectives on Socialism I: The Socialist Party Revisited," ibid., 245. For Hoan and Berger, see Booth, "Municipal Socialism and City Government Reform," and Sally M. Miller, *Victor Berger and the Promise of Constructive Socialism, 1910–1920* (Westport, CT: Greenwood Press, 1973). See also, Cecelia Bucki, *Bridgeport's Socialist New Deal, 1915–36* (Urbana: University of Illinois Press, 2001).

20. She printed her speech in *The Coming Nation* (March 1914). For how her ideas meshed with those of nonsocialist progressives, see Maureen A. Flanagan, *Seeing with Their Hearts: Chicago Women and the Vision of the Good City, 1871-1933* (Princeton, NJ: Princeton University Press, 2002) and Daphne Spain, *How Women Saved the City* (Minneapolis: University of Minnesota Press, 2001).

When women socialists ran for office in Los Angeles after women received the vote in California, they ran as representatives of the working class, but as one scholar has put it, "they emphasized the need to elect women to office as representatives of their sex, in order to further gender equality and to ensure that women's concerns would find representation and serious consideration in policymaking bodies." They also emphasized the "maternalist and feminist goals in their campaigns." Quite possibly it was their influence that helped make California the leading state in passing legislation "advocated by mainstream women's groups."[21] When socialist Estelle Lawton Lindsey ran for a seat on the Los Angeles City Council in 1915, she made the specific point that she would bring "woman's point of view . . . the humanitarian point of view" into government. Another female socialist political candidate in Los Angeles, Mila Tupper Maynard, pointedly argued that the social issues that most concerned women were considered "side issues" by men, who had to be made to see that these social issues were indeed the important ones for government. Context made the difference in Kaneko's losing bid for office and Lindsey's successful one. No women won municipal office in Chicago that first year of municipal suffrage. Beyond that, however, although the program may have sounded the same, coming from the mouth of a firm socialist undoubtedly made women of the very middle–class ward from which she was running shy away from her. Another difference was that Chicago's Democratic Party had a strong labor base and a ward system that empowered members of the city council, so socialist candidates made little headway into the local political structure. This was not the situation in Los Angeles. There Lindsey drew support from both labor and women, but she won election not running as a socialist candidate but running as an independent.[22]

The SPA did make some inroads in the political system in the Progressive Era. Labor leader Eugene Debs was the party's quadrennial presidential candidate and socialist candidates were being elected on local levels in many parts of the country. Yet, threat of socialist political power was more feared than real. Much of organized labor was ambivalent about socialism. In the 1908 presidential campaign, Samuel Gompers led the AFL to support Democratic candidate William Jennings Bryan, although he could not carry all organized labor for Bryan, who many workers suspected was more interested in farmers than laborers. After the administrations of Theodore Roosevelt it was also plain to most Americans that both the Republican and Democratic parties were adopting progressive reforms. For many in the working class, and a number of

21. Sherry Katz, "Redefining 'the Political': Socialist Women and Party Politics in California, 1900–1920," in *We Have Come to Stay: American Women and Political Parties, 1800–1960*, Melanie Gustafson, Kristie Miller, and Elisabeth I. Perry, eds. (Albuquerque: University of New Mexico Press, 1999), 23–32, quote 28.

22. Ibid., 28 and 29. See also, Flanagan, *Seeing with Their Hearts* and "The Predicament of New Rights: Suffrage and Women's Political Power from a Local Perspective," *Social Politics: International Studies in Gender, State, and Society*, 2 (Fall 1995): 305–30; and Jennifer Koslow, "Putting It to a Vote: The Provision of Pure Milk in Progressive Era Los Angeles," *Journal of the Gilded Age and Progressive Era*, 3 (April 2004): 111–44 for her discussion of the conflict between middle-class and socialist women in the pure milk campaign in that city.

middle-class adherents, socialism was indeed a preferred alternative, but it never attracted sufficient numbers to pose a serious threat to mainstream progressivism. In 1911, socialist mayoral candidate Job Harriman won 37 percent of the vote, but the socialists did not win any municipal offices. Despite electing several hundred socialist candidates to local offices throughout the country in 1911, the majority of Americans preferred reform through the two regular parties where radicalism was less likely to hold sway. The historian Eric Rauchway has probably best articulated the problem thwarting socialists gaining more headway against mainstream progressives in the political sphere:

> progressivism became a way of thinking and speaking about social problems that could be addressed through any political party or none. . . . What made progressivism was not social class, occupation, or economic interest, but rather a belief about human nature and modern environment, as revealed in one's experience . . . contact with others vastly different from oneself.

Whether socialist proposals resembled those of nonsocialist progressives, socialists could not overcome the fear that the majority of Americans had of their potential radicalism. Proposals for social welfare coming from socialist women such as Kaneko and Lindsey may well have been easier for other Americans to accept than any such proposal promoted by male socialists. And, in fact, when male socialists were elected to office, they tended to support main labor issues and not social welfare ones like those proposed by female socialists.[23]

SOCIAL POLITICS IN THE POLITICAL REALM

Woman Suffrage

For a country that considered itself the most democratic of all to refuse to grant woman suffrage was a scandal in the eyes of many progressives. The two wings of the woman suffrage movement had united in 1890 to form the National American Woman Suffrage Association (NAWSA). Through this organization, suffragists worked simultaneously to gain the vote on the state level as well as to pass the Susan B. Anthony suffrage amendment through Congress. Success came gradually in states, although mainly west of the Mississippi River. The amendment stalled in Congress with neither party getting behind it, and the Democrats, the party of the South, firmly opposed to it.

Many male progressives who supported woman suffrage did so because they believed it was a right of democratic citizenship. They rejected the nineteenth-century idea of separation of citizenship in which men represented the family in public and women had private citizenship. Naturally, many female

---

23. The most extensive work on Eugene Debs remains Nick Salvatore, *Eugene V. Debs: Citizen and Socialist* (Urbana: University of Illinois Press, 1982). For Los Angeles, see Daniel J. Johnson, "'No Make-Believe Class Struggle': The Socialist Municipal Campaign in Los Angeles, 1911," *Labor History* 41 (February 2000): 25–45. See also, Eric Rauchway, *Murdering McKinley: The Making of Theodore Roosevelt's America* (New York: Hill and Wang, 2003), 210. See Katz, 30, for behavior of male socialists in the California State Assembly from 1912 to 1916.

progressives also rejected this idea and demanded equal rights of citizenship. Good government progressives of both genders wanted women to vote so that middle-class voters could enact specific types of progressive reforms.[24] Yet, most female progressives wanted the vote not only as a symbol of equal citizenship but in order to advance their political program of social politics on the local and national levels. Working women and immigrant women needed the vote to be able to protect themselves. The NAWSA in 1904 had specifically extended its work toward securing not just the vote but complete equality when it demanded that all constitutional and legal barriers to women's equal individual or personal freedom be abolished.

Women's political equality leagues formed all across the country in a pyramid structure as part of the progressive movement. From the bottom, urban women created new organizations. The Chicago Woman's Club formed the Chicago Political Equality League in 1894. The Denver Equal Suffrage League (DESL) was formed in 1893 after activist women in the city received a letter from national organizer Lucy Stone urging them to "organize the city's leading citizens for suffrage." Within weeks, the women reported, "the DESL was formed, composed almost entirely of wealthy club women and socialites." Across the following years, women in Seattle, San Antonio, Tampa, St. Louis, and Houston, just to name a few, organized political equality or equal suffrage leagues. Working women formed wage-earners' and working-women's suffrage leagues. Settlement houses organized immigrant women to promote suffrage. Every state had its suffrage association into which it drew these local groups. The NAWSA stood at the top of the pyramid, sometimes directing the work of the state and local leagues, but these latter often set their own agendas.[25]

---

24. For examples of women allied with male good government groups, see Gayle Gullett, *Becoming Citizens: The Emergence and Development of the California Women's Movement, 1880-1911* (Urbana: University of Illinois Press, 2000) and James Connolly, *The Triumph of Ethnic Progressivism: Urban Political Culture in Boston, 1900–1925* (Cambridge, MA: Harvard University Press, 1998) for Boston Equal Suffrage Association for Good Government.

25. Sara Hunter Graham, *Woman Suffrage and the New Democracy* (New Haven, CT: Yale University Press, 1996) is the most recent overview of the national movement, quote on Denver, 36. For aspects of local suffrage movements, see Flanagan, *Seeing with Their Hearts*, 74–75, 77, 80–84, 125–29, 194–95; Nancy Hewitt, *Southern Discomfort: Women's Activism in Tampa, Florida, 1880s–1920s* (Urbana: University of Illinois Press, 2001), esp. 231, where she lists women's efforts to end child labor, promote health and environmental issues, etc., and their conviction that "all of these efforts would be enhanced if women gained the vote"; Judith McArthur, *Creating the New Woman: The Rise of Southern Women's Progressive Culture in Texas, 1893–1918* (Urbana: University of Illinois Press, 1998); Ellen Carol DuBois, "Working Women, Class Relations, and Suffrage Militance: Harriot Stanton Blatch and the New York Woman Suffrage Movement, 1894–1909," *Journal of American History*, 74 (June 1987): 34–58; and Elinor Lerner, "Immigrant and Working Class Involvement in the New York City Woman Suffrage Movement, 1905–1917: A Study in Progressive Era Politics" (Ph.D. diss., University of California, Berkeley, 1981). Socialist women's suffrage organizations connected to the nonsocialist movement but never became part of NAWSA. See the various documents in Sally Miller, ed., *Race, Ethnicity and Gender in Early Twentieth Century Socialism* (New York: Garland, 1996), esp. 253–62. See also, Steven M. Buechler, *The Transformation of the Woman Suffrage Movement: The Case of Illinois, 1850–1920* (New Brunswick, NJ: Rutgers University Press, 1986), and Marjorie Spruill Wheeler, ed., *Votes for Women! The Woman Suffrage Movement in Tennessee, the South, and the Nation* (Knoxville: University of Tennessee Press, 1995).

In the first decade of the twentieth century, suffrage organizations throughout the country moved out of their meeting rooms and into the streets. They began to hold open-air, street corner meetings, and beginning in 1908 organized suffrage parades in cities across the country. Thousands of women marched in these parades, often dressed totally in white, and carrying American flags, banners, and placards demanding the vote. Working-class women marched with middle-class women. Black and white women were generally segregated in parades, as in most other areas of suffrage agitation—mainly at the insistence of southern women. But Chicago suffragists insisted on having Ida B. Wells-Barnett, who had organized the Alpha Suffrage Club in Chicago, march with them in Washington, D.C., in 1913 and Irene McCoy Gaines marched alongside Ruth Hanna McCormick in the 1914 Chicago parade.[26]

Behind much of women's suffrage activity lay their desire to promote social politics. In the midst of the depression of 1893, the Colorado Equal Suffrage Association had appealed to women to support suffrage on the basis of the reforms they might bring to society:

> Are you not interested in politics when in spite of the strictest economy want creeps into the household, when the mother is forced to pinch and save and deny her children; when the self-supporting woman sees her wages reduced, and when on every side arises a long, low undertone of sorrow, the cry of the suffering poor? No matter how hardly economic conditions press upon men, except in the cases of a few favored ones they press harder on women. It is the duty of every true daughter of Colorado to come to the rescue: to bend every power of mind and heart to the solving of the social problems that surround us. Charity can never do it. Only right laws, rightly executed can reform social conditions.

For Florence Kelley and Jane Addams, suffrage was the means to their desired end of totally reforming American society. Kelley in particular believed that only with the power to vote could immigrant and women workers advance their own demands. In fact, many of the women who believed in these ideals split from the NAWSA after 1914, believing that the organization no longer combined social issues of industrial safety, legal equality for all women, and equal pay for equal work with suffrage. Labor leader Leonora O'Reilly later aptly summed up why socially oriented progressive women needed the vote: "to do justice to our work as home-keepers. Children need pure milk and good food, good schools and playgrounds, sanitary homes and safe streets."[27]

---

26. See DuBois, "Working Women, Class Relations, and Suffrage Militance" and Flanagan, *Seeing with Their Hearts*.

27. Colorado Equal Suffrage Association, "To the Women of Colorado," *Leaflet 3* (1893) posted on website http://womhist.binghamton.edu/colosuff/doc20.htm. Graham, *Woman Suffrage and the New Democracy*, 29–30 and 82. O'Reilly quoted in Foner, *The Story of American Freedom*, 156. Although African American women obviously faced different problems with or without suffrage, members of the Woman's Convention of the Baptist Church often used similar language to that of white women's organizations to support suffrage. See Evelyn Brooks Higginbotham, *Righteous Discontent: The Women's Movement in the Black Baptist Church, 1880–1920* (Cambridge, MA: Harvard University Press, 1993), 226–27.

The Election of 1912

The presidential election of 1912 catalyzed the progressive backers of social politics. After four lackluster losing campaigns from 1896 through 1908, the Democrats moved decisively beyond their earlier populist agenda to seek a candidate with progressive credentials: they found him in Woodrow Wilson, the governor of New Jersey.[28] But, the most significant factor of this election was Theodore Roosevelt's return to the national political scene through the newly formed Progressive Party.

The Republican Convention in Chicago that summer was a contentious affair. Taft was the incumbent. Roosevelt was back in play and the darling of progressive Republicans, although he had competition from Senator Robert LaFollette, who considered himself the true progressive candidate because he had been fighting the battles in Congress while Roosevelt had been off killing big game in Africa. In 1911, a group of progressive men had formed the National Progressive Republican League and they came to the convention prepared to nominate LaFollette and spurned Roosevelt's bid for their support. Yet, they underestimated Roosevelt's charisma. Despite the Wisconsin delegation's convention chant

We do not need the Taft smile /
Nor Teddy's toothsome grin; /
LaFollette once; LaFollette twice; /
LaFollette til we win!

regular Republicans would have nothing to do with LaFollette and his only votes came from his small group of followers. Roosevelt did not fare much better. He was too radical for the party that was now dominated by businessmen. The regulars preferred Taft and renominated Taft. Fights broke out in the floor of the convention between progressive and regular Republicans whom the progressives charged with stealing delegate votes. In high dudgeon, the progressives marched out of the convention and announced they were forming their own party: the Progressive, or Bull Moose, Party.[29]

The progressives then held their own convention in August, again in Chicago, and not surprisingly nominated Roosevelt for president and California Governor Hiram Johnson for vice-president. Jane Addams proudly seconded Roosevelt's nomination, claiming that this "new party has become the American exponent of a world-wide movement toward juster social conditions, a movement which America, lagging behind other great nations, has been unaccountably slow to embody in political action." She specified that the party stood for social politics: protection of children, care of the aged, relief of overworked girls, safeguarding of burdened men. Despite Addams' optimism, the party platform, in fact, left a lot to be desired for progressive

---

28. Bryan had been the candidate in 1896 and 1900. Alton B. Parker, their candidate in 1904, had proved such a dismal candidate that the Democrats returned to Bryan in 1908.

29. Nancy Unger, *Fighting Bob LaFollette: The Righteous Reformer* (Chapel Hill: University of North Carolina Press, 2000), 194 and 217–20. The split between LaFollette and Roosevelt over progressive leadership did not end after the convention and would trouble the new party.

women. Even Addams, as she left the convention with progressive Mary Wilmarth, lamented the party's militarism in the face of female protest. "How frail a barrier woman's influence seemed to be in spite of its vaunted power," Wilmarth mused to her companion. And Addams later recounted that she found it "very difficult to swallow those two battleships" that were included in the party platform.[30]

Roosevelt's "New Nationalism" was not precisely what many female progressives wished either. The rhetoric was all about the public interest, but at heart it was an economic agenda. Roosevelt now polished his earlier ideas about regulating the economy in the public interest into a shiny creed to bring immigrants and women together with big businessmen, hoping to elicit a "voluntarism" that would eliminate rapacious capitalism in "the name of an American national interest." This was not the younger, moderately "trustbusting" Roosevelt. By 1912, he had determined that economic consolidations were here to stay so now what was needed was a way to regulate them so as not to deprive other Americans of economic opportunity. The party's Declaration of Principles emphasized:

> This country belongs to the people who inhabit it. Its resources, its business, its institutions and its laws should be utilized, maintained or altered in whatever manner will best promote the general interest. . . . Behind the ostensible government sits enthroned an invisible government, owing no allegiance and acknowledging no responsibility to the people. To destroy this invisible government, to dissolve the unholy alliance between corrupt business and corrupt politics is the first task of the statesmanship of the day.

There was political method at work here. The Progressive Party would not survive unless it drew significant numbers of voters away from both the Democrats and Republicans. Roosevelt's rhetoric about using government "as the steward of economic productivity" so as to "enroll rich or poor, whatever their social or industrial position, to stand together for the most elementary rights of good citizenship" was calculated to build a lasting new political party from the disaffected members of both old parties.[31]

Because it was open to women and progressive women's issues, and it endorsed women suffrage when the Republican and Democratic parties did not, the 1912 campaign indeed drew prominent progressive women into the Progressive Party. Frances Kellor of New York supported Roosevelt, as did Ruth Hanna McCormick, the daughter of Republican party politico Mark Hanna who had engineered the McKinley campaigns. Lillian Wald, Mary Simkhovitch, Harriet Vittum, Grace and Edith Abbott, and Margaret Dreier Robins (president of the NWTUL) and numerous other female progressives who had social politics

---

30. Addams, "Why I Seconded Roosevelt's Nomination," *Woman's Journal*, 43 (August 1912): 257; Addams, "Mary Hawes Wilmarth," in *The Excellent Becomes the Permanent* (New York: Macmillan, 1932), 106–07; and Addams, "My Experiences as a Progressive Delegate," *McClure's Magazine*, XL (November 1912): 13. The platform called for building two battleships every year.

31. Rauchway, *Murdering McKinley*, 189–200, quote from 195. See also, Robyn Muncy, "Trustbusting and American Manhood, 1898–1914," *American Studies*, 38 (Fall 1997): 21–42 for an analysis as to how trustbusting was primarily a white male issue.

at heart joined the Progressive Party.[32] On the one hand, the party's platform committee adopted virtually all of the social progressives' proposed "Social Standards for Industry." It called for minimum wage standards, regulation of hours of work, worker compensation, and abolition of child labor. Interestingly, it also endorsed developing a National Health Service, although by this it meant a service to regulate in the public health, not provide for a national system of public health services. On the other hand, platform members such as Charles Merriam of Chicago and Charles McCarthy of Wisconsin, who came from the political progressive wing more concerned with expertise than social welfare, determined the overwhelming majority of planks. These focused on moderate federal government regulation of business and industry and development of a national infrastructure. "Big government working in harmony with big economic interests to regulate corporations, guarantee the rights of labor, and protect the weak" is the best overall description of the Progressive Party platform.[33]

Progressive women, especially Addams, were also upset when Roosevelt refused to seat African American "black-and-tan" delegations from Alabama, Florida, and Mississippi, and the platform committee turned down the request that the party come out for racial equality. The Republican Party in the South was determined to make itself into a "lily-white" organization, and unfortunately the progressive wing was not terribly better. Addams and other cofounders of the NAACP did support W.E.B. DuBois' protest asking the progressive leadership instead to adopt the following statement:

> The National Progressive party recognizes that distinctions of race, or class, or sex in political life, have no place in a Democracy. Especially does the party realize that a group of 10,000,000 people, who have in a generation changed from slavery to a free labor system, re-established family life, accumulated $1,000,000,000 of real property, and reduced their illiteracy from 80 to 30 percent, deserve and must have justice, opportunity, and a voice in their own government.

When the party refused, DuBois turned to the Socialist Party as the only "party which openly recognizes Negro manhood." Unhappy with the socialists, however, by the time of the election he and several other northern black leaders, including women who joined the Women's National Wilson and Marshall Organization, endorsed Wilson and the Democrats. Other black progressives drifted back into the Republican camp, reluctant to desert the party of Lincoln.[34]

---

32. Allen F. Davis, "The Social Workers and the Progressive Party, 1912–1916," *American Historical Review*, 69 (April 1964): 671–88. For names of more women in the Progressive Party, and the part they played at the convention, see Melanie Gustafson, *Women and the Republican Party, 1854–1924* (Urbana: University of Illinois Press, 2001), ch. 4. The text of the entire platform can be found on the website http://www.pbs.org/amex/presidents/26_roosevelt/psources.

33. Arthur S. Link and Richard L. McCormick, *Progressivism* (Arlington Heights, IL: Harlan Davidson, 1983), 42–43.

34. Text of DuBois' statement was printed in the *New York Times*, August 7, 1912. See also, ibid., August 18 and 21, 1912, and the *Crisis* (November 1912) for DuBois urging African American support for Wilson, and Gustafson, *Women in the Republican Party*, ch. 5, for accounts of these events and Jane Addams' subsequent decision to stay in the Progressive Party.

The decision not to support racial equality could have been seen as a purely political ploy—he wanted to make inroads into Democratic strength in the southern states—but Roosevelt's actions must be seen in the context of his already well-formed ideas about an American race. In private correspondence he indeed argued that southern African Americans were readily corruptible and thus a danger to the party's desire to become a nationwide movement. Even worse, he argued they were of "very grave harm, to their own race." The best way from them to "progress" would be under the protection and guidance of the "best white men in the South." As to northern African Americans, he welcomed the "best colored men" into the progressive Party, saying that he did not believe they could be manipulated by white politicians.[35]

Finally, socially oriented progressives feared that Roosevelt was taking too much advice from George Perkins, a partner in J.P. Morgan and Co. and the organizer of International Harvester Company (formerly the McCormick Reaper Works). The millionaire Perkins was funding much of the party's campaign and other progressives had a hard time allying with a man who seemed so inimical to their social justice agenda, and who had influenced the big business, big government orientation of the party platform. But the Progressive Party was the best choice on offer, so progressives focused on what they believed was a common outlook among party members: that they all wanted "a government of the people, by the people, and for the people," as stated in the party's Declaration of Principles.

The 1912 election, then, was a four-way race. Taft for the Republicans, Roosevelt for the Progressives, Wilson for the Democrats, and Eugene Debs again for the SPA. The election came on the heels of the Triangle fire, the Lawrence textile strike, and socialist gains in local-level elections in 1910 and 1911, all of which were producing a restless electorate. Various reforms had strengthened the powers of the presidency, so it seemed even more crucial now to control that office in order to advance a preferred agenda. Taft and the regular Republicans stuck to their big-business-first agenda, which included maintaining the high tariff. Debs and the SPA were unlikely to draw too large a number of votes, but these could be taken away from the progressives by voters desiring more radical changes than Roosevelt was promising. The Democrats wanted the White House back. The election in a very real sense was a referendum on progressivism, how far it had come, and how far it would continue to go.

Roosevelt and Wilson were vying for the voters who wanted something between Taft and Debs. Wilson and the Democrats drew from their old populist agenda and promised both the middle class and the working class that, once in power, their goal would be to keep opportunity wide open for them to advance by curbing the power of big business. Wilson's promised "New Freedom" exhibited a traditional distrust of the power of big business and monopoly, which he saw as causing the growing gap between the "haves" and the

35. Roosevelt's reasoning is cited in Gustafson, *Women in the Republican Party*, ch. 5. For the idea of the "best men," see Glenda Gilmore, *Gender and Jim Crow: Women and the Politics of White Supremacy in North Carolina, 1896–1920* (Chapel Hill: University of North Carolina Press, 1996). This also includes discussion of how, before Jim Crow, black men attempted to use the "best men" ideology to their own political advantage.

"have nots." Wilson's task was formidable, as he had to draw together the southern Democrats and northern industrial working class. His "New Freedom" was meant to appeal to these disparate groups.

The election results showed that reform was clearly what Americans wanted. More than ten million of the almost fifteen million ballots cast went to Wilson and Roosevelt. Wilson received the highest number of popular votes and ran away with the electoral votes. Yet, if the Republicans had not split, Wilson would have lost. Between them, Roosevelt and Taft took 7.5 million votes, whereas Wilson took 6.2 million. Debs received the highest percentage of votes ever for a socialist candidate: 6 percent.

Progressive Party members were keenly disappointed with the outcome. Yet most of them thought they could live with Wilson even if his New Freedom rarely addressed using government to advance social welfare. His inaugural speech in March 1913 at least mentioned some of their social agenda. "Society," he declared,

> must see to it that it does not itself crush or weaken or damage its own constituent parts. The first duty of law is to keep sound the society it serves. Sanitary laws, pure food laws, and laws determining conditions of labor which individuals are powerless to determine for themselves are intimate parts of the very business of justice and legal efficiency.

Still, he propounded the antimonopoly theme as the basis for social justice:

> There can be no equality or opportunity, the first essential of justice in the body politic, if men and women and children be not shielded in their lives, their very vitality, from the consequences of great industrial and social processes which they can not alter, control, or singly cope with.

In terms of the historical understanding of progressivism, it is interesting to note that Wilson's most prolific biographer, the historian Arthur S. Link, in his volume on the New Freedom chose to include only the parts of the speech that stressed business enterprise. He accompanied this with a newspaper illustration celebrating Wilson's progressivism. The caption at the top reads "The President" and it shows a man standing with arms raised to the rising sun within which was written the word "opportunity," and on the man's shirt back appears the word "enterprise." Around his feet are the broken chains and shackles of "money trust," "monopoly," and "Wall Street Intimidation."[36]

Republican social progressives took heart from their belief that the campaign itself had injected their concerns so far into the political system that they could never be ignored. To keep up the pressure a group of them put together the National Progressive Service, intending it as a means for drafting new social progressive legislation and as a mechanism through which to build a

---

36. Arthur S. Link, *Wilson: The New Freedom* (Princeton, NJ: Princeton University Press, 1955), 58–56.

strong Progressive Party. Jane Addams encouraged Roosevelt to focus on the positive:

> the tremendous impulse the campaign has given to social reform measures . . . which have never before seemed to become so possible of fulfillment as at the present moment. I had never dared hope that within my life-time thousands of people would so eagerly participate in their discussion. I am sure you have been in a large measure responsible for this outcome.

Unfortunately for these progressives, Roosevelt failed to share their optimism of an ongoing political party. Theirs was a movement that lacked clear direction and leadership after 1912. Roosevelt quickly moved away from the more socially oriented progressives toward the likes of George Perkins. While the former were drafting resolutions to demand public ownership of utilities and other social welfare reforms as part of a Progressive Party platform, the latter were still focusing on regulating trusts.[37]

By 1914, as Progressive Party candidates were defeated in local and state elections across the country, the barely nascent party was already dying. Wilson had significantly lowered the tariff, to the delight of all but big business. Robert LaFollette was working hard in the Senate to pass elements of a progressive agenda. He helped Wilson shepherd through Congress the Clayton Anti-Trust Act and the Federal Trade Commission, even though he was unhappy that Wilson was not pushing for more social reform measures. With ratification of the 16th and 17th Amendments, essential elements of a progressive political agenda had been passed, even as social reforms in areas such as child labor, working hours, housing, and national health seemed doomed to fail as national reforms.

37. Rauchway, *Murdering McKinley*, 201–03, Addams quoted 201–02. See also, Davis, "The Social Workers and the Progressive Party," 684–88.

There is a story told, although it may well be apocryphal, that President Roosevelt was converted to government regulation and oversight of industry while eating breakfast one morning. According to this tale, he was reading a just-published novel, Upton Sinclair's *The Jungle*, as he was tucking into his breakfast sausages. Sinclair's exposé of Chicago's packing houses described them using "everything about the hog except the squeal" in turning out their pork products—not an image guaranteed to make the president's breakfast go down easily. Going further into the book, Roosevelt would have read even worse accounts of packing-house practices, perhaps of how they disposed of "downer" cows:

> It was late, almost dark, and the government inspectors had all gone, and there were only a dozen or two of men on the floor. That day they had killed about four thousand cattle, and these cattle had come in freight trains from far states, and some of them had got hurt. There were some with broken legs, and some with gored sides; there were some that had died, from what cause no one could say; and they were all to be disposed of, here in darkness and silence. "Downers," the men called them; and the packing house had a special elevator upon which they were raised to the killing beds, where the gang proceeded to handle them, with an air of businesslike nonchalance which said plainer than any words that it was a matter of everyday routine. It took a couple of hours to get them out of the way, and in the end Jurgis saw them go into the chilling rooms with the rest of the meat, being carefully scattered here and there so that they could not be identified. When he came home that night he was in a very somber mood, having begun to see at last how those might be right who had laughed at him for his faith in America.*

By the end of *The Jungle*, the members of Sinclair's immigrant family who had come to the United States with so much hope were either dead or broken in body and spirit.

---

*Upton Sinclair, *The Jungle* (New York: Doubleday Page and Co., 1906), chs. 3 and 4 for quotes.

CHAPTER 7

The Battle Against Monopoly Capitalism

The right to regulate the use of wealth in the public interest is universally admitted.

—THEODORE ROOSEVELT

THE POLITICAL ECONOMY OF DEMOCRACY

Upton Sinclair was a "muckraker." He and other writers were so called because they were accused of, or celebrated for, depending on the perspective of the reader, exposing the muck of American society. These writers took on municipal corruption, life in the urban slums, and child labor, but industrial production and monopoly were the favored targets of many of them. For Sinclair it was the meat-packing industry. Ida Tarbell exposed the workings of the Standard Oil Company. Frank Norris attacked the railroad industry. The groundwork for them had been laid earlier by such writers as Henry Demarest Lloyd, whose book *Wealth Against Commonwealth* had attacked the prerogatives enjoyed by private industries and the harm they were doing to ordinary people. According to Lloyd:

> They assert the right, for their private profit, to regulate the consumption by the people of the necessaries of life, and to control production, not by the needs of humanity, but by the desires of a few for dividends. The coal syndicate thinks there is too much coal. There is too much iron, too much lumber, too much flour—for this or that syndicate. . . . The majority have never been able to buy enough of anything; but this minority have too much of everything to sell. . . . Liberty produces wealth, and wealth destroys liberty.[1]

---

1. Ida M. Tarbell, *The History of the Standard Oil Company* (New York: McClure's, 1904); Frank Norris, *The Octopus: A Story of California* (New York: Sun Dial Press, 1901); Lloyd, *Wealth Against Commonwealth* (New York: Harper & Brothers, 1894). See also, Lincoln Steffens, *The Shame of the Cities* (New York: McClure's, 1904); Jacob Riis, *How the Other Half Lives* (New York: Charles Scribner's Sons, 1890); and Louis Filler, *The Muckrakers* (University Park: Pennsylvania State University Press, 1976) for a broad overview.

141

Unlike earlier writers such as Lloyd, the muckrakers of the twentieth century were crusading, investigative reporters more than anything else. Even when they wrote fiction, as did Sinclair in *The Jungle*, the story was based on fact and experience, not on philosophy. Sinclair went to work in the Chicago stockyards to gather information for his book. He walked the streets of packingtown in that city to see how people lived. This made their writing accessible to average readers, who could also compare the events and problems described by the muckrakers to those they encountered in everyday life.

Once these stories were published, the problems they exposed had to be addressed. Whether or not the Roosevelt story was true, millions of other Americans would have been thinking the same questions—How safe is my food? What am I serving to my children? Why is industry allowed to slaughter diseased animals and sell their meat to the unsuspecting public? Why does the law always seem to side with producers and not workers or consumers? This was a problem that hit home for all Americans. Urban, industrial society removed control of daily life and labor from the individual's hands. The public at large could not protect itself from predatory business practices. If that were the case, then how could the individual's, and by extension the public's, welfare be safeguarded? And, how might democratic opportunity be restored? In trying to answer these questions, proposals for economic progressivism fell into three broad categories: revolution, reform, and regulation.

1. Revolution

The fundamental premise of capitalism that the marketplace should determine all economics, combined with the "corrupt bargain" between industrialists and politicians, convinced at least a small cadre of Americans that capitalism itself *was* the problem with American society. It was a political economy that would, by its very nature, exploit the human and natural resources of society, exhausting all of them for the purposes of the few wealthy and powerful who controlled the economic, political, and legal systems. For Marxist socialists, only a revolutionary economic and social order, brought about through the class struggle, would free the working class to develop its own capacities and opportunities. Socialist Labor Party leader Daniel DeLeon articulated the difference between reform and revolution to a meeting of workingmen in Boston in 1896. Take a poodle, he told his audience: you could keep its coat long or shave it; it could have a shaved tail with a tassel of hair on the end; it could have a red bow on its head, or a brass collar around its neck. But no matter how its appearance was changed, he claimed, "essentially, a poodle he was, a poodle he is and a poodle he will remain. . . . That is reform." So, he went on, "with society. . . . Whenever a change leaves the internal mechanism untouched, we have reform; whenever the internal mechanism is changed, we have revolution."[2]

---

2. Richard Schneirov, "New Perspectives on Socialism II," *The Journal of the Gilded Age and Progressive Era*, 2 (October 2003): 351–60, gives a brief overview of both Marxist and revisionary socialism. Daniel DeLeon, "Reform or Revolution," January 26, 1896.

The program of the SLP was foremost an economic one bent on destroying "despotic" capitalism and replacing it with socialist industrialist unionism. According to this plan, the working class would take control of all industry and elected representatives from all sectors of industry would administer society through a socialist industrialist union. During the Progressive Era, the SLP ran presidential candidates, but they never received as many as 40,000 votes for president. Socialist candidates were significantly more successful in local elections. But more threatening to the American public than the SLP as a political party was the Industrial Workers of the World (IWW), also known as the Wobblies. Extremely dissatisfied with the elitism and "reactionary" stance of the AFL, union organizers such as Mary "Mother" Jones, William "Big Bill" Haywood of the radical Western Federation of Miners, and anarchist Emma Goldman met in Chicago in 1905 to form this "One Big Union." The IWW preamble stated frankly that there could never be any reform of the system:

> The working class and the employing class have nothing in common. There can be no peace so long as hunger and want are found among millions of the working people and the few, who make up the employing class, have all the good things of life. Between these two classes a struggle must go on until the workers of the world organize as a class, take possession of the means of production, abolish the wage system, and live in harmony with the Earth.

Although official IWW membership reached around 100,000 by 1917, it was most popular in the western states, where its leaders and adherents were violently treated and some, such as Joe Hill, were killed. Hill was later immortalized in the song "I Dreamt I Saw Joe Hill Last Night" with its metaphoric line that he [the dream of socialism] had never died. But, in truth, the IWW never made terribly much headway even among laborers. Some of that was undoubtedly due to political and legal oppression. But the milder Debsian socialism of the Socialist Party of America (1901) simply was more attractive to more American workers. Much of the reason for that, as the next section explores, is that it had a democratic component that was more appealing to them. In most progressive movements, democracy and capitalism seemed so American that progressives could not imagine one without the other. The question for them, instead, was how far to reform capitalism.[3] It is in this regard that some aspects of American socialism can be viewed as part of progressivism.

2. Reform

Socialist Party of America

Although reform and regulation might seem to mean the same thing, in the context of economic progressivism they are in fact different concepts.

---

3. The best analysis of the IWW is Melvyn Dubofsky, *We Shall Be All: A History of the Industrial Workers of the World* (Urbana: University of Illinois Press, 2nd edition, 1988). See also, Joyce L. Kornbluh, *Rebel Voices: An I.W.W. Anthology* (Ann Arbor: University of Michigan Press, 1964). Debs attended the convention, and supported the members of the IWW, but was never active in the union.

Reform proposals of the American socialist movement intended to change both fundamental ideas about capitalism as well as its mechanisms. Historians of American socialism continue to disagree on the exact meaning of Debs' socialism as leader of the SPA, as well as that of other socialist party leaders such as early union organizer Morris Hillquit and Congressman Victor Berger. But recent work in this field is moving toward a general consensus that Debsian socialism rejected the IWW's advocacy of violence and sabotage in favor of using the ballot box and changing the law. Changing the law meant more than passing new laws to protect workers and to stop courts from issuing strike injunctions. The courts would have to change how they interpreted the Constitution. To accomplish such a change would also require that the courts shift significantly their ideas about capitalism. Both the SPA and socialist labor unions set out to move courts away from upholding the laissez-faire doctrines that they believed had led to favoring business over labor.

The progress of worker compensation laws in Montana is an example of how this worked. In that state, the Socialist Party based in the city of Butte combined with the Montana Federation of Labor (MFL) to secure a state worker compensation law beginning in 1909. At first, they were defeated in several attempts by employers and their legislative allies who argued that it would infringe upon the rights of business and overreach the police power of the state. But since the leader of the MFL believed that "no subject is engaging the attention of the workers . . . as much as that which has become known as the Workingmen's Compensation," the group kept working. Finally, in 1914, the combined MFL and Socialist Party used the political reforms of the initiative and referendum to put the measure to a popular vote. The voters approved and the law came into force the following year.[4] By 1914, Montana, other states, and the Supreme Court had accepted the idea that laissez-faire capitalism did not work. Business was no longer to have an entirely free hand and states had to accept some responsibility toward their residents.

By working to change law and its interpretation, by formulating new legislation to protect workers, and by working within the political system, American socialism participated in economic progressivism. It helped change the relationship between business and labor to give labor far more protection and rights, and it put a healthy dent in the doctrine of freedom of contract. The American socialists who moved in this direction have been termed "evolutionists" to distinguish them from "revolutionary" socialists. Although the latter believed that workers must overthrow capitalism, the evolutionists believed

---

4. The essays in two special issues of the *Journal of the Gilded Age and Progressive Era* are an excellent source for understanding the historiography of American socialism and the newest interpretations. Not all historians of socialism will agree with these essays, of course, but they are intended also to situate American socialism within the context of the Progressive Era. See *Journal of the Gilded Age and Progressive Era*, 2 (July 2003 and October 2003). For the Montana example, see John P. Enyeart, "Revolution or Evolution: The Socialist Party, Western Workers, and Law in the Progressive Era," 2 (October 2003): 377–402, quote, 401.

that in working through the system they would gradually "socialize" American society. Although Debsian socialists clearly distinguished themselves from mainstream economic progressives, whom they accused of having an insufficient critique of the ills of capitalism, their political impulses were fundamentally democratic. Snippets of the speech that Debs gave in Chicago to open his 1912 presidential campaign give a taste of this combination and the optimism Debs, the "socialist citizen" as his biographer called him, had about a peaceful evolution of America into "democratic socialism." "The laws of evolution have decreed the downfall of the capitalist system," he assured his listeners.

> The handwriting is upon the wall in letters of fire. The trusts are transforming industry and next will come the transformation of the trusts by the people. Socialism is inevitable. Capitalism is breaking down and the new order evolving from it is clearly the Socialist commonwealth. The present evolution can only culminate in industrial and social democracy . . . the coming social order [will be] based upon the social ownership of the means of life and the production of wealth for the use of all instead of the private profit of the few.

Socialism will triumph and bring economic peace and abundance, Debs predicted. Socialism will end "the brute struggle for existence . . . the millions of exploited poor will be rescued from the skeleton clutches of poverty and famine." Other social problems would be solved. Socialism would end prostitution and white slavery. Debs wrapped up his speech with a call to arms reflecting his optimism:

> Comrades and friends, the campaign before us gives us our supreme opportunity to reach the American people. They have but to know the true meaning of Socialism to accept its philosophy and the true mission of the Socialist party to give it their support. Let us all unite as we never have before to place the issue of Socialism squarely before the masses. For years they have been deceived, misled and betrayed, and they are now hungering for the true gospel of relief and the true message of emancipation.[5]

Despite such optimism, Debs recognized the strength of his enemies. When members of the IWW, including "Big Bill" Haywood, were charged with murder in Idaho in 1906, he gave a rousing address to workers that expressed his anger and determination to wrest control of the country from the capitalist tyrants: "There have been twenty years of revolutionary education, agitation and organization since the Haymarket tragedy, and if an attempt is made to repeat it, there will be a revolution and I will do all in my power to precipitate it."[6] Debs continued to lead the SPA through the years of World War I, but after the 1912 presidential campaign, other leaders such as Hillquit and Berger increasingly moved the party even more into a democratic posture.

---

5. Nick Salvatore, *Eugene V. Debs: Citizen and Socialist* (Urbana: University of Illinois Press, 1982), 220, 224–25. Eugene V. Debs, "Opening Speech, the Campaign of 1912," pamphlet printed by *Chicago Daily Socialist* of speech from June 16, 1912, at Riverview Park, Chicago, Illinois.

6. "Arouse, ye Slaves!" *Appeal to Reason* (March 10, 1906).

The underlying premise of socialism, derived from Karl Marx, was that the solidarity of an oppressed working class would ultimately overthrow capitalism. Because the myth of a classless society still held sway in the Progressive Era, the idea that there might be a permanent working class arrayed against other classes was a difficult one for many Americans to accept. Middle-class progressives feared that there was a growing divide in opportunity between themselves and the working class. Eradicating this divide, rather than fighting to maintain their position, was one of the progressives' aims. From the perspective of the working class, there were also problems with the class solution to capitalism. First, quite a large percentage of the working class simply did not adhere to socialism. Skilled workers were organized into the AFL; others seemingly believed more in the possibilities of democratic reforms through universal white male suffrage, an option not truly open to workers in European industrial societies.

Second, the SPA faced the problems of racial, gender, and ethnic divisions in trying to forge a solid working class. Even Debs, who often condemned discrimination against African American workers, thought mainly about white workers. As his biographer concluded, "his central message focused on expanding and strengthening the self-perception of America's white working-men and women." African American socialists had a difficult time finding a place in the party that, as Debs asserted, had no "particular message for African Americans as a race." A number of prominent black ministers encouraged their communities to join the party, and special efforts produced decent numbers of black votes for party candidates in New York City and in Oklahoma, for example. But racism permeated the SPA, even if it was not as virulent as that among other groups in the United States.[7]

Gender issues were, if anything, more difficult for the SPA. Because the emphasis was on class, the SPA recognized no particular gender problems. According to the party's class analysis, once the working class had triumphed, working-class women would be taken care of. Party publications often referred to "wives of toilers," and woman suffrage was looked upon as divisive for the class struggle. The "woman question," as with the "race question," was considered secondary to the "class question." For their part, socialist women such as Josephine Kaneko and May Wood Simons pushed the party to support suffrage as a necessary and separate issue. They helped establish a Woman's National Committee (WNC) inside the party structure in 1908. The work of the WNC helped expand women's membership in the party, but the party's national leadership never really accepted this separate endeavor. Women were almost never members of the National Executive Committee, and in 1914 it withdrew all its support for the WNC. Unfortunately for female socialists, concepts such as solidarity, worker, or proletariat applied mainly to class and gender was viewed as a "digression" from class. "The Woman's National

---

7. Salvatore, *Eugene V. Debs*, 228, and Sally Miller, "For White Men Only: The Socialist Party of America and Issues of Gender, Ethnicity, and Race," *Journal of the Gilded Age and Progressive Era*, 2 (July 2003): 283–302.

Wearing the Red Scarves: Women Socialists, May Day, New York City (1910)
Source: Library of Congress, Prints & Photographs Division, LC-USZ62-51009

Committee where women for a few years developed their own networks and somewhat circumvented patriarchal supervision was grudgingly tolerated only briefly."[8]

Finally, unlike so many European socialist parties, ethnicity always troubled the SPA. Many of the party's leaders were either native born—Debs hailed from Terre Haute, Indiana—or were German or east European Jewish immigrants who spoke English. New immigrants often did not speak English and they had brought with them their national socialist organizations and culture. Some of the ethnic socialist groups had a split identity: they were as concerned with problems of the working class back in Europe as in the United States. In response, some SPA leaders became caught up in the immigration restriction debates. Morris Hillquit advocated restriction of some immigrant groups and Victor Berger even drafted an anti-Asian immigration resolution. The SPA never adopted this resolution, but questions of ethnicity and immigration bedeviled the SPA. So, beyond violence against socialists and the American aversion to accepting hard and fast class lines, the SPA itself found it difficult to confront both American ethnicity and the separate movements for racial and gender equality that were important components of progressivism.[9]

---

8. Miller, "For White Men Only," 290. See also, Ava Baron, "Gender and Labor History: Learning from the Past, Looking to the Future," in *Work Engendered: Toward a New History of American Labor*, Ava Baron, ed. (Ithaca, NY: Cornell University Press, 1991), 11–24.

9. Miller, "For White Men Only."

The Regional Experience: The South and the West

Regional differences also characterized progressive attacks on monopoly capitalism, although generalization does not give complete justice even to the varieties of progressive experience within regions. The legacy of slavery and the ensuing racial segregation and discrimination obviously shaped southern progressivism. There was the "New South" of cities such as Birmingham, Alabama, with a thriving steel industry, but overall the South lagged well behind in industrialization and remained a heavily agricultural economy. Feeling disadvantaged by economic competition and tariff policies that encouraged industrial production, the South was more eager to cling to an older antimonopoly, "trustbusting" tradition than were other areas of the country.[10]

Political progressivism had different patterns in western and southwestern cities due in some measure to later settlement patterns. Portland, Oregon, led in the movement to expand popular democracy. In that city, William R. U'Ren promoted the initiative and referendum, which Oregon adopted in 1902, and the graduated income tax. Mayors Harry Lane and Will Daly attacked streetcar monopolies and public utilities for gouging the citizenry. Portland was also the home of Curt Muller, the laundry owner who challenged the state law limiting women's hours of work in laundries, a man whom most progressives would never have included as one of their own. A recent study of Portland by historian Robert Johnston, however, argues that these different people and groups who followed them ought to be included within progressivism for their attacks on corporate capitalism and for instituting a commission-style municipal government that worked for the people and not the elites. Johnston's Portland "progressives" were found mainly among the "middling" classes: small business owners, shopkeepers, etc.[11]

On the other hand, it is not yet clear whether we should call what was occurring in Portland a forward-looking progressivism or a backward-looking type of populist democracy. The Portland experience, as Johnston admits, centered in the middling classes of a not very diverse or industrialized city. These people were oriented toward the idea of property-owning equality, something that may well have harkened back to an earlier nineteenth-century ideal of a republic of property owners. This was the context of Curt Muller's objection to the hours law: he saw it as government depriving him of his property. In this sense, he would seem a bit closer to industrialists than to even middle-class economic progressives in wanting no government interference with property. Moreover, as immigration continued Portland developed a rather strong Ku Klux Klan movement by the early 1920s. What the Portland experience does demonstrate, however, is how deeply embedded in American society was the concept of popular democracy and the anger against big business for threatening democracy and opportunity. Unfortunately, the rise of the KKK also demonstrates that not all Americans were to be included in that democracy and opportunity. The Port-

---

10. Samuel P. Hays, *The Response to Industrialism, 1885–1914* (Chicago: University of Chicago Press, rev. ed., 1995).

11. Robert D. Johnston, *The Radical Middle Class: Popular Democracy and the Question of Capitalism in Progressive Era Portland, Oregon* (Princeton, NJ: Princeton University Press, 2003).

land experience may be an anomaly, which we will not know until more studies are done on western cities, but it does present an interesting case of how certain Americans responded to the reform waves of the Progressive Era.[12]

Farmers as Capitalists

Rural and agricultural movements during the Progressive Era also aimed to reform the economic system. In some measure this can be seen in the formation of new farmers' cooperatives. Farmers since the Civil War period had felt themselves increasingly "victimized" by the market forces of laissez-faire capitalism. They believed that they were at the mercy of the railroads for shipping charges, the middlemen who now brokered farmers' products for faraway markets, and banks that charged whatever they wished for the loans that farmers often needed to get through the seasons of bad weather and poor crops.

Rather than depend solely on government regulation, farmers in the agricultural regions in the Midwest first sought ways to control their own destinies through cooperation. After early-twentieth-century attempts to pool their crops as a way of controlling the price received failed, farmers' groups switched to organizing networks of grain elevator, dairy, and fruit-growers cooperatives through which they hoped to escape being at the mercy of the marketplace. Minnesota, Iowa, Wisconsin, and California were in the forefront of this movement. Agrarian progressives traveled to Europe, where such schemes were already well under way. In the same way that American cities could still be built outward, agrarian reformers believed there was land to start new agricultural settlements formed around economic and social collectivity that would break down the individual isolation of farmers. Such cooperation, if it had spread through the economic system and been sustained over time, would have challenged some of the very foundations of capitalism. Yet, a minority report filed by the American Commission on Agricultural Cooperation and Rural Credit concluded after a visit across Europe that agricultural cooperation would never match that of Europe. American farmers were too divided by race, religion, and ethnicity and lacked any sense of mutuality. They were, the report concluded, "ambitious, individualistic, and desirous of acquiring means and property." American farmers were capitalists at heart. They could not envision actually moving outside the system into one of true social democracy.[13]

Agrarian progressivism instead produced large regional cooperatives, such as the California Fruit Growers' Exchange in 1917, to help control market prices. The difference between cooperative agriculture and cooperative marketing was significant. The latter movement accepted capitalism. It donned "the clothes of the big-business trust." By the mid 1920s, such cooperatives

---

12. Theodore H. Moore, "Capital Cities: Planning, Politics, and Environmental Protest in Lansing, Michigan and Salt Lake City, Utah, 1920–1945" (Ph.D. diss., Michigan State University, 2004) has identified some similarities between Portland and the later environmental crusades in Salt Lake City.

13. Daniel Rodgers, *Atlantic Crossings: Social Politics in a Progressive Age* (Cambridge, MA: Harvard University Press, 1998), 325, 331–38, 338 for commission report.

shipped 50 percent of the livestock going into Chicago's stockyards and one-third of the country's cheese. Farmers outside the cooperatives would find it harder and harder to compete in the capitalist agricultural economy. [14]

Social Democracy/Social Justice

Social justice progressivism for its part contained an economic dimension that intended to reform capitalism to make it function in the public interest. For Jane Addams, this meant recognizing that the collective rather than the individual's voice had to be decisive. Americans, she wrote, had to realize "that a large manufacturing concern has ceased to be a private matter; that not only a number of workmen and stockholders are concerned in its management, but that the interests of the public are so involved that the officers of the company are in real sense administering a public trust."[15] Her definition of the collective concern, thus, went beyond the special interests of either business or labor. It denied business claims to sole control of their establishments, and rather than envision worker control of their labor as the end result of reform, it made the good of society as a whole the goal.

Kate Barnard struggled to convince her fellow Oklahomans that social justice and economic progressivism were an entwined endeavor. The Oklahoma experience is an interesting angle on regional variation because progressivism there advanced simultaneously with the territory's preparation for statehood. Barnard, a stenographer, was in many ways a typical social justice progressive who came to progressivism through concern for poor children, especially working children, and then went on to draw more groups together to work for reform. She first revived a moribund charity organization, the United Provident Association, and then organized the Oklahoma City Child Labor League. Extending her concerns to laboring women, Barnard formed a coalition of women's organizations and labor organizations. She founded the Federal Union #12374 for unskilled laborers as well as a chapter of the Women's International Union Labor League. Barnard seized upon Oklahoma's preparation for statehood, which it achieved in 1907, as the opportunity to advance her progressivism. As a delegate to the convention that drew up the constitution for statehood, she was largely responsible for including an antichild labor statute in it. She received solid support from labor and the Democratic Party for this statute, but she also muted farmer concerns about restricting child labor by pointing out that this would only apply to "labor injurious to health and morals," not to children working on family farms.

In campaigning for adoption of the constitution she put together a unionist-social reformer coalition that carried the day for the constitution. It was this labor-social reformer alliance that she thought was most important for securing progressive reforms: "the best way to help workers is to get into their organizations and work with them; instead of standing aloof . . . and trying to work for them," she told her nonlabor allies. One hostile newspaper account de-

---

14. Ibid., 340–42.
15. Addams, *Democracy and Social Justice* (1902; reprint, Urbana: University of Illinois Press, 2002), 65.

scribed her as this "little ninety-six pound bunch of nerves" who frightened all the politicians because she was so well connected to labor. Indeed, because she was state Commissioner of Charities and Corrections, these connections helped her secure passage of one of the most advanced state laws against child labor, a juvenile court law, and new laws reforming the penal system. Yet, for Barnard, the anti–child labor statute in the new state constitution was clearly about social justice and the rights of children. When she was asked to give a woman's opinion on the constitution, she responded by saying that she viewed it from a mother's standpoint: "from the standpoint of the dearest thing on earth to women—her immortal child . . . [child labor and compulsory education would] not only protect our little ones from a man's labor, but assure them that degree of education which enables them to come in touch with the higher thoughts and nobler impulses of the world." As with Portland, the Oklahoma case may stand alone. Barnard and her allies had little success when they tried to convince other southern labor organizations to ally with social reformers in a crusade against child labor. Nonetheless, Barnard and the Oklahoma situation expose how some progressives wished to reform the economic system by having Americans imagine that capitalism could function within a social democracy. "Oklahoma," she optimistically declared in 1910, "is ruled today by what is really a labor party."[16]

Still other progressives, whom we might term early feminists, believed that economic reform was tied to eradicating gender expectations and rearranging family life. The tireless crusader, public speaker, and writer Charlotte Perkins Gilman declared that true economic reform required freeing women from domestic servitude and giving them equality of economic opportunity. Confining women to the home, according to Gilman, made them "economic parasites" and "social idiots" who could not contribute to the well-being of society at large. Her solution was to make domestic activities into communal endeavors: if there were communal laundries, nurseries, and cafeterias, she argued, women would be freed from domestic drudgery and gain economic independence. The result, she believed, would be a new society in which

> we shall not move from the isolated home to the sordid shop and back again, in a world torn and dissevered by the selfish production of one sex and the selfish consumption of the other; but we shall live in a world of men and women humanly related, as well as sexually related, working together, as they were meant to do, for the common good of all.

A few feminist groups tried to carry out Gilman's ideas. They built apartment houses with communal areas that freed working women from having singly to do many of the daily domestic chores. Harriot Stanton Blatch approached the problem from a different angle. She believed that women would always work

---

16. Keith L. Bryant, "Kate Barnard, Organized Labor, and Social Justice in Oklahoma During the Progressive Era," *Journal of Southern History*, 35 (May 1969): 145–64, quotes from 153, 161–62, 152 respectively, and 163 for final quote. See also, Lynn Musslewhite and Suzanne Jones Crawford, *One Woman's Political Journey: Kate Barnard and Social Reform, 1875–1930* (Norman: University of Oklahoma Press, 2003), 45 for quote on children.

and to help working women gain both political and economic equality, she organized the Equality League of Self-Supporting Women in New York City. Such efforts were rare, of course, as they so squarely contradicted prevailing gender assumptions about women's role in society. Both kinds of undertakings were attacked by elements of labor who stressed that the site for economic reform needed to be the workplace, not the home. As the living wage became "an emblem of manliness," feminist economic reform proposals for social democracy were perceived as threatening to the male worker. Many middle-class female progressives also shunned such ideas as those of Gilman and Blatch. They supported, instead, the concept of the family wage that would allow men to support their families so that women did not have to do double-duty as workers outside and inside the home.[17]

3. Regulation and the "New Freedom"

Regulation of capitalism was the preferred route to reform, especially among those who already wielded political power and did not wish to surrender it. After Roosevelt's defeat in 1912 and the Progressive Party's subsequent demise, Wilson and the southern-controlled Democratic Party pursued antimonopoly regulation on the national level. Wilson's "New Freedom" promised to restore competition to business and not to expand federal government power so as to interfere with states' rights. As was the case with most southern Democrats, Wilson shied away from any commitment to social issues. During 1913 and 1914, Wilson kept to this program. He refused to support woman suffrage, ignored African American calls for a commitment to racial equality, blocked passage of a rural farm credits bill, and refused attempts to exempt organized labor from the 1890 Sherman Anti-Trust Act. The focal points of the New Freedom in these two years were regulation of banking, currency, and trade, and new antitrust legislation. Although almost everyone agreed that each of these economic problems had to be addressed, there was no agreement among economic progressives as to how far to insert government into such regulation. The arguments over banking and currency regulation highlight some of these divisions.

Federal Reserve System

As Wilson came into office, the United States had 7,000 individual banks with no central coordination. Currency was a mixture of gold and silver coins and certificates, greenbacks, and national bank notes issued against government bonds. There was no official mechanism to increase the money supply. Aside perhaps from the House of J.P. Morgan, which a congressional banking subcommittee found to be in control of an "astounding concentration of control

---

17. Charlotte Perkins Gilman, *Women and Economics: A Study of the Economic Relation between Men and Women As a Factor in Social Evolution* (Boston: Small, Maynard & Co., 1898; New York: Harper & Row, 1966 edition), quote 313. See also, Eric Foner, *The Story of American Freedom* (New York: W.W. Norton, 1998), 144–46.

over credit resources of the country," almost no one believed that the situation could continue as it was. The U.S. Senate made the first move in 1908 when it passed the Aldrich-Vreeland Act, creating a National Monetary Commission to study the problem. Four years later, it issued the Aldrich Plan for a National Reserve Association overseen by a Board of Directors of private businessmen and bankers. Dissent was immediate. Bryan Democrats charged that this would mean Wall Street control, not an unreasonable assumption since a prime architect of the plan was Paul Warburg, a partner in a major investment firm associated with J.P. Morgan. Progressive Republicans demanded stronger government control, as they had in their 1912 party platform. This was the situation as Wilson came into office determined to break the power of the "Money Trust."[18]

Banking reform was a quintessential struggle between the adherents of laissez-faire and those demanding popular control by democratic government. As various bills and amendments were proposed and as Wilson moved toward accepting the need for shared public and private control, the language used signified how profoundly each side believed in its rights. Southern and western agrarians, following in the spirit of Bryan populism, wanted the "Money Trust" destroyed before any new regulation emerged. They charged that any private control over banking would create an "oligarchy of boundless wealth" that would control "the politics of the Nation in order to protect its own proper interests as well as to govern the financial destiny of the Nation." They argued that any new regulation would also have to include mechanisms for agricultural credits to farmers to weather the vicissitudes of climate and marketplace. The opponents of public control were even more vituperative in their comments. One of Wall Street's chief spokesman declared that any "provision for Government currency and an official board to exercise absolute control over the most important of banking functions is covered all over with the slime of Bryanism." *The New York Times* editorialized against the agrarian position, saying that "it is just as well that these uncouth ideas should come to the surface. They are like the impurities in the blood—the cutaneous eruption may be unsightly, but the patient is the better for getting rid of his peccant humors."[19]

Once the House passed the Federal Reserve Bill favored by Wilson, and supported by Secretary of State Bryan, the real battle began. Bankers rallied against the measure that proposed government control of a Federal Reserve Board and made Federal Reserve notes into U.S. obligations. One banker from Chicago declared that it was both Anglo-Saxon and true Americanism "that capital must be managed by those who supply it." Another, from San Antonio, declared the bill to be "communistic." A Des Moines banker warned that "we

---

18. Nell Irvin Painter, *Standing at Armageddon: The United States, 1877–1919* (New York: W.W. Norton, 1987), 273.

19. Arthur S. Link, *The New Freedom* (Princeton, NJ: Princeton University Press, 1955), ch. 7, provides an excellent summary of the battles over banking and currency and an explanation of the various proposals. Quotes from 202 ("astounding concentration"), 218–19 ("oligarchy"), 216 ("slime of Bryanism"), and 212 (*NYT*).

are facing proposed legislation which I can hardly regard as less than an invasion of the liberty of the citizen in the control of his own property."[20] It took months of political wrangling before the Federal Reserve Act finally passed Congress in late December 1913. The Federal Reserve system that it created was in the end a compromise. It did not go nearly as far as radical progressives had wanted toward federal control of banking, destroying the "Money Trust," or giving agrarian interests extensive benefits. It did not, in fact, destroy laissez-faire, redistribute the wealth, or seize property, as its opponents had charged. But it did remove exclusive control of the money supply from private hands, gave benefits to farmers, and attempted "to create a fine balance between private management and public supervision."[21]

In its desire to straddle the line between public and private power, the Federal Reserve Act resembled the progressive compromise to regulate public utilities rather than enact municipal ownership. Louis Brandeis, who had acted as one of Wilson's chief advisors over the "Money Trust" question, was leery of giving too much power to government. Brandeis feared that too much state power would be as dangerous to individuals as unregulated big business. Progressives such as Brandeis constantly walked a tightrope between controlling corporate greed and preserving individual democratic freedoms.[22]

The role of agrarians in shaping the Federal Reserve is interesting. Older historical accounts accurately describe the role of the congressmen from agricultural regions in holding up the bill until they were sufficiently satisfied with it. But these accounts neglect to mention the pressure that farmers' organizations were putting on their congressmen. Newer work might exaggerate the role of agrarian movements as constituting "the most important political force driving the development of the American national state in the half century before WWI," and in constructing a "producer-friendly state" through government regulation. Yet, there is no doubt that they influenced the final shape of the Federal Reserve Act.[23]

The Federal Trade Commission and Clayton Anti-Trust Act

Wilson and Roosevelt had clashed during the campaign over the proper function of big business in the U.S. economy. Roosevelt had moved away from trustbusting and was now advocating strong regulation of business practices by a federal commission. Wilson was keeping staunchly to his antimonopoly

---

20. Ibid., 225 and 229.

21. Ibid., 238. See similar conclusions in Alan Dawley, *Struggles for Justice: Social Responsibility and the Liberal State* (Cambridge, MA: Harvard University Press, 1991), 147, and *Changing the World: American Progressives in War and Revolution* (Princeton, NJ: Princeton University Press, 2003), 67–70; and Painter, *Standing at Armageddon*, 275–76.

22. See Louis Brandeis, *Other People's Money, and How the Bankers Use It* (New York: Stokes, 1914) for his articulation of the problem.

23. For older accounts, see Link, *The New Freedom*; for newer accounts, see Elisabeth Sanders, *The Roots of Reform: Farmers, Workers, and the American State, 1877–1917* (Chicago: University of Chicago Press, 1999), 1 and 410.

stance, rejecting such an increased role for the government in economic affairs. Wilson believed that the existing Sherman Anti-Trust Act contained enough teeth to dismantle big business and its interlocking directorates. His attorney general, James McReynolds, used the act to attack U.S. Steel, American Telephone and Telegraph, and the railroad monopolies controlled by J.P. Morgan. Once Wilson was in office, however, and realized that Congress was leaning toward regulating trusts rather than breaking them up, he supported the proposed new Clayton Anti-Trust Act as well as a proposal to create a Federal Trade Commission (FTC). What finally emerged in both these cases was a compromise toward regulation that, at least at the time, did not seriously disrupt much business as usual.

The original proposal to regulate trade practices, the Covington Bill, would have established an independent Interstate Trade Commission to investigative trade practices, but without administrative authority. Wilson hailed this measure as "no dangerous experiment." But Brandeis and many Rooseveltian progressives wanted an agency with more popular control. They feared that business would easily control an independent agency and objected to the fact that the bill defined unfair practices. They wanted the concept of unfair practices to remain undefined to be able to take into account any new practices that emerged in the future. The compromise legislation created an independent Federal Trade Commission, but with the power to issue cease and desist orders whenever it found unfair trade practices. It also did not define what these practices were, leaving the commission constantly able to contend with new issues and practices as the economy grew. The final compromise to the legislation was to give courts the power to review cease and desist orders so that this would be the place where unfair practices would ultimately be defined, not within the commission itself. A commission that lacked enforcement power, and depended on the whim of appointees and judicial oversight, disappointed Brandeis, who called the working of the commissioners in their first few years a "stupid administration."[24]

The proposed Clayton Anti-Trust Act brought the AFL squarely into the struggle over economic regulation. Business and courts had used the Sherman Anti-Trust Act to declare unions as a restraint of trade. Gompers now demanded that any new antitrust legislation give labor unions, farm, and cooperative organizations an antitrust exemption, as well as give them immunity from criminal prosecution and labor injunctions. Despite intense pressure from the AFL, the National Farmer's Union, and the railroad brotherhoods, Wilson rejected these demands as class legislation. He did agree to an amendment saying that unions were not per se conspiracies in the restraint of trade and allowing labor the right to "peaceful" and "lawful" actions. The final version of the legislation opened a door for labor organizing by specifying that "the labor of a human being is not a commodity." Yet, these provisions were so weak that business continued its virtually unchallenged assault on labor

---

24. Link, *The New Freedom*, 425–30, 435–42. Brandeis quoted in Painter, *Standing at Armageddon*, 278.

organizing through the 1920s. One congressman who had favored stronger antitrust measures bitterly complained that the new law was "a sort of legislative apology to the trusts, delivered hat in hand, and accompanied by assurances that no discourtesy is intended."[25]

Earlier histories of progressive economic regulation, and Wilson's role in it, tended to view the Federal Reserve, the FTC, and the Clayton Act as major victories for progressivism. Wilson's chief biographer concluded that the FTC was "hailed by progressives of all political faiths as the beginning of a new era in constructive federal regulation of economic life." Later studies have asked "constructive for whom" and have offered a different interpretation. Brandeis and LaFollette had been enthusiastic supporters of the FTC, but the final result disappointed them in not creating the means for more popular control. Brandeis had wanted a board with power to respond to public complaints. Instead he got a Wilsonian vision of a board that was "a counselor and friend to the business world."[26] Despite the nod to workers, the Clayton Act and FTC continued to impede union organizing and workers' activities, although such progressive reforms were the foundation on which the New Deal would build for expanding worker and union rights.

In the final analysis, the conservative, middle-of-the-road economic progressives won the day. Rather than destroying capitalism, they protected much of its emphasis on private property. By assuming that government needed to have a hand in directing its growth, new progressive regulation helped eradicate the cutthroat practices of big business and thereby achieved that aim. At the same time, however, economic progressivism of regulation "created a new bureaucratic nexus that linked corporate executives and public administrators in what later came to be called the fourth Branch of government." Events of later 1914 would bear out this conclusion. A global economic recession begun in late 1913 caused U.S. production to drop and unemployment to rise. By the summer of 1914, Wilson convened a meeting with businessmen and bankers to decide how to respond to these events. The result was a round of appointments of conservative businessmen and financiers to regulatory bodies such as the Interstate Commerce Commission and Federal Reserve Board. Wilson considered that enough legal barriers had been erected against unfair competitive practices so that now he and business could work together to advance the economy.[27] When war broke out in Europe in August 1914 Wilson became even less engaged with promoting more economic regulation. As war progressed, as subsequent chapters will explore, the fears of progressives such as Brandeis or old populists such as

---

25. Link, *The New Freedom*, 429–30. See also, Foner, *The Story of American Freedom*, 144. Quote from Painter, *Standing at Armageddon*, 277.

26. Link, *The New Freedom*, 442, is laudatory; Nancy Unger, *Fighting Bob LaFollette: The Righteous Reformer* (Chapel Hill: University of North Carolina Press, 2000), 231, discusses the disappointments of Brandeis, LaFollette, and other progressives.

27. See Dawley, *Changing the World*, 70, for quote; Dawley, *Struggles for Justice*, 148–49; Link, *The New Freedom*, 448–51; and Unger, *Fighting Bob LaFollette*, 231.

Bryan that a strong regulatory government would align itself with business would seem borne out.

THE REGULATORY ECONOMY AND THE PRESIDENCY

Theodore Roosevelt's presidency, combined with the first two years of Wilson's first administration, established the power of the presidency to direct the economy. Despite the fact that much of progressive economic reform came after his terms of office, Roosevelt had begun the process of breaking down the obstinacy of both the Senate and the Supreme Court toward regulation. It was not just that he inserted the presidency more forcefully into the picture, but how he did it that helped change the nature of the office. He was the first president to appeal directly to voters, using his "bully pulpit" to incite public pressure against Congress and the courts. He also took a "hands-on" approach dealing with Congress, brokering deals between Democrats and Republicans. Once Wilson assumed office, he was able to build on both of these techniques. Over issues of the Federal Reserve, Clayton, and the FTC, for example, he was in constant communication with congressional leaders of all factions. It was his mediation that produced the final version of each of these measures. He called leaders of the relevant congressional committees to meetings at the White House, he informed the press of what he intended to demand from Congress, he kept in contact with leaders of business and labor organizations.[28]

Wilson also clearly exercised the power of the presidency to shape a Supreme Court more amenable to his ideas. In 1916, he appointed Brandeis, described "as easily the leading progressive lawyer and most effective critic of big business and finance," to the Supreme Court. Even before a death of a justice gave Wilson this opportunity, he had signaled his intentions in a speech before the Gridiron Club:

> I have known of some judges who seemed to think that the Constitution was a strait jacket into which the life of the nation must be forced, whether it could be with a true regard to the laws of life or not. But judges of that sort have now gently to be led to a back seat and, with all respect for their years and lack of information, taken care of until they pass unnoticed from the stage. And men must be put forward whose whole comprehension is that the law is subservient to life and not life to law.

Conservatives, and bigots, were appalled that "a slimy fellow of this kind," and Jewish to boot, could be so chosen. The *New York Times* railed that "It need never be said, and cannot rightly be said that the court needs among its members some advocate of 'social justice.'" Former president William Howard Taft saw this as a direct attack on the Court's ability to uphold property rights. He called Brandeis "utterly unscrupulous" toward getting what he wanted and

---

28. Eric Rauchway, *Murdering McKinley: The Making of Theodore Roosevelt's America* (New York: Hill and Wang, 2003), 185–86, and Link, *The New Freedom*, chs. 13 and 14.

"of much power for evil."[29] The depth of hostility toward Brandeis, as well as the joy expressed over his nomination by progressives such as LaFollette, organized labor, and social justice progressives, demonstrate how controversial the changes undergone in the Progressive Era still were in 1916, and how bitterly elements of American society attempted to cling to their previous control of American society.

Brandeis' appointment also demonstrates why it is unrealistic to try to define *a* "progressivism," or even to try to limit it to a consistent ideology. Wilson was dead set against social welfare legislation of the kind that Brandeis ardently supported and would attempt to uphold if laws were ever passed. Yet, as his speech to the Gridiron Club exposed, Wilson did not believe in strict legal formalism, so his appointment of Brandeis contributed to the growing cause of legal realism that supported social legislation. In another example, Wilson consistently opposed any literacy test to control immigration as a betrayal of democratic principles of equal opportunity, but he had no feeling for racial equality. He refused to support the idea of an interracial National Race Commission to examine the status of African Americans and supported the segregation of the federal government in the face of vehement protests from social justice progressives. Oswald Garrison Villard, editor of *The Nation*, mourned this "lamentable betrayal of democratic principles." But Wilson countered with the progressive logic of regulation, saying that segregation "was for the benefit and the best interests of both races in order to overcome friction."[30] Moreover, Wilson was an advocate of states' rights, so he could stand aloof from interfering in lynching and segregation inside states under the claim of following the Constitution. Not until the 1954 Supreme Court decision of *Brown v. Board of Topeka, Kansas* that began to overturn *Plessy v. Ferguson* would federal law begin to trump states' rights in issues of discrimination. Wilson voted for woman suffrage in a referendum in his home state of New Jersey but refused to commit the Democratic Party to support a national amendment—a situation that would cause him much embarrassment during his second administration. Even liberal progressives could fall back on states' rights when a particular proposal, such as the federal abolition of child labor, struck them as giving national government too much power.

Even in its mildest form, economic progressivism raised into public discussion the idea of the rights of private property versus the public good. Once raised, it would not remain confined to "big" issues such as regulating railroads or the money supply but would permeate every aspect of American society. Nevertheless, for many progressives, economic regulation was not nearly enough reform. Upton Sinclair wrote *The Jungle* to inspire socialism.

---

29. Arthur S. Link, *Wilson: Confusion and Crises, 1915–1916* (Princeton, NJ: Princeton University Press, 1964), 324–27 and *Wilson: Campaigns for Progressivism and Peace, 1916–17* (Princeton, NJ: Princeton University Press, 1965), 141, for more on Taft's response.

30. Villard quoted in Link, *The New Freedom*, 250; Wilson, in Morton Keller, *Regulating a New Society: Public Policy and Social Change in America, 1900–1933* (Cambridge, MA: Harvard University Press, 1994), 255.

Instead, it inspired the Meat Inspection Act. This was a good thing—although a century later the problem of "downer" cows is still with us. But the divide between what Sinclair had hoped to accomplish and the lessons Roosevelt and other progressives took from his book explains much about which progressives ultimately controlled national economic progressivism and how they defined the public interest.

The Tuolumne River flows in a valley through Yosemite National Park in the Sierra Nevada Mountains of eastern California. At the turn of the last century, there was a natural meadow along the river in this valley called Hetch Hetchy. Prior to 1913, it was a quiet valley nestled between tall mountain peaks, traversed by a narrow river running through a deep gorge, and dotted with trees, waterfalls, and climbing trails. It was a peaceful, remote wilderness, filled with flora and fauna that beckoned hearty nature lovers to witness its unspoiled beauty. West of Yosemite, on the other side of the mountains and on the Pacific coast, was the growing city of San Francisco.

San Francisco residents, indeed much of the West, needed water and the government was seeking ways to provide it. In 1899, the U.S. Geological Survey (founded in 1879) surveyed Yosemite, which had been created as a national park in 1890, to determine whether the Hetch Hetchy site would be an appropriate place for a water reservoir. The survey decided that it was and that a dam and reservoir there could give San Francisco "an unfailing supply of pure water." Mayor James Phelan jumped at the possibility and secured from Congress permission to enter the park for the purposes of damming the river and flooding the valley.

Opponents who wanted to preserve this wilderness setting, led by John Muir and the Sierra Club, fought for the preservation of the area as it was and argued that there was a public interest in preserving nature for the future. San Francisco countered that the city desperately needed water if it were to progress. The opponents charged that flooding the valley would sacrifice a broad public interest to satisfy a narrow local interest. The official statement of the Sierra Club, issued in 1907, declared that "we do not believe that the vital interests of the nation at large should be sacrificed and so important a part of its National Park destroyed to save a few dollars for local interests." In 1908, the Secretary of the Interior James Garfield countered that supplying San Francisco with water was "the highest use to which water and available storage basins . . . can be put" and that this would serve a great public interest. Behind the arguments of both sides lurked economics. The Sierra Club charged that the city itself had admitted that it could find other sources of good water, but flooding Hetch Hetchy would be cheaper. Another opponent reminded Congress that there was economic value in scenery and urged it to save the valley for tourism. The city argued that its residents and businesses ought to be guaranteed affordable water.*

San Francisco won the battle. In 1913, Congress passed and President Wilson signed the Raker Act allowing the city to construct a dam and reservoir in the Hetch Hetchy valley. By 1923 the O'Shaughnessy Dam was completed, the valley was flooded, pipelines and power houses were in place, and water from the Hetch Hetchy reservoir, as well as electric power generated by the dam, were flowing into the city. Hetch Hetchy, depending on one's viewpoint, was either a victim, or a splendid example, of the Progressive Era.

---

*Holway R. Jones, *John Muir and the Sierra Club: The Battle for Yosemite* (San Francisco, 1965), quotes from 88, 95–96, and 99.

CHAPTER 8

The Competing
Publics of Conservation
and Environmentalism

[Reduction] fascinates the business man in America because
you can extract money out of the garbage.
                                    —MARY MCDOWELL, 1913

THE 1890 FEDERAL census discovered that there was no longer any census
tract inside the United States without white or black settlement. The frontier, Frederick Jackson Turner intoned in 1893, was closed. Turner believed that
the rugged individualism of the frontier experience, combined with the absence of nearby authority, had shaped the country's democratic values. With
the nation now settled, with the forces of law and order extended across the
continent, and with corporate industrialization the engine of economic development, Americans, Turner thought, would need to consider what values they
would apply to the future development of their democracy. At precisely the
same time, other Americans were arguing that consideration of the public interest and the common welfare were integral democratic values that had to replace individualism. This argument became embedded in questions about
how to deal with the natural environment and the built environment of an industrial economy.

THE CONSERVATION OF NATURE

Wilderness and the idea of nature had always played an important role in how
Americans thought about themselves. The clash between nature and the industrial machine was a trope played over and over again in the American
imagination. Scholars and writers such as Roderick Nash, Leo Marx, and

161

Henry David Thoreau, just to give a small sample, pondered how this clash led
to a dichotomous American identity that gloried in the magnificent natural
world of the continent, but that was also willing to destroy nature in the name
of economic progress.[1] This dichotomy became particularly evident as European settlement advanced across the western territories and artists became
fascinated by the landscape there. Paintings such as Albert Bierstadt's "Scene
in Yosemite Valley" and "Early Morning, Merced River," Thomas Hill's
"Yosemite Falls" and "Yosemite Valley," and John Mix Stanley's "Western
Landscape" portrayed the West as an unspoiled pastoral Eden. Bierstadt even
painted Hetch Hetchy valley with the sun streaming into the gorge and deer
pacifically grazing in the foreground. But relentless westward movement
brought the machine into the garden. Native Americans were ruthlessly dis-
possessed from the lands that they had used for survival, not development. In
1869 the transcontinental railroad linked the country and the race was on to
lay steel track all across the West. By the end of the century the iron horse dominated the landscape from St. Louis to San Francisco, from Phoenix to Seattle.
Settlers rushed to clear land for agriculture; urban residents clamored for
growth and progress; water was needed for the West's many arid areas as well
as for the growing cities; timber, gold, silver, copper, and other mineral resources were quickly mined for economic development.

In the rush to settle and develop the West, Congress gave away western
lands and mineral and grazing rights without developing any coherent policy.
It simply operated under the understanding that development was a good
thing. Unlike in Europe, where usable land had long ago been inhabited, settlement of the western areas of the United States proceeded simultaneously
with new ideas about progress and organization. By the late nineteenth century, groups of Americans organized to challenge unregulated development,
especially to consider how to conserve the natural environment. As with most
every issue in the Progressive Era, there were competing visions of what it
meant to conserve the natural environment.

1. Preservation or Conservation

John Muir was a naturalist and wilderness explorer who had settled in California in 1868. As a naturalist, he experienced firsthand the western landscape that
others only saw in artistic rendering and he was determined to put saving the
aesthetic beauty of wilderness areas ahead of exploiting them for economic
purposes. To this end, he founded the Sierra Club in 1892, dedicated to preserving the natural environment of the West and saving it from being overwhelmed
by westward settlement and development. Although Muir and the Sierra Club
were in the forefront of the preservation movement, they were not alone.
In 1904, the American Park and Outdoor Art Association and the American
League for Civic Improvement combined to form a new group, the American

---

1. Roderick Nash, *Wilderness and the American Mind* (New Haven, CT: Yale University Press,
1967); Leo Marx, *The Machine in the Garden: Technology and the Pastoral Ideal in America* (New York:
Oxford University Press, 1964; reprint, 2000); and Henry David Thoreau, *Walden: Or, Life in the
Woods* (Boston: Ticknor and Fields, 1854).

Civic Association. This organization united urban residents with professional landscape architects concerned about environmental preservation and urban beauty. The General Federation of Women's Clubs was also an active participant in the preservation movement from grand projects, such as opposing the destruction of Hetch Hetchy, to local efforts to build parks and preserve open land against development.[2]

Muir's work and writings attracted the attention of President Roosevelt. Roosevelt had earlier in life spent time in the West recovering from the deaths of his mother and first wife. That sojourn had imbued a lifelong appreciation for the life and landscape there and made him an eager listener to Muir's paeans to preservation. After Roosevelt spent three nights camping in Yosemite with Muir in 1903 he was enthralled:

> The first night was clear, and we lay down in the darkening aisles of the great Sequoia grove. The majestic trunks, beautiful in color and in symmetry, rose round us like the pillars of a mightier cathedral than ever was conceived even by the fervor of the Middle Ages. Hermit thrushes sang beautifully in the evening, and again, with a burst of wonderful music, at dawn.[3]

Even before the campout Roosevelt had been an advocate for western environmentalism. During his time in office he developed a reputation as the "conservation" president, creating five new national parks, a number of game and bird reserves, and withdrawing millions of acres from possible private economic use. He appointed a Public Lands Commission to study and formulate policy as to who could use, own, and develop public lands.

Early accounts of the conservation movement, as with many of the first interpretations of the Progressive Era, tended to see it as a struggle of the people against greedy corporations to control all the land and resources. The fact that the federal government had virtually given away millions of acres of western lands in the decades following the Civil War lent credibility to that story. The rhetoric used by Muir and the Sierra Club as they attempted to thwart projects such as the Hetch Hetchy reservoir helped perpetuate this idea, adding to it the twist of selfish local interests versus the broader public good. The so-called Ballinger-Pinchot controversy, when Chief Forester Gifford Pinchot fought against the plan of President Taft's Secretary of the Interior Richard Ballinger to make millions of acres of public land available to private leases, added to the picture of rapacious business interests being thwarted by public-regarding conservationists. Louis Brandeis, acting as lawyer for the Pinchot side in the affair, succeeded admirably in depicting Ballinger and his side as the "agents of rapacious capital." Yet Pinchot also clashed forcefully with Muir and the Sierra Club. There were thus two sides to the conservation movement: those taking

---

2. See Donald Worster, "John Muir and the Modern Passion for Nature," *Environmental History*, 10 (January 2005): 8–19, for a nice discussion of Muir's background. For the urban preservationists, see William H. Wilson, *The City Beautiful Movement* (Baltimore: Johns Hopkins University Press, 1989) and Maureen A. Flanagan, "The City Profitable, The City Livable: Environmental Policy, Gender, and Power in Chicago in the 1910s," *The Journal of Urban History*, 22 (January 1996): 163–90.

3. Theodore Roosevelt, *An Autobiography* (New York: Macmillan, 1913), 332–33.

the aesthetic approach—the preservationists—versus those who considered themselves practical conservationists. Writing to Horace McFarland, the president of the American Civic Association, about Hetch Hetchy, Pinchot declared that "the aesthetic side of conservation could not 'at this stage of the game . . . go ahead of the economic and moral aspects of the case.'" Congressman William Kent of California was more blunt. He told Pinchot that he believed that the Hetch Hetchy opponents were "misinformed nature lovers and power interests who are working through the women's clubs."[4]

2. Scientific Management and Rational Planning

As much as Roosevelt waxed ecstatic over the glories of sleeping under the cathedral spires of the Sequoias of Yosemite, his administration was firmly grounded in the reality of development through regulation. His Public Lands Commission, appointed in 1906, was a response to Pinchot's idea that public management of western lands controlled by the government was the most effective way to conserve nature and its resources. Pinchot and Roosevelt took it for granted that these lands would be settled and used. Just as Frederick Jackson Turner had considered the frontier a primary resource for the development of a democratic character, Roosevelt believed that American democracy could be maintained only if the United States carefully conserved the resources essential for economic progress.

Early in his career, Pinchot had gone to England, where he encountered specialists in forest management, a profession that did not exist in the United States at the time. He returned home determined to apply the lessons of scientific forestry that he had learned in Europe. The principal objective of this scientific forestry was to realize that forests were a crop. Forests were not to be viewed merely as things to be preserved, but rather they had to be managed to make them pay financially.[5] As head of the U.S. Forestry Service, Pinchot carried out his ideas so successfully that he can be viewed as primarily responsible for Progressive Era conservation policy. Decisions over the management of timber and water resources exemplify how conservation became a "market-based" endeavor. Pinchot convinced private landowners to work with his Bureau of Forestry, a division of the Department of Agriculture, in a private-public management relationship. Large lumber companies such as Weyerhaeuser and railroads such as the Northern Pacific owned millions of acres of timberland. With the western lands now occupied by farmers, ranchers, and extractive industries, Pinchot convinced these industries that it was

4. Nell Irvin Painter, *Standing at Armageddon: The United States, 1877–1919* (New York: W.W. Norton, 1987) for Brandeis; Samuel P. Hays, *Conservation and the Gospel of Efficiency: The Progressive Conservation Movement, 1890–1920* (Cambridge, MA: Harvard University Press, 1959), 194, for Pinchot and Kent quotes.

5. Brian Balogh, "Scientific Forestry and the Roots of the Modern American State: Gifford Pinchot's Path to Progressive Reform," *Environmental History*, 7 (April 2002): 198–225. For more on Pinchot, see Char Miller, *Gifford Pinchot and the Making of Modern Environmentalism* (Washington, D.C.: Island Press/Shearwater Books, 2001). See also, Pinchot's autobiography, *Breaking New Ground* (New York: Harcourt Brace, 1947).

in their best economic interests to adopt techniques of scientific management in order to conserve future supplies. Efficiency of management and conservation was the key progressive concept that Pinchot applied to natural resources. Pinchot's ideas were so appealing to lumbermen that they even raised the money to endow a chair in the Yale Forestry School, Pinchot's alma mater.[6]

Beyond conservation through regulation, providing water for the West was one of the Roosevelt administration's main concerns. Here too Pinchot was influential in applying scientific management based on a cost-benefit analysis. Even before he became president, Roosevelt had been influenced by Pinchot. Once in office, Roosevelt invited Pinchot to make suggestions. The new president then pronounced in favor of the irrigation strategies supported by Pinchot and Nevada Congressman Francis Newlands. Under this plan, irrigation would be financed by the federal government through a Reclamation Fund from proceeds of the sale of western public lands. Newlands believed that only federally directed irrigation could ensure the economic growth of Nevada and much of the rest of the West, and that only scientific expertise directed from Washington could prevent interstate rivalries from derailing irrigation projects. Congress passed the Newlands Reclamation Act in 1902 to carry out this plan. Once put into effect, the federal government was able to implement efficiency by centralizing control of natural resources formerly in the hands of overlapping state or local authorities. Although the federal government controlled public land sales, states had controlled water laws, and the different agencies under the Departments of Agriculture and Interior had competed with one another to implement policies. Newlands argued that this system did not work because there were too many conflicting interests at work. Moreover, Newlands was most concerned with providing water to farmers, and part of his plan was to facilitate the settlement of small farms rather than having western lands gobbled up by big farm interests.[7] The new law did not immediately function as smoothly as Newlands had hoped when the Reclamation Service created by the 1902 Act became part of the Interior Department in 1907. President Taft and his Secretary of the Interior Richard Ballinger reversed the Roosevelt administration's policy of withdrawing public lands containing water power sites from development without a permit. Ballinger preferred to cede water power sites to individual states to develop as they saw fit. This was one example of the friction that was subsequently labeled the Ballinger-Pinchot affair. Almost all of Ballinger's preferred policies flew in the face of Pinchot's idea of scientific management. Ballinger left office and was replaced in early 1912 by Walter L. Fisher, a Chicago progressive who

---

6. See Balogh, "Scientific Forestry," for Pinchot and market-based management and Hays, *Conservation and the Gospel of Efficiency*, 29–31, for Pinchot and lumber companies. But also see Hays, 173–74, about not underestimating the role of others in the conservation movement.

7. See Donald Pisani, *Water and American Government: The Reclamation Bureau, National Water Policy, and the West, 1902–1935* (Berkeley: University of California Press, 2002), 32, for the problem of overlapping authorities, and Hays, *Conservation*, 11–15 and 101. See also, Donald Worster, *Rivers of Empire: Water, Aridity, and the Growth of the American West* (New York: Oxford University Press, 1992).

favored the concept of scientific expertise. With the Interior Department again in the hands of a progressive manager, the conservation movement was then almost totally given over to scientific management and rational planning for the economic use of natural resources.[8]

Because by far the most controversial aspect of water control was damming of rivers and creating reservoirs, the following years provoked continuing conflict over the economic value of water and who should benefit. Two California projects besides Hetch Hetchy demonstrate how scientific water conservation in the Progressive Era privileged economic development. The first of these again involved a growing city's need for water, this time Los Angeles. Two hundred miles east of that city in the Sierra Nevada Mountains was the agricultural area of Owens Valley. Leading men in Los Angeles starting buying up land and water rights in the valley, planning to build an aqueduct to bring water in from the Owens River. At the same time, the Reclamation Service was studying plans for an irrigation project to water the valley. The service dropped its plan and L.A. developers were given the right to build the aqueduct, despite forceful protests by valley farmers.

The second conflict returns us to the northern Sierra Nevada, where the privately owned Great Western Power Company (GWP) proposed to build a hydroelectric dam on the Feather River and flood Big Meadows. The justification for this project, which would destroy the small town of Plattville and surrounding ranching areas, was to provide "economical power everlasting" for the San Francisco Bay area and simultaneously irrigate the Sacramento Valley. According to GWP's perspective, using the river in this way "will give its highest value for all purposes, will bring into active use all its great dormant resource, and will add enormously to the development of California." The livelihoods of the people of the Big Meadows area quickly lost out against these claims for economic progress and efficient use of nature.[9]

Despite voicing strong support for preserving rural life when he appointed a Commission on Country Life in 1908, Roosevelt approved the L.A. project over a competing proposal to irrigate the valley. And when the farmers of the Owens Valley tried to stop the aqueduct, their activities were met with force on the part of the government. There was little opposition to the Big Meadows project, and despite the strenuous protests of the Sierra Club and women's clubs, Hetch Hetchy was also dammed and flooded, with the approval of President Wilson. Progressive ideas of scientific management and efficiency drove the conservation movement. Engineers were captivated by the possibility of constructing dams that would serve multiple ends from one source of water. Rivers could be made navigable and flood control measures implemented, and this would provide both water for irrigation and hydroelectric power by ap-

---

8. Hays, *Conservation and the Gospel of Efficiency*, 160–71.

9. For Los Angeles and the Owens Valley, see Rebecca Ewan, *The Land Between: Owens Valley, California* (Baltimore: Johns Hopkins University Press, 2000). For the story of Big Meadows, see Jessica Teisch, "The Drowning of Big Meadows: Nature's Managers in Progressive-Era California," *Environmental History*, 4 (January 1999): 32–53, GWP quotes from 40 and 42.

plying efficiency through centralized planning and expert direction. "Unharnessed rivers flowing to the ocean without being used by man were deplored as wasteful," according to historian Samuel Hays, because "they could be made far more productive if brought under control by large-scale public works such as dams and reservoirs."[10]

Of course it did not hurt that in the cases of both the L.A. aqueduct and Hetch Hetchy, the person making the final decision had an interest in the relevant city. The engineer for the Reclamation Service who decided in favor of the aqueduct was also a consultant to the Los Angeles Water Commission, and Wilson's Secretary of the Interior Franklin Lane, who gave final permission for Hetch Hetchy, was San Francisco's former city attorney and a close friend of former Mayor Phelan. Progressive scientific management of land and resource use thus created a new type of interlocking directorate. Economic progressives had fought to dismantle these economic empires in private enterprise, yet they were creating a group of scientific managers who would move among positions both inside and outside of government exercising their professional expertise, much as businessmen had been doing with corporate growth. The scientific managers, for their part, claimed that this was the best means for serving the public good. By granting private companies such as GWP the rights to build on public lands, conservation policy also led to the creation of public utility monopolies. By 1912, for example, GWP and five other corporations already controlled almost 90 percent of California's commercial water power.[11]

Western conservation policies were inevitably linked to the development of federal government policy toward Indians. Parcels of land being fought over by various conservation forces, including in national parks and forests, were actually often occupied by Native Americans. For decades Native Americans and settlers had clashed over how to use the land. The American idea of progress taught that land had to be owned and cultivated in some manner that would yield economic advancement. The concept of private landownership was foreign to indigenous peoples; land for them was to yield enough for survival, not to be exploited for profit. Those conservationists who favored preservation admired the Indian approach to the land, and because they wrote about it, many Americans at the time developed a "romantic" vision of Indians and their way of life. Yet, the victorious conservationist vision was driven by the vision of expert use of land, so the development of Indian policy and thus Native American life often became a byproduct of conservation policy. Pinchot's plan for timberland, which Roosevelt approved, was to transform timbered lands on Indian reservations into national forests. As this plan proceeded, Indians lost control of those lands to the Forestry Service. Developing national parks as tourist sites deprived Indians of access to traditional hunting grounds and other

10. Samuel P. Hays, *Essays: Explorations in Environmental History* (Pittsburgh: University of Pittsburgh Press, 1998), 5.
11. Teisch, "The Drowning of Big Meadows," 43.

traditional means of survival. Forced off the lands that they had previously been able to use, having their lands opened up to tourists, and having nowhere else to go, groups of Indians in the West became economically dependent on the tourist trade for survival.[12] Thus, treaties and land allotments that had been forged in the nineteenth century were summarily abrogated so that conservationists such as Pinchot could manage land and its resources. The new commercial tourist trade—not the wilderness preserved for nature lovers that John Muir had envisioned—became another thriving economic enterprise in the West.

3. Conservation and Class

Native Americans were not the only residents on lands that the conservationists wanted to set aside for rational economic planning and for tourism. The drive to regulate and regularize land use also drove subsistence-level settlers off the lands and barred them from the hunting, fishing, and timber cultivation they had relied on to supplement their meager incomes. Such innovations were not confined to western lands. The Superior National Forest was established in 1909 in northern Minnesota, ostensibly to save its timber from being overharvested. Once it had been established, the forest was declared a state game preserve and game wardens and park rangers were employed (as they were elsewhere) to thwart now-illegal hunting and fishing. This was a severe blow to the people living on or near the forest who had been accustomed to living off the land. Many of these residents were either former miners who had been blacklisted after a particularly violent strike in 1907 or Indians from nearby reservation lands. On the other hand, the area's merchants and wealthier property owners quickly capitalized on the forest's appeal as a tourist site from which they could secure economic gain. Although it is generally very hard to find evidence for precisely how the lower classes thought about their land, oral interviews from the Superior Forest area suggest that both the European immigrants and Native Americans there thought of the land as something to be used for subsistence, not necessarily for economic profit. The Superior Forest is an example of how, by placing scientific land use policy throughout the country in the hands of government, the idea that land was for economic profit, not for living, was institutionalized into the American governing system.[13]

---

12. Hays, *Conservation and the Gospel of Efficiency*, 158. See also, Karl Jacoby, *Crimes Against Nature: Squatters, Poachers, Thieves and the Hidden History of American Conservation* (Berkeley: University of California Press, 2001), 151, for the Havasupai and Grand Canyon National Park as an example. See also, Arthur F. McEvoy, *The Fisherman's Problem: Ecology and Law in the California Fisheries, 1850–1980* (Cambridge, UK: Cambridge University Press, 1986), ch. 3, for his account of what happened to Indians there once they had to compete with commercial fishermen.

13. See Jacoby, *Crimes Against Nature* for the Adirondacks, Yellowstone, and Grand Canyon areas, and Benjamin Haber Johnson, "Conservation, Subsistence, and Class at the Birth of the Superior National Forest," *Environmental History*, 4 (January 1999): 80–99.

THE BUILT ENVIRONMENT

Imagine opening your daily newspaper and seeing a man and a chicken actually standing on water! This was the sight greeting readers of the *Chicago Daily News* in spring 1911. The water was the city's notorious Bubbly Creek, an offshoot of the south branch of the Chicago River located at the north end of the stockyards area. For decades, local industries dumped industrial wastes and raw sewage into the creek until it had become so crusted with sewage that it could be walked on by humans and fowl. The purpose of both pictures was to show that industry had been allowed to pollute the creek until it could no longer be seen as water. In the age well before digital manipulation, the photos were true. Not only was it unsightly to see a person standing on water, but one might wonder whether the chicken was going to be somebody's dinner after walking on sewage and how near the creek was to other sources of food. The paper also printed stories about the city's garbage dumps, accompanied by

A Menance to Health: Man Standing on the Encrusted Water of Bubbly Creek, Chicago (1911)
Source: *Chicago Daily News negatives collection*, DN-0056839. Courtesy of the Chicago Historical Society

photographs that conjure up modern-day images of poor, overcrowded cities in the developing world. One picture showed people walking through an enormous garbage dump on the city's west side, where light industry and housing intermingled. In other photos, people were digging through garbage dumps on the South Side, searching for anything salvageable, and children were shown playing in alleys filled with garbage, refuse, and the carcasses of dead animals.[14]

The situation in any other big city during the Progressive Era was similar. Bodies of water were polluted by industrial and human wastes. Thick black smoke poured out of chimneys. Poorer inhabitants lived crammed together in unhealthy, unsanitary tenements, with little access to clean water, eating and drinking suspect food. Rural life was not much better. Infant mortality rates remained higher there than in big cities, access to medical care was rare, and community and farm household sanitation were still pretty wretched.[15]

Settlement houses, social workers, and women's organizations had been attacking these problems for a number of years, in the process developing a new attitude toward the built environment of cities and towns, re-envisioning a common welfare fostered by a clean environment. The progressive environmental movement, however, was not confined to these groups and their ideas. It was driven by an amalgam of professional, technological, sociological, and civic and human values whose practitioners all believed in environmental determinism but saw different roads to achieving a good built environment. Historian Martin Melosi sees progressive environmentalism as motivated by a "shared view that a good society was 'efficient, organized, cohesive'" and "that the good in people would prevail if the evils produced by imperfect social, political, and physical circumstances were eliminated."[16] New professional urban planners studied how to design the built environment. Engineers believed that application of new technologies was the correct approach to environmentalism. Businessmen and politicians emphasized profitability and who should benefit and why and who should pay for environmental improvements. Laborers wanted to protect jobs. Women and their organizations collapsed the presumed divide between the private world of the home and public worlds of economics and public spaces.

Melosi's technological approach to environmentalism undervalues the economic rationales advanced for new environmental policies and problems that other progressives encountered in pursuing human-centered ideas of environmentalism. Although many of those progressives involved in environmental

---

14. See *Chicago Daily News*, April 19, 1911; October 13, 1913. There is an online searchable catalog of *Chicago Daily News* photo negatives that contains more than 55,000 images of photographs taken by the paper's photographers between 1902 and 1933. Most are of Chicago and its surrounding area: http://memory.loc.gov/ammem/ndlpcoop/ichihtml/cdnhome.html.

15. See descriptions in Lynne Curry, *Modern Mothers in the Heartland: Gender, Health, and Progress in Illinois, 1900–1930* (Columbus, OH: Ohio State University Press, 1999), 65–78. Her statistics on infant mortality were taken by U.S. death registration area, so they extended beyond Illinois.

16. Martin Melosi, *The Sanitary City: Urban Infrastructure in America from Colonial Times to the Present* (Baltimore: Johns Hopkins University Press, 2000), 106–07.

issues argued for reform of the environment based on social justice, in the end those progressives interested in technology, expertise, and economics drove much reshaping of the built environment. Arguments about the public health threats from water and air pollution, for example, lost salience as technology professionals came to define pollution as an economic problem in which property rights and economic waste and efficiency were the highest priority in decision making.[17]

1. Technology, Science, Professionalism, Business

During the Civil War, the U.S. Sanitary Commission had expressed grave concern for the state of the public health. Over the succeeding decades, the idea that there might be a public interest in protecting and fostering health grew alongside medical and scientific developments in understanding the sources of disease and its prevention. Sanitary engineers, medical and scientific researchers, and urban planners shared an interest in fashioning a more orderly built environment. Their expertise produced significant advances in building sewer systems, laying water pipes to bring water into houses and tenements, controlling the discharge of pollutants into bodies of water, and in finding better ways to collect and dispose of garbage and refuse.[18] At every step in these processes, professional expertise and cost efficiency guided developments in the built environment. In Chicago, engineer Lyman Cooley supervised construction and opening of the Ship and Sanitary Canal in 1900. The original idea for the canal was to carry waste away from the city's drinking water supply, Lake Michigan, and to clean up the Chicago River. Yet, Chicago's leaders quickly envisioned it as an economic waterway that would connect shipping from the city all the way to the Gulf of Mexico. Decades before, Chicago's leaders had guaranteed the city's economic prominence over its nearest rival, St. Louis, by ensuring that trains from every point in the country came into Chicago. Now they sought to keep that economic advantage with waterways. Even their support for enhancing the public health was driven by economic motivations as city leaders feared that periodic outbreaks of typhoid would discourage new business development.[19]

---

17. David Stradling, *Smokestacks and Progressives: Environmentalists, Engineers, and Air Quality in America, 1881–1951* (Baltimore: Johns Hopkins University Press, 1999), 5, ch. 6. See also, Flanagan, "The City Profitable, The City Livable."

18. John Duffy, *The Sanitarians: A History of American Public Health* (Urbana: University of Illinois Press, revised edition, 1990) and *A History of Public Health in New York City*, 2 vol. (New York: Russell Sage Foundation, 1968–74); and Melosi, *The Sanitary City* and relevant essays in Melosi, ed., *Garbage in the Cities: Refuse, Reform, and the Environment, 1880–1980* (College Station: Texas A&M University Press, 1981) and *Effluent America: Cities, Industry, Energy, and the Environment* (Pittsburgh: University of Pittsburgh Press, 2001).

19. Harold L. Platt, "Chicago, the Great Lakes, and the Origins of Federal Urban Environmental Policy," *The Journal of the Gilded Age and Progressive Era*, 1 (April 2002): 122–23, and Carolyn Shapiro-Shapin, "'A Really Excellent Scientific Contribution': Scientific Creativity, Scientific Professionalism, and the Chicago Drainage Case, 1900–1906," *Bulletin of the History of Medicine*, 71 (Fall 1997): 389–90.

Residents of St. Louis fought against the canal, convinced that the Chicago sewage dumped into it would flow into the Illinois River and downstream to their city. As soon as the canal was opened, St. Louis brought legal action against Chicago. Universities had pioneered in new sanitation and medical discoveries, as they had in developing new social and economic theories. Both Chicago and St. Louis now brought in scientific "experts" from MIT, Washington University, the University of Chicago, and Northwestern University to testify. The question that most occupied these scientists, and around which the case revolved, was the best means for purifying water of bacteria. The new professionals saw Chicago's canal project as a chance to test their theories, publicize them, and then compete to have them accepted as scientific truth.[20]

Scientific advice, technological know-how, and economic impact thereafter were the triple benchmarks for much environmental decision making. Among the defects of this emphasis on expertise was that it crowded out other concerns. When the germ theory moved to the forefront of concerns about pure water, for instance, water polluted in other ways was ignored. Industrial wastes flowed through the rivers of every industrial city, but because the professionals did not connect this always with bacteria, moves to clean up these waterways slowed down. Chicago's Bubbly Creek was horribly polluted in 1911 but ignored because it did not affect drinking water, nor flood directly into basements. When concerns over such wastes did finally become a public concern, technology and cost-benefit analysis tended to drive policy. In Connecticut public agitation over the dumping of industrial wastes into the state's rivers resulted in 1917 in the creation of a Board of Industrial Wastes to recommend solutions. The board included two representatives from manufacturing and two engineers, along with two members of the state Board of Health, but only one member to represent the public. Not surprisingly, the board's decisions were the result of economic and expert recommendations. Manufacturers had used the threat of "economic peril" to thwart any measures they thought too stringent and the board sought "profitable means of reducing pollution." In the impasse over this issue, the board ultimately settled for hoping that "technology and science could provide a means of transcending a potentially intractable conflict between economic development and a clean environment."[21]

Professional planners also competed to have their expertise recognized in the contestation over the built environment. Planners believed preserving nature in the city was a key element to fostering public health. Almost every city plan advanced in the Progressive Era featured large, open public spaces, carefully spaced housing, destruction of unsightly and insalubrious areas, systems of parks and boulevards, and zoning to separate business and residential areas

20. Shapiro-Shapin, "A Really Excellent Scientific Contribution," 387–88 and 396–400. See also, Melosi, *The Sanitary City* and *Garbage in Cities*; Stradling, *Smokestacks and Progressives*; Robert Dale Grinder, "The Battle for Clean Air: The Smoke Problem in Post-Civil War America," in *Pollution and Reform in American Cities, 1870–1930*, Martin V. Melosi, ed. (Austin: University of Texas Press, 1980); and Harold L. Platt, "Invisible Gases: Smoke, Science, and the Redefinition of Environmental Policy in Chicago, 1900–1920," *Planning Perspectives*, 10 (1995): 67–97.

21. John T. Cumbler, "Conflict, Accommodation, and Compromise: Connecticut's Attempt to Control Industrial Wastes," *Environmental History*, 5 (July 2000): 314–35, quotes from 326 and 327.

of the city. Frederick Law Olmsted is best known for laying out Central Park, but he also created planned suburbs such as Riverside, Illinois. Along with Olmsted, and then his sons, men such as John Nolen, Harland Bartholomew, and George Kessler were hired by cities as diverse as Bridgeport, Connecticut, Lansing, Michigan, and San Diego, California, to provide them with a comprehensive plan for city growth. Cities generally either adopted modified versions of such plans or rejected them altogether. Businessmen wanted plans for more economic development rather than open park lands preserving nature. Opponents of the proposed San Diego plan argued that "city planning was a cosmetic to beautify the city at the cost of its economic prosperity" and satirized the backers of such planning as "geraniums."[22]

2. Environmental Justice

As good progressives, planning experts, sanitary engineers, and scientific researchers all couched their findings and recommendations in the language of serving the public good. Urban planners believed that scientific application of their ideas to the built environment could solve human needs. "Intelligent city planning," John Nolen said in 1909, " is one of the means toward a better utilization of our resources, toward the application of the methods of private business to public affairs, toward efficiency, toward a higher individual and collective life."[23] Many urban residents and social justice reformers countered that the primary concern for a better built environment ought to be to guarantee the health of all citizens. Professional experts were treated to a profound skepticism that they were more interested in promoting their theories than in safeguarding human health. A St. Louis newspaper put to verse doubts that running water cleansed bacteria and thus that the sewage from Chicago's Ship and Sanitary Canal would not pollute St. Louis waters:

> Of deaths at the dawn and the twilight,
> Of sickness at morning and noon,
> We'd learn, if the current could whisper
> Of germs that will poison us soon!
> Of danger and death and destruction,

---

22. For a broad overview of urban planning, see Stanley K. Schultz, *Constructing Urban Culture: American Cities and City Planning, 1800–1920* (Philadelphia: Temple University Press, 1989). For planning in specific cities, see Eric Sandweiss, *St. Louis: The Evolution of an American Urban Landscape* (Philadelphia: Temple University Press, 2001); Patricia Burgess, *Planning for the Private Interest: Land Use Controls and Residential Patterns in Columbus, Ohio, 1900–1970* (Columbus: Ohio State University Press, 1994); Bruce R. Stephenson, *Visions of Eden: Environmentalism, Urban Planning, and City Building in St. Petersburg, Florida, 1900–1995* (Columbus: Ohio State University Press, 1997); Robert K. Fairbank, "Rethinking Urban Problems: Planning, Zoning, and City Government in Dallas, 1900-1930," *Journal of Urban History*, 25 (September 1999): 809-37; and John Hancock, "'Smokestacks and Geraniums': Planning and Politics in San Diego," in *Planning the Twentieth-Century American City*, Mary Corbin Sies and Christopher Silver, eds. (Baltimore: Johns Hopkins University Press, 1996), 172–73.

23. Stanley K. Schultz and Clay McShane, "To Engineer the Metropolis: Sewers, Sanitation, and City Planning in the Late Nineteenth Century," *The Journal of American History*, 65 (September 1978): 389–411, Nolen quoted on 389.

Of weariness, worry and woe,
We'd hear, like the damning of demons,
If the waters could speak as they flow!

Suspicions about who would benefit from environmental solutions also occasioned skepticism, as seen in the dry comment of Mary McDowell that began this chapter. McDowell and a group of women reformers had traveled to Germany to study its method of disposing of garbage and refuse by incineration. Returning to Chicago, McDowell then presented her findings supporting incineration as the most healthful means to dispose of garbage. Chicago businessmen, for their part, cited expert opinion on reduction as a safe and sanitary method. The reduction method produced marketable byproducts for whomever held the franchise on garbage disposal—hence McDowell's comment that one could make money out of garbage. The reduction method also produced the huge refuse dumps that the *Daily News* had photographed. McDowell and many social settlement workers believed that these sites bred disease in the surrounding areas and also drew poor Chicagoans into them in search of anything salvageable, thereby endangering even further the health of the poor. Reduction, she believed, would perpetuate such areas and do little to enhance the health of the city. Chicago's political leaders tried to finesse the issue by assuring the supporters of incineration that they would tighten the regulations on the reduction company's franchise.[24]

Progressive reformers such as McDowell did not reject scientific expertise; rather they wanted it used to benefit people's needs and health first. Dr. Alice Hamilton, for example, was an expert in bacteriology and industrial health who taught at both Northwestern and Harvard Universities. She applied her scientific expertise differently from the men who had consulted for Chicago and St. Louis on the canal case. Hamilton was not interested in the scientific discovery per se so much as using discoveries in bacteriology to benefit the public health directly. During a 1902 typhoid outbreak in Chicago she and Jane Addams found the typhoid bacillus in the city's water supply and presented this as evidence that neither the Ship and Sanitary Canal nor the city's overall engineering system had cleaned up the water. The two women also discovered a circle of institutionalized corruption surrounding the city's water pollution ordinances. City engineers, politicians, health inspectors, and property owners had colluded in not enforcing these ordinances in poor neighborhoods. They uncovered a secret log, called the "stay book," kept by city officials that listed hundreds of complaints against the health department that had never been pursued as a "courtesy" to anyone with political connections. For environmental justice progressives such as Hamilton and Addams, depending solely on applying professional expertise to reform the built environment would always breed evasion and corruption, unless it were motivated by a desire to provide social justice. Preservation of

---

24. Refrain reprinted in Shapiro-Shapin, "A Really Excellent Scientific Contribution," 401. For McDowell, see Maureen A. Flanagan, *Seeing with Their Hearts: Chicago Women and the Vision of the Good City, 1871–1933* (Princeton, NJ: Princeton University Press, 2002), 96–98.

a public health, according to many social justice progressives, had to be the first purpose of environmentalism.[25]

The environmental progressivism of many women reformers differed in another important way from that of professional planners and male scientific experts. These women explicitly connected the inside and outside environments. The municipal housekeeping metaphor that they applied to justify their public work included their desire to make the household benefit from progressive reform. Ellen Swallow Richards, the first woman admitted to MIT, was a trained scientist. In 1884 she was appointed an instructor there in sanitary chemistry, where she worked to develop better sanitary conditions for food and clean water. She was instrumental in developing sewage treatment and promoting food inspection laws in Massachusetts. But her deepest concern was to raise American consciousness about the need for sanitation inside the household in order to foster public health. She pioneered what was then called the home ecology movement (later home economics) to advocate "scientific housekeeping." Private and public were explicitly connected when she worked with the Boston Women's Education and Industrial Union to establish public kitchens that by 1912 were serving lunch to almost 10,000 public school children daily in that city's South End.[26]

Both Hamilton and Richards applied their expertise toward achieving end results that were more appreciated by groups of women than professional men. Rural women used Richards' ideas to demand better public health standards in their communities and inside their own households. Illinois farm women challenged the Department of Agriculture policy of supporting the modernization of outdoor agricultural work and not that of household modernization such as indoor plumbing and electrification. They also demanded better education in, and access to, health care, especially for their children. As early as 1898, Illinois farm women belonging to Farmers' Institutes had organized themselves into a separate department of "household science." Their discussions and investigations focused on domestic hygiene, child nutrition, and community and household sanitation. These were the same ideas that urban women were bringing to their progressive crusades against smoke pollution and garbage dumps and that Richards was promoting through her household environmentalism. The built environment for these progressive women was inside the home as well as outside; one could not flourish without the good of the other being taken care of. Public attention and public

25. Barbara Sicherman, *Alice Hamilton: A Life in Letters* (Cambridge, MA: Harvard University Press, 1984). See also, Harold L. Platt, "Jane Addams and the Ward Boss Revisited: Class, Politics, and Public Health in Chicago, 1890–1930," *Environmental History*, 5 (April 2000): 203–09. Schultz and McShane, "To Engineer the Metropolis," 408, acknowledged this type of collusion as a general urban problem.

26. For Richards, see Margaret Rossiter, "'Women's Work' in Science, 1880–1910," *Isis*, 71 (September 1980): 381–98; Dolores Hayden, *The Grand Domestic Revolution: A History of Feminist Designs for American Homes, Neighborhoods, and Cities* (Cambridge, MA: Harvard University Press, 1981), 150–62; and Daphne Spain, *How Women Saved the City* (Minneapolis: University of Minnesota Press, 2001), 187–88.

funding had to be directed toward both and not just given on the basis of economic development.[27]

Because women's work on public health environmentalism in the Progressive Era did not fit well into the "expertise" concept as defined by male progressives, most scholars of progressivism marginalized Richards' ideas about home ecology and "scientific housekeeping" as just about housework, not real environmentalism. They similarly dismissed the "municipal housekeeping" work of progressive women. But these women were progressive pioneers in the idea that public health decisions had to be made on the basis of environmental justice, not merely, or even primarily, on economics, and in understanding that private and public spaces could not be separated from one another in the modern world. Rural women, encouraged by educated health reformers, including the Children's Bureau after its founding, also adopted these ideas, so this was not merely an urban middle-class movement. Rural women participated actively in the so-called "Better Baby Contests" that were often held at state and country fairs. The purpose of these demonstrations was to encourage better infant health practices and to provide advice about health and hygiene. Across the southern Appalachians, rural women, including those living in mining camps, flocked to Baby Week contests to acquire information on child care, home hygiene, and better sanitary practices. Mary Breckinridge, a relative of Sophonisba, founded the Frontier Nursing Service in Kentucky that she kept funded through donations from women's clubs around the country.[28]

Rural southern African American women, were organized into the home demonstration department of the Negro Cooperative Extension Service. This initiative was launched by Booker T. Washington to function like the Cooperative Extension Work in Agriculture and Home Economics, created by the 1914 Smith-Lever Act that was benefitting mainly white Americans. The women of the home demonstration department cultivated home gardens, planted trees and flowers, and disseminated information on soil conservation and scientific housekeeping techniques throughout the South. They taught one another in their local organizations, as did middle-class white women in the North, and they educated each other in these techniques at institutions such as the Hampton Institute. These women applied principles of efficiency and scientific management to the work of rural African American women, but always from their

---

27. For Illinois farm women, see Curry, *Modern Mothers in the Heartland*, 77–84.

28. Ibid., 101–104. Curry notes the discomfort of the Children's Bureau with calling these "contests" as if they might be akin to livestock competitions and whether these contests were looked upon as part of eugenics. But she also notes (104–05) that she has found evidence that most of those involved were concerned more "with promoting lifesaving health and hygiene measures than 'selective human breeding.'" Sandra Barney, "Maternalism and the Promotion of Scientific Medicine During the Industrial Transformation of Appalachia, 1880–1930," *NWSA Journal*, 11 (Fall 1999): 68–92. For a social history of the germ theory and its applicability to these issues, especially that the home ecology movement was not intended to affect just the private world, see Nancy Tomes, *The Gospel of Germs: Men, Women, and the Microbe in American Life* (Cambridge, MA: Harvard University Press, 1998).

perspective that the health and hygiene of family, home, and community were all important for maintaining and advancing public health.[29]

In other cases, African American women stepped in when racial prejudice left their communities outside other organized progressive health campaigns. In Atlanta, black residents were more than twice as likely to die from tuberculosis as white residents of the city, but their health needs were less likely to be met. Lugenia Burns Hope of the Neighborhood Union led African American women in an antituberculosis movement. In 1914 Hope allied with white Atlanta public health worker Rosa Lowe to construct a citywide public health program that would benefit blacks as well as whites. Hope and Lowe both "shared belief that physical health was fundamental to citizenship." In Richmond, Virginia, the death rate of black residents from tuberculosis was also twice that of their white neighbors, yet the city's public health administration and its doctors ignored the black community and focused on treating the individual white tuberculosis patient. On the other hand, the white public health nurses in that city viewed public health as a social welfare issue, not one of individual health, so they took it upon themselves to minister more to black residents of the city than to white residents.[30]

In addition to working to better public health among African Americans in Atlanta, Lugenia Burns Hope saw this as an opportunity to shatter the prevailing myth of black genetic inferiority. She hoped to prove that if given proper share of health care and other public environmental goods, they would be as resistant to tuberculosis as any other group of Americans. Playing an active role in these health matters was essential for African American women because the organized antituberculosis campaign was targeting both African Americans and Mexican migrants as genetically inferior breeders of tuberculosis. By the 1920s, Los Angeles city officials, for example, were actively campaigning to expel any Mexicans with tuberculosis from the city as both genetically inferior and an economic drain.[31]

Frederick L. Hoffman, vice-president of the Prudential Insurance Company, was simultaneously working to discriminate against African Americans in life insurance plans. Hoffman's use of statistics to try to prove his theories was certainly part of progressivism. But so too were the challenges that he

---

29. Dianne D. Glave, "'A Garden So Brilliant with Colors, So Original in Its Design': Rural African American Women, Gardening, Progressive Reform, and the Foundation of an African American Environmental Perspective," *Environmental History*, 8 (July 2003): 395–411. For rural Tennessee women, black and white, and home improvement campaigns, see Mary S. Hoffschwelle, *Rebuilding the Rural Southern Community: Reformers, Schools, and Homes in Tennessee* (Knoxville: University of Tennessee Press, 1998).

30. Sarah Mercer Judson, "Civil Rights and Civic Health: African American Women's Public Health Work in Early Twentieth Century Atlanta," *NWSA Journal*, 11 (Fall 1999): 93–111, esp. 97–99, and Steven J. Hoffman, "Progressive Public Health Administration in the Jim Crow South: A Case Study of Richmond, Virginia, 1907–1920," *The Journal of Social History*, 35 (Fall 2001): 177–94, 183–86 for public health nurses and tuberculosis.

31. Emily K. Abel, "From Exclusion to Expulsion: Mexicans and Tuberculosis in Los Angeles, 1914–1940," *Bulletin of the History of Medicine*, 77 (Winter 2003): 823–49.

was manipulating data to prove a theory he had already developed.[32] The conclusions of Hoffman and other health officials that the inbred weakness of certain groups made them more susceptible to disease or a higher risk for life insurance policies were challenged by arguments of social justice reformers that social conditions were responsible for higher levels of disease and illness among groups of people, not genetic inferiority.

Yet, as often was the case in the Progressive Era, statistical data proffered by male experts overrode the counterarguments of female progressives. So despite women's environmental reform efforts, the voices of those male progressives who approached environmentalism in terms of economics, inefficiency, and jobs eclipsed those of environmental justice advocates. In Birmingham, Alabama, businessmen succeeded in weakening air pollution ordinances by finding engineers and physicians to testify in their favor. The former produced reports concluding that antismoke ordinances were not practical; the latter denied that smoke was a health hazard. When reformers in Chicago campaigned to electrify railroads to eliminate smoke pollution from coal-burning engines, the railroad executives who resisted were supported by locomotive firemen who feared loss of jobs. The gender dimension of this issue was made clear in one fireman's declaration that "this looks to me like a woman's ordinance."[33] A bulletin of the Department of the Interior in 1912 encapsulated the economic perspective of the Progressive Era smoke pollution issue. It defined problems caused by urban smoke as economic waste, damage to buildings, loss of light, but not as a direct threat to people's health. It congratulated Chicago for seeing smoke pollution as an engineering problem and saw no problem with the ordinances of Denver and Louisville, for example, that allowed smoke pollution if there were "no known" practical devices to prevent it.[34]

Environmental justice reformers definitely made some headway toward their vision of a good environment. Without their efforts, the overall health of Americans would have continued to deteriorate. Poor and minority Americans would have continued to suffer even more disproportionately from the effects of environmental pollution than they did. But in the end there is no denying that theirs were the minority voices—not in numbers, possibly, but certainly in the realm of developing public policy. Male experts and the economics of environmental policy took precedence over environmental justice. The conclusion that "as cities turned toward a technological solution to the air

---

32. Beatrix Hoffman, "Scientific Racism, Insurance, and Opposition to the Welfare State: Frederick L. Hoffman's Transatlantic Journey," *Journal of the Gilded Age and Progressive Era*, 2 (April 2003): 150–90.

33. Stradling, *Smokestacks and Progressives*, ch. 6, for both the Birmingham and Chicago efforts, quote, 122. See also, Stradling, "Dirty Work and Clean Air: Locomotive Firemen, Environmental Activists, and Stories of Conflict," *The Journal of Urban History*, 28 (November 2001): 35–54, for the example of Cincinnati in the early 1920s and for his conclusion that, particularly for working-class men, "urban space remained largely about work," 47. Despite Stradling's contention otherwise, this also applied generally to middle-class men.

34. Department of the Interior, U.S. Bureau of Mines, "City Smoke Ordinances and Smoke Abatement," *Bulletin*, 49 (1912).

pollution problem, the issue of economic waste, both for consumers of coal and victims of soot, gained in salience" is correct.[35] The only comfort that proponents of environmental justice might have taken if they could see into the future was that once raised, ideas about environmental justice did not disappear entirely from the public discourse.

---

35. David Stradling and Peter Thorsheim, "The Smoke of Great Cities: British and American Efforts to Control Pollution, 1860–1914," *Environmental History*, 4 (January 1999): 6–31, quote, 21.

In 1913, New York City was dancing to new tunes. The turkey trot, the bunny hug, the Texas Tommy, and more were the rage of public dance halls, cabarets, and ballrooms. The staid waltz of the later nineteenth century in which the partners' bodies did not touch—six inches apart was the prescribed distance to be maintained—and prescribed steps were the only allowable movements had given way to rhythm and romance. Dance partners whirled, twirled, and hugged. They shook their shoulders and wiggled their hips. They took "advantage of the dances to embrace." The new dance craze crossed all sectors of society. The younger generation, as might be expected, was its prime enthusiast. "We went dancing . . . every night except Monday. . . . Because . . . the dance hall was closed on Monday," one working woman recalled of her new urban experience. For the working class, dancing and other forms of cheap public entertainment provided welcome relief from long, arduous workdays. Public dancing also freed them from supervision. But middle-class and wealthy young people, married couples as well as unmarried singles, eagerly joined in this new public nightlife.

Other forms of new urban mass entertainment were definitely on the rise and bridging class in popular culture that same year. Woodrow Wilson had barely been inaugurated when he threw out the first ball in a Washington/New York baseball game in early April 1913. This was the first game the New York team played under its new name: the "Yankees." The first feature movie on sexuality was released that year: *Traffic in Souls* was about prostitution and "white slavery." Within a year, New York City would open the first movie "palace," the Strand in Times Square, seating more than 3,000. Two years later Wilson also had the distinction of being the first president to have a moving picture shown in the White House. Unfortunately, the picture he chose was the blatantly racist *Birth of a Nation*.

In 1913, the International Exhibition of Modern Art, popularly known as the "Armory Show," opened in Manhattan. There the Cubist paintings, especially Marcel Duchamp's "Nude Descending a Staircase No. 2," shocked, outraged, and fascinated visitors accustomed to admiring the Grand Masters or landscape artists. Even the paintings of Henri Matisse did not escape the wrath of art critics. But the world of art was changing, as was that of recreation. Stylized and formalized art was giving way to new forms but also to new audiences. The Armory Show inaugurated changing ideas about high culture. It was no longer just to be admired; it was to be marketed and consumed. Old Masters could only be purchased by the very wealthy. The work of up-and-coming artists could be purchased by the middle class. The artists themselves participated in this new "mass-marketing" of culture.*

*Lewis Erenberg, *Steppin' Out: New York Nightlife and the Transformation of American Culture, 1890–1930* (Westport, CT: Greenwood Press, 1981), 148–51; Joan M. Jensen, "'I'd Rather Be Dancing': Wisconsin Women Moving On," *Frontiers: A Journal of Women Studies*, 22:1 (2001): 1–20, quote from 1; Martin Green, *New York 1913: The Armory Show and the Paterson Strike Pageant* (New York: Macmillan, 1988).

CHAPTER 9

⊸◈⊷

Money, Morals, and Modernity
The Consumer Society

> The difference between the theater and the big amusement
> park is the difference between the Sunday-school and the
> Sunday-school picnic.
>
> —FREDERIC THOMPSON, 1908

THE LATE NINETEENTH century had been the era of capital goods production: steel rails, railroad cars and mass transit cars, manufacturing and industrial plants, and large machinery to run the mills and plants of an industrial economy, such as those that had been exhibited at the 1893 Fair. Yet, by the turn of the twentieth century, infrastructure developments such as railroads, bridges, sewer and water pipes, telephone lines, and street railway lines were in place in many areas of the country, and the western lands were settled. Railroad building still went on, of course, and cities kept expanding as in-migration continued. New housing, bridges, roads, and sewer and water systems were in constant demand, and upgrading production always required new and better machinery. Yet, the capital goods market was reaching a critical saturation point. It could not by itself keep the economy growing. There were only so many new railroad cars or new steel plants to be needed every year. Consumption of high culture and low culture was thus part of the changing capitalist economy of the Progressive Era. By the first decade of the twentieth century, big cities had established glamorous department stores for the upscale, presumably female, consumer. The motto of Marshall Field and Company in Chicago was "Give the Lady What She Wants." Along with a steady stream of new fashions, factories were churning out new household appliances. Vacuum cleaners and washing machines were available to all who could afford them. The growth of the mail-order catalog stores, Montgomery Ward and Sears and Roebuck, offered small town and rural Americans a chance to participate in this consumption. New consumer items were not just for inside the house. In 1908, Sears and Roebuck began marketing a mail-order house. In 1909, the Model T rolled off Henry Ford's production line and by the end of the second decade of the century, Americans owned more than eight million automobiles.

Continued economic growth through the Progressive Era would come to depend on production and regulation of a new consumer goods economy. Who produced consumer goods and how, who bought them, who consumed the new forms of leisure, how mass consumption was changing the nature of both public and private relations—these were all concerns for progressives. Emerging as it did alongside so many other changes made this shifting economic world seem dangerous but also made it a perfect context for promoting reforms. For some progressives, Theodore Dreiser's *Sister Carrie* was a cautionary tale about what might happen to young women lured to the city by promises of materialism and popular entertainment. When Carrie went to look for work in a Chicago department store, she

> passed along the busy aisles, much affected by the remarkable displays of trinkets, dress goods, stationery, and jewelry. . . . She could not help feeling the claim of each trinket and valuable upon her personally. . . . There was nothing there which she could not have used—nothing which she did not long to own. The dainty slippers and stockings, the delicately frilled skirts and petticoats, laces, ribbons, hair-combs, purses, all touched her with individual desire.

Carrie's experience with shoppers who could afford all these items and the shop girls selling them also filled her with envy, ultimately transforming her pursuit of a living into a quest for the good life of acquisition, one in which family and social responsibility meant virtually nothing.[1] Consumption and leisure, many progressives also worried, were producing new opportunities for vice, undermining public morality, and putting young women in danger in work and leisure activities. But many of them also perceived that rising consumption could provide the perfect opportunity for convincing Americans that all workers had to be accorded rights and protections by society and government. All of these fears and hopes were intertwined in the progressives' approach to dealing with the new consumer society.

CONSUMPTION AND LABOR

The National Consumers' League led by Florence Kelley immediately recognized the connections between labor and the new consumerism. When Kelley became the league's first national secretary in 1899, she laid out the organization's vision and purpose. "The underlying principles of the Consumers' League are simple," she declared. "They are partly economic and partly moral." "The first principle of the League is universality," she went on to say, and it is worth recounting in her own words what she meant by this principle:

> It recognizes the fact that in a civilized community every person is a consumer . . . we all make daily and hourly choice as to the bestowal of our means. As we do so,

---

1. For overviews of the growth of a consumer culture, see *The Culture of Consumption: Critical Essays in American History, 1880–1980*, Richard Wightman Fox and T.J. Jackson Lears, eds. (New York: Pantheon, 1983). Dreiser, *Sister Carrie*, ch. 3.

we help to decide, however unconsciously, how our fellow-men shall spend their time in making what we buy. . . . The Consumers' League then acts upon the proposition that the consumer ultimately determines all production, since any given article must cease to be produced if all consumers ceased to purchase it.

The NCL turned to woman power to confront this aspect of the changing economy. Using rationale similar to that which later produced the 1960s sloganeering "if you're not part of the solution, you're part of the problem," the NCL urged women as the main shoppers for their families not to frequent department stores that exploited their female employees. But it also announced that it would investigate how specific consumer goods were produced and publicize the results so that shoppers could avoid buying from certain manufacturers. Making explicit the connection between consumption and women, Kelley announced that its first investigation would be into the manufacture of women's "white muslin underwear."[2]

By 1904, there were sixty-four leagues in twenty states. The leagues had 30,000 members by 1913. As the NCL pursued its work it also sought to involve consumers directly in a campaign for a minimum wage for female workers. The organization connected wage labor with consumption and urged a collectivist response by proposing that a board of employers, workers, and "representatives of [the] consuming public" be established to set wages. The NCL created a "grassroots phalanx of consumers [who] became thoroughly implicated in the conditions under which goods were produced."[3]

The coal strikes of 1902 and 1913 also forced Americans to think about the connection between consumption and labor. It was one thing if laborers in an industry peripheral to mass consumption—for example, cigar makers—struck and short supply increased the price. It was quite another to weather long strikes in an industry that consumers depended on for daily life. As prices for coal rose dramatically in both strikes, consumers realized that they were not removed from the problems of workers. They began to demand government intervention in the relations between employers and employees. They were also becoming convinced by organizations such as the NCL that unless workers received decent wages, there would be continuous labor strife.

But the NCL did not achieve its goal of consumer participation in wage decisions. Other progressives urged different solutions and they had more political clout than the NCL. The American Association of Labor Legislation focused on new legislation such as worker compensation and workplace regulation. By

---

2. Florence Kelley, "Aims and Principles of the Consumers' League," *The American Journal of Sociology*, 5 (November 1899): 289–304, quote, 289–90. See also, Kathryn Kish Sklar, "Two Political Cultures in the Progressive Era: The National Consumers' League and the American Association for Labor Legislation," in *U.S. History As Women's History: New Feminist Essays*, Linda Kerber, Alice Kessler-Harris, and Kathryn Kish Sklar, eds. (Chapel Hill: University of North Carolina Press, 1995), 36–62, and "The White Label Campaign of the National Consumers' League, 1898–1918," in *Getting and Spending: European and American Consumer Societies in the Twentieth Century*, Susan Strasser, Charles McGovern, and Matthias Judt, eds. (Cambridge, UK: Cambridge University Press, 1998), 17–36.

3. Sklar, "Two Political Cultures in the Progressive Era," 59–60, quote, 49. Florence Kelley, "Minimum-Wage Boards," *The American Journal of Sociology*, 17 (November 1911): 303–14.

1917, thirty-seven states had enacted worker compensation laws that were to be administered privately, with the states having the power to decide if an accident was "compensable" but no more than that. The few attempts to enact state insurance systems failed as businessmen and the AFL both opposed such measures. The AFL, representing very few women workers, wanted wages set through collective bargaining and opposed most NCL initiatives. The willingness of Gompers to work with businessmen and politicians on labor issues made the wishes of the AFL more palatable to those holding economic and political power. Unfortunately for the NCL and the Women's Trade Union League, the AFL maintained its stubborn resistance to organizing women workers. Although female-headed organizations supported the largely female garment worker strikes in New York City and Chicago in 1909, 1910, and 1915, for example, and gains were definitely made for women workers within the industry on the basis of this collective activity, organized male workers in the AFL remained the primary beneficiaries of most progressive national labor legislation.[4]

Other progressives, such as David Phillips and Father John Ryan, promoted the concept of a moral principle of wages. In his 1906 book on the subject, Ryan somewhat obliquely connected consumption and production. He contended that there was an American standard of living that was a "natural and absolute" right of citizenship. His declaration left a door wide open for defining what constituted an "American" standard of living. As consumer production increased across the coming years, the idea of a living wage increasingly came to mean the right to earn enough money to purchase an array of consumer items.[5]

CONSUMPTION OF LEISURE

When Florence Kelley argued in 1905 that everyone had a right to leisure, she meant time off from work. No one, she believed, should have to work seven days a week without rest. By the following decade, a right to leisure had acquired a whole new meaning. Leisure was becoming a public, commercial activity, and Americans were consuming it as fast as they could. Large public dance halls replaced private dance venues. Nickelodeons accommodated up to 300 patrons; newer movie palaces increased that number tenfold. Amusement parks opened in cities everywhere. Baseball fever swept through the country, attracting black and white Americans to new, large stadiums.

Coney Island in Brooklyn, Riverview Park in Chicago, Manhattan Beach in Denver, Ponce de Leon Park in Atlanta, and The Chutes in San Francisco drew millions of patrons eager to enjoy thrilling new rides, the midway of games, refreshments, exotica from around the world, and the tunnel of love, where

---

4. Sklar, "Two Political Cultures in the Progressive Era," and Morton Keller, *Regulating a New Society: Public Policy and Social Change in America, 1900–1933* (Cambridge, MA: Harvard University Press, 1994), 199–202, for worker compensation laws. Although unions such as the ILGWU supported, and even led, garment workers' strikes, the AFL had more political power to influence the course of any labor legislation.

5. Father John A. Ryan, *A Living Wage* (New York: Macmillan, 1906). See also, Eric Foner, *The Story of American Freedom* (New York: W. W. Norton, 1998), 145.

young people cruised in the dark without adult supervision. Advertisements for the amusement parks titillated patrons with the possibility of a new sexual freedom. Picture postcards showed women's bare legs and young couples embracing. Young men were lured onto rides with suggestions that young women might throw their arms around them. For those young women, the anonymity of the amusement park released them from family and neighborhood supervision. A worker at one of the rides expressed the sexual thrill that was promised: "Men like it because it gives them a chance to hug the girls, the girls like it because it gives them a chance to get hugged."[6]

What seems tame at the turn into the twenty-first century were dramatically changing ideas about sexuality and proper behavior that American society was undergoing at the turn of the previous century. Amusement parks and other places of public leisure were breaking down the separate worlds of female and male culture that had characterized nineteenth-century middle-class notions of propriety. These older notions were being replaced by a heterosexual social culture in which the sexes mingled, but in which young women, especially working women who now had money of their own, exercised new social freedoms and chose their own forms and places of leisure. By the end of the first decade of the twentieth century, there were more than 500 dance halls in the New York area. By the 1920s, dance palaces such as the Grand Central and Roseland in New York, the Aragon in Chicago, and the Hollywood Palladium in Los Angeles accommodated as many as 3,000 dancers at a time. Dance halls promised these women "laughter and liberty galore." Dance halls and amusement parks also rearranged patterns of urban dating. Some young women frequented these new places of leisure hoping to "pick up" men who would "treat" them to an evening's fun. "Gold digging" became a new phrase in the American vocabulary. Men, for their part, were seen as "preying" upon young innocent women. "I didn't know men were bad, all bad—where a girl is concerned," recounted one young woman who ended up a prostitute after being "tempted by lies and overpowered by the evil in men."[7]

"Nickle madness" also swept through the country. Cheap nickelodeon theaters drew large audiences and especially appealed to women as a counterpoint to the male space of the saloon. Nickelodeon owners played to this appeal by advertising they were "aiming to please the ladies." They encouraged women to bring their children and assured that "ladies without escorts cordially invited." Movie theaters were not necessarily sites of a new sexual arrangement between young men and women, as these appeals demonstrate. But movies themselves presented new images of sex and sexuality: romance, flirtation, glamour, and sexual intrigue were common themes. In *It's a Shame to*

---

6. John Kasson, *Amusing the Million: Coney Island at the Turn of the Century* (New York: Hill and Wang, 1978) and Kathy Peiss, *Cheap Amusements: Working Women and Leisure in Turn-of-the-Century New York* (Philadelphia: Temple University Press, 1986), quote, 134.

7. Peiss, *Cheap Amusements*, quote, 126; Randy D. McBee, *Dance Hall Days: Intimacy and Leisure among Working-Class Immigrants in the United States* (New York: New York University Press, 2000), 55–56 for dance palaces; and Joanne Meyerowitz, *Women Adrift: Independent Wage Earners in Chicago, 1880–1930* (Chicago: University of Chicago Press, 1988), 102–03.

Take the Money, a shoeshine boy considered the sight of a woman's ankles sufficient payment for shining her shoes. *The Boarding House Bathroom* had peep-
ing toms peering through a keyhole at a young woman. Conspicuous consumption was also emphasized and cleverly linked to personal freedom for
women by showing them smoking and drinking and wearing glamorous
clothing.[8]

New music halls called cabarets (the early incarnation of the nightclub) provided live entertainment, including dancing, along with dinner and drinking.
Unlike the dance halls that catered heavily to the working class, the cabarets
required more spending money so habitués could feel they were out on the
town in grand style. The cabaret imitated the French café in decor and atmosphere, and in this setting the middle class was treated to "an image of cosmopolitan European fun." Cabarets became the place to see and be seen; the place
to spend conspicuous amounts of money on the consumption of leisure. They
were also a way for different social groups to mingle on the basis of that
money. Socialites and theater people, businessmen and gamblers, Irish, Jewish,
and Anglo-Saxon came together at the cabaret. "In the cabaret and night world
of New York, the gambler could easily fit into a crowd that was learning to
spend impulses more freely."[9]

African Americans could not patronize "white" cabarets, so they built their
own, to which whites were also drawn. Such interracial cabarets were known
as "black and tans." Harlem in New York City and the Stroll in Chicago were
perhaps the best known of these cabaret areas, but San Francisco's Barbary
Coast cabarets were very popular on the West Coast. Heavyweight boxing
champion Jack Johnson open his "black and tan" Café de Champion on
Chicago's South Side in 1912. Its three stories accommodated an enormous
barroom and main area for orchestras, singers, and dancers as well as a private
dining and drinking space. Although the Café closed two years later when
Johnson was convicted of violating the Mann Act—an antivice law that made
it illegal to transport a woman across state lines for "immoral purposes"—
other cabarets opened on the Stroll and in cities across the country. The growth
of cabaret nightlife was spurred by the popularity of a new type of music—
jazz—being brought from the South by African Americans. Black musicians
played jazz to interracial audiences at the Dreamland Café, the DeLuxe, the
Elite, and the Royal Gardens in Chicago and Purcell's Elite Café and Olympia
Café in San Francisco.[10]

Not only big-city people were captivated by jazz. Groups of young white
men began to form jazz bands in cities as remote from the big time as Butte,

---

8. Peiss, *Cheap Amusements*, 148–57, quotes, 148–49.

9. Erenberg, *Steppin' Out*, ch. 4, provides a very good introduction to the life of the cabaret,
quotes, 117 and 139.

10. Robin F. Bachin, *Building the South Side: Urban Space and Civic Culture in Chicago, 1890–1919*
(Chicago: University of Chicago Press, 2004), 269–79, and Douglas Henry Daniels, *Pioneer Urbanites: A Social and Cultural History of Black San Francisco* (Berkeley: University of California Press,
1990), 147–48. Erenberg, *Steppin' Out*, considers the different circumstances in New York City
where African American cabarets opened in Harlem in the 1920s with black entertainers catering to
white audiences.

Montana. As jazz entered into working-class dance halls, racist attitudes came into play. Police in Butte raided a New Year's Eve party in 1922 at one so-called "joint." The newspapers carried sensational stories of finding white women "dancing with negroes to the jazz music of a colored orchestra" and white men "jazzing it" with black women. Although this particular "joint" already had a reputation for various forms of vice, what appalled many of the city's white residents was that the white women dancing at the club were "respectable" working women from "good" families. It wasn't just the sexy dance moves of jazz that were the problem. Interracial dancing upset the proper citizens of Butte and other cities.[11]

Baseball emerged in the Progressive Era as the first mass professional spectator sport. The ballpark was theoretically ecumenical and democratic: middle class and working class, men and women, young and old, every religious and ethnic group—even African Americans at some parks—who could afford the price of a ticket could see a baseball game. New ballparks seating tens of thousands were built in northern and midwestern cities. Charles Comiskey, owner of the Chicago White Sox, opened Comiskey Park in 1910. Called the "Baseball Palace of the World" for its size and amenities, the new park seated 35,000 and included 7,000 twenty-five cent bleacher seats. No previous ballpark had anywhere near that number of cheap seats. Detroit's Navin Field (later renamed Tiger Stadium) opened two years later, seating 23,000; within a decade that was expanded to 30,000. Fenway Park in Boston opened that same year seating 35,000. Yankee Stadium was not built until 1923, when its seating capacity of 53,000 made it the largest baseball park. Supply met the demand as millions of Americans every year bought tickets to see the "Georgia Peach" Ty Cobb steal bases for the Detroit Tigers, "Shoeless" Joe Jackson hit for the White Sox, the "Babe" pitch and then hit home runs for Boston and the Yankees. The economic gamble of baseball team owners paid off handsomely as owners made profits in the hundreds of thousands of dollars.[12]

Baseball remained segregated on the field because of an 1898 agreement among owners to bar black players. Nonetheless, baseball's popularity sustained black baseball leagues, although until 1920 most of the owners were white. That year Andrew "Rube" Foster organized the Negro National League with mainly black businessmen as owners, making the league a source of cultural pride and economic profit for African American communities. Despite being more economically precarious, the Negro league became the dominant spectator sport of urban blacks who thrilled to the base stealing prowess of James "Cool Papa" Bell in St. Louis and the overpowering pitching of Smokey

---

11. Mary Murphy, *Mining Cultures: Men, Women, and Leisure in Butte, 1914–1941* (Urbana: University of Illinois Press, 1997), 85, 88–89. See also, Kevin Mumford, *Interzones: Black and White Sex Districts in Chicago and New York in the Early Twentieth Century* (New York: New York University Press, 1997).

12. Steven A. Riess, *Touching Base: Professional Baseball and American Culture in the Progressive Era* (Westport, CT: Greenwood, 1980; Urbana: University of Illinois Press, rev. edition, 1999) and *City Games: The Evolution of American Urban Society and the Rise of Sports* (Urbana: University of Illinois Press, 1989), 118–20 for black players and leagues and 197–98 for profitability; and Bachin, *Building the South Side*, 226–29 and 234–35, for class, ethnicity, and race at Comiskey Park.

Joe Williams and Wilbur "Bullet Joe" Rogan in Kansas City. Baseball brought money into urban black communities.[13]

Baseball had been played in cities, towns, and rural areas for decades before the Progressive Era, but its professionalization and business culture were new, as was its increasing identification as the "urban" national pastime. Such changes did not please all Americans, who perceived that once baseball became a big business it was subject to similar economic centralization and potential corruption as other businesses. In fact, all baseball owners had political connections in their cities that they used to get approval for Sunday games, low license fees, and preferential treatment for municipal services. Bribery earned baseball parks special fire and police protection. Baseball and professional gambling grew together. As long as it was a local, amateur, or semiprofessional game no one had been much bothered by these issues. Once it was identified as the "national pastime," once it was rhapsodized as the game that "exercises and purifies all of our emotions, cultivating hope and courage when we are behind, resignation when we are beaten, fairness to the other team when we are ahead, charity for the umpire, and above all the zest for combat and conquest," Americans and team owners became less nonchalant. Game-fixing investigations were already under way in most major league cities when the 1919 "Black Sox" scandal broke wide open and exposed the ugly connections between the two. Baseball had become too profitable a business for owners to ignore the scandal. Their solution was very progressive: they turned to expertise and created the office of Commissioner of Baseball to oversee and regulate its activities. The new commissioner, Judge Kenesaw Mountain Landis, immediately expelled the eight White Sox players who had been accused of fixing the outcome of the 1919 World Series, even though they had been acquitted in a jury trial.[14]

CONSUMPTION AND COMMERCIALIZED VICE

The Black Sox scandal was merely a speed bump on baseball's road to becoming an integral part of American leisure and the country's economy. By the 1920s, owners had restored faith in baseball as a fair game and crowds were larger than ever as more Americans could afford to buy tickets. Receiving an antitrust exemption (which it still holds), which might have raised a red flag for another industry, helped baseball owners to present the sport as

---

13. Robert W. Peterson, *Only the Ball Was White* (Englewood Cliffs, NJ: Prentice Hall, 1970); Rob Ruck, *Sandlot Seasons: Sport in Black Pittsburgh* (Urbana: University of Illinois Press, 1987); Daniel J. Lerner, "Visions of a Sporting City: 'Shadowball' and Black Chicago, 1887–1951" (Ph.D. diss., Michigan State University, 2002); and Michael Lomax, "Black Entrepreneurship in the National Pastime: The Rise of Semiprofessional Baseball in Black Chicago, 1890–1915," *The Journal of Sport History*, 25 (1998): 43–65.

14. Robin Bachin, "At the Nexus of Labor and Leisure: Baseball, Nativism, and the 1919 Black Sox Scandal," *The Journal of Social History*, 36 (Summer 2003): 941–62, quote of Morris Cohen, 949. See also, Eliot Asinof, *Eight Men Out: The Black Sox and the 1919 World Series* (New York: Holt, Rinehart, Winston, 1963). Among the charges had been conspiracy to defraud the public and injure the business of owner Charles Comiskey.

organized, well regulated, and controlled by respectable businessmen. Other spectator sports suffered more from progressive revulsion to gambling. Boxing and horse racing were betting sports, especially the latter. Antigambling (or gaming as it was also called) forces secured laws either limiting or banning boxing and horse racing altogether. Class and ethnic prejudice provided partial motivation for outlawing boxing. The sport was most popular in major urban areas and among working-class ethnic groups. But both sports were also perceived as connected to prostitution and liquor, and thus a triple threat to standards of public morality. In trying to dampen interest in boxing, reformers also had to contend with the influence of other forms of mass entertainment. After a 1912 federal law made it illegal to send fight movies through the mail, one particularly enterprising group set up a movie projector on the Canadian side of the border to show the film of a 1915 boxing match to Americans standing on their side of the border. A federal judge ruled it illegal to show the film, although why he thought he could prevent Canada from doing what it wanted can only be imagined as a case of American moralizing run amok.[15]

Other areas of popular leisure had even tougher going than spectator sports. Tales of "white slavery"—young women and girls being forced into prostitution—circulated rapidly throughout the country. Some of these tales were the kind of hysterical response that usually accompanies social change, especially when women challenge societal norms, as they were obviously doing. Committees were organized in cities to investigate the connections between new forms of popular culture and vice. New York's Committee of Fourteen, a private citizens' association founded early in the century, visited dance halls, restaurants, and massage parlors in search of commercialized prostitution. Chicago had its Committee of Fifteen, led by lawyer Clifford Roe, who specialized in spreading lurid tales of white slavery in which unsophisticated young women were "treated" to dinner by unscrupulous slave traders who drugged and raped them and then sold them into prostitution and "debt peonage," from which they could never escape. Official vice commissions were also appointed in cities to investigate the growth of commercial vice districts: New York's Tenderloin, Chicago's Levee, New Orleans' Storyville, and San Francisco's Barbary Coast were found to be alive with saloons, gambling dens, brothels, and suspect hotels.

Movies played a double role in stimulating a "panic" over sexuality and vice. On the one hand, the sexuality depicted in movies made what was previously private into a public issue. But movies such as *Traffic in Souls* and *Inside the White Slave Traffic* were also used to manipulate public outrage over vice.[16] Antivice reformers often used the familiar language of the Progressive Era in their crusades. They declared that commercialized vice was a big business, controlled by a Vice Trust. The movie, *Smashing the Vice Trust* depicted the antivice movement as an assault on organized moneymaking from vice. Reformers

---

15. Keller, *Regulating a New Society,* 112–15.

16. Mara L. Keire, "The Vice Trust: A Reinterpretation of the White Slavery Scare in the United States, 1907–1917," *The Journal of Social History,* 35 (Fall 2001): 5–41, esp. 10–15.

charged that a wealthy few were exploiting the public's desire for leisure, same as the Beef Trust exploited workers' and consumers' need for wages and food. Reformers declared that urban prostitution was being centralized into corporate capitalism wherein real estate speculators, lawyers, liquor interests, and brothel owners were making money by exploiting the needs of young women for a way to earn a living. Moreover, prostitution was becoming an organized big business, with "business methods, bookkeeping, and cash registers and checks." The money invested in it, and profits made from it, ranged from those of smaller cities such as Kansas City, with $400,000 in capital investments in its red light district; to a $15 million business in prostitution in Chicago; to estimates that Storyville produced $1 million a week. The prostitutes themselves saw very little of this money. With so much money to be made, it seemed only reasonable to municipal officials that they should share in the profits. Politicians and police solicited bribes to ignore prostitution, illegal drinking, and gambling. Leading citizens and politicians invested in property in red light districts and then secured low tax assessments on that property, simultaneously making money and depriving the city of tax revenue. Ward officials often had a hand in running vice operations in their districts. One of the largest financial trust companies in the West financed an enormous "house of assignation" in San Francisco. As Chicago activist Ellen Henrotin remarked, "The modern tendency towards centralization has not passed by so promising a field for exploitation."[17]

Precisely because it had become big business, and because many antivice reformers wanted to eliminate prostitution and outlaw red light districts, progressive antivice reformers never attained their goal of ending prostitution. By comparison, Britain and other European countries had moved toward either decriminalization or regulation of prostitution rather than elimination. Failing to end prostitution, American reformers turned to relocating vice, often by segregating prostitution and other vice activities into African American neighborhoods. Or vice practitioners found a more amenable city in which to work, as when Chicago cracked down on vice operations and many of them simply moved to Detroit, which was considered a "wide open" city. Antivice reformers did succeed in something that the antichild labor advocates never managed. In 1913 the Supreme Court upheld the Mann Act, declaring it to be within Congressional power to regulate the movement of women in interstate commerce, similar to regulating food and drugs, or forbidding the use of the mail for lotteries or obscene literature.[18]

Economics also played a role in the temperance movement. The Woman's Christian Temperance Union, antisaloons leagues, and a Prohibition Party had been working for decades to ban the sale of alcohol and had experienced some

17. Ibid., 15, for Henrotin quote. See also, Ruth Rosen, *The Lost Sisterhood: Prostitution in America, 1900–1918* (Baltimore: Johns Hopkins University Press, 1982), quote, 42, and 71–73 for figures, and Keller, *Regulating a New Society*, 122 for San Francisco and 117–125 for activities and laws regulating prostitution and its big-business aspect.

18. Bachin, *Building the South Side*, 256–59; Victoria W. Wolcott, *Remaking Respectability: African American Women in Interwar Detroit* (Chapel Hill: University of North Carolina Press, 2001), 102–03; and Keller, *Regulating a New Society*, 123.

moderate success in a few states. But enforcing the Sunday closings of saloons in heavily immigrant cities had been an uphill, and generally losing, battle for prohibitionists in these areas. Breweries, saloon keepers, and a powerful Brewers' Association obviously resisted attempts to regulate alcohol sale, let alone outright prohibition. But many cities also depended on licensing revenues and other monies derived from the sale of alcohol. On the other hand, some businesses supported temperance thinking that more sober workers would be more efficient. Large companies began to pass their own measures to regulate their workers' drinking habits, especially to forbid alcohol in the workplace. Even the AFL supported such restrictions. Nevertheless, it seems certain that national prohibition would not have been enacted if not for racism and World War I. Many southerners who identified themselves as progressives connected abolishing the sale of liquor with control of African Americans. Well before the 18th Amendment, many areas of the South were already dry. Still, powerful economic interests throughout the country might have staved off complete prohibition if World War I did not give the well-organized Anti-Saloon League new life. During the war, prohibitionists would tie temperance to national preparedness, and business again stressed that prohibition would make workers more productive and efficient. Of course, once prohibition was enacted, this form of vice too relocated into African American areas of cities, or as in Tampa, Florida, continued in the Latino neighborhoods of Ybor City, generally with white businessmen owning the establishments.[19]

CONSUMPTION AND PUBLIC MORALITY

Attacking prostitution, gambling and gaming, and liquor was a reflection of a sober Protestant sense of morality. These were bad things to do and therefore they had to be stopped. But there were also Catholic temperance forces and Jewish antivice reformers, so the concerns with new public entertainments, although an aspect of morality, cannot be merely lumped in with antivice. Prostitution, for example, was defined as the *Social Evil*, but for many progressives sports, movies, dance halls, and cabarets were more complicated issues. They recognized that society was changing, so the issue for them was to regulate these forms of entertainment as other elements of society were being regulated.

When the dance hall craze and other new amusements hit New York and working girls found cheap and welcome ways to put fun into their arduous workdays, young women's public roles changed dramatically. Before the opening of dance halls, amusement parks, and movie theaters, most girls and young women had not gone out in public without a family member or approved escort. As more young women were working and earning their

---

19. Keller, *Regulating a New Society*, 125–39. See also, Jack S. Blocker, *Retreat from Reform: The Prohibition Movement in the United States, 1890–1913* (Westport, CT: Greenwood Press, 1976); Norman H. Clark, *Deliver Us from Evil: An Interpretation of American Prohibition* (New York: W.W. Norton, 1976); and James H. Timberlake, *Prohibition and the Progressive Movement, 1900–1920* (Cambridge, MA: Harvard University Press, 1963). See Nancy Hewitt, *Southern Discomfort: Women's Activism in Tampa, Florida, 1880s–1920s* (Urbana: University of Illinois Press, 2001), 233–34.

own money, they were now going out on their own, making their own friends and decisions. Many female progressives feared that the new sites of public leisure were leaving young women open to being preyed upon by unscrupulous men who could ultimately lead too many of them into prostitution. Publications such as that of Louise DeKoven Bowen, *The Road to Destruction Made Easy in Chicago*, warned of such dangers. Progressive Belle Israels Moskowitz had begun working at the New York City settlement the Educational Alliance (formerly the Hebrew Institute) in 1900. Quitting the alliance when she married, she then joined the Council of Jewish Women. Through the council, she organized a Committee on Amusements and Vacation Resources for Working Girls. Like good progressives, Moskowitz and her female compatriots investigated and gathered statistics that confirmed their fears. They did not want to close dance halls but to pass new laws that would make them more orderly and safer places for working girls. They also looked for ways to organize other types of amusements in different venues where they believed these women would be safer. Jane Addams held her generation to blame for not understanding the extent of changes in work and lifestyle for young people and for trying to restrict their activities rather than regulate them to make them safer. Addams saw theaters as a natural release from the drudgery of life for so many young people, who often went to work at age fourteen:

"Going to the show" for thousands of young people in every industrial city is the only possible road to the realms of mystery and romance; the theater is the only place where they can satisfy that craving for a conception of life higher than that which the actual world offers them.

But it was also a temptation because, as she viewed it, the themes presented in these spectacles were often of the wrong sort—murder, revenge, robbery were celebrated—and could lead young people to exalt crime.[20]

Reformers such as Bowen, Moskowitz, and Addams were accused by some Americans at the time, and by historians thereafter, of trying to impose their moral standards on young people.[21] Yet, the world of young women especially had been transformed so quickly, and the money to be made from their desire for freedom and entertainment was sufficient to draw too many unsavory types into these industries. Furthermore, many of these reformers' concerns about young women were realistic in the sense that birth control was extremely hard to obtain, there were no effective treatments for venereal disease, and unmarried mothers were treated as "fallen" women. African American

---

20. Bowen (Chicago: Hale-Crossley Printing, 1916); Elisabeth Israels Perry, *Belle Moskowitz: Feminine Politics and the Exercise of Power in the Age of Alfred E. Smith* (New York: Routledge, 1987); and Jane Addams, *Spirit of Youth and City Streets* (New York: Macmillan, 1909; Urbana: University of Illinois Press, reprint edition, 1972), 75–103, quote, 75–76.

21. Damning with faint praise is one of the more recent assessments of Moskowitz. "Even such determined progressives as Belle Moskowitz conceded that human beings . . . needed to play." Such a statement implies that progressivism and play were mutually incompatible. See Michael McGerr, *A Fierce Discontent: The Rise and Fall of the Progressive Movement in America, 1870–1920* (New York: The Free Press, 2003), 273.

women in Chicago discussed "the temptations that await the girls who go un-protected after dark." African American women in Detroit were equally con-cerned about the temptations open to young migrant women and the lack of more "respectable" alternatives. The YWCA in that city opened a social center for young working women in 1918 and shortly reported that 500 women were availing themselves of the facilities. African American settlements in Chicago organized dance clubs and other types of entertainments, hoping to persuade younger people to attend those gatherings rather than regular dance halls and cabarets. In Chicago, reformers in the Juvenile Protective Association per-suaded a group of dance hall owners to form the Dance Hall and Ballroom Managers' Association, the members of which promised to maintain "decent" halls. Between 1910 and 1913, cities across the country passed new dance hall ordinances, the same as they were regulating other public activities. New reg-ulations included licensing fees, closing hours, and alcohol restrictions.[22]

On the other hand, dance hall reformers were largely unsuccessful at cen-soring dance and music styles that they believed were immoral. Jazz was here to stay, there was money to spend, and even the middle class was adopting the new public entertainment. The modern age had arrived and there was no turn-ing it back. The working girls who belonged to the National League of Women Workers' clubs basically ignored the "Rules for Correct Dancing"—including no "undue conspicuous display of hosiery"—that the organization's Executive Board tried to impose. Dance hall owners themselves staved off imposed cen-sorship by posting their own rules and regulations about dancing. Reforms through adaptation and regulation were pursued rather than abolition. Pro-gressives also began to realize that movies and theater could send positive messages to the public and could be family entertainment. This had been part of Addams' message in *The Spirit of Youth and the City Streets*. The People's In-stitute in New York City formed a National Board of Censorship of Programs of Motion Picture Shows (later called the Board of Review) to which movie producers agreed to voluntarily submit their movies for review.

With so much concern about the sexuality of young women circulating through progressive movements, birth control also became a more public and contested issue. Birth control reformers did make some slow progress in their crusade to make contraception openly available to women. When Margaret Sanger was prosecuted in 1917 for supplying contraceptive devices at her clinic, public opinion sided with Sanger. Mary Ware Dennett's National Birth Control League (1915) and local affiliates challenged all legal impediments to dispensing contraception and to setting up birth control clinics. Legal progress was painfully slow as a majority of states maintained anti–birth control laws and Congress refused to repeal the Comstock Act (1873) that made it illegal to send obscene literature through the mail. Information on contraception was deemed obscene and it took until 1933 for federal courts to rule that contracep-tives were not obscene products. On the other hand, prosecution of offenders

---

22. Perry, *Belle Moskowitz*, 55–57; Anne Meis Knupfer, *Toward a Tenderer Humanity and a Nobler Womanhood: African American Women's Clubs in Turn-of-the-Century Chicago* (New York: New York University Press, 1996), 102; Wolcott, *Remaking Respectability*, 68–69; and Louise DeKoven Bowen, *Growing Up with a City* (New York, 1926; Urbana: University of Illinois Press, reprint, 2002), 122–24.

was generally lax. Despite official disapprobation, birth control for many Americans remained a private issue and not one of public morality.[23]

THE FAMILY AS CONSUMER

The new forms of public leisure also decentered the family and community as the sites of leisure. Older forms of recreation, such as those revolving around picnics and church socials or saloons and home visiting, had also tended to be "homosocial" leisure that segregated the sexes, with men's leisure being public and most women's being private. Both of these changes were especially true for the working class, who had not been able to afford to spend much money on entertainment and men (not women) had generally consumed what small sums were available for recreation. Now, dance halls brought together young working men and women with their own money to spend free from family supervision. Amusement parks provided entertainment for young single people but also changed the nature of family entertainment. Amusement parks had rides, sometimes bathing beaches, and circus or carnival attractions for all family members. Going to the amusement park was not a community-oriented recreation, as picnics and church socials had been. Amusement park entrepreneurs such as Frederic Thompson worked to create something that could be advertised as wholesome family entertainment. Visitors to amusement parks, he observed, "are not in a serious mood, and do not want to encounter seriousness. . . . What is presented to them must have life, action, motion, sensation, surprise, shock, swiftness or else comedy." Hence Thompson likened the amusement park to the Sunday-school picnic where enjoyment, not moralism or seriousness, was the purpose, and by doing so he sought to persuade Americans that it was a perfectly respectable form of leisure.[24]

Family consumption involved far more than popular entertainments. Consumer spending for clothing and household goods and appliances was also required for supporting a consumer economy. The "ethical" consumption of the National Consumers' League was being replaced by the ethic of consumption. The country was growing richer every year, thanks in large part to economic regulation and the application of scientific management to production. The

---

23. The most extensive treatments of the birth control movement are David Kennedy, *Birth Control in America: The Career of Margaret Sanger* (New Haven, CT: Yale University Press, 1970), Linda Gordon, *The Moral Property of Women: A History of Birth Control Politics in America* (Urbana: University of Illinois Press, 2002), and *Woman's Body, Woman's Right: A Social History of Birth Control in America* (New York: Penguin, 1976). See also, Keller, *Regulating a New Society*, 30–33; McGerr, *A Fierce Discontent*, 271–74; and Priscilla Murolo, *The Common Ground of Womanhood: Class, Gender, and Working Girls' Clubs, 1884–1928* (Urbana: University of Illinois Press, 1997), 132.

24. Peiss, *Cheap Amusements*, 5–6, ch. 1 and 23 for spending money; Kasson, *Amusing the Million*, quote, 66. See also, Roy Rosenzweig, *Eight Hours for What We Will: Workers and Leisure in an Industrial City, 1870–1920* (Cambridge, UK: Cambridge University Press, 1983) and Francis G. Couvares, *The Remaking of Pittsburgh: Class and Culture in an Industrializing City, 1877–1920* (Albany: State University of New York Press, 1984).

cost of a new Model T dropped from $850 in 1908 to $316 in 1916, the year in which 1.5 million automobiles were sold in the United States. Upscale and bargain department stores throughout the country were thronged with shoppers. Two thousand women were described in 1909 as scrambling for merchandise at F.W. Woolworth and Adler department stores in Brooklyn, knocking aside salespersons and other shoppers to get the best bargains. Department stores advertised themselves as the place for young people to come learn how to shop, hoping to instill the consumption habit in them early in life. They encouraged mothers to bring their children along so that they too could learn the art of shopping. New inventions such as the phonograph, and the radio by the 1920s, began to appear in every middle-class household, and often in those of the working class. Baseball and radio came together in 1922 when radio first broadcast the World Series.[25]

The right to consume became identified as a right of American citizenship. The focus on consumer protections that had driven the earlier Meat Inspection Act and the Food and Drug Act had morphed into the new consumerism by the 1920s. Consumers became an interest group seeking not just assurances of safety for what they bought but an abundant supply of goods at affordable prices. Advertising took off as a new profession, marketing consumer goods to Americans as individuals and as family members. For some progressives the consumer had even been seen as the essential element to reform. Walter Lippmann had written that he believed that consumers, rather than businessmen or workers, represented the real public interest. "With the consumer awake neither the workers nor the employer can use politics for his special interest." Still, the ability to consume became tied to labor union membership as workers and their families sought higher incomes to afford more goods. "We find ourselves simply swamped by our desires," the wife of a union member wrote. "Without the union earning power, we would not have had the money to buy the radio or countless other things."[26] Yet, great segments of the consumer economy was built on middle-class consumption. Industrialists continued to resist unions and all attempts to implement collective bargaining for workers through the 1920s so that wages did not keep up with consumer desires.

---

25. McGerr, *A Fierce Discontent*, 230; "Women Madly Riot at Bargain Sales," *New York Times*, April 25, 1909, cited in Alison Isenberg, *Downtown America: A History of the Place and the People Who Made It* (Chicago: University of Chicago Press, 2004), 78; Susan Porter Benson, *Counter Cultures: Saleswomen, Managers, and Customers in American Department Stores, 1890–1940* (Urbana: University of Illinois Press, 1986), 100–02; and Riess, *Touching Base*, 233. See also, Richard W. Fox and T. J. Jackson Lears, eds., *The Culture of Consumption: Critical Essays in American History, 1880–1980* (New York: Pantheon, 1983).

26. Lippmann, *Drift and Mastery* (New York: M. Kennerley, 1914), quoted in Alan Dawley, *Changing the World: American Progressives in War and Revolution* (Princeton: Princeton University Press, 2003), 203; Foner, *The Story of American Freedom*, quote, 148. See also, Lizbeth Cohen, "Citizens and Consumers in the Century of Mass Consumption," in *Perspectives on Modern America: Making Sense of the Twentieth Century*, Harvard Sitkoff, ed. (New York: Oxford University Press, 2001), 146–47 and David Thelen, *The New Citizenship: Origins of Progressivism in Wisconsin, 1885–1900* (Columbia: University of Missouri Press, 1972).

CONSUMING HIGH CULTURE

Finally, we return to the Armory Show of 1913. The very formal and conservative National Academy of Design had controlled the production and dissemination of art until 1912, when a small group of artists and patrons formed the Association of American Painters and Sculptors (AAPS). These were the "modernists." They wanted Americans to see art that broke away from the restrictions of formalism, much as popular culture was breaking free of the strictures of "proper" behavior. Opening day of the exhibit drew 4,000 spectators—not a baseball-size crowd, to be sure, but something shockingly new for the world of high culture. Its location in the enormous Armory of the 69th New York Regiment was specifically chosen to accommodate such crowds. Total attendance over the exhibit's four weeks was estimated at 90,000. The high world of art disapproved. The *New York Times* review of the show warned that "this movement is surely a part of the general movement, discernible to all of the world, to disrupt, degrade, if not destroy, not only art but literature and society too."[27]

Two months later, another show opened in New York that melded high culture with working-class issues. Striking silk workers from Paterson, New Jersey, marched into the city, where they held a pageant at Madison Square Garden to publicize the workers' demands. The pageant was a collaboration between the strikers and New York intellectuals such as Mabel Dodge, John Reed, and Max Eastman. Both groups hoped that the pageant would not only help end the strike favorably for the workers, but that it would create a bridge between the working class and the middle-class intellectuals of socialist leaning, many of whom had gathered around the radical publication, *The Masses*. Fifteen thousand spectators watched the pageant, whose actors were all striking silk workers. Like the Armory show, the Paterson Strike Pageant exploded cultural traditions. It had no plot: it was "the self-recorded life of the strikers" that "turned the lives of masses of men . . . into a spectacle." It also encouraged the audience to interact with the actors and to respond sympathetically to the strikers' plight. The *Times* savaged the pageant, calling it "a series of pictures in action . . . shown with the design of stimulating mad passion against law and order and promulgating the gospel of discontent." A more sympathetic critique described the pageant as exposing "the possibilities of a vital and popular art." The *Times'* worries were unfounded. The Pageant did not lead to revolution as the IWW, which was leading the Paterson strike, had hoped when it publicized the pageant as "a battle between the working class and the capitalist class." The majority of silk workers had not belonged to the IWW and when the owners offered to negotiate, most strikers capitulated. They were less interested in overthrowing capitalism than in securing better wages within it.[28]

27. Martin Green, *New York 1913: The Armory Show and the Paterson Strike Pageant* (New York: Macmillan, 1988), 171–91, quote, 179. See also, McGerr, *A Fierce Discontent*, 240–42.

28. Green, *New York 1913*, 195–215, quotes, 204 and 205; Steve Golin, *The Fragile Bridge: The Paterson Silk Strike, 1913* (Philadelphia: Temple University Press, 1988), 170–77; and Anne Huber Tripp, *The I.W.W. and the Paterson Silk Strike of 1913* (Urbana: University of Illinois Press, 1987).

But the pageant itself helped inspire a new genre: art in the service of social causes. The progressive publication *The Survey* celebrated it for conveying "what speech and pamphlet, picture and cartoon, fiction and drama fall short of telling": that the strikers were human beings struggling to survive in the industrial economy.[29]

The failure of the Paterson strike to inspire a more revolutionary ending began the downfall of the IWW. By 1915, the IWW presence in the eastern United States had virtually disappeared, although it remained very active in the western states. When war broke out in Europe in late summer 1914, attention turned to rethinking America's role in the world. As entering the war became more of a possibility, it enhanced patriotism and "Americanism." In this context, radical unionism, let alone revolutionary movements, would be unable to survive for long.

---

29. *The Survey* quote in Tripp, 146–47.

Building the Panama Canal (1906). Source: Library of Congress, Prints & Photographs Division, LC-USZ62-96773

Vino del mar, a Panamá,
  a trabajar en la selva y a construir el Canal.
Le pagaron en plata
  al hombre blanco le pagaron en oro
  y la fiebre amarilla se llevó el alma de todos.

Mi abuelito fue un hombre, Antillano,
  y vivió y murió en Panamá.

Hombre Antillano, quiero reconocer tu
  voluntad de hierro, tu sacrificio.
Diste la vide para construir un camino
  que uniese a los océanos
  dentra del corazón de Panamá.

El tiempo ha transcurrido
  pero la discriminación continúa;
  debemos trabajar juntos hasta encontrarle
  una cura.

Hombre Antillano, vino del Caribe y encontró
  una casa y un nuevo comienzo en Panamá.
Mi abuelito fue un hombre, Antillano,
  y vivió y murió en Panamá.

He came from the sea, to Panama
  to work in the jungle and to build a Canal.
They paid you in silver
  and paid the white man in gold
  and the yellow fever took the souls of all.

My grandfather was a West Indian man,
  and he lived and died in Panama.

West Indian man, I want to recognize your
  iron will, your sacrifice.
You gave your life to build a road
  that united the oceans
  through the heart of Panama.

Time has passed
  but discrimination continues;
  we have to work together to find
  a cure.

West Indian man, came from the Caribbean and found
  a home and a new beginning in Panama.
My grandfather was a West Indian man,
  and he lived and died in Panama.*

Hombre Antillano by Rubén Blades

   In 1914, the first ships passed through the Panama Canal. Opening the canal enhanced the American quest to become the leading economic power in the world. The transcontinental railroad lines had opened overland transport from coast to coast. How to move goods quickly by sea had remained a problem. Now the canal united the Atlantic and Pacific Oceans. Because the United States also controlled the strip of land along either side of the canal, the so-called Panama Canal Zone, 1914 also culminated almost two decades of the country's efforts to control the Caribbean and perhaps even establish hegemony over economic trade and development from the Canadian border to the tip of Central America and throughout the surrounding waters. Controlling the canal also gave U.S. naval ships unfettered and quick passage between the two coasts and out onto the oceans. But uniting the two oceans also meant, as Rubén Blades put it in his song to his grandfather, expropriating other peoples' lands and exploiting them for the benefit of U.S. development.

*Copyright 1992 Ruben Blades Publishing. All rights administered by Sony/ATV Music Publishing, 8 Music Square West, Nashville, TN 37203. All rights reserved. Used by permission.

CHAPTER 10

Bringing Democracy to the World

We will not renounce our part in the mission of our race,
trustee, under God, of the civilization of the world.
— SENATOR ALBERT BEVERIDGE, 1900

BEFORE THE END of the nineteenth century, the United States did not have a foreign policy as we would think of it today. Since the time of President Jefferson, the United States had eschewed "entangling" foreign alliances, practicing isolationism rather than foreign affairs. There was tariff policy, but that was developed domestically, not in conjunction with other countries. There were occasional foreign spats through the nineteenth century, including, of course, the War of 1812. Treaties were signed with other countries as the need developed. There had been "incidents" to which the United States had had to respond, as when groups of Americans tried to invade Canada or when several Italian immigrants were lynched in New Orleans in 1891 and there had been a brief severing of diplomatic relations with Italy. The famous "54°40' or fight" sloganeering of the 1844 presidential campaign over the northern border of the United States had ended in a peaceful treaty agreement with England. President Monroe in 1823 had promulgated the "Monroe Doctrine" that warned European powers to refrain from any further ventures into the Western Hemisphere, and conflicts over the southern borders had produced the 1848 war with Mexico. The acquisition of the lower pieces of Arizona and New Mexico with the Gadsden Purchase of 1853 completed the continental United States. That same year, the U.S. Navy, under the command of Admiral Matthew Perry, sailed into Tokyo Bay on a mission to "open" Japan to foreign trade. Since the 1840s, the United States had declared that it had a "special relationship" with the Hawai'ian Islands, a situation developed from the settlement there of white businessmen.

Yet, there was no official foreign policy apparatus inside the State Department. Foreign affairs were largely those incidents to which the United States responded on a need-to basis. In fact, the distinction that nineteenth-century Americans had made between foreign and domestic affairs, and how they thought of foreign affairs, was institutionalized in different cabinet positions: secretary of state, secretary of war, and secretary of the navy. Besides, Americans had been so busy pushing West and building the country that there seemed no need to pay much attention to the rest of the world. Economic growth, however, demanded constant expansion and as the western United States became settled and "civilized," the doctrine of "manifest destiny" that had been formulated to justify conquest of the continental territory offered the possibility of justifying foreign expansion. Bringing democracy to the world became the justification for economic expansion. As white Americans had justified seizing Indian territories to "civilize" these people, they now justified expanding democracy as their motive for colonizing other groups.

In the Progressive Era, strategic foreign expansion and the policy to carry it out were driven by a combination of perceived economic needs, ideas of cultural and racial superiority, and progressive ideas about reforming the world. None of these can be separated from each other, because in every area where the United States moved out into the world, these three elements intertwined.[1] Whether they approved or not of specific foreign policy developments, progressives had to come to terms with the new role America was playing in the world. For some of them, this meant justifying imperialism as a "progressive" movement; for other progressives, it meant recognizing how the United States was now part of a larger world in which the ideas of progressivism ought to be applied internationally.

MOVING THE BOUNDARIES

From 1898 to 1914, the United States engaged in an imperial endeavor outside its continental boundaries. Beginning with the 1823 Monroe Doctrine, the United States had looked upon the Caribbean basin as its own preserve. The western islands of the Caribbean were close to the eastern coast of the United States. Mexico bordered the United States and railroads had linked the two countries by the end of the century. The tiny nations of Central America were only a short distance from the southern United States by boat. The United

---

1. For overviews and interpretations of the development of U.S. foreign policy, see Walter LaFeber, *The American Age: The United States Foreign Policy at Home and Abroad Since 1750* (New York: W.W. Norton, 1989); *The New Empire: An Interpretation of American Expansion, 1860–1898* (Ithaca, NY: Cornell University Press, 1963; new edition, 1998); and "The 'Lion in the Path': The U.S. Emergence as a World Power," *Political Science Quarterly*, 101:5 (1986): 705–09 for analysis of foreign policy development by the late nineteenth century. See also, Ernest R. May, *Imperial Democracy: The Emergence of America as a Great Power* (New York: Harper & Row, 1973); Robert L. Beisner, *From the Old Diplomacy to the New, 1865–1900* (New York: Crowell, 1975); Emily S. Rosenberg, *Spreading the American Dream: American Economic and Cultural Expansion, 1890–1945* (New York: Hill and Wang, 1982); and Robert E. Hannigan, *The New World Power: American Foreign Policy, 1898–1917* (Philadelphia: University of Pennsylvania Press, 2002).

WELL, I HARDLY KNOW WHICH TO TAKE FIRST!

McKinley Gobbles It Up: Cuba Steak, Porto Rico Pig, Philippine Floating Islands (1898)
Source: Library of Congress, Prints & Photographs Division, LC-USZ62-55890

States coveted the natural resources of the entire area: from sugar and tropical fruits to oil and coal. A stable Caribbean region would make it possible to exploit these resources for American production and would assure easy access to much of South America for goods produced in the United States. Roadblocks to U.S. desires, however, were European control of many Caribbean islands and indigenous revolutions there. Opportunity for change came with the insurrection of Cubans against Spanish rule in 1898. Using the explosion aboard the U.S. warship, *The Maine*, in Havana Harbor as a pretext for entering the insurrection on the side of the Cubans, a combination of U.S. military and Cuban insurgency defeated the Spaniards within a few months. Having won the "splendid little war,"[2] declared in support of the Cuban people's right to democratic freedom, the United States now had to construct a peace. Annexation was clearly out of the question, so the United States neatly finessed the question with the 1901 Platt Amendment to the peace treaty. With the amendment,

---

2. I am going to avoid using any name for this war. American historians comfortably called it the Spanish-American war for decades, but this designation has been challenged because it does not recognize that the United States also practiced war against the peoples it colonized. At its most expansive, it has lately been referred to as the Spanish-American-Filipino-Cuban-Puerto Rican War.

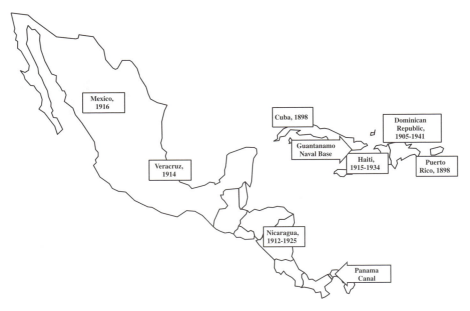

Caribbean Incursions, 1898–1941

Cuba agreed to accept limitations to its diplomatic and financial relations with other countries, gave the United States the right to intervene in its affairs when necessary to preserve order on the island, and leased Guantánamo to the United States for a naval base. Puerto Rico came in the bargain: the autonomous government that had been established by its citizens' rebellion against Spain was abolished, the island was thereafter declared a U.S. territory, and its residents were granted U.S. citizenship in 1917. Spaniards living on the island, on the other hand, had been granted immediate citizenship, a reflection of the racial thinking that was in vogue during the Progressive Era.[3]

Despite this consolidation of U.S. interests in Cuba and Puerto Rico, the Caribbean basin remained unstable. Unrest in the Dominican Republic, Haiti, Nicaragua, and Mexico, for example, threatened U.S. interests. Across the following years, the United States sent troops into these areas to restore order. At times the United States even took control of a country's assets, as was the case with the Dominican Republic in 1905: from 1916 to 1922, the Department of the Navy actually governed that country. The building of the Panama Canal was the crowning jewel in dominating the Caribbean and securing the area for American commerce.[4]

---

3. The lease to Guantánamo was renewed in 1934 and can only be abrogated with the consent of both countries. Thus, the United States maintains its presence on Cuban soil to this day. For Puerto Rico, see Michael González-Cruz, "The U.S. Invasion of Puerto Rico: Occupation and Resistence to the Colonial State, 1898 to the Present," *Latin American Perspectives*, 25 (September 1998): 7–26.

4. Samuel P. Hays, *The Response to Industrialism, 1885–1914* (Chicago: University of Chicago Press, 1957), 174, and Nell Irvin Painter, *Standing at Armageddon: The United States, 1877–1919* (New York: W.W. Norton, 1987), 174.

On the Pacific side of the country, American sugar plantation owners who had settled in Hawai'i pressured Congress to annex the islands permanently to the United States in order to guarantee economic stability for business interests. In 1893, these businessmen—aided by a landing force of U.S. sailors and marines—seized control of the islands from Queen Lili'uokalani. Congress was reluctant to annex the islands and inclined toward heeding the petitions for independence submitted to it by the Hawai'ian Patriotic Leagues (one male, one female). In the wake of other events in 1898, however, President McKinley succeeding in securing passage of legislation permanently annexing them. Two years later, Hawai'i was declared a territory of the United States. Unlike the rhetoric that would surround the coming conquest of the Philippines, the reasons for annexing Hawai'i were bluntly economic: "We need Hawaii just as much and a great deal more than we did California. It is manifest destiny," President McKinley declared.[5]

Before he resigned his position as assistant secretary of the Navy to be commissioned in the military and bring his "Rough Riders" to Cuba, Theodore Roosevelt launched an initiative to seize the Philippines from Spain. U.S. commercial ships needed ports in Pacific islands where they could refuel for their long journeys across that ocean. Annexing Hawai'i was a stepping-stone across the Pacific.[6] If Spain could be ousted from its possessions in that part of the world, a piecemeal approach to secure commerce in the Pacific would no longer be necessary. Admiral George Dewey, commander of the Pacific Fleet, quickly defeated the Spanish fleet in Manila Bay. The United States took control of the Philippines, and along with them secured the other Spanish possession of Guam, an island located between Hawai'i and the Philippines. The Philippines were officially annexed to the United States in 1899. Ideas about race were prominent in arguments about this act of imperialism. Filipinos were declared ignorant, barbaric, degenerate, and semicivilized people whose seven-year rebellion against American occupation was "proof" that they were incapable of self-government. Mark Twain, always the satirist but this time with an edge of despair, wrote of the Philippines:

> Extending the Blessings of Civilization to our Brother who Sits in Darkness has been a good trade and has paid well. . . . But the "Blessings of Civilization" ("JUSTICE, CHRISTIANITY, EDUCATION. . . and so on") are just an outside cover. . . . The real contents (the "Actual Thing") of Western civilization are the poverty of New York slums and the slaughter in South Africa and the Philippines, where "Civilization" was being resisted. . . . Is there no salvation for us but to adopt Civilization and lift ourselves down to its level?[7]

---

5. Copies of the 556–page petitions with more than 21,000 signatures of native Hawai'ians are preserved at the National Archives and Records Administration, in Records of the U.S. Senate, Record Group 46. McKinley quoted in Painter, *Standing at Armageddon*, 150.

6. The United States occupied the uninhabited Midway Islands in 1867; it negotiated a treaty with Germany in 1899 to occupy half of the Samoan islands, including the port of Pago Pago, which is now called American Samoa.

7. Mark Twain, "To the Person Sitting in Darkness," *The North American Review* (February 1901), quoted in Painter, *Standing at Armageddon*, 156.

The ultimate target of Pacific expansion was Asia. Despite the obvious cynicism of the old adage penned by nineteenth-century French author Alphonse Karr, "Plus ça change, plus c'est la même chose" ("the more things change, the more they stay the same"), when it comes to China the adage holds a certain truth. At the turn to the twentieth century, China was viewed as an enormous marketplace, just as it is today. But European powers already controlled large portions of China, and Japan was moving in as well. To confront the China "problem," U.S. Secretary of State John Hay proposed to these various powers the "Open Door Policy" under which all nations would have a right to free trade with China. Although no one replied affirmatively to this initiative, Hay simply declared that his proposal had been accepted. In the wake of a nationalist uprising in China—the so-called Boxer Rebellion—and fearing Russian encroachment into China, President McKinley in 1900 sent 55,000 U.S. troops into China to help quell the rebellion. From that point, the United States became inextricably bound up in Asian affairs. When President Roosevelt brokered the peace to the Russo-Japanese War (for which he received the Nobel Peace Prize), he further altered the political and economic landscape of Asia. The following year a treaty between the United States and Japan gave the latter a free hand in Korea in exchange for the former's control of the Philippines.[8]

The final frontier of U.S. foreign policy in the early years of the century was a detente of sorts with England. Despite ongoing friction between the United States and England since the revolutionary era, now leading politicians and businessmen in both countries were speaking of a common political, cultural, and economic heritage that made the two countries natural allies. England had been the predominant world power, controlling an empire that stretched across every continent. But its resources were stretched thin trying to maintain the empire, and the United States was looking to overtake it as the world's economic powerhouse. As the two countries were being drawn closer together economically, their individual foreign actions influenced one another. When Secretary of State Hay informed the British of U.S. intentions to go to war against Spain, England replied that it would be "guided [on Cuban issues] by the wishes of the President."[9] Similarly, the United States maintained a neutral stance during the Anglo-Boer War in South Africa (1899–1902), even though much popular opinion sided with the Boers as defenders of their liberty against British economic imperialism. What else could the United States do? If it criticized British policy in South Africa, it would leave itself wide open for criticism of its policies in the Caribbean and Pacific.[10]

Moreover, Britain and the United States were in the process of signing treaties of agreement and noninterference in each other's affairs. In the 1901 Hay-Pauncefote Treaty, for instance, Britain acknowledged the rights of the United States to build the Panama Canal. In return, the United States agreed to provide equal access to the canal for ships of all nations. When the Taft admin-

---

8. Hays, *The Response to Industrialism*, 180–81.

9. Thomas Paterson, "United States Intervention in Cuba, 1898: Interpretations of the Spanish-American-Cuban-Filipino War," *The History Teacher*, 29 (May 1996): 341–61, quote from 344.

10. Richard B. Mulanax, *The Boer War in American Politics and Diplomacy* (Lanham, MD: University Press of America, 1994).

istration mandated lower tolls for U.S. ships, England vigorously protested that this violated the treaty. The Wilson government had to deal with this protest and convinced Congress to repeal this legislation. But U.S. relations with England were not just over the canal and that particular treaty. Wilson believed it imperative to satisfy England on this issue because England was unhappy with U.S. involvement in Mexican affairs that had begun in the Taft administration. Repeal of exemptions for American ships, Wilson hoped, would solidify Anglo-American relations.[11]

EXPANSIONISM AND PROGRESSIVISM

This imperial expansionism was driven by a combination (and some might say a perversion) of progressive ideas. Imperialism was an extension of the movement to order and regulate society, economics, and government. The mission of civilization that had rationalized treatment of Native Americans now was internationalized and applied to people throughout the world. Regulation of other societies, many Americans now believed, would make the world more orderly for Americans. The urge to foster everlasting opportunity and progress for the American people and for American capitalism underlay all foreign policy development. Historians have at times tried to disentangle the various elements of progressivism from one another in domestic as well as foreign developments.[12] In the end, the development and implementation of foreign policy up to and including World War I exposes how American ideas of capitalism and democracy were becoming inextricably linked in the minds of so many people. The progressive urge to save capitalism by lessening its worst aspects would now be put into play around the world. Not all progressives agreed with this linkage, nor with expansionism. But behind this new imperialism lay many of their ideas.

1. Order, Regulation, and the World Economy

By 1900, the United States dominated the world market in production of items ranging from petroleum and agricultural machinery to sewing machines and cameras. Its foreign investments rose dramatically from $700 million in 1897 to $2.5 billion in 1908; and again to $3.5 billion by 1914. By 1913, U.S. businesses controlled 78 percent of the silver, lead, and copper mines in Mexico, as well as 58 percent of its oil production. Total U.S. investment in Mexico alone was approaching $1 billion.[13]

American interests in this new international marketplace needed protection from the vicissitudes of laissez-faire policies in the same way that regulation

---

11. Arthur S. Link, *Woodrow Wilson: The New Freedom* (Princeton, NJ: Princeton University Press, 1956), 304–12, gives an extensive accounting of the canal toll issue.

12. See Daniel Rodgers, "In Search of Progressivism," *Reviews in American History*, 10 (December 1982): 113–32, for an excellent discussion of why not to try to discern one element of "progressivism" in any of the era's reform movements.

13. LaFeber, "The 'Lion in the Path,'" 711, and Painter, *Standing at Armageddon*, 285.

and order had been needed for domestic production and markets. The 1912
Progressive Party platform had declared it "imperative to the welfare of our
people that we enlarge and extend our foreign commerce." This statement was
meant to bolster the platform's plank for two new battleships a year—hence
the disillusionment of some of the women at the convention—and clearly signified that leading progressive men intended to use military power to regulate
foreign relations. Theodore Roosevelt railed against President Taft for not in-
tervening in Mexico to protect U.S. oil interests there. When Mexican revolutionaries overthrew the dictatorship of Porfirio Díaz and threatened American
interests there, progressive followers of Roosevelt's New Nationalism called
for massive intervention in order to "defend property and order against revolutionary chaos." When U.S. ships invaded the port of Veracruz in 1914, these
progressive imperialists thought the action was insufficient. They rejoiced
when Wilson finally sent the army into Mexico in 1916 under General "Black
Jack" Pershing. Herbert Croly's 1909 book, *The Promise of American Life*, encapsulated why these progressives believed in the need to order and regulate the
world:

> The American nation, just in so far as it believes in its nationality and is ready to
> become more of a nation, must assume a more definite and a more responsible
> place in the international system. . . . In all probability no American international
> system will ever be established without the forcible pacification of one or more
> centers of disorder. . . . The United States has already made an effective beginning
> in this great work both by the pacification of Cuba and by the attempt to intro-
> duce a little order into the affairs of the turbulent Central American countries.

Croly's additional remark that the work had also been helped along by having
a strong dictator in Mexico would presage the progressive support for U.S. intervention policies that would stabilize governments and economies in the
Caribbean across the coming years.[14] In the same way, President Wilson would
be able to draw many progressives into supporting U.S. entry into World War
I, that "European" conflict. Patriotic nationalism demanded international interventionism to secure an orderly world and to defeat any forces that threatened to disrupt this order.

Ordering world affairs cannot be separated out from economic interests, of
course. Because so many progressives had connected economic prosperity to
progress on the domestic scene, it made sense to some of them to practice it internationally. While in office, President Taft consciously practiced "Dollar Diplomacy": if something on the international scene benefitted U.S. economic interests, his administration pursued it. The expansion of state-centered power as an
aspect of progressive ideas about a domestic political economy, thus, was
brought into foreign policy. New Nationalist Republicans, following Roosevelt's
lead, envisioned this as bringing order and stability to the world of property and

---

14. See Alan Dawley, *Changing the World: American Progressives in War and Revolution* (Princeton,
NJ: Princeton University Press, 2003), 42–43; and William Leuchtenberg, "Progressivism and Imperialism: The Progressive Movement and American Foreign Policy, 1898–1916," *The Mississippi Valley Historical Review*, 39 (December 1952): 483–504. Croly quoted 501–02, from Herbert Croly, *The
Promise of American Life* (New York: Macmillan, 1909), 209, 302–03.

economics. Other progressives, however, remained so focused on specific social problems that they paid little attention to foreign developments outside their area of interest. Right up to the moment that war erupted in August 1914, progressives working on housing reform, urban planning, workmen's compensation, etc., were traveling in Europe. They thought more about being "citizens of the progressive world" than about international expansionism. In their minds, social politics overshadowed nationalist politics, and it is probably true that these progressives did not have "an economic understanding of the path to war deep enough." When war broke out they were genuinely surprised and hard-pressed to understand why it had happened.[15]

2. Expansion as Progress

Seeing expansion as an aspect of ordering and regulating the United States only partially accounts for the foreign policy pursued during the Progressive Era. Progress was becoming defined also as pushing American ideas and American values out into the world.

Moralism

An element of moral superiority underlying Progressive Era foreign policy sometimes coincided with, sometimes fought against, involvement in other countries' affairs. Assessments that Woodrow Wilson and William Jennings Bryan believed themselves to be "missionaries of democracy," or that both Theodore Roosevelt and Wilson were "Christian moralists," are correct. And, as with most missionaries, these men believed in their own righteousness. It has been said of Wilson and Bryan that they were "inspired by the confidence that they knew better how to promote the peace and well being of other countries than did the leaders of those countries themselves." Such language had already been used in 1904 when Roosevelt promulgated his Corollary to the Monroe Doctrine, claiming for the United States the right to exercise international police power to end chronic unrest or wrongdoing in the Western Hemisphere. Roosevelt had couched his so-called Roosevelt Corollary in moralistic terms:

> All that this country desires is to see the neighboring countries stable, orderly, and prosperous. Any country whose people conduct themselves well can count upon our hearty friendship. If a nation shows that it knows how to act with reasonable efficiency and decency in social and political matters, if it keeps order and pays its obligations, it need fear no interference from the United States. . . . It is a mere truism to say that every nation, whether in America or anywhere else, which desires to maintain its freedom, its independence, must ultimately realize that the right of such independence can not be separated from the responsibility of making good use of it.

---

15. Cyrus Veeser, *Dollar Diplomacy and America's Rise to Global Power* (New York: Columbia University Press, 2002); Dawley, *Changing the World*, 102–03; and Daniel Rodgers, *Atlantic Crossings: Social Politics in a Progressive Age* (Cambridge, MA: Harvard University Press, 1998), 268–75, quotes, 268 and 275. See also, Emily S. Rosenberg, *Financial Missionaries to the World* (Cambridge, MA: Harvard University Press, 1999).

In making the case for this interventionism, Roosevelt was referring to the United States as helping Cuba to become a "just and stable civilization" through the Platt Amendment.[16]

Wilson also spoke in moralistic terms when dealing with Mexico. When revolutionaries seized the Mexican government in 1913, he refused to follow the traditional practice of recognizing whatever government was in place. For Wilson, it was an immoral government, installed through revolution and violence. Despite pleas of railroad and oil interests that recognition and non-interference would protect U.S. economic interests in Mexico, he withheld recognition for all of 1913 and into 1914 while trying to force the Mexican government to hold new elections. Wilson did not believe that Mexicans were incapable of better self-government, as some of those Americans with economic interests in Mexico believed. "When properly directed," he said, "there is no people not fitted for self-government." Yet he justified his interference in Mexican affairs by saying that "I do not hold that the Mexican peons are at present as capable of self-government as other people—ours for example." Secure in his own moral righteousness, Wilson believed it was his duty to bring better government to Mexico. When a minor incident involving an American warship gave Wilson the excuse to order U.S. marines and sailors to occupy the port city of Veracruz, he was so certain of his position's morality that he was surprised when the Mexicans seemed to forget their internecine quarrels and turned on the American invaders.[17] On a sliding scale of one to ten as to how negative were the ideas of progressive moralism—ten being the most negative—Wilson's can probably be judged at about a three. His deep roots in Protestantism—his father was a minister—had imbued him with a messianic sensibility. This does not excuse his paternalistic moralism toward other groups of people, but the genesis of such moralism was in social gospel progressivism. As the religious-based morality of the social gospel had preached attaining the Kingdom of God on earth for the United States, Wilson now sought to bring the Kingdom of God to the entire world.[18]

Mission of Civilization

Other progressives turned foreign policy into a mission to civilize other people by conquering them, such as had been the idea behind "civilizing" the Native Americans. As with Native Americans, the idea of civilizing them generally meant taking their land and occupying them more for U.S. benefit than for their own. The sardonic Mark Twain had a quip for this tendency also: "There must be two Americas: one that sets the captive free and one that takes a once-captive's new freedom away from him."[19]

---

16. Dawley, *Changing the World*, 79; Link, *The New Freedom*, 278; President Theodore Roosevelt, "Annual Message to Congress," December 6, 1904.

17. Link, *The New Freedom*, 394.

18. See John Morton Blum, *Woodrow Wilson and the Politics of Morality* (Boston: Little, Brown, 1956) and Malcolm D. Magee, "Above the Mountains of the Earth: The American Presbyterian Roots of Woodrow Wilson's Foreign Policy" (Ph.D. diss., Michigan State University, 2004).

19. Twain quoted in Dawley, *Changing the World*, 18.

The first articulation of this policy came with the occupation of the Philippines after the "splendid little war" ended in 1898. Senator Albert Beveridge was a fervent progressive whose causes included the abolition of child labor, the eight-hour day for labor, and government regulation of corporations. Beveridge also ardently supported annexing the Philippines, providing instructive example of how an arch-progressive could also promote imperialism by drawing upon the former crusades to justify the latter through an amalgam of racist ideology, ideas about the greatness of American democracy, and economic progress. As soon as Spain surrendered in 1898, Congress debated whether to occupy or to leave the Philippines. Beveridge immediately opted for occupation: "The opposition tells us that we ought not to rule a people without their consent. I answer, the rule of liberty, that all just governments derive their authority from the consent of the governed, applies only to those who are capable of self-government," he declared in a public speech. Two years later, in the midst of the Filipino uprising against the occupation, Beveridge again compared the Filipino people to children not capable of self-government, but now he went a bit further: "They are not capable of self-government. How could they be? They are not of a self-governing race. They are Orientals, Malays . . ." His racial thinking, messianic belief in American democracy, and the ideas of progress all came tumbling out in this speech:

> Mr. President, this question is . . . elemental. It is racial. God has not been preparing the English-speaking and Teutonic peoples for a thousand years for nothing but vain and idle self-contemplation and self-administration. No! He has made us the master organizers of the world to establish system where chaos reigns. . . . And of all our race He has marked the American people as His chosen nation to finally lead in the regeneration of the world. This is the divine mission of America . . . We are trustees of the world's progress.

The average American may not have heard Beveridge's speeches, but a concrete vision was presented to the visitors to the 1904 St. Louis World's Fair. The exhibit dedicated to the Philippines there was intended to show that Filipinos were not yet ready for self-government.[20]

Populist crusader Bryan challenged Beveridge's ideas of a divine mission of civilization in his speech to the Democratic Convention of 1900. "If true Christianity consists of carrying out in our daily lives the teachings of Christ," he declared, "who will say that we are commanded to civilize with dynamite and proselyte with the sword?"[21] Yet, Bryan's entire speech shows that he was most concerned that imperialism would benefit big business and would impose intolerable military burdens on farmers and workers to maintain an empire. After several upheavals in the Caribbean, Bryan, as secretary of state

---

20. Leuchtenberg, "Progressivism and Imperialism," 484 for first Beveridge quote. Beveridge speech from *Congressional Record*, 56th Cong., 1st Sess., 704–12. See also, George F. Becker, "Conditions Requisite to Our Success in the Philippine Islands," address delivered before the American Geographical Society, February 20, 1901, *Bulletin of the American Geographical Society* (1901): 112–23 for similar ideas; and Matthew Frye Jacobson, *Barbarian Virtues: The United States Encounters Foreign Peoples at Home and Abroad, 1876–1917* (New York: Hill and Wang, 2000), 227 for discussion of the 1904 Fair.

21. William Jennings Bryan, *Speeches* (New York, 1909).

under Wilson, even gave up his anti-imperialist stance. He supported intervention in Latin American countries in order to be a benevolent tutor in the arts of self-government to backward people.[22] Other progressives responded less enthusiastically to imperialist conquest and intervention, but many of them shared the common belief that other groups of people were not yet ready to assume responsibility for their own progress, let alone contribute to the progress of the world.

The Panama-Pacific International Exhibition, held in 1915 in San Francisco to celebrate the opening of the Panama Canal, clearly represented the idea of expansion as progress. The locations of three major exhibitions held in the United States from 1876 to 1915 metaphorically celebrated the expansion of the continental United States: from Philadelphia to Chicago to San Francisco, the United States was complete from coast to coast.[23] The San Francisco Exhibition, held in a city on the rim of the Pacific, also celebrated the U.S. extension out into the world. The 1915 Exhibition transformed the 1893 Exposition's "Court of Honor" into the "Court of the Universe" on which western, but particularly American, progress was displayed. In other regards, the layout remained the same as before so that the hierarchy of civilization was clear to everyone attending. One of the main entrances to the exhibition led along the Avenue of Progress, where the visitor could admire the "Palaces" of Mining and Metallurgy, Machinery, and Varied Industries. Another main entrance led into the "Court of the Universe" surrounded by the Agriculture, Liberal Arts, Manufactures, and Transportation "Palaces." The Panama Building was relegated to a small distant pavilion on a street named Cortez Way. Whether intentional or not, locating the Panama Building on a street named for a sixteenth-century European conqueror fittingly captured the American sense of western progress over lesser peoples.

"Americanizing" White Manhood

The connection of Americanism to racial ideals was quickly applied to foreign policy. It is easy to imagine that first in line to articulate this idea was Theodore Roosevelt. When the Filipinos revolted against occupation, Roosevelt urged a vigorous response to the conflict in a speech to a men's club in Chicago:

> We cannot avoid the responsibilities that confront us in Hawaii, Cuba, Porto [sic] Rico, and the Philippines. . . . I preach to you, then, my countrymen, that our country calls not for the life of ease but for the life of strenuous endeavor. The twentieth century looms before us big with the fate of many nations. If we stand idly by, if we seek merely swollen, slothful ease and ignoble peace, if we shrink from the hard contexts where men must win at hazard of their lives and at the risk of all they hold dear, then the bolder and stronger peoples will pass us by, and will win for themselves the domination of the world.

Vigor, courage, strenuous work were the attributes of American manhood in Roosevelt's eyes. He and other like-minded Americans also compared this vigorous manhood against that of the men of the new colonies. Social geographer George Becker likened Filipinos to adolescents: "Any close observer finds among them a lack of the sense of responsibility and an absence of settled

---

22. See also, Dawley, *Changing the World*, 80–81.
23. The 1904 St. Louis Fair celebrated the centennial of the Louisiana Purchase.

principles of action not dissimilar to those with which we are familiar among American boys in their teens."[24]

Unlike Roosevelt, Becker was not an admirer of war. He and others who considered themselves progressives, however, justified imperialism by thinking about benevolent progress as brought to the world by the United States. This caused them, either consciously or unconsciously, to construct a mental image of occupied peoples as lesser human beings. The fact that the Cubans themselves had not only rebelled against Spain but had played a significant role in the success of their insurrection was all but ignored by the press and leading political figures at the time. American will and willingness to fight and die were celebrated as the cause of victory and the reason for America's growing dominance in the world. The press portrayed the Cuban rebels sympathetically. They were courageous men revolting against the despicable Spaniards, but the American military was depicted as rushing to their rescue. Most accounts at the time would also neglect to mention how many of the U.S. military in Cuba were African Americans and Native Americans. Four black units of the regular army were among the first troops readied for the Cuban campaign. Rather ironically, these were units that had been used in the west to subdue Native Americans.[25] But Roosevelt's flamboyance and gift for self-promotion—he was even given the honorific thereafter of "Colonel" after his 1898 exploits—attracted the American press in Cuba to report on his exploits more than those of the regular army.

Roosevelt had also had a hand in trying to build a "white" army, by which is meant not just skin color but ideals of white manhood. In his personal account of his exploits he explained how he had filled the Rough Riders with men from the West and Southwest, those who came from the areas of the country "most recently won over to white civilization." Following his theory of "hybridity" he mixed in with them men from other European backgrounds and some mixed-blood Indians. He refused to admit any Asian or African American volunteers to the Rough Riders. Moreover, the "honor" of American manhood was invoked to justify war in 1898, just as it would be in 1914 when Wilson intervened in Mexico. Senator Beveridge even argued that it was government's purpose to "manufacture manhood." Empire was the new frontier that could build character among (white) American men.[26]

---

24. Speech of Theodore Roosevelt to Chicago, 1899, printed in Roosevelt, *The Strenuous Life: Essays and Addresses* (New York: The Century Company, 1903); and Becker, "Conditions Requisite to Our Success in the Philippine Islands," 116. But see also, Chapter 12 of this book for the different perspective of an American woman living in Mexico at the time.

25. Willard B. Gatewood, Jr., "Black Americans and the Quest for Empire, 1898–1903," *Journal of Southern History*, 38 (November 1972), 547. Thanks to Dawn Ottevaere for pointing me to this essay.

26. For invaluable insight into the aspect of manhood and Cuba and the Philippines, see Kristen L. Hoganson, *Fighting for American Manhood: How Gender Politics Provoked the Spanish-American and Philippine-American Wars* (New Haven, CT: Yale University Press, 1998). Theodore Roosevelt, *The Rough Riders* (New York: Charles Scribner's Sons, 1900), 22–23, quoted in Gary Gerstle, *American Crucible: Race and Nation in the Twentieth Century* (Princeton, NJ: Princeton University Press, 2001), 27–28. See also, Gail Bederman, *Manliness and Civilization: A Cultural History of Gender and Race in the United States, 1880–1917* (Chicago: University of Chicago Press, 1995). For Cubans, see Louis A. Pérez, *The War of 1898: The United States and Cuba in History and Historiography* (Chapel Hill: University of North Carolina Press, 1998). Albert Beveridge, *The Young Man and the World* (New York: Appleton, 1905), 338.

The building of the Panama Canal, as Rubén Blades sang about it, depicts this racial understanding of manliness and imperialism. Building the canal was dangerous, unhealthy work. Yellow fever epidemics had plagued its progress from the start and had contributed to a French company abandoning the initial attempts to build a canal. Despite medical advances in understanding the causes of the fever, the canal construction company took few chances of an epidemic among American workers. It employed many Caribbean men to do the actual hard work while white men did the supervising. Caribbean men were considered less "manly" in other regards: their labor was not equal to that of "white" men. As Blades correctly wrote, white men were paid in gold; Caribbean men in silver. Silver was worth half as much as gold. So, the land and the men of the Caribbean were exploited for American progress, and the people there were not deemed as valuable as were "whites." The United States could claim that it was bringing democracy to the world, but once again democracy was not equal for everyone, nor did it accord equal recognition to the work, sacrifices, and hopes of other people. As Blades recounted it: his grandfather went to make a new life in Panama. He helped build the canal. He and other Caribbeans lived and died in Panama, but their contributions to "progress" have rarely been recognized.[27]

PROGRESSIVE INTERNATIONALISM

Not all progressives welcomed imperialism. A group of Bostonians founded the Anti-Imperialist League in late 1898. Within a year its membership reached 30,000. Anti-imperialism was the glue of the league, but it meant different things to its different members. On the one hand, there were those members who objected to having anything to do with people of different "races." Many other anti-imperialists were concerned with the undemocratic nature of imperialism, not only with how it was being practiced, but also that it would harm democracy in the United States. In a letter to Susan B. Anthony, Senator George Hoar (R-MA) feared that "the sense of justice and righteousness and the love of liberty which abolished slavery . . . and gave citizenship and suffrage to the colored people seems dead." Some suffragists compared the Filipino people's struggle for freedom to American women demanding suffrage: both were yearning for democratic equality and freedom. Other suffragists were anti-imperialists because they opposed war as brutal and undemocratic. Jane Addams was in the forefront of such anti-imperialism. Introducing her series of essays that were published as *Newer Ideals of Peace*, she consigned war to an outmoded and unreformed way of acting in the world that did not consider the lessons of collective global responsibility that progressivism was preaching. She also implicitly attacked the linkages being made between imperialism, war, and manhood.

> We are much too timid and apologetic in regard to this newer humanitarianism, and do not yet realize what it may do for us in the way of courage and endurance.

---

27. For exploitation of Caribbean men, see Dawley, *Changing the World*, 90–91. See also, Bederman, *Manliness and Civilization*.

> We continue to defend war on the ground that it stirs the nobler blood and the higher imagination of the nation, and thus frees it from moral stagnation and the bonds of commercialism. We do not see that this is to borrow our virtues from a former age and to fail to utilize our own.

Robert LaFollette remained a fervent anti-imperialist who saw war, aggression, and conquest as part of capitalism's attempt to conquer democracy. When President Wilson repudiated a major loan agreement negotiated with the assistance of the J.P. Morgan Company with a consortium that wished to build a railroad in China, he rejoiced with this "rejection of Dollar Diplomacy. Humanity is to be placed higher than property in our international affair."[28]

Addams and LaFollette, indeed most anti-imperialists, were internationalists, not isolationists. They had a very keen sense of the connections of the United States in the world and believed that progressivism was a worldwide cause. Many American progressives recognized that a multitude of problems facing their own society were part of a worldwide system, the defects of which could be resolved by regulating the marketplace economy, practicing mutuality and collectivism across national borders, and spreading democratic principles. They did not believe that expansionism was the means for reforming the conditions of the world. This sense of internationalism drove them to construct international progressive networks.

For African American progressives, internationalism and imperialism were difficult issues to confront. On the one hand, participation in the 1898 war was seen as a chance to prove both black manhood and black citizenship. Supporting the Cuban insurgency also presented the opportunity to free the "non-white" population of Cuba from white oppressors. On the other hand, anti-imperialist African Americans argued that because they were oppressed at home they had no business fighting for someone else's freedom before their own. The fact that the army was racially segregated also rankled even those African Americans who supported the war as their civic duty. The call for a Pan-African Conference to be held in England in the summer of 1900 to bring together people of African descent everywhere in the world presented African Americans with a new way to confont imperialism. W.E.B. DuBois and black Americans responded, joining delegates from Africa, North and South America, and the West Indies at this conference. DuBois drafted the conference "Address to the Nations of the World" and he declared "race uplift" to be a "progressive doctrine." Ida B. Wells-Barnett, and the writer Anna Julia Cooper who attended the 1900 Conference, both also saw the position of African Americans as part of a worldwide problem. As DuBois articulated it, the position of African Americans was "but a local phase of a world problem." Speaking in terms that would have been recognized by any progressive, DuBois asserted

---

28. Kristen Hoganson, "'As Badly-Off as the Filipinos': U.S. Women's Suffragists and the Imperial Issue at the Turn of the Twentieth Century," *Journal of Women's History*, 13 (Summer 2001): 9–33, 13 for Hoar; Addams, *Newer Ideals of Peace* (New York: Macmillan, 1907), 26–27; for LaFollette, Link, *The New Freedom*, 286, originally from *LaFollette's Weekly*, 5 (March 29, 1913), 1. For an illuminating comparison of the peace ideas of William James and Jane Addams, see Linda Schott, "Jane Addams and William James on Alternatives to War," *Journal of the History of Ideas* (April 1993): 241–54.

that the "color line" of imperialism merely "transferred the reign of commercial privilege and extraordinary profit from the exploitation of the European
working class to the exploitation of backward races under the political domination of Europe." When war came to Europe, he again saw its imperial and
racial implications. He charged that the white working class was being encouraged to support the war to show their superiority to the lesser peoples of
the world.[29]

For other progressives, preoccupation with social politics, as mentioned
earlier, had produced a certain euphoria that international cooperation was
overcoming nationalism. In 1914, more than 200 international conferences
were scheduled to be held in Europe. These conferences, and the variety of reforms that were to be discussed at them, fostered an optimism among progressives that they were on the verge of constructing an international civic society:
"a common, public sense, with institutions and visual forms matched to it."
When war came in August of that year, most progressives were totally surprised and very dismayed. Before too long, however, American progressives
rallied around the idea that the war experience in both Germany and England
was producing an orderly and disciplined society. American progressives began to speak of a "war socialism," a collectivism that was altering the political
economies of Europe into ones in which the state assumed control of crucial
parts of the economy. Order, regulation, and controls on laissez-faire capitalism were celebrated by some progressives as achievements that would remain
once the absurdity of war was finished. Editors of the progressive *New Republic* began to wonder "how much longer would the United States 'hang back in
the nineteenth-century industrial chaos?'" On the brink of U.S. entry into the
war Walter Lippmann exalted that "the progressive nations have discovered
that the old unorganized competitive profiteering is unsound and wasteful."[30]

From August 1914 until the United States officially entered the war in April
1917, different streams within progressivism had varying responses to the conflict. Progressives saw signs within the United States that war was having a
salutary effect on reform. Wilson appeared now agreeable to promoting a domestic reform agenda that embraced more social welfare. The Keating-Owen
Child Labor Act passed Congress; railroad workers gained the eight-hour day
with the Adamson Act; a new tax act of 1916 increased levies on the wealthy
and enacted a federal inheritance tax. Wilson appointed to the Supreme Court
Louis Brandeis, the man whose progressive attacks on big business and support for social welfare measures had earned him the label of "the people's
lawyer." Progressives called his nomination "a landmark in the history of

---

29. Gatewood, "Black Americans and the Quest for Empire," 548–55. J.R. Hooker, "The Pan
African Conference of 1900," *Transition*, 46 (1974): 20–24, 24 for DuBois and "progressive doctrine."
See also, Robin D.G. Kelley, "'But a Local Phase of a World Problem': Black History's Global Vision,
1883–1950," *Journal of American History*, 86 (December 1999): 1045–77, DuBois quotes 1054. See
W.E.B. DuBois, "The African Roots of War," *The Atlantic Monthly*, 115 (May 1915): 707–14, for his
complete critique. For more on DuBois, see *W.E.B. DuBois: A Reader*, David Levering Lewis, ed.
(New York: Henry Holt, 1995).

30. Rodgers, *Atlantic Crossings*, 268–79, quotes, 273, 278.

American democracy"; American Jews were overjoyed; labor greeted the nomination enthusiastically. Wall Street and big business were appalled.[31] All of this happened in the context of Wilson's moves to prepare the United States for the possibility of entering the "European" conflict. If entering the war were to become inevitable, then some progressives believed they could take heart at the signs that war would facilitate greater domestic reform.

None of these successes meant that all progressives would automatically support the decision to go to war. They did, however, prepare them for accepting Wilson's arguments that this war was an outgrowth of democratic progressivism. He claimed it would be a war to save the world for democracy. Siding with the victor would give the United States a chance to be the ultimate peace broker who could bring about true democracy and internationalism once the war was won. A snippet from Wilson's war address to Congress reveals his thinking:

> It is a fearful thing to lead this great peaceful people into war, into the most terrible and disastrous of all wars, civilization itself seeming to be in the balance. But the right is more precious than peace, and we shall fight for the things which we have always carried nearest our hearts—for democracy, for the right of those who submit to authority to have a voice in their own governments, for the rights and liberties of small nations, for a universal dominion of right by such a concert of free peoples as shall bring peace and safety to all nations and make the world itself at last free.

Such rhetoric could allow progressives to believe that once the war was won with American power, which they were sure would be the case, nationalistic individualism would be shattered and a new internationalism would take its place. They believed that winning a war over tyranny, as they came to see it, would allow them to break free from a narrowly defined idea of progressivism as "American" and construct it as universal. Winning the war would bring the United States more fully into a world of shared values.[32]

Moreover, the ideas now espoused by progressives such as Lippman and the editors of *The New Republic* about the need for a strong, regulatory state heralded a shifting focus among their progressivism. They were replacing ideas about collectivism and government action in the public interest with calls to a new sense of civic nationalism that spoke about the national interest.[33] This may seem at first glance an arbitrary distinction, but it was not. Defining a "public" interest had always been a slippery problem for progressives. Whose public interest was always a question. If one governed in the national interest instead, the definitional problem could seemingly be solved as the nation theoretically covered all of the public. Yet, as opponents of war

---

31. Arthur S. Link, *Woodrow Wilson: Confusions and Crises, 1915–1916* (Princeton, NJ: Princeton University Press, 1964), 323–28, quote, 327; Dawley, *Changing the World*, 120–21 and 234.

32. *Congressional Record*, 65th Cong., 1st sess., 102–04. Rodgers, *Atlantic Crossings*, 279. See also, James Livingston, "The War and the Intellectuals: Bourne, Dewey, and the Fate of Pragmatism," *The Journal of the Gilded Age and Progressive Era*, 2 (October 2003): 431–50.

33. Dawley, *Changing the World*, 122–23, discusses this matter.

would object, governing from a national interest could allow any group or any idea to dominate others and perhaps inevitably lead to defining any objection as anti-American. Republican progressive Robert LaFollette perceived it this way. He had enthusiastically backed the domestic reform agenda of the Democrat Wilson, but LaFollette's progressivism saw no public interest in interventions, war, or the U.S. entry into it, only a business interest. For LaFollette, the enemy remained big business and its exploitation of the public interest. The interventions in the Caribbean, he thought, had "reduced the U.S. Marines to a collection agency for Yankee creditors." He decried the willingness of nations to "sacrifice lives for private gain." He believed that the $50 million loaned to France by J.P. Morgan and Company in 1915—indeed the more than $2 billion that U.S. banks had lent to France and England by 1917—had more to do with war profiteering than with promoting democracy. If Germany won the war, England and France would never repay the loans. He was one of six senators who voted against going to war, declaring that "the poor, sir, who are the ones called upon to rot in the trenches, have not organized power" to resist. Progressive Senator George Norris feared that "We are going into war upon the command of gold . . . I feel that we are about to put the dollar sign on the American Flag."[34]

The idea of war and conflict as enhancing American manhood was ever-present in the rhetoric surrounding war. Theodore Roosevelt was keen to go to war and to enact compulsory male military service. He declared that "the military tent where they all sleep side by side will rank next to the public school among the great agents of democratization." As usual, he did not mean to include African American, Native American, or Hispanic men. But even the non-belligerent progressive Raymond Robins was won over to accepting this kind of reasoning. As the Republican Convention of 1916 was considering whether to include a war resolution and whether to call for male military service, Robins concluded that compulsory military training "will do more in one generation to break down class and section prejudice, develop disciplined, vigorous and efficient citizenship, and to unify the diverse groups of our national life in a vital Americanism than all other forces combined."[35]

It is true, as historian Daniel Rodgers has written, that the war brought social progressives "en masse into government and quasi-government service," where they could play a role in reorganizing the relationships between state and society. Florence Kelley and Josephine Goldmark, working through the Children's Bureau and the National Consumers' League, were important consultants to the government.[36] Once the United States became an actual bel-

---

34. Nancy Unger, *Fighting Bob LaFollette: The Righteous Reformer* (Chapel Hill: University of North Carolina Press, 2000), 235–40. See Dawley, *Changing the World*, 32, for quote on U.S. Marines and his staunch anti-interventionism. For Norris, see David Kennedy, *Over Here: The First World War and American Society* (New York: Oxford University Press, 1982), 21.

35. Robins quoted in Leuchtenberg, "Progressivism and Imperialism," 497; Roosevelt in Kennedy, *Over Here*, 17.

36. Rodgers, *Atlantic Crossings*, 283–84.

ligerent in the war, most progressives hoped that by working with the government during war they would be active participants in restructuring society in the aftermath. It had been growing increasingly evident to many of them that domestic progressivism had not solved many of the country's racial, labor, or gender problems. They hoped that the collective wartime activities and new cooperative measures that they were able to implement would carry over afterwards. These hopes would be sorely disappointed.

It was early springtime that the strike was on
They moved us miners out of doors
Out from the houses that the company owned
We moved into the tents at old Ludlow.

We were so afraid they would kill our children
We dug us a cave that was seven foot deep
Carried our young ones and a pregnant woman
Down inside the cave to sleep.

That very night you soldiers waited
Until us miners fell asleep
You snuck around our little tent town
Soaked our tents with your kerosene.

You struck a match and the blaze it started
You pulled the triggers of your gattling guns
I made a run for the children but the fire wall
  stopped me
Thirteen children died from your guns.

We took some cement and walled that cave up
Where you killed those thirteen children inside
I said, "God bless the Mine Workers' Union"
And then I hung my head and cried.*

"The Ludlow Massacre"
Woody Guthrie

The mining town of Ludlow, Colorado, sat alongside the Purgatory River in the foothills of the Sangre de Cristo Mountains. The Colorado Fuel and Iron Company, the property of John D. Rockefeller, owned the mines of Ludlow. Mining was a hazardous occupation and Colorado Fuel and Iron was not particularly concerned to protect its employees. Between 1904 and 1914, around 200 miners were killed in its mines, where they labored for less than $2 a day, often paid in scrip that they could only redeem at company stores. They lived in houses owned by the company. The Western Federation of Miners had tried to organize the Colorado mines early in the century, but with the help of the forces of law and order the companies had thwarted their attempts. In late 1913, about 9,000 miners walked off their jobs. Evicted from company houses, they set up tent colonies and refused to be moved.

On April 20, 1914, the tent colony at Ludlow was attacked by the state militia, sent into the area by the governor at the urging of the company. When the onslaught was over, there were twenty dead bodies in the colony. Two women and eleven children were among the dead; they had burned or suffocated to death when the attackers set fire to the tents. Enraged miners descended on Ludlow and battled the company and the militia until President Wilson was forced to call in the army to restore order. When order was restored, the strike was effectively broken. Miners were either blacklisted or returned to their jobs with no concessions from the company.

That same April 20, Wilson had ordered the military assault on Veracruz, Mexico, near the Tampico oilfields in which Rockefeller was a major stockholder. The June 1914 issue of the radical magazine *The Masses*, with its blood-red cover featuring a huge miner firing a rifle and holding a dead child in his other hand, had two main stories: Ludlow and Mexico. The message was clear. Despite all progressive reform, business still controlled the country. The location of Ludlow was perhaps prophetic: it was purgatory for the miners and the Sangre de Cristo (blood of Christ) was surely running.

---

*"The Ludlow Massacre" by Woody Guthrie. © Copyright 1958 (renewed) by Sanga Music, Inc. All rights reserved. Used by permission.

CHAPTER 11

Domestic Troubles, Foreign Engagement

Political democracy can only exist where there is industrial democracy.
—COMMISSION ON INDUSTRIAL RELATIONS, 1912

God Gave Me My Money.
—JOHN D. ROCKEFELLER, 1905

T HE YEAR 1914 was not an especially auspicious one for progressives interested in social reform. Try as they might to warm to Woodrow Wilson, his New Freedom still did not pursue the social reform agenda that many of them wanted. He had acquiesced in the racial segregation of the federal government, resisted federal government social policies that would restrict states' rights, refused to support national woman suffrage, and had only intervened in the Colorado mine strike after failing personally to convince Rockefeller to compromise with the miners.

One reason the Colorado miners' strike was so intransigent was that a global business recession had begun late in 1913. With the United States now tied into the world marketplace, it could not escape the recession that was, in part, caused by events in Europe. In response, production in the United States dropped and unemployment rose. These events forced Wilson to reconsider his idea that the country would be reformed by breaking up monopolies. He now began to move closer to Roosevelt's position that big business was here to stay and that government and business should work together on economic regulation. A stream of businessmen, including J.P. Morgan, flooded into the White House for chats, in which the president assured them that he was on their side. Robert La Follette was distressed as Wilson appointed conservatives to the Interstate Commerce Commission (ICC) and the Federal Reserve Board, fearing that "progressive" control of these key areas of regulation was about to end. When a coalition of conservative Democrats and Republicans confirmed

219

the ICC nominations, LaFollette charged that Wilson had triumphed "over progressive Democrats and progressive Republicans by securing the support of all that remains of the old Aldrich oligarchy."[1]

The Democrats lost seats in the congressional elections of 1914, although they maintained control of Congress. Wilson put an optimistic face on the results. He expressed the opinion that so much economic regulation had been accomplished, including much better relations between labor and business, that the country was well along the road to progress. Yet, 1914 showed that was clearly not the case. The right of workers to organize unions was being forcefully rejected by business, as Ludlow exposed again to the public. By the winter of 1914–15 the war in Europe had worsened the economic picture in the United States. Unemployment made that winter especially cruel and tumultuous. Nationally, about 11.5 percent of the workforce was unemployed. In industrial cities the total was higher: more than 13 percent in Chicago and above 20 percent in Duluth, Minnesota. The U.S. Labor Bureau estimated unemployment in New York City at slightly above 16 percent in early 1915. "Armies" of unemployed men began marching to Washington again as they had done in the depression of 1893–94. Outbreak of war in August 1914 further exacerbated domestic conditions as food prices began rising: the cost of bread, for example, rose 20 percent. The Women's Trade Union League was organizing marches of unemployed women. The IWW was making gains in the western states and leading unemployment marches. Socialists were rallying against the war. Women had organized a Peace Party that was not only marching against the war, it was connecting with female peace activists all across Europe.[2]

In the face of growing disorder and radical agitation, social justice progressives struggled to maintain their reform agenda of collectivity and democracy. Hull House held meetings of the unemployed, with Addams still hoping that the collective voice would make an impression on the city's employers. But when the unemployed marched through the streets without a permit they were beaten and several were arrested by the police, including seven women. As they had done in the past, wealthy Chicago women such as Mary Wilmarth bailed out many of those arrested, and Sophonisba Breckinridge declared that she would testify on their behalf at any trial. But even at Hull House more radical elements began to seize the upper hand. At a following meeting protestors resolved to continue using the public streets to

> [demonstrate] our poverty to the world, and by so doing forcing the authorities to do something for the unemployed and their dependents . . . we the unemployed of Chicago, are determined to use the liberty of the public streets, and shall continue to use the public streets and fight for the rights of same until we have acquired our purpose—namely: the cry for bread and work be heeded.

---

1. Arthur S. Link, *Woodrow Wilson: The New Freedom* (Princeton, NJ: Princeton University Press, 1956), 447–50, for the ICC appointment and LaFollette's losing fight to stop it; quote, 450, originally from *LaFollette's Weekly*, 6 (April 18, 1914): 9.

2. Nell Irvin Painter, *Standing at Armageddon: The United States, 1877–1919* (New York: W.W. Norton, 1987), 295–96.

Major Strike Areas, 1886–1919

Despite the pleas of Addams and Breckinridge not to do so, these demonstrators had again poured into the streets carrying banners crying "Starvation or revolution, which?" or "Why should we starve in the midst of plenty?"[3]

WORLD WAR I

Given the volatility of domestic conditions, the war in Europe was a mixed blessing both for the Wilson administration and for many progressives. On the one hand, the economy slowly recovered by the spring of 1915, largely due to orders for war supplies from Europe. American banks prospered as loans to the belligerents reached $2.25 billion by 1916. Merchant ships carried a steady stream of American goods across the Atlantic as Wilson pronounced the United States neutral and declared that the United States was free to trade with whomever it wanted. He also declared that American ships should be inviolate in the Atlantic and that Americans should be free to travel across the ocean without fear of harm. In hindsight these policies could only have led to disaster. The bulk of American loans went to Britain and France. If they lost the war, those loans would go unpaid and American banks would collapse. As the

---

3. *Chicago Tribune*, February 1, 1915.

German side grew more desperate, American shipping came increasingly under fire and American property and lives were lost in the new submarine warfare. Each incident put more pressure on Wilson's neutrality policy, but his administration held firm to the principle that American business should be free to trade unimpeded with any European country. In the 1916 presidential campaign Wilson and the Democrats pledged not to go to war, yet early in 1915 Wilson had started a "preparedness" campaign that many progressives feared would lead the United States into war. He authorized construction of new warships for the navy and almost tripled the size of the regular army. He sent the army into Mexico in mid-1916.

In the administration, only Wilson's secretary of state, the old populist William Jennings Bryan, objected to these policies. In June 1915, he resigned his position and began a peace crusade. In speeches across the country he warned Americans that a new fight was now on "between the people and the special interests." Progressive Frederic Howe attacked business and war-profiteering and Robert LaFollette declared profit as the chief motive behind all of Wilson's international policies. He demanded an immediate embargo on selling armaments to the belligerents.[4]

Radicals charged that preparedness was causing even more labor injustice. The socialist Kate Richards O'Hare furiously denounced the war as a capitalist venture. "The Congress of the United States," she declared, "has the power to stop the war in Europe almost instantly by forbidding the exportation of food and ammunition." "Money," she went on to say

> that has been stolen by corrupt officials and worse than wasted on armament and preparation for war would provide funds to give labor to every unemployed man and make possible all manner of public industries . . . the constitutional power to issue money with which to wage a war of destruction could just as readily be invoked to wage a war on poverty and unemployment.[5]

Socialists and the IWW, led by the Italian-American anarchist Carlo Tresca, conducted a bitter labor strike in 1916 in the iron ore mines of the Mesabi Range in northern Minnesota. The mining company, a subsidiary of U.S. Steel, refused to negotiate. The strikers suffered beatings, arrests, and deaths, until the strike was broken. Preparedness required steel and the Wilson administration was not about to intervene on the part of the strikers. The chances that socialism, a minor movement in the United States, could actually succeed in keeping the United States out of war were even further diminished as European socialist movements succumbed to nationalist sentiment and supported the war. So American socialists were fighting a lonely ideological battle against the inexorable pull of war.

Progressive women formed the Women's Peace Party in 1915 to try to prevent U.S. involvement in the war, and there would be an important gender di-

---

4. Arthur S. Link, *Wilson: Confusions and Crises, 1915–1916* (Princeton, NJ: Princeton University Press, 1960), 30–33; Alan Dawley, *Changing the World: American Progressives in War and Revolution* (Princeton, NJ: Princeton University Press, 2003), 118; and Nancy Unger, *Fighting Bob LaFollette: The Righteous Reformer* (Chapel Hill: University of North Carolina Press, 2000), 235–40.

5. Kate Richards O'Hare, "I Denounce," *The National Rip-Saw*, 12 (March 1915).

Protesting the Violence Against the Striking Minnesota Miners (1916)
Source: Library of Congress, Prints & Photographs Division, LC-USZ62-21716

mension to their response to war as there was to that of socialist Josephine Conger Kaneko. As she expressed it, war was "a thoroughly masculine quantity."[6] This gender dimension to foreign policy will be discussed in detail in Chapter 12 so that it can receive the attention it deserves. Before that, the rest of this chapter will consider the impact of war on the country and progressivism, beginning with the challenge of the presidential election of 1916.

PROGRESSIVISM AND WAR

1. The 1916 Presidential Campaign

By the November 1916 election, war had been raging in Europe for more than two years. Wilson was certain to be renominated by the Democrats, but antiwar sentiment still ran high in the United States, so the Democrats needed to promise peace. Despite his preparedness campaign, Wilson pronounced himself the candidate of peace and ran on the slogan "He kept us out of war." He emphasized his neutrality toward Europe and the peace made with Mexico by

6. Mari Jo Buhl, *Women and American Socialism, 1870–1920* (Urbana: University of Illinois Press, 1983), 312.

the time of the convention. He defended his interference in Mexico as a just cause, proclaiming that he was "more interested in the fortunes of oppressed men and pitiful women and children than in any property rights whatsoever." For progressives disheartened by his foreign policy, he pointed to his support of the Keating-Owen Child Labor Act, a workmen's compensation act for federal employees, and the Adamson Act for railroad workers. All Wilson's points in the campaign emphasized fighting oppression at home and abroad, a goal that he would reiterate in his later war message. Finally, Wilson promised that his second administration would "build an America in which the nations of the world 'shall at last come to see upon what deep foundation of humanity and justice our passion for peace rests.'"[7]

By portraying the Democrats as the true party of progressivism who were now promoting social welfare legislation and direct government amelioration of labor relations, Wilson undercut progressivism in the Republican Party. Republican nominee Charles Evans Hughes played into the Democrats' hands, first by attacking the Adamson Act as government interference in the rights of business to control labor and then attacking the neutrality campaign and labeling the president's preparedness campaign as too weak. In contrast to Wilson's themes of humanity and justice, the Hughes campaign called for an "America first and America efficient."[8]

In the 1916 campaign both parties had to take account of the growing numbers of women voters. Four million women were now eligible to vote for president. Both parties endorsed women suffrage, but neither promised to support the national suffrage amendment and neither candidate was forthcoming with personal promises to support the amendment's passage. Progressive women were torn between the two candidates. Frances Kellor opted for Hughes and headed a Women's Committee of the National Hughes Alliance. Other prominent progressives Harriet Vittum and Margaret Dreier Robins of Chicago also supported Hughes. The women of the Hughes committee had staunchly backed Theodore Roosevelt in 1912 and even though the party no longer seemed to be pursuing social welfare they could not break away altogether from the Republican Party. The women's committee organized and financed a women's campaign train that left New York on October 2, making "whistle-stops" in cities across the country. Other former Progressive Party women did, however, switch parties, saying they were making the best choice out of a bad bargain. In Illinois, Jane Addams and Mary Wilmarth voted for Wilson. Wilmarth wrote to her friend Ellen Gates Starr that she was "oppressed with the call for decision as to my first vote for President." She vehemently objected to his Mexico policy, his military build up, and his segregation of the federal government. On the other hand, she welcomed other aspects of his policy that emphasized social justice: his willingness to work with Julia Lathrop as head of the Children's Bureau and support for anti–child labor. She also disliked Hughes' statements about Ameri-

7. Arthur S. Link and William M. Leary, "Election of 1916," in *The Coming to Power: Critical Presidential Elections in American History*, Arthur M. Schlesinger Jr., Fred L. Israel, and William P. Hanson, eds. (New York: Chelsea House Publishers, 1972), 296–321; and Maureen A. Flanagan, "The Election of 1916," in *American Presidential Campaigns and Elections*, vol. 2, Ballard C. Campbell and William G. Shade, eds. (New York: Sharpe Reference, 2003), 646–62.

8. Link and Leary, "Election of 1916," 307.

canism and applauded Wilson for having vetoed yet another attempt to enact a literacy test for immigrants. Lillian Wald declared for Wilson also. Whether women controlled the outcome is hard to say because we do not have voting statistics to tell us. But of the women suffrage states, Hughes won only Illinois. He even lost California, where women had voted since 1911. California was among the most progressive of states and the progressive Republican Hiram Johnson was elected governor in that same election.[9]

The really thrilling victory for women in 1916 was the election in Montana of Jeannette Rankin to Congress. Rankin won despite being a Republican in a state that voted for Wilson. Rankin had engaged in social justice causes for several years and her campaign platform promised that she would work for the eight-hour day for women, maternal and child health care, and the national suffrage amendment. She also pledged to support a strong national defense. In spite of this last pledge, a few days after being seated in Congress, she demonstrated her peace credentials and voted against going to war.[10]

2. Progressives and War

Unfortunately, those progressives who had voted for Wilson on the basis of his peace proclamations saw their hopes dashed within a short time. Wilson's neutrality policy grew increasingly useless as Germany had continued to pursue a strategy of submarine warfare that threatened American shipping, property, and lives. Under heavy pressure from businessmen and bankers as well as members of his own administration he broke relations with Germany and asked for congressional support in arming U.S. merchant ships. Finally, on April 2, 1917, he asked Congress for a declaration of war.

As soon as Wilson had declared his preparedness campaign, progressives had organized to oppose it, fearing that it would lead to war and disaster for their reform crusades. In late November 1915, a group gathered at Lillian Wald's Henry Street Settlement and formed an Anti-Militarism Committee, soon renamed the American Union Against Militarism (AUAM). Its members included Wald, Addams, Kelley, Howe, and Paul Kellogg, the editor of *The Survey*, the journal of the social-science-oriented progressives. Wald declared that war was "inevitably disastrous to the humane instincts which had been asserting themselves in the social order." Howe warned that war "is usually identified with a reaction at home. It checks social legislation."[11] The AUAM announced that it would fight against any budget increases to be used for

9. Molly M. Wood, "Mapping a National Campaign Strategy: Partisan Women in the Presidential Election of 1916," in *We Have Come to Stay: American Women and Political Parties, 1860–1960*, Melanie S. Gustafson, Kristie Miller, and Elisabeth Israels Perry, eds. (Albuquerque: University of New Mexico Press, 1999) and Mary Hawes Wilmarth to Ellen Gates Starr, October 21, 1916, Ellen Gates Starr Manuscript Collection, Sophie Smith Collection, Smith College Library. See also, Melanie S. Gustafson, *Women and the Republican Party, 1854–1924* (Urbana: University of Illinois Press, 2001), ch. 6, and Jo Freeman, *A Room at a Time: How Women Entered Party Politics* (Latham, MD: Rowman and Littlefield, 2000), 76–80.

10. Freeman, *A Room at a Time*, 80.

11. David Kennedy, *Over Here: The First World War and American Society* (New York: Oxford University Press, 1980), 33–34. The AUAM set up a civil liberties bureau that ultimately evolved into the American Civil Liberties Union (ACLU).

armaments and then campaigned across the country against the growing militarism, holding frequent antiwar rallies, distributing leaflets and press releases, and mounting an exhibit titled "War Against War," the centerpiece of which was "a huge armored dinosaur symbolizing the military establishment lumbering along with a peasized brain"—the antiprogressive.[12]

As events of early 1917 seemed to bear out the fears that war was now in the offing, Jane Addams and an antiwar group, the Emergency Peace Federation, called on Wilson in late February to try to convince him not to go to war. Yet, progressives were not unified in thinking that war would bring disaster. The editors of the progressive *New Republic* were moving toward supporting war, using the progressive language of internationalism:

> We must recognize that we are one great community and act as a member of it. Our entrance into it [the war] would weight it immeasurably in favor of liberalism and make the organization of a league for peace an immediately practicable object of statesmanship. By showing that we are ready now, as well as in the theoretical future, to defend the western world, the cornerstone of federation would be laid.[13]

Addams recalled that at her meeting with Wilson, he spoke in the same vein: "As head of a nation participating in the war the President of the United States would have a seat at the Peace Table," he told the delegation. "But if he remained the representative of a neutral country he could at best only 'call through a crack in the door.'"[14]

Wilson, the men of the *New Republic*, and many other progressives believed that war had become inevitable and that by entering it they would be able to bring progressive order and regulation to it. Paul Kellogg now abandoned the antimilitarism movement and wrote to Lillian Wald that "the time is ripe . . . to take both the war scare and the lesson which the military leaders of Europe are giving us in developing human and natural resources, as two motive factors in pushing through a program for human conservation and national growth that might otherwise take years to develop." Wald may not have been of total accord with such sentiments, but in July 1917 she too resigned from the AUAM.[15]

Once progressives had accepted the war as fact, they set out to bring order into the war effort and to tie winning the war to advancing a progressive domestic agenda. The National Women's Trade Union League sent Wilson a message outlining its war program. The women wanted nationalization of the railroads, strengthened rights of labor to organize and bargain collectively, and a heavy tax on the wealthy to finance the war. Walter Lippman declared that after the war was won "we shall stand committed as never before to the

---

12. Alan Dawley, *Changing the World: American Progressives in War and Revolution* (Princeton, NJ: Princeton University Press, 2003), 117. *The Survey* (January 1, 1916): 370–71.

13. "Justification," *The New Republic*, 10 (February 10, 1917) and "Defense of the Atlantic World," ibid. (February 17, 1917), quoted in Arthur S. Link, *Woodrow Wilson: Campaigns for Progressivism and Peace* (Princeton, NJ: Princeton University Press, 1965), 304.

14. Jane Addams, *Bread and Peace in Time of War* (Urbana: University of Illinois Press, revised edition, 2002), 38.

15. Kennedy, *Over Here*, 34.

realization of democracy in America. . . . We shall turn with fresh interest to our own tyrannies—to our Colorado mines, our autocratic steel industries, our sweatshops and our slums."[16]

Seeing war in this light allowed many progressives to contribute centrally to the war effort at home. Appeals were made to them to work in areas that particularly interested them. Florence Kelley, Josephine Goldmark, and Grace Abbott took positions overseeing the treatment of women workers and the enforcement of child labor provisions. Julia Lathrop helped to draft a new type of insurance policy for military members, which progressives hoped would be a prelude to new types of social insurance after the war. Labor leader and bootmaker Mary Anderson worked for the Women's Branch in the Army Ordnance Department, where she inspected the working conditions of women in the country's arsenals. Pauline Goldmark headed the Women's Service Section of the Railroad Administration. Goldmark took charge of bettering the condition of female railway workers but also acted as the unofficial advocate for women's rights in the industry. Samuel Gompers was given a spot on the National War Labor Board. New federal agencies recognized collective bargaining and the eight-hour day; better working conditions for women and children were mandated. To meet the needs for housing for war workers who began to flood into the shipyards and industries most necessary for the war effort, government actually began to enact housing policies. Progressive urban planners such as John Nolen were engaged to draw up plans and designs for new communities under two new agencies, the Emergency Fleet Corporation and the United States Housing Corporation. Progressives in individual cities promoted new housing plans, not just because housing was needed, but from their idea that democracy required that social space be well ordered and organized. For some progressives it could, and did, seem as if they had finally captured the national attention for their agenda that had eluded them for years.[17]

Other groups of progressives and their organizations carried on their reform work during the war. Social justice progressives used the military's discovery that young American males were not particularly healthy to continue working for maternal and child health care. The Women's City Club of New York made exposing this problem one of its top priorities. It investigated health conditions in the city, prepared statistical reports, and compared infant mortality rates unfavorably with those in other industrial countries. Earlier progressive campaigns to clean up cities and enact provisions for pure food and milk had made some headway in attacking health problems. Still, the United States had only the 18th lowest maternal death rate and 11th lowest infant mortality rate in the

---

16. Ibid., 39–40; Lippmann quote originally from "The World Conflict in Relation to American Democracy," *Annals*, 72 (1917): 1–10.

17. Daniel Rodgers, *Atlantic Crossings: Social Politics in a Progressive Age* (Cambridge, MA: Harvard University Press, 1998), 283–85, 288–89; Allen F. Davis, "Welfare, Reform, and World War I," *American Quarterly*, 19 (Autumn 1967): 516–33; and Maurine Weiner Greenwald, *Women, War, and Work: The Impact of World War I on Women Workers in the United States* (Ithaca, NY: Cornell University Press, 1980), 61–86. See also, Robert Macieski, "'The Home of the Working Man Is the Balance Wheel of Democracy': Housing Reform in Wartime Bridgeport," *The Journal of Urban History*, 26 (September 2000): 715–32.

world. Business leaders and the AFL had continued to resist any national health insurance programs while European countries had been enacting them.[18]

In other places, women used the state-organized Councils on Defense or local defense councils to promote progressivism. In Illinois, Addams, Mary McDowell, Alice Hamilton, Sophonisba Breckinridge, and Louise DeKoven Bowen headed a Committee on Sanitation, Medicine and Public Health and used the war rhetoric to their advantage: the committee dedicated itself to "one of the most pressing home-front duties . . . to conserve the health of children as a vital strategic measure for winning the war." They succeeded in establishing a Child Welfare Department inside the Council of Defense, which they hoped would outlast the war itself. Black and white women's clubs in Atlanta used their role in organizing the home front to pursue their concerns about vice and protection for young women to reorganize public space in the city. African American clubwomen also used the war effort to demand more equal protection from the federal government. The women from the Neighborhood Union wrote directly to Wilson in spring 1918 demanding an end to lynching, pointing out that this was a type of undemocratic evil that the war was supposedly being fought to conquer. "While we are sacrificing the best blood of our sons upon our Nation's altar to help destroy Prussianism beyond the seas, we call upon you to use your high offices to destroy the lynching institution at our doors." Unfortunately for these women, Wilson was far too preoccupied with foreign affairs to engage in such a domestic crusade.[19]

These progressives' faith that victory in war would prolong progressivism and enhance democracy at home emanated from their beliefs in the power of publicity and education. Despite previous evidence to the contrary, progressives continued to believe that once social ills were demonstrated to Americans through social scientific evidence, they would welcome proposed reforms. Progressivism had always depended on the power of publicity: making the best case for the justice of what was being proposed to convince people to support the cause. It was not so much the progressive faith in publicity that was mistaken, but what the American people could be convinced to support. The Wilson administration took the idea and applied it to promoting the war effort. The president constituted a Committee on Public Information (CPI) headed by George Creel, a progressive muckraker who had endorsed the social centers movement as well as the popular democratic reforms of initiative and referendum. The CPI was charged with "selling the war" because, as Wilson declared, "It is not an army we must shape and train for war, it is a nation." Creel responded to his charge with fervor, declaring that his task was to bring

---

18. "Maternity Protection," *Bulletin*, Women's City Club of New York (June 1917) from WCCNY, Archives and Special Collections, Hunter College, New York, N.Y. (WCCNY microfilm, reel 17, frame 20). See Morton Keller, *Regulating a New Society: Public Policy and Social Change in America, 1900–1933* (Cambridge, MA: Harvard University Press, 1994), 194–96. Of the 30 percent of recruits rejected as unfit for service, the majority were suffering the ill effects of childhood disease.

19. Lynne Curry, *Modern Mothers in the Heartland: Gender, Health, and Progress in Illinois, 1900–1930* (Columbus: Ohio State University Press, 1999), 111, and Sarah Mercer Judson, "'Leisure Is a Foe to Any Man': The Pleasures and Dangers of Leisure in World War I Atlanta," *The Journal of Women's History*, 15 (Spring 2003): 92–115, quote from 106–07.

The Committee for Public Information Sets the Tone
Source: Library of Congress, Prints & Photographs Division, LC-USZ62-71272

about "no mere surface unity, but a passionate belief in the justice of America's cause that should weld the people of the United States into one white-hot mass instinct with fraternity, devotion, courage, and deathless determination." At the beginning of his work, he thought that persuasion, not coercion, was the democratic way. In addition to official publications from his office, he constituted a group he called "Four-Minute Men," who were to give short patriotic speeches in local communities. As the war dragged on, however, the methods of the CPI turned cruder. The agency began to exhort people to turn in anyone they suspected of being unpatriotic. It encouraged the Four-Minute Men to use atrocity stories to whip up war support.[20]

Every war stirs up fervent support and engenders dissent. Repression of dissenters in wartime always results from the need to convince a democratic people of the justice of violent slaughter of other people. That Wilson, Creel, and other fervent participants in the CPI campaign thought it so necessary to have such unity of "passionate belief" reflects in part on the American need to create an identity. When Alexis de Tocqueville had toured the United States in the 1830s, he found it a country where "genuine independence of mind and real freedom of discussion" was essentially absent. Americans, he observed, seemed to feel a tremendous need to assure that they all agreed on values. Accepting this observation makes sense of the deep repression of dissent that would come during the war years. It was not sufficient for Wilson to have general agreement; he wanted the hearts and minds of all Americans behind him so that he would be certain of his values, certain that he was leading a just cause.[21]

The progressive faith in educating a democratic public was also turned to use for the war. In 1908, peace advocates had organized the American School Peace League to encourage the teaching of peace in public schools. With the outbreak of war, other forces now advocated using the schools for military training. The rhetoric of "strenuous masculinity" used to promote such training in schools would have delighted Theodore Roosevelt. Public schools and teachers were instructed to inculcate "patriotism, heroism, and sacrifice" in school children. They were told to portray the war in patriotic, democratic terms, to stress the differences between American democracy and German autocracy. Any teacher who resisted, or refused to take a loyalty oath, could be summarily fired. In one case in New York City, a Quaker pacifist with eighteen years of experience who resisted instructing her students in militarism was dismissed for "behavior unbecoming a teacher."[22]

Faith in education and publicity were "comforting beliefs in a society wracked by new social ills but reluctant to repudiate the laissez-faire, anti-

---

20. Kevin Mattson, *Creating a Democratic Public: The Struggle for Urban Participatory Democracy During the Progressive Era* (University Park: Pennsylvania State University Press, 1998), 106–07, for Creel and Wilson, and Kennedy, *Over Here*, 60–62. See also, George Creel, *How We Advertised America* (New York: Harper & Brothers, 1920).

21. Tocqueville's observations cited in Kennedy, *Over Here*, 47. See also, 63 for more on Americans' longing for "a single consensual set of values."

22. Susan Zeiger, "The Schoolhouse Versus the Armory: U.S. Teachers and the Campaign Against Militarism in the Schools, 1914–1918," *The Journal of Women's History*, 15 (Spring 2003): 150–179, see esp. 158–59 and 167–68. See also, Kennedy, *Over Here*, 54–55.

Patriotic but Segregated: African American Infantry in France (1918)
Source: Library of Congress, Prints & Photographs Division, LC-USZ62-116442

statist heritage that Americans prized," according to one assessment. It might usefully have included the reluctance of Americans to repudiate racist and exclusionary ideologies to this illusion. Even the radical Ida B. Wells-Barnett, whose son served with the army in France, believed that participation in the war effort would finally result in a recognition of equal citizenship. W.E.B. DuBois had supported Wilson's decision to go to war and later urged African Americans to close ranks with "our own white fellow citizens," although union leader A. Philip Randolph opposed the war. DuBois' internationalism convinced him that this was essentially a colonial war, but that minority and colonized peoples around the world would benefit more if the Allies won rather than Germany. African Americans did have some reason for hope. Even before U.S. entry into the war, increasing numbers of industrial jobs created to meet European war orders as well as the promise of political equality were pulling tens of thousands of African Americans northward and away from the legally segregated South. With jobs contributing to the war effort, and African American men enlisting and answering the draft, African American progressives could be optimistic. On the other hand, there were ominous signs against such optimism. When black leaders had appealed to Wilson in 1917 for protection in the midst of a racial riot in East St. Louis, Illinois, Wilson ignored their pleas.[23]

DEMOCRACY FOR THE WORLD, COERCION ON THE HOME FRONT

Despite hopes that war would provide an occasion for implementing some of their reform agendas, progressives could not overcome two critical aspects to war mobilization: the appeal to support the war became wrapped in ideas of "Americanism" and the war became defined as in the national interest. Events produced by these two issues helped to mute the long-term possibilities of a progressive agenda after the war. Moreover, Americans were treated to the spectacle of a foreign war to save the world for democracy being accompanied by coercion, violence, and the curtailment of free speech and the right to dissent at home.

1. 100 Percent Americanism

Both Wilson and Hughes had injected the rhetoric of "Americanism" into the 1916 campaign. Progressive Mary Wilmarth had been dismayed that Hughes' speech on Americanism put "policy above principle," she wrote to her friend Ellen Gates Starr. Wilmarth noted that Hughes had proclaimed that "whoever supports me supports an American *policy and absolutely nothing else*" and she then pointed out that there had been an "American policy in slave holding" and that communities in the country practiced slavery as a policy. Finally, she rejected his implication that America was "an equivalent word to United States of America." She could not countenance this kind of thinking, and her fears were prescient considering what was to come. Yet, Wilson was also speaking about Americanism, but at least in 1916 Wilmarth and other progressives could credit him with reforms that were creating a more humane society. Hughes, for his part, kept stressing American efficiency and economics.[24]

When war was declared, too many average Americans heard "Americanism" equated with patriotism and supporting the war. It became important not just to define oneself as a patriotic American, but to root out those who might not be American enough. In a country with millions of immigrants, many of whom came from one side or the other of the European belligerent nations, ethnicity of the wrong sort was enough to put people under suspicion. Germans, of course, were the easiest target. Some of the reaction was silly. Anything German was suspect as un-American and sharply contrasted with American values. Sauerkraut, for example, was renamed liberty cabbage—Germans might

23. Kennedy, *Over Here*, 47, 279, 283. See Mark Ellis, "'Closing Ranks' and 'Seeking Honors': W.E.B. DuBois in World War I," *Journal of American History*, 79 (June 1992), 96–124. DuBois quote "Close Ranks," *The Crisis*, 16 (1918): 111. Elliot M. Rudwick, *Race Riot at East St. Louis, July 2, 1917* (Carbondale: Southern Illinois University Press, 1964).

24. Mary Hawes Wilmarth to Ellen Gates Starr, letter of October 21, 1916, Ellen Gates Starr Manuscript Collection, Box 12, folder 43, in Sophia Smith Collection, Smith College Library.

eat sour cabbage, but real Americans ate liberty cabbage. (Most Americans probably did not know that in renaming French fries as freedom fries after France refused to support the Iraq invasion in 2003, they were repeating past history.) But repression of a much worse variety became all too common. German language teaching was forbidden in many schools. The governor of Iowa forbade the speaking of German on the telephone and in any public place. Perfectly law-abiding German-Americans and their shops and businesses were attacked. The mayor of New York City declared that there were only two kinds of people: "Americans and traitors." To sort them out, he constituted a Committee on National Defense to give loyalty oaths to all municipal employees, including teachers. The American Protective League (APL) recruited 250,000 volunteers committed to watch for, and report to the Department of Justice, any "disloyalty" in their communities.[25]

Self-appointed vigilante groups went in search of suspects. In April 1918, a crowd of 500 cheering "Americans" lynched a young German immigrant coal miner in Collinsville, Illinois—not far from St. Louis with its large German community—for no discernable reason other than his heritage. The victim was bound in the flag, and when the mob's leaders were brought to trial they wore red, white, and blue. Their defense was that this was a "patriotic" murder. The jury acquitted them in less than an hour. It took Wilson over three months after this episode to condemn "mob violence" generally and he seems mainly to have been concerned that the German press was using this lynching for its own propaganda purposes.[26] By the time the war ended, it was clear that the campaign for 100 percent Americanism would carry over. "The war carried much further the shift from sympathy to fear, from cosmopolitan democracy to jealous nationalism," wrote historian John Higham.

> By threat and rhetoric, 100 percent Americanizers opened a frontal assault on foreign influence in American life. They set about to stampede immigrants into citizenship, into adoption of the English language, and into unquestioning reverence for existing American institutions.

The wartime Americanism fervor showed how little progress progressives such as Jane Addams and Lillian Wald had made toward convincing Americans that mutual respect and acceptance of difference was the best way to construct an America where all could find a home. Although Addams and Wald, as well as John Dewey, continued to plead for a recognition that immigrant cultures had good things to offer American society, the forces behind 100 percent Americanism were victorious when they finally succeeded in passing the immigrant literacy bill over Wilson's veto.[27]

---

25. Kennedy, *Over Here*, 67–68, and Painter, *Standing at Armageddon*, 329–30.

26. See Christopher Capozolla, "The Only Badge Needed Is Your Patriotic Fervor: Vigilance, Coercion, and the Law in World War I America," *The Journal of American History*, 88 (March 2002): 1354–83, 1354 for Wilson and this episode.

27. John Higham, *Strangers in the Land: Patterns of Nativism, 1860–1925* (New Brunswick, NJ: Rutgers University Press, rev. edition, 2002), 236–53, quote from 247. Even Frances Kellor, whose sympathies were generally with immigrants, urged in a 1916 book, *Straight America*, that Americanization was vital for the national interest.

2. 100 Percent Loyalty

During a 1916 preparedness parade in New York City, participants marched under an electric sign that read "Absolute and Unqualified Loyalty to Our Country." President Wilson led such a parade in Washington, D.C., carrying the American flag. As with concepts such as national interest or public interest, loyalty became a contested issue during wartime. For many Americans, absolute and unqualified came to be defined as brooking no dissent, no negative word, no going against anything declared by the government. Legislation backed by military and public enforcement of this concept took hold quickly.

Congress passed the Espionage Act in June 1917. The act outlawed any obstruction of military operations during wartime and forbade the use of the mails to disseminate any material advocating treason, insurrection, or forcible resistance to any law of the United States in violation of this act. The U.S. Postmaster assumed authority for deciding which publications or mail might violate this law. He interpreted it broadly, even barring single issues of a publication that expressed an opinion that he judged inappropriate. Socialist publications, of course, were immediately banned from the mail and African American publications were investigated for potential subversion. States also applied the law to a whole range of cases, and individuals were convicted even for discussing whether conscription was constitutional. Almost as soon as war was declared, the AUAM wrote to Wilson expressing the organization's

Patriotism from the Top: Woodrow Wilson Carries the Flag in a Preparedness Parade, Washington, D.C. (1916)
Source: Library of Congress, Prints & Photographs Division, LC-USZ62-109786

concern "lest America, having declared a state of war, should sacrifice certain safeguards fundamental to the life of her democracy" and urging him to take a strong stand against any signs of repression. Wilson, unfortunately, was already moving in the other direction.[28]

Within a year the progressives who were worried about democratic rights had even more reason for concern. The Espionage Act was strengthened by amendment, referred to as the Sedition Act, that made it easier, as the attorney general had requested, to prosecute any "disloyal utterances." The Act was breathtaking in its attack on free speech. It declared it unlawful for anyone to

> willfully utter, print, write, or publish any disloyal, profane, scurrilous, or abusive language about the form of government of the United States, or the Constitution of the United States, or the military or naval forces of the United States, or the flag of the United States, or the uniform of the Army or Navy of the United States, or any language intended to bring the form of government of the United States or [any of the above] into contempt, scorn, contumely, or disrepute . . .[29]

Under its provisions the Socialist Party leader Eugene Debs was arrested and tried for a speech in which he had defended the rights of the IWW and criticized corporate and government leaders. The case against him was so weak that the U.S. Department of Justice, which had wanted the Sedition Act, refused to prosecute. The U.S. attorney for northern Ohio, where the speech had been given, took up the prosecution, however, and pursued it vigorously. At his trial, Debs simply cited a litany of patriots from the Revolution through the abolitionists who had dissented from government policy and defended freedom of speech in a democracy. The judge was unimpressed and sentenced Debs, who was in ill health, to ten years in prison.[30]

The loyalty of workers, many of whom were immigrants, and some of whom had ties to socialism or the IWW, was also questioned. Wilson had requested, and Gompers and the AFL leadership had agreed to, a no-strike pledge from labor (although Gompers did soon repudiate it). But the AFL could never guarantee the cooperation of all its members, let alone the majority of workers who did not belong to the AFL. What happened to copper miners in Bisbee, Arizona, and Butte, Montana, most of whom had affiliated with the IWW-sponsored Metal Mine Workers Industrial Union, illustrates how these repressive laws inspired citizen vigilance and enforcement.

In mid-July thousands of the miners went out on strike against the Phelps-Dodge Corporation in Bisbee. Two citizens' vigilante committees, combined with the corporation's private police, were deputized to round up on charges of "vagrancy, treason, and of being disturbers of the peace . . . all those strange men who have congregated here." Men, women, and children were

---

28. See letter of Lillian Wald, et al. to the President of the United States, April 16, 1917, accessible from the Jewish Women's Archives website, http://www.jwa.org. Original letter at the New York Public Library, Manuscript and Archives Division.

29. Kennedy, *Over Here*, 26, 75, and 79–80; and Ellis, "'Closing Ranks' and 'Seeking Honors,'" 99 and 102.

30. Nick Salvatore, *Eugene V. Debs: Citizen and Socialist* (Urbana: University of Illinois Press, 1982), 294–95. Also arrested under these provisions were socialists Kate Richards O'Hare, Rose Pastor Stokes, Victor Berger, and more. O'Hare was sentenced to five years in prison.

indiscriminately rounded up, placed under armed guard, marched at gunpoint into sealed boxcars, and deported to a desert town in New Mexico. The Citizens' Protective League thereafter issued passports to Bisbee residents who were able to demonstrate their loyalty. No one could live, work, or obtain a draft exemption in Bisbee without taking a loyalty oath. The Wilson administration disapproved of this vigilantism, which it distinguished from vigilance, and the president had appointed a mediation commission to attempt to resolve this dispute, but such a mechanism failed to change things in Bisbee or to prevent future violence against miners. In Butte, Montana, troops and vigilantes took control of the town in the aftermath of a mine disaster that killed 164 miners. The vigilantes mutilated and then lynched Frank Little, a half-Indian IWW organizer. The events of Bisbee and Butte may not have pleased Wilson, but such actions were certainly inspired by his administration's emphasis on unquestioning and absolute loyalty.[31]

The draft was also used to compel Americans to support the war. Men of draft age—which was lowered from 21 to 18 in 1918—were expected to register voluntarily. In the first rounds of registration this went rather well. But even so, Wilson encouraged all citizens to help make sure that all eligible men registered. As the military losses in France began to mount, the Selective Service in mid-1918 issued a "work or fight order" that ordered local boards to draft immediately anyone not engaged in work essential to the war effort—or any workers going out on strike. Members of the APL also conducted "slacker" raids looking for eligible men who were avoiding the draft.[32]

In an ironic twist, the emphasis that progressives had put on the local community now worked toward coercion of loyalty. The progressive social center advocates had thought of the neighborhood as the place where all people could decide together and their decisions would flow upward to create a better society. The shifting emphasis toward nationalism and the national interest changed the flow. Local draft boards became part of a hierarchy in which decisions flowed downward from the federal government to the neighborhood.[33] The Selective Service was run by local boards who had more opportunity to coerce. But by making the draft a local task, people could be more easily convinced that the draft was not so much federal intrusion as local decision making. Local boards could also practice favoritism. In some areas, significantly more white men received exemptions than black men. So, while some progressives descended on Washington hoping that wartime centralized regulation would bring further social reforms that would make society more democratic, other progressives watched their ideas of local democracy vanish.

31. Capozolla, "The Only Badge Needed Is Your Patriotic Fervor," 1365–69 provides a short summary of these events and also places them in the context of an American concept that democratic citizenry required social vigilance to keep law and order. See also, Dawley, *Changing the World*, 161–62.

32. Kennedy, *Over Here*, 150, 165–66.

33. Mattson, *Creating a Democratic Public*, 106–09.

AFTERMATH

As the war was ending in late 1918, several issues coalesced to determine the course of reform for the future. First, the government quickly disbanded several federal agencies that some progressives had hoped would be the vanguard of continuing social reconstruction. Second, the Democrats suffered significant losses in the November congressional elections, revitalizing the Republican Party and demonstrating the weakness of the Democrats. Third, Wilson was far more preoccupied with winning the peace abroad than in domestic issues. Finally, 100 percent Americanism had a firmer grip on the American people than did ideas about continuing social reform. The Bolshevik Revolution in Russia begun in 1917 had increased suspicion of anything foreign.

The fact that the wartime agencies disbanded so quickly, some within a few days of the armistice, demonstrated that social reconstruction accomplished through state agency had not sunk deep roots during the war. As late as June 1918, progressive writer Will Durant had confidently declared that "the new social order is coming and that is all there is to it." For his part, Wilson quickly abandoned any tentative plans for constituting a postwar Reconstruction agency and settled for saying there would only need to be "readjustment" while admitting at the same time that "he had little to recommend" in this regard. Yet, many progressives remained optimistic into 1919 and took the lead by forming their own reconstruction committees. Social workers, housing activists, children's welfare advocates, and public health promoters all kept working to reconstruct the country through established agencies and committees such as the Children's Bureau and the American Association for Labor Legislation. They traveled to England to study that country's reconstruction plans, conducted their own meetings, and showed up at government-sponsored hearings that were determining whether to retain or abandon wartime measures such as nationalization of the railroads. Labor lawyer Glenn Plumb (whose wife was a progressive activist in Chicago) proposed both that government continue to run the railroads and that their operation be guided by a tripartite association of labor, government, and the public. The railroad brotherhoods and agrarian interests supported the proposal; Gompers and the AFL rejected it, believing that wartime measures such as the eight-hour day and higher wages would carry on after the war. Steeply rising union membership during the war helped promote this sense of security. Then, when Wilson sent Gompers and other labor leaders to Europe as advance men for his peace proposals as soon as the war ended, labor's optimism increased. At home, a special industrial commission was convened to try to bring business and labor together. But when labor demanded that it have an equal voice in all future economic decision making, the commission failed. Then the *New York Times* attacked the Plumb Plan as "a very large step toward the principles of Lenin and Trotsky." Waves of labor strikes swept through the country across 1919 and enduring business, government, and even public hostility toward labor helped doom any further social reconstruction on the part of government.[34]

Wilson's inattention to domestic affairs and his fear that additional Republicans in Congress would block his international peace plans made him leery of promoting social reconstruction. In fact, he had never been the reformer that many progressives had hoped he would be. At base, his progressivism had always been of the antimonopoly variety and his social and economic reforms had either been intended to break up monopolies or had been made necessary by the exigencies of preparedness and war. What he had earlier told Jane Addams was thus true. His attention was focused on entering the war so that he would have a seat at the peace table in order to promote his two primary aims of his Fourteen Points for peace: a League of Nations that would arbitrate international disputes and prevent international monopolies, and a pledge of self-determination for all people. Democratic losses in the 1918 elections made him even more reluctant to seek domestic reforms. To Wilson's bewilderment over what seemed to him to be the public's rejection of his leadership, George Creel reminded him of the effect of his domestic repression: "All the radical or liberal friends of your anti-imperialism war policy were either silenced or intimidated. . . . There was no voice left to argue for your sort of peace." Or as another progressive, Amos Pinchot, put it: Wilson had put "his enemies in office and his friends in jail."[35]

Wilson sailed for Europe and the Versailles Peace Conference with the Democrats in disarray, the Republicans attacking him on both domestic and foreign policy, and a country descending into reaction. Nearly four million workers went out on strike in 1919, ranging from a general strike that began with a longshoreman's strike in early January in Seattle to a strike that virtually shut down the steel industry; even the Boston police struck for the right to join the AFL. Business and government aligned against labor, calling in militia and the military to break strikes. Across 1919 and into fall of the following year, federal troops were used twenty times to break strikes. The steelworkers, who often toiled seven days a week for as long as twelve hours a day, were denounced as disloyal foreigners and so-called progressives in Wilson's Cabinet authorized the army to intervene. Wilson had even considered enacting a peacetime sedition act to deal with such upheavals. As it was, the army marched into Gary, Indiana—the home of U.S. Steel—and declared martial law.[36]

---

34. Rodgers, *Atlantic Crossings*, 299–303 and 298 for quote of Will Durant and 305 for quote from the *New York Times*; see also, Kennedy, *Over Here*, 256–58; Julie Greene, *Pure and Simple Politics: The American Federation of Labor and Political Activism, 1881–1917* (Cambridge, UK: Cambridge University Press, 1998); and Dawley, *Changing the World*, 262–64 and 283.

35. Kennedy, *Over Here*, 250 and 89.

36. Dawley, *Changing the World*, 265–66 and Kennedy, *Over Here*, 87. See also, David Brody, *Labor in Crisis: The Steel Strike of 1919* (Urbana: University of Illinois Press, rev. edition, 1987); David Montgomery, *The Fall of the House of Labor: The Workplace, the State, and Labor Activism, 1865–1925* (Cambridge, UK: Cambridge University Press, 1987); and Dana Frank, *Purchasing Power: Consumer Organizing, Gender, and the Seattle Labor Movement, 1919–1929* (Cambridge, UK: Cambridge University Press, 1994).

The aftermath of the war indeed brought little good news for African Americans either. Demobilized white soldiers returned to industrial cities to claim back the jobs that African American migrants had taken during the war. Scaled-back production and the economic recession that started by early 1920, combined with racism, resulted in black men and women workers being fired and replaced by white men and women.[37] Almost twice as many African Americans were lynched in 1919 as had been in 1917. Northern cities where southern migrants had headed for the promise of economic and political opportunity now also faced a housing crisis that had been ignored during the wartime emergency. African American soldiers returned home determined to claim their rights as citizens having now served their country in wartime. What they found instead was white intransigence that led to racial rioting. Cities as diverse as Knoxville and Omaha witnessed these riots, but one of the worst outbreaks came in Chicago in the hot summer of 1919, when a white man threw rocks at a black boy swimming in Lake Michigan who had drifted into "white" territory. The boy died, police failed to charge the white attacker, and white and black residents fought each other in the streets, attacked streetcars, and burned homes and businesses. When the fighting stopped more blacks had been killed and injured than whites, and more black businesses and homes destroyed. Yet, the state's attorney declined to prosecute any of the white rioters.[38]

Nor were African American hopes realized that the war might bring a new internationalism that would end imperialism and racism. As the war was ending, a National Equal Rights League meeting chose delegates to send to Europe to participate in peace gatherings that were taking place. Because Gompers and representatives of other areas of American society were being sent to Europe, the members of the Equal Rights League believed they were entitled to representation. But, as Ida B. Wells-Barnett reported, "none of us got to go because President Wilson forbade it." William Monroe Trotter and DuBois managed to get to Versailles but had little or no influence on the outcome. When the final version of the treaty maintained colonial rights, hopes of African Americans were even further dashed.[39]

Part of this backlash against labor and African Americans reflected the fears produced in the United States by the 1917 Russian Revolution and socialist uprisings in Germany and elsewhere in Europe that followed war. Indeed, even during the war the army had drawn up "War Plans White," a secret plan to thwart revolution that targeted whole groups of Americans: "Presumed enemies

37. Gareth Canaan, "'Part of the Loaf': Economic Conditions of Chicago's African-American Working Class During the 1920s," *Journal of Social History*, 35 (Fall 2001): 147–74.

38. William Tuttle, *Race Riot: Chicago in the Red Summer of 1919* (Urbana: University of Illinois Press, 1996 edition) and for wartime background, see Tuttle, "Contested Neighborhoods and Racial Violence: Prelude to the Chicago Riot of 1919," *Journal of Negro History*, 55 (October 1970): 266–88. See also, Tim Madigan, *The Burning: Massacre, Destruction, and the Tulsa Race Riot of 1921* (New York: St. Martin's Press, 2001) and Rudwick, *Race Riot at East St. Louis* for other wartime and postwar racial rioting.

39. *Crusade for Justice: The Autobiography of Ida B. Wells*, Alfreda M. Duster, ed. (Chicago: University of Chicago Press, 1970), 379.

included the entire population of immigrant Italians, Austrians, Hungarians, Poles, and other East European 'racial groups.'" African Americans were not to be trusted because of "their class consciousness, racial instincts, poverty, instinctive hostility to the white race and susceptibility to propaganda." Southern and east Europeans were suspected of bringing socialism and anarchism to the United States. After the war, the successes of Bolshevism abroad meant that every kind of political dissent inspired fears of revolution at home. In this hysterical environment, extreme measures became common. Following a series of dynamite bombs, including one sent to the home of Attorney General A. Mitchell Palmer, the new Justice Department bureau was authorized to round up suspected terrorists and to invade meetings of any presumed radical groups. The Justice Department kept the anarchist labor agitator Carlo Tresca under close surveillance during the early 1920s, trying to discover whether he was a naturalized American citizen. The letters in the FBI surveillance file make it clear that the department was hoping to find that he was not and then to deport him. By the beginning of 1920, around 4,000, mainly immigrant "suspects" had been arrested. Almost 600 were eventually deported to Russia, including the professed anarchist Emma Goldman. Patriotic groups attacked meetings of presumed radicals. Business was able to wield these fears as a weapon against strikers. The mayor of Seattle, Ole Hanson, requested that federal troops be sent to the city, saying that the 60,000 strikers there were "deep Red revolutionists" who intended to seize government and implement Russian anarchy. Others claimed that labor agitation was being directed from Moscow. The House of Representatives refused to seat socialist Victor Berger, who had been elected from Wisconsin in 1918. Robert LaFollette raged helplessly against the hypocrisy of proclaiming to be making the world safe for democracy while persecuting people at home. He labeled Wilson's proposed League of Nations as just another aspect of an alliance of the powerful to subjugate and exploit the losers, just as winners had done after every other war.[40]

Eugene Debs ran for president from jail in 1920 and earned almost one million votes. Still, these were only 3.4 percent of the total vote. The threat of a socialist takeover of the United States was never realistic. But the dream of industrial democracy that the Commission on Industrial Democracy had earlier proclaimed as vital for a democratic nation died in the ashes of World War I. So did many other progressive dreams. Health insurance plans were scuttled amid cries of bolshevism. The Keating-Owen legislation was overturned and a proposed child labor amendment failed. Plans to continue a national housing policy faded. The railroads were denationalized. Schemes for new agricultural colonies that would absorb returning soldiers and avoid the corporatization of agriculture secured only tepid support, and their rejection of African American or Asian American applicants further doomed any such programs. The Senate rejected the Versailles Peace Treaty and with it membership in the new League

---

    40. Kennedy, *Over Here*, 288–92, gives a brief overall account of these events. The most thorough exploration remains Robert K. Murray, *Red Scare: A Study in National Hysteria, 1919–1920* (Minneapolis: McGraw Hill, 1964). For LaFollette, see Unger, *Fighting Bob LaFollette*, 265–73. For Tresca, see his FBI surveillance file at http://foia.fbi.gov/foiaindex/tresca.htm.

of Nations. Nationalism of a virulent variety usurped the progressive ideas of mutuality and collectivity. In 1919 the Supreme Court, led by Justice Oliver Wendell Holmes, upheld several of the wartime convictions, including that of Debs. This ruling set a new precedent that a determination of "clear and present danger" could be applied according to circumstance to limit freedom of speech. When Frederic Howe as commissioner of immigration for the port of New York delayed in deporting alien radicals he was forced out of his position. A progressive argument that social reconstruction was the cure for Bolshevism was lost in the Red Scare of 1919.[41] If other businessmen were not as blunt as Rockefeller about God's provenance, they securely reasserted their control over the economy with the Republican victory of 1920.

---

41. Rodgers, *Atlantic Crossings*, 349–50, 313, and 301; and Kennedy, *Over Here*, for the Supreme Court.

Peace, Not War: Women's Peace March, New York City (1914)
Source: Library of Congress, Prints & Photographs Division,
LC-DIG-ggbain-17020

On August 29, 1914, 1,500 women, many clad in black mourning dress and others wearing black armbands, marched down Fifth Avenue in New York. To the beat of muffled drums, and led by a young woman carrying a banner picturing a dove and an olive branch and the word PEACE, these women were marching silently against war. The parade had been organized by Lillian Wald. Heading the marchers was Fanny Garrison Villard, the seventy-year-old daughter of the abolitionist William Lloyd Garrison. Among those in the march were well-known progressive figures Wald and Addams, Mary Dreier and Leonora O'Reilly of the National Women's Trade Union League, suffrage leaders Anna Howard Shaw and Carrie Chapman Catt, and more radical feminists Charlotte Perkins Gilman and Crystal Eastman. There was a contingent of 100 nurses from the Henry Street Settlement, "more than 100 socialist women, a group of 20 black women, and, in traditional dress, a Native American woman and a Chinese woman." What bound these disparate women together was a common rejection of war. War, as Jane Addams had earlier declared, was the old way of solving problems, not the progressive way. War meant nationalism, not internationalism. War was disastrous for women and children. War did not further democracy, rather, "war itself destroys democracy wherever it thrives and tends to entrench militarism."*

*For the parade, see Nell Irvin Painter, *Standing at Armageddon: United States, 1877–1919* (New York: W.W. Norton, 1987), 296–97, and Kathryn Kish Sklar, "'Some of Us Who Deal with the Social Fabric': Jane Addams Blends Peace and Social Justice," *Journal of the Gilded Age and Progressive Era*, 2 (January 2003): 91. Jane Addams, Emily Greene Balch, and Alice Hamilton, *Women at the Hague*, Harriet Hyman Alonso, intro. (Urbana: University of Illinois Press, 2003 reprint), 37. See also, Alonso, *Peace as a Women's Issue: A History of the U.S. Movement for World's Peace and Women's Rights* (Syracuse, NY: Syracuse University Press, 1993).

CHAPTER 12

━━▅◣▐▌◢▅━━

Gender and Democracy
in War and Peace

We do not admire the man of timid peace.
—THEODORE ROOSEVELT, 1899

Peace and bread had become inseparably connected in my mind.
—JANE ADDAMS, 1922

EDITH O'SHAUGHNESSY WAS married to a U.S. diplomat posted to Mexico from 1911–1914, the crucial years in the relationship between Mexico and the United States between the overthrow of the Díaz regime and the landing of U.S. troops at Verzcruz. O'Shaughnessy went to Mexico thinking that the people there surely needed American help to overcome their backwardness. Her initial thoughts about Mexicans in many ways mirrored those of geographer Edward Becker. Other people were like children in need of help from the grown-up and responsible United States.

But her world was not that of the diplomat whose task was to carry out policy, nor was it that of the professional social scientist constructing theories around social structures. Hers was the everyday life of families, both hers and those of the women she employed as household help and the children that they often brought with them to work. Hers was also the world of deep poverty, encountered daily on the streets around her home. Home, parent, child were the three concepts around which her view of the world revolved. Seeing the world in this way, she began to believe that it was not Mexicans' inability to govern themselves, as some progressives and conservatives were charging and giving as the reason for U.S. intervention, but that it was precisely too much foreign intervention that was making it impossible for Mexicans to establish a stable government. She concluded that the United States "had used Mexico 'only as a quarry' for oil and precious metals." The United States—the parent—was not helping to create a home for the child—Mexico. Instead it was exploiting the country's turmoil to enrich itself.[1]

---

1. Molly M. Wood, "A Diplomat's Wife in Mexico: Creating Political, Professional, and National Identities in the Early Twentieth Century," *Frontiers: A Journal of Women's Studies*, 25:3 (2004): 104–33, 116 for quote.

Her thinking is clearly paternalistic (or better put, maternalistic), but it caused her to have far more sympathy with Mexico and to abhor Wilson's Mexico policy more than most male progressives. William Jennings Bryan, for example, had turned in favor of more imperialism in the wake of continuing troubles in the Caribbean. O'Shaughnessy wanted the United States to emphasize the human needs of the Mexican people rather than the extraction of minerals and protection of U.S. property in developing a policy toward Mexico. On this basis she would campaign strenuously against Wilson in 1916.

One can deride the maternalistic instincts expressed by O'Shaughnessy and by other American women who traveled as diplomatic wives, religious missionaries, or educators to new U.S. possessions or other nonwestern countries.[2] It was the rare American who did not believe that she had more to offer than to gain from foreign residence. Yet, it is inescapably true that progressive women's emphasis on home, family, and children, their burgeoning belief in mutuality and collectively, and their rejection of the rhetoric of masculinity led many of them to oppose much U.S. foreign policy and especially World War I. Once the United States had entered the war and for years afterwards this belief in peace and internationalism would subject women peace advocates to continuing derision and to charges of subversion and even communism.

Addams' four stated objections to war—it is not progressive, it is not internationalistic, it is disastrous for women and children, and it destroys democracy—characterized an important gender distinction in progressivism that had run through all foreign policy development of the Progressive Era. This distinction would become more apparent as the United States was drawn ever nearer to becoming a co-belligerent. It would also contribute in great part to determining the fate of progressivism through the war years and after.

THE WOMEN'S PEACE PARTY

In the opening months of war in Europe Emmeline Pethwick-Lawrence from England and Rosika Schwimmer from Budapest toured the United States. Although they represented the opposing sides in the conflict, both women declared that war was the enemy of mankind. They urged American women to form a peace party that could help formulate reasonable peace terms to end the war and protest against the uselessness of war for settling international disputes. American women responded to this appeal: in January 1915, 3,000 women met to form the WPP. They named Jane Addams to chair the party and adopted an eleven-point platform detailing their ideas of the nature and purposes of foreign policy. The WPP dedicated itself to:

- An immediate convention of neutral nations in the interest of early peace
- Nationalization of armaments manufacture

2. For examples of work on American women and their foreign travel and impact, see Manako Ogawa, "'Hull-House' in Downtown Tokyo: The Transplantation of a Settlement House from the United States into Japan and the North American Missionary Women, 1919–1945," *The Journal of World History*, 15 (September 2004): 359–87; and Jane Hunter, *The Gospel of Gentility: American Women Missionaries in Turn-of-the-Century China* (New Haven, CT: Yale University Press, 1984).

- Organized opposition to militarism
- Education of children in the ideals of peace
- Democratic control of foreign policies
- Women suffrage to further humanize governments
- A concert of nations rather than balance of power diplomacy
- Reorganization of the world to substitute law for war
- Use of economic pressure rather than armies and navies
- Removal of the economic causes of war
- Securing a government-appointed commission of men and women with an adequate appropriation to promote international peace

At the founding meeting Jane Addams bluntly stated why she believed that women were more concerned than men about peace: "I do not assert that women are better than men," she said, "but we would all admit that there are things concerning which women are more sensitive than men, and that one of these is the treasuring of life."[3]

Forty-seven American women accepted an invitation from English, Dutch, and Belgian women to participate in an International Women's peace conference at The Hague. Making this journey were Jane Addams, Emily Greene Balch, Alice Hamilton, Mary Simkhovitch, and Leonora O'Reilly. Florence Kelley wished to attend, but the State Department denied her a passport. One thousand women representing twelve countries met from April 28 to May 1, 1915, and declared their two inseparable goals were to gain political equality and achieve international peace. They agreed at the conference to adhere to two principles: that henceforth all international disputes were to be resolved by "peaceable means"; and that the franchise for all women was indispensable for changing the means and method of foreign affairs. War, they declared, was a "horrible violation of women" and that what the world must have was a permanent peace "based on principles of justice." Jane Addams afterwards clarified that she did not believe that women were biologically or essentially against war, but that experience inclined them that way: "women, who have brought men into the world and nurtured them until they reach the age for fighting, must experience a peculiar revulsion when they see them destroyed, irrespective of the country in which these men may have been born."[4]

Other women believed that men actively stood in the way of peace. Speaking at a peace conference in July 1915 in San Francisco, Indiana suffrage activist May Wright Sewall declared to great applause that there was no disappointment that can compare with "the disappointment that the women of the world feel, that, at this stage of its development, the men of the world still continue to use armies as their instruments of rule; still continue

---

3. Jane Addams, *Peace and Bread in Time of War* (Urbana: University of Illinois Press, reprint edition, 2002), ch. 1, briefly outlines the events that led to forming the Woman's Peace Party and the planks of the WPP platform.

4. For the international congress, see Jane Addams, Emily Greene Balch, and Alice Hamilton, *Women at the Hague*, Harriet Hyman Alonso, intro. (Urbana: University of Illinois Press, reprint edition, 2003), xv, xviii, and 60–61. For the denial of a passport to Kelley, see Kathryn Kish Sklar, "'Some of Us Who Deal with the Social Fabric': Jane Addams Blends Peace and Social Justice," *Journal of the Gilded Age and Progressive Era*, 2 (January 2003): 94.

to believe that war is a proper method of adjusting their disagreements with other peoples." Addressing the same conference, WPP leader Harriet Thomas also spoke about the differences between men's and women's experiences that led to the formation of the women's party. "Because the women were free, because they were not bound by tradition and all these ancient ideas that men cling to in regard to this superstition of war, women were able to make this protest and this demand, and so the Women's Peace Party was organized."[5]

The Women's Peace Party preamble, which stated baldly that women were "the mother half of humanity," emphasized gender experiences over nationalism. Such sentiments caused the Wilson administration concern that women would continue to oppose war once the United States entered it, especially because the WPP had registered 40,000 members within a year of its organization. Wilson had additional cause for concern because of the popularity of a new song titled "I Didn't Raise My Boy to Be a Soldier." The chorus of the song emphasized women's potential opposition to war:

> I didn't raise my boy to be a soldier,
> I brought him up to be my pride and joy,
> Who dares to put a musket on his shoulder,
> To shoot some other mother's darling boy?
> Let nations arbitrate their future troubles,
> It's time to lay the sword and gun away,
> There'd be no war today,
> If mothers all would say,
> I didn't raise my boy to be a soldier.

Theodore Roosevelt's manly retort to this song was that the proper place for women who opposed the war was "in China—or by preference in a harem—and not in the United States."

When the draft was enacted, the administration especially feared that women, as mothers, would obstruct it. The antipeace sentiment that was building well before mid-1917 specifically connected pacifism with feminine weakness. Theodore Roosevelt, of course, played his part in promoting such an idea. So did an ultraconservative male organization, the National Security League, composed largely of businessmen and financiers. When Jane Addams had returned from the Hague conference in 1915 she was surprised by the virulent antipacifism expressed in many newspapers. Even so, once the United States went to war, she admitted that she was unprepared for "the general unwillingness to admit any defect in the institution of war as such" and that it was even considered "unpatriotic . . . to discuss the very issues for which the war was being fought."[6]

---

5. For the San Francisco conference, see May Wright Sewall, "Women, World War and Permanent Peace," *Proceedings of International Conference of Women Workers to Promote Peace*, July 4–7, 1915 (San Francisco, 1915), 16 and 97.

6. Jane Addams, *Bread and Peace in Time of War*, 63. Song lyrics, and quote from Roosevelt, at http://historymatters.gmu.edu/d/4942/.

The cinema was used as a popular culture means to counteract women's professed pacifism and to bring all women, and not just peace activists, into line behind the war effort. The nascent film industry contributed to whipping up patriotism by producing several films in which "motherly love" was portrayed as women's domination of men; women's opposition to war was depicted as "hysterical, misplaced, and uncontrolled." Additional films then juxtaposed this image of the "bad mother" to that of the "good mother": she was the one who was now willing to sacrifice her son in service to his country.[7] In fact, with the exception of anarchist Emma Goldman's "No Conscription" campaign, very few female peace workers tried to stop conscription once it was law. Jane Addams wrote of how painful it was that after having advised immigrant men to become citizens, she now had to watch them register for the draft. But she did so, even when one of them remonstrated against her for the consequences of having taken her advice. What Addams and the women's peace movement wanted was broader than opposing conscription and this war. And in the long run what they wanted was perhaps even more threatening. They wanted to de-glorify and de-legitimize war as the instrument for the settlement of international disputes. After the Hague conference, they formed the Women's International Committee for Permanent Peace to work for this goal. This committee spent the war seeking to convince the belligerents that the way to end hostilities was through international arbitration conducted by neutral nations, not by physically defeating the enemy. Because neutral nations had no nationalist interests at stake, the women believed that a conference of peoples from these nations could broker a peace that would satisfy both sides. But Addams and other women also believed that war could only be avoided for the future if all nations recognized their international interest in resolving hunger and exploitation around the world. Hence the title of her book on this subject, *Peace and Bread in Time of War*.

Such ideas directly contradicted the wartime ideas of Wilson. Wilson wanted to win the war so that he might impose a peace that would in turn impose democracy on the world. With democracy, he believed, international problems would be resolved. Addams wanted a peace that would bring "equality of social and economic conditions around the world"—an idea that can be understood as emanating directly from the ideals of social justice progressivism.[8] The leaders of Wilson's administration and other men who vigorously supported going to war feared women's opposition and its potential influence in foreign affairs. On the one hand, this shows the progress women had made during the Progressive Era. Men now considered women a force to be reckoned with, even in foreign affairs. On the other hand, in their wartime propaganda and then in actions afterwards, men clearly tried to reassert their control over women.

---

7. For the popular culture, including cinema, depiction of women, see Susan Zeiger, "She Didn't Raise Her Son to Be a Slacker: Motherhood, Conscription, and the Culture of the First World War," *Feminist Studies*, 22 (Spring 1996): 6–39. See also, Kathleen Kennedy, *Disloyal Mothers and Scurrilous Citizens: Women and Subversion during World War I* (Bloomington: Indiana University Press, 1999).

8. *Women at the Hague*, 64.

WOMAN SUFFRAGE

In the lead-up to the war, the woman suffrage amendment was languishing in Congress and Wilson refused to endorse it. The NAWSA, led by Carrie Chatman Catt, continued its campaign of persuasion, but suffragists who were unsatisfied with the slow progress being made by the NAWSA broke away in 1913 to form a new suffrage group they named the Congressional Union. In 1917, they changed the name to the National Woman's Party (NWP). With neither political party committing itself to the amendment in the 1916 presidential campaign, the NWP and its leader Alice Paul used Wilson's statements about democracy as a bludgeon to make him support woman suffrage. In early January 1917, NWP members and sympathizers, including NACW leader Mary Church Terrell and her daughter, began picketing the White House demanding passage of the suffrage amendment. The women displayed banners and signs accusing Wilson and the Democrats of fighting for democracy abroad while refusing to support it for American women. One of their banners asked "Mr. Wilson, how long must American women wait for liberty?" Other signs used Wilson's statements about entering the war for democratic reasons directly against him for not supporting the amendment.

After one particularly embarrassing episode for Wilson where a visiting delegation from Russia witnessed these pickets and signs, the women were ac-

Making Their Stand: Woman Suffrage Pickets Line the White House Fence (1917)
Source: *Women of Protest: Photographs from the Records of the National Woman's Party*, photograph by Harris & Ewing. Manuscript Division, Library of Congress, Washington, D.C.

cused of damaging international relations and police were ordered to begin arresting pickets. In response, Paul released a statement to the press declaring that:

> it is those who deny justice, and not those who demand it, who embarrass the country in its international relations . . . the responsibility, therefore, is with the government and not with the women of America, if the lack of democracy at home weakens the government in its fight for democracy 3000 miles away.

In the atmosphere of 100 percent Americanism and loyalty, the behavior of the pickets soon became intolerable to the administration and to Wilson supporters. The right to peaceful assembly was attacked; pickets were arrested and physically thrown into jail; several were sentenced to jail on the charge of obstructing the sidewalk. Every time the women were arrested and then released the pickets returned to the White House despite police, public, and administration hostility. The finale of this "suffrage rioting," as it came to be called, was when several were arrested and jailed and Alice Paul was put into a psychiatric ward in solitary confinement. The jailed suffragists began a hunger strike and after several days prison authorities began to force-feed them. The reports of the women's treatment aroused so much public protest that the administration was forced to capitulate. In late 1917, Paul and the other women were released, and Wilson finally called for passage of the amendment.[9]

It is impossible to know how much longer women might have had to wait for the right to vote without World War I. It was clear in the state ratification campaign, however, that southern states remained adamantly opposed to passing suffrage in their individual states, so forcing the national amendment surely hastened all women receiving the right to vote. It is also clear that woman suffrage did not bring complete political and legal equality to women. Into the 1920s, the majority of states refused to allow women to serve on juries, or discriminated against them where allowed, as did one judge who excluded blondes from juries saying they were "fickle." Many states maintained discriminatory laws against married women's property rights and rights to children.[10] To attack this continuing democratic inequality, the NWP would propose the Equal Rights Amendment, a move that would make it difficult to construct a solid woman's movement through the 1920s.

---

9. A good short description of the NWP picketing and the administration's response to it can be found in Sally (Sara) Hunter Graham, "Woodrow Wilson, Alice Paul, and the Woman Suffrage Movement," *Political Science Quarterly*, 98 (Winter 1983): 665–79. See also, Nancy Cott, "Feminist Politics in the 1920s: The National Woman's Party," *The Journal of American History*, 71 (June 1984): 43–68, esp. 43–47.

10. Morton Keller, *Regulating a New Society: Public Policy and Social Change in America, 1900–1933* (Cambridge, MA: Harvard University Press, 1994), 305–07. See also, Christine Lunardini, *From Equal Suffrage to Equal Rights: Alice Paul and the National Woman's Party, 1910–1928* (New York: New York University Press, 1986), for the NWP after suffrage and its promotion of the Equal Rights Amendment.

BACKLASH AGAINST SOCIAL JUSTICE

The majority of progressive activist women and women's organizations across the country supported the war effort, if not always the war itself. Those who went to Washington, or actively worked for the local defense councils, often viewed their war work as an opportunity to further their ideas of social justice domestically in hopes that these would carry over into peacetime and out into the world. Women kept up their pressure on the local level for reforms on infant and maternal health, pure food and milk, and clean air. At the Children's Bureau, Julia Lathrop declared that "the abolition of poverty is a necessity of the democratic State, and not an unattainable luxury." The Bureau and the Woman's Committee of the National Defense Council, pointing out the poor physical condition found among military recruits, lobbied for more attention to children's health care as part of the war effort. Wilson declared 1918 to be "Children's Year" and gave the Bureau $150,000 from the wartime Defense Fund to implement children's programs, and women's organizations in many states responded enthusiastically and increased their child welfare work. New Mexico's women's clubs, for example, were finally able to establish a state Child Welfare Service. Wilson further cooperated with women's efforts by agreeing to hold a White House Conference on Children in the spring of 1919.[11]

When the Women's Bureau became a permanent part of the Department of Labor in 1920 and the suffrage amendment passed, progressive women believed they had reason to be optimistic for the future. Yet a backlash against many progressive women's reform proposals had begun to take shape during the war. The pro-peace and pro-suffrage challenges of the WPP and the NWP were easy targets. The NAWSA had not helped when, after declaring total support for the war effort, it advocated censoring the NWP. Women quickly discovered that the backlash was not just for these stances but against women's ideas and their determination to insert them into public policy. Nevertheless, the integral role women had played in supporting the war effort made them believe that, having done their part, they were now entitled to participate in the peace process. Meeting a month after hostilities ceased, the NWTUL issued a document titled "Women and Reconstruction." The document declared that "the world-wide struggle for freedom and justice has not ended" and laid out the group's standards for attaining peace and justice in the world that it wanted to see created by the peace treaty. These women pointedly called it the "Treaty for Peace" to distinguish it from a treaty merely to end the war. Following in the footsteps of the WPP, the NWTUL believed that real peace could

---

11. Lathrop quoted in Robyn Muncy, *Creating a Female Dominion in American Reform, 1890–1935* (New York: Oxford University Press, 1991), 98. See also, Kriste Lindenmeyer, *"A Right to Childhood": The U.S. Children's Bureau and Child Welfare, 1912–46* (Urbana: University of Illinois Press, 1997), 72–74; Jessica B. Peixotto, "The Children's Year and the Woman's Committee," *Annals of the American Academy of Political and Social Science,* 79 (September 1918): 257–62; and Sandra Schackel, *Social Housekeepers: Women Shaping Public Policy in New Mexico, 1920–1940* (Albuquerque: University of New Mexico Press, 1992), 14. See also, Judith McArthur, *Creating the New Woman: The Rise of Southern Women's Progressive Culture in Texas, 1893–1918* (Urbana: University of Illinois Press, 1998), 124–27, for the work of Texas women.

not be gained unless the means to social justice were part of the postwar world. They called for a peace treaty that would resolve problems facing both belligerent and neutral nations. They wanted a treaty to enact new wage, hour, and health standards for labor; that would acknowledge the right of self-government of industry (meaning more worker control and unions); that would require universal woman suffrage; and that would enforce social protections for women and children, public ownership of natural resources, and demobilization plans that would not result in vicious competition for jobs. The NWTUL further called for an International Congress of Working Women to fight for and monitor the application of such standards.[12]

As the Versailles Peace Conference was meeting in 1919, the Women's International Committee for Peace met in Zurich hoping also to influence the negotiations. These women represented both the belligerent and neutral nations and were united in their concern for the postwar condition of women and children, especially the suffering caused by the widespread hunger that war had produced. So, while the men at Versailles argued over reparations and the ongoing blockade of German ports, the women at Zurich demanded an immediate end to the blockade and charged that the current conditions in Europe were a "disgrace to civilization." They

> urged the Governments of all the Powers assembled at the Peace Conference immediately to develop the interallied organizations formed for purposes of war into an international organization for purposes of peace, so that the resources of the world—food, raw materials, finance, transport—shall be made available for the relief of the peoples of all countries from famine and pestilence.

When they learned the details of the proposed treaty, the women were dismayed at its pronounced nationalism and its failure to consider the human elements of hunger and disease. They warned that "by the financial and economic proposals [of the treaty] a hundred million people of this generation in the heart of Europe are condemned to poverty, disease and despair which must result in the spread of hatred and anarchy within each nation."[13]

Peace activist women's dismay at the treaty's neglect of human suffering deepened as they realized that the war's end would not bring international progressivism, yet they did not abandon their cause despite the refusal of the men at Versailles to listen to them. In 1919, they formed a permanent organization, the Women's International League for Peace and Freedom (WILPF). In doing so, and by continuing to work for internationalism, these women became ready targets in the nationalist and anticommunist hysteria of the early 1920s. The NWTUL encountered suspicion and hostility when it attempted to form ties to an International Federation of Working Women. Hostility to women's internationalism was magnified because many Americans believed

---

12. "Women and Reconstruction: Being the Report of the Committee on Social and Industrial Reconstruction of the National Women's Trade Union League, Meeting in New York, December 9–12, 1918" (Chicago, 1919). A copy of this report can be found at the following: http://ocp.hul .harvard.edu/ww/outsidelink.html/http://nrs.harvard.edu/urn-3:FHCL:409249.

13. For accounts of the Zurich conference and quotes, see Addams, *Bread and Peace in Time of War*, ch. 8.

that women were now meddling in affairs that were rightly none of their concern—that is, foreign policy. But disapprobation did not deter women such as Jane Addams and Emily Greene Balch. They kept agitating to replace power politics with internationalism and social justice without which, they believed, there could be no lasting peace. Addams also condemned U.S. occupations in the Caribbean and Central America and warned that U.S. imperialism was increasing "militarism" in the world. Balch journeyed to Haiti with a delegation of African American women representing the International Council of Women of the Darker Races and reported that occupation of Haiti was also increasing imperialism and militarism.[14]

On the home front, much of women's progressive agenda was thwarted, as national legislation to institutionalize social justice progressivism continued to elude them. In part this failure reflected divisions within women's national organizations that had formed the Women's Joint Congressional Committee in 1920. Women, for example, did not unanimously support a 1921 proposal to create a Department of Public Welfare to oversee education, public health, child welfare, and other social issues that President Warren G. Harding endorsed to bring expertise and efficiency to coordinate social issues. This emphasis on efficiency and expertise troubled women's organizations, which worried that it would automatically place social issues into the hands of male bureaucrats and politicians. This was not paranoia on women's part: since 1919, the male-dominated Public Health Service had been trying to take over the Children's Bureau. They also feared that with so many problems to contend with, the proposed department would ignore one or more of them. The General Federation of Women's Clubs, for instance, preferred either a Department of Health or a "distinct sub-division" of any Department of Welfare that would deal directly with children's health issues.[15]

Women progressives continued to favor new legislation to implement social policy rather than leaving social issues to be decided upon by a government bureaucracy more concerned with efficiency than with social justice. When Congress passed the Sheppard-Towner Maternity and Infant Welfare bill in 1921, women celebrated a major step in that direction. Jeannette Rankin had first introduced the bill in 1918. Now it was reintroduced by congressmen who were scrambling to figure out the impact women voters might have in coming elections. Sheppard-Towner would provide federal funds for maternal and infant care to every state that passed enabling legislation to provide additional state funds. All but three states—Illinois, Massachusetts, and Connecticut—eventually complied, although in many states women had to fight hard for its accep-

---

14. Alan Dawley, *Changing the World: American Progressives in War and Revolution* (Princeton, NJ: Princeton University Press, 2003), 240–42, 299–301. See also, Mary Renda, *Taking Haiti: Military Occupation and the Culture of U.S. Imperialism, 1915–1940* (Chapel Hill: University of North Carolina Press, 2001), 191–92, 267.

15. Keller, *Regulating a New Society*, 180–81; Lucetta C. Chase, "The Social Program of the General Federation of Women's Clubs: One Index of Fifty Years of Progress," *Journal of Social Forces*, 1 (May 1923): 465–69. See also, "A National Department of Public Welfare: A Debate," *Journal of Social Forces*, 2 (March 1924): 377–81. Muncy, *Creating a Female Dominion*, 143–45 for Public Health Service maneuvers.

tance. The general arguments against it were the familiar ones that social justice progressives had long struggled against: opponents charged that it would raise taxes; that it was not a proper function of the federal government to involve itself in health care; and, according to the American Medical Association (AMA), that it intruded on their area of expertise. On the other hand, the Medical Woman's National Association enthusiastically supported the measure. State legislatures, however, were still overwhelmingly male, as were entrenched professional organizations such as the AMA that wanted any available money to come their way. When New York's Governor Nathan Miller spoke against the measure as a financial drain on the state, Florence Kelley warned him that as he had just appropriated $125,000 of state funds for new hog barns at the state fairgrounds, at the next election women voters might not appreciate "that swine shelters appeal to him more strongly than dying mothers and babies." When Miller was defeated for reelection the following year, the new governor, Al Smith, listened to his advisor Belle Moskowitz and immediately ratified it.[16]

Sheppard-Towner was only a partial victory for social justice progressives. The legislation was a "sunset" law. It would run for five years, after which Congress would consider whether to renew it. Women obviously hoped that the program would show such good results that renewal would be no problem. Women's organizations throughout the country worked in their states to set up programs to administer the funds. They used the money to fund health conferences, set up prenatal care centers, distribute literature to pregnant women, and employ visiting nurses and female doctors. They initiated programs to train and license midwives to increase the safety of delivery among immigrant and rural white and black women where few physicians were available and among whom midwifery was a significant part of the culture. The $17,430 they received from the first Sheppard-Towner funds enabled women in the geographically large and highly rural state of New Mexico to fund their first public health nurses to travel the state holding clinics for mothers and children. Thanks to Sheppard-Towner, between 1922 and 1929 infant mortality fell from 75 to 64 deaths per 1,000 live births, whereas maternal deaths fell from 67 to 62 per 1,000; the general death rate, by contrast, was actually rising.[17]

Further improvement was still possible: England's maternal death rate was half that of the United States and New Zealand had an infant death rate of 36 per 1,000. Yet the program was barely renewed in 1927 and in 1929 it was allowed to die.[18] One can find obvious suspects as reasons for dropping federal

16. Kelley quoted in Lindenmeyer, *"A Right to Childhood,"* 94. See also, J. Stanley Lemons, "The Sheppard-Towner Act: Progressivism in the 1920s," *The Journal of American History,* 55 (March 1969): 776–86; Molly Ladd-Taylor, *Mother-Work: Women, Child Welfare, and the State, 1890–1930* (Urbana: University of Illinois Press, 1984); and Muncy, *A Female Dominion.* For Smith and Belle Moskowitz, see Elisabeth Israels Perry, *Belle Moskowitz: Feminine Politics and the Exercise of Power in the Age of Alfred E. Smith* (New York: Routledge, 1987). Lathrop had made the case that what she had in mind for Sheppard-Towner was exactly the same kind of funding that the Smith-Lever had made available to states to subsidize rural county agent extension work.

17. Lindenmeyer, *"A Right to Childhood,"* 95–97, and Schackel, *Social Housekeepers,* 31–33.

18. See Lemons, "The Sheppard-Towner Act," 786 and Lindenmeyer, 100 and 104–05 for statistics.

funding for infant and maternal health care. Distrust of big government, appeals to states' rights, and dislike of government intrusion into private life
were all elements that helped to kill this program. But, to a great extent, the
reasons are rooted in reaction against women, the lack of support that male
progressives were willing to give to social justice programs, and to a backlash
against any "un-American" ideas that had resulted from World War I. By the
time of its renewal in 1927, President Coolidge did not support it, the AMA
and the Public Health Service were adamantly opposed, and conservative
women's groups argued that it was the work of "communist" women of the
Children's Bureau.[19]

Although many "patriotic" and conservative organizations had attacked
social reforms sponsored by women's organizations themselves, some of the
most sustained and vicious attacks on women's progressivism after the war
came from other groups of women. One particular group that had opposed
woman suffrage kept up the attack through its newsletter called the *Woman Patriot*. Yet, these attacks could not have succeeded if men in power had been
more sympathetic to a social justice agenda. In 1924, Henry Ford's publication,
The Dearborn Independent, printed a chart prepared by the Department of War's
Chemical Warfare Bureau that accused the Women's Joint Congressional Committee and its various member organizations of being enmeshed in the "spi-
der's web" of Bolshevism. The headline to the chart read: "The Socialist-
Pacifist Movement in America Is an Absolutely Fundamental and Integral Part
of International Socialism." In effect, the chart accused all the major national
and international women's organizations, and individuals such as Florence
Kelley, Margaret Dreier Robins, and Belle LaFollette, among others, as belonging to this international conspiracy against democracy. The following week,
the paper followed this up with a headline, "Are Women's Clubs Used by Bol-
shevists?" Carrie Chapman Catt, who had advocated censoring the NWP in
wartime, now repudiated these "attacks made upon individuals, any individuals, who have appealed to public opinion on behalf of world peace." She categorically rejected the charges being made that "the masses [sic] women
within the many well-known organizations were being weakly played upon
by a few women in 'key positions' who were linked to world communism and
its aim to overturn all governments."[20]

By 1929, the backlash against organized women sabotaged any chance of
extending the Sheppard-Towner Act. The AMA remained in staunch, well-
organized and well-funded opposition. *The Woman Patriot* sent out a thirty-
six-page petition and letter on the "Bolshevist origins of the entire progressive program for children." It urged the end to Sheppard-Towner, charging
that it, the Children's Bureau, child labor laws, and the child labor amendment were part of a "conspiracy to sovietize the United States." The petition
described Florence Kelley as "the ablest legislative general Communism has
produced" and went on to denounce Addams, Julia Lathrop, the Parent

---

19. Lindenmeyer, 101–02 and Muncy, *Creating a Female Dominion*, 146–47.
20. *The Dearborn Independent*, March 15 and 22, 1924, and Carrie Chapman Catt, "Poison Propaganda," *The Women Citizen* (May 31, 1924): 32–33.

Teacher Association, the League of Women Voters, the Women's Bureau, the Children's Bureau, the WCTU, and all the member organizations of the Women's Joint Congressional Committee as part of this plot.[21] Virtually the entire women's social justice network, with its millions of members, was thus denounced as communist and its social welfare objectives were pronounced a threat to democracy. The Sheppard-Towner Maternity and Infant Welfare Program died as a national program. Some states continued to fund their own programs, but more federal funding for children's welfare had to wait until New Deal legislation.

WHY NO SOCIAL WELFARE STATE?

Why the United States did not adopt a national social welfare network before the New Deal, as happened across western Europe, remains a much debated question.[22] Although Americans' suspicion of a centralized national state played a role in this outcome, many progressive reforms had already been enacted that vastly strengthened the federal government, including the income tax, the federal reserve, antitrust legislation, and the many economic regulations and their new federal bureaucracies. Yet, national health insurance, maternal and child medical care, an amendment against child labor, or a national housing policy to provide funds for cheap decent housing somehow remained unacceptable. The courts continued to obstruct welfare legislation, as when the Supreme Court ruled that the interstate powers of Congress could not be extended to limit child labor. And, unlike in European countries, there was no Labor Party to promote a social welfare program. Organized labor adamantly opposed national health insurance and male workers resisted any insurance program that would deduct contributions from their wages. Arguments that Sheppard-Towner was inappropriate because it invaded private life are disingenuous in that the country readily ratified the Prohibition Amendment that surely invaded private life and, as many charged, impinged upon the personal liberty that Americans so dearly cherished.[23]

To a great extent the failure of progressive proposals to create a social welfare state can be attributed to prevailing ideas about gender.[24] Robyn Muncy's book, *Creating a Female Dominion in American Reform*, draws this conclusion. Women, especially through the Children's and Women's Bureaus, were not

---

21. Lemons, "The Sheppard-Towner Act," 784–85.

22. The best transnational comparison can be found in Daniel Rodgers, *Atlantic Crossings: Social Politics in a Progressive Age* (Cambridge, MA: Harvard University Press, 1998). See also, Keller, *Regulating a New Society* and various essays in *Mothers of a New World: Maternalist Politics and the Origins of Welfare States*, Seth Koven and Sonya Michel, eds. (New York: Routledge, 1993).

23. For this, and other conclusions as to why so little social welfare, see, for example, Keller, *Regulating a New Society*, 178–80, 196, and 207. See also, Rodgers, *Atlantic Crossings*, 244, for worker resistance and Muncy, *Creating a Female Dominion*, 132. See also, the essays in Michel and Koven, *Mothers of a New World* and Theda Skocpol, *Protecting Soldiers and Mothers: The Political Origins of Social Policy in the United States* (Cambridge, MA: Harvard University Press, 1992).

24. The issue of race and the welfare state in the early 1920s will be discussed in Chapter 13.

only the leading advocates of social welfare reforms, they wanted both a voice in creating new legislation and the power to implement it—they wanted their own dominion. Men in power refused to give way to women. The Sheppard-Towner Act had not given the male medical profession control over the funds, nor decisions on hiring and procedures. It had conferred much of it on the Children's Bureau and other women's organizations. The AMA referred to the women doctors working within Sheppard-Towner as social workers, not as doctors, to undercut public perception of them as medical authorities. Other opponents attacked the women of the "dominion" for stepping out of a woman's proper place. Sheppard-Towner opponent Senator James Reed railed against the "female celibates" in the Children's Bureau for daring to promote female professionalism. Furthermore, women's professionalism was seen as a threat because it was not predicated on business efficiency or on making money. Public service and cooperation were the driving forces behind the work of the Children's Bureau and the women working with Sheppard-Towner funds. Business values and the profit motive "were central to that of the AMA leadership," as they had been to most male organizations and businessmen throughout the Progressive Era. These conflicting sets of values had traveled along the paths of progressivism before the war but could not share a single road when national policy was at stake afterwards.[25]

Female progressives had faced other difficult obstacles to promoting social welfare. Progressive women such as Kate Barnard had been able to make alliances with organized labor to enact child labor restrictions in Oklahoma. In Chicago, the WTUL had a good friend in John Fitzpatrick, the head of the Chicago Federation of Labor. Yet overall, organized labor had remained firmly against social welfare through government. Samuel Gompers declared compulsory health insurance as an alien concept that should be rejected because it originated in Germany, where the people's acceptance of authority and regulations was "far different from the spirit and the genius and the ideals of the American people. It is a difference of race psychology." Organized labor also resisted progressive pressure for old-age social insurance, objecting to any proposal that would deduct from workers' wages. Capitalism also thwarted compulsory health insurance. By wartime, there was a booming private insurance sector that was determined to stop any attempts to take insurance out of corporate hands. As was so often the case in the Progressive Era, the entire issue was clouded by conflicting social science statistics. For the insurance industry, Frederick Hoffman published *Facts and Fallacies of Compulsory Health Insurance*, purporting to prove that it would not work.[26]

25. Muncy, *Creating a Female Dominion*, 108, 125–35, and 139–50. See also, Skocpol, *Protecting Mothers and Soldiers*, 518, for list of women's organizations supporting continuation of Sheppard-Towner and Schackel, *Social Housekeepers*, 34–36 and 38–40. For the fate of national health insurance through the twentieth century, see Colin Gordon, *Dead on Arrival: The Politics of Health Care in Twentieth-Century America*, (Princeton, NJ: Princeton University Press, 2003).

26. Beatrix Hoffman, "Scientific Racism, Insurance, and Opposition to the Welfare State: Frederick L. Hoffman's Transatlantic Journey," *The Journal of the Gilded Age and Progressive Era*, 2 (April 2003): 150–90, Gompers quoted 179, and Rodgers, *Atlantic Crossings*, 220–21, 242–44, 252–54, and 257–59.

Female progressives could see from early on that securing national health or old-age insurance would be a challenge. They also feared that, even if passed, such legislation would provide minimal benefits for women. Because so many working women moved in and out of the workforce for childbirth and other family reasons, they would never accumulate enough insurance to help them in old age. Women also doubted that any general insurance plans would ever cover pregnancy, childbirth, or child-care needs of women workers. For female progressives, mothers' pensions to help support poor women who were widows or deserted wives was a viable alternative. Historians have generally dismissed mothers' pensions programs because they reached small numbers of women, often involved means testing, did not pay enough to keep these women from having to work outside the home also, and were racially discriminatory when enacted.[27] On the other hand, within the context of progressive possibilities, mothers' pensions to protect some of the most vulnerable women was one of the few programs that they could hope to achieve. Moreover, in many places women were not even the original promoters of such laws and, once enacted, were not always happy with how they were carried out. In 1917, Sophonsiba Breckinridge complained that the idealism behind the concept of widows' pensions was compromised by means testing built into the system: "A pension granted only on proof of destitution after searching investigation and under continued supervision is not what most wage-earners wish for their wives and children." Daniel Rodgers' assessment that "the guiding tropes of the mothers' pension movement were sentiment and women's weakness" undoubtedly explains why some men supported this kind of welfare but not those that would have covered male workers. Such a blanket assessment does not necessarily hold for many female social justice reformers.[28]

Social justice progressives labored under severe political limits also. The Children's Bureau may be faulted for rejecting a recommendation from the 1917 Conference on Infant and Maternal Welfare in Wartime that daycare facilities be provided for women working in war industries. The bureau believed that it was better for children if mothers not work, and argued that "local patriotic effort" should be used to avoid mothers having to work. Yet, there was absolutely no political likelihood of achieving state-funded child care in a society that would not even fund child health care nor abolish child labor.[29]

---

27. For a variety of assessments of the idea of mothers' pensions, see Joanne L. Goodwin, *Gender and the Politics of Welfare Reform: Mothers' Pensions in Chicago, 1911–1929* (Chicago: University of Chicago Press, 1997); Sonya Michel, *Children's Interests/Mothers' Rights: The Shaping of America's Child Care Policy* (New Haven, CT: Yale University Press, 1999); Ladd-Taylor, *Mother-Work*; Barbara J. Nelson, "The Origins of the Two-Channel Welfare State: Workmen's Compensation and Mothers' Aid," in *Women, the State, and Welfare*, Linda Gordon, ed. (Madison: University of Wisconsin Press, 1990); Michael Willrich, "Home Slackers: Men, the State, and Welfare in Modern America," *The Journal of American History*, 87 (September 2000): 460–89; and Rodgers, *Atlantic Crossings*, 240–41. According to Katz, "Redefining 'the Political,'" 28, Los Angeles socialist women supported mothers' pensions.

28. Goodwin, *Gender and the Politics of Welfare Reform*, and Rodgers, *Atlantic Crossings*, 241 for quote. Breckinridge quoted in Michel, *Children's Interests/Mothers' Rights*, 82. Original in Edith Abbott, "The Experimental Period of Widows' Pension Legislation," *Proceedings of the National Conference of Social Work* (1917): 163–64.

29. Lindenmeyer, *"A Right to Childhood,"* 72–73.

The Supreme Court's refusal to extend hours of labor protection to all workers had narrowed women's choices. The "entering wedge" strategy employed in the *Muller v. Oregon* case produced two divisive, and likely unintended, consequences for the future of progressive reform and for women's position in American society. Injecting a gendered notion of citizenship into economics made unavoidable an eventual split with those feminists who believed in total equal rights. The National Consumers' League, the NWTUL, and the NAWSA (and then the League of Women Voters) rejected the NWP and the Equal Rights Amendment, and the women's movement fractured. Progressive women's choice to focus on the rights and protections of women and children allowed progressive men thereafter to define women as being interested in social work while men were doing real politics. Chicago reformer George Sikes, for example, told the Illinois League of Women Voters that the men of the Chicago City Club could not support the "social issues" of the ILWV because the agenda of the City Club was "entirely political." His wife, Madeleine Wallin Sikes, was a leading figure in the ILWV. Another Chicago reformer, Charles Merriam, succinctly summed up the male view:

> In my experience women have shown the keenest interest in the problems of schools, recreation, health, city waste, housing, the protection of women and children, the case of the immigrant, and in general all measures for the protection of the weak and helpless. Questions of finance, engineering, most public works, industrial controversies, and public utility problems, have been of less interest, although not without capable students.

In Seattle, men ridiculed the administration of Mayor Bertha Knight Landes as "petticoat rule" and when she stood for reelection her opponent refused to debate her on the issues.[30] When Mary (Molly) Dewson gathered the evidence for the 1,138-page brief arguing in favor of maintaining Washington, D.C.'s, minimum-wage law for women workers in 1923, she tried to change the debate. Women deserved a minimum wage, she argued, because they had been socially and economically disadvantaged in the past and they needed a minimum wage guaranteed so that they would not keep falling into poverty. The Supreme Court overturned the law, ruling that "now that women had the vote, they were no longer a dependent class, excluded from freedom of contract, but equal to men."

In the 1923 *Adkins* case, Dewson and progressive women's organizations tried to make a case for industrial equality that acknowledged that gender differences required different provisions for the workplace. Men, after all, did not get pregnant, go through childbirth, and have major child-care responsibilities. Social justice progressives did not think that women should be punished for

---

30. Interview with George Sikes, Illinois League of Women Voters Manuscript Collection, Box 6, folder 41, at Chicago Historical Society; Charles Merriam, *Chicago: A More Intimate View of Urban Politics* (New York: Arno, 1929), 156; and Sandra Haarsager, *Bertha Knight Landes of Seattle: Big-City Mayor* (Norman: University of Oklahoma Press, 1994), 226–27. See also, Maureen A. Flanagan, *Seeing with Their Hearts: Chicago Women and the Vision of the Good City, 1871–1933* (Princeton, NJ: Princeton University Press, 2002) and Kristi Andersen, *Women in Partisan and Electoral Politics Before the New Deal* (Chicago: University of Chicago Press, 1996).

reproducing humanity. Not only did such arguments fail to impress the jurists, they continued to uphold more laws based on women's unequal nature. In 1924, the Court upheld a New York state law banning women's night work in restaurants in large cities. In *Radice v. New York* the Court cited the need for the state to protect "women's health and the public welfare." As historian Nancy Woloch has put it, with these two rulings working women were caught in a trap of men's making: "False paternalism (which deprived New York waitresses of high tips at night) and false equality (which denied Washington, D.C., workers a 'living wage') could coexist."[31]

Florence Kelley had understood that without labor legislation, women's equality would be linked to male standards within which women could never be equal.[32] By the early 1920s, Kelley perceived that the entire political, social, and economic structure of the country was set to a male standard of what was natural and what was deviant. As long as that standard prevailed, women would always be judged as unequal even with their new political rights. What the social justice reformers of the women's dominion wanted was to change the rules on how society was organized. They wanted Americans and the law to acknowledge that gender difference did not mean inequality of democratic citizenship.[33]

In the final analysis, the significance of gender for the meaning of democracy within progressivism came down to the following. Social justice progressives believed that social justice legislation and its enforcement would bring about real democracy. As Jane Addams had said, there could be no peace without bread. Florence Kelley believed there could be no democracy without social justice. Political and economic progressives such as Woodrow Wilson believed that a capitalist democracy, with safeguards against economic exploitation, would ultimately produce social justice. For these latter progressives, the forms of democracy were sufficient to produce democracy. To return to the two quotes that began this chapter, the idea of not admiring the "man of timid peace" as the way to organize society and the idea that both "bread and peace" must be guaranteed could not stand easily together.

---

31. For an assessment of the Washington, D.C., case, in the ruling *Adkins v. Children's Hospital*, see Nancy Woloch, *Muller v. Oregon: A Brief History with Documents* (Boston: Bedford Books of St. Martin's Press, 1996), 52–57.

32. Joan G. Zimmerman, "The Jurisprudence of Equality: The Women's Minimum Wage, the First Equal Rights Amendment, and *Adkins v. Children's Hospital*, 1905–1923," *The Journal of American History*, 78 (June 1991): 224–25 and 203 for Kelley.

33. For an excellent argument in this regard, see Wendy Sarvasy, "Beyond the Difference versus Equality Policy Debate: Postsuffrage Feminism, Citizenship, and the Quest for a Feminist Welfare State," *Signs* (Winter 1992): 329–62.

In April 1920, a group of men held up a payroll truck in South Braintree, Massachusetts. They got away with $15,000 but in the process killed the two guards. A short while later, Nicola Sacco and Bartolomeo Vanzetti were caught in a police trap that had actually been set for someone else. The two men were subsequently charged with the robbery and murder. Sacco and Vanzetti were Italian immigrants and professed anarchists. They had fled the country during World War I to avoid the draft and upon returning resumed their associations with other known anarchists. They claimed innocence, but they were convicted and then executed in August 1927.

For more than eighty years, the question of their guilt or innocence in the robbery and murder has taxed historians and legal scholars. At the time, serious questions were raised about whether there was sufficient evidence to prove them guilty, as their accusers claimed, or whether they were convicted because they were anarchists, as their supporters maintained. Fellow anarchists and socialists were certain that they were martyrs to the Red Scare and anti-immigrant sentiment. "The names of the 'good shoe-maker and poor fish-peddler' have ceased to represent merely two Italian workingmen. Throughout the civilised world Sacco and Vanzetti have become a symbol, the shibboleth of Justice crushed by Might," claimed Emma Goldman and Alexander Berkman, writing from France after their deportations from the United States. Conservative organizations such as the Industrial Defense Council (IDC), whose membership and goals resembled those of the wartime National Security League, were not only certain that they were guilty but also that any "Red" was an enemy of the country. Speaking before the Kiwanis Club of Lawrence, Massachusetts, two months before the execution, IDC member Frank Goodwin, referring to that city's breaking of the IWW-involved textile strike of 1912, praised the businessmen of that city for demonstrating "that you knew how to take care of [Red murderers]."

On the other hand, some very respectable Americans were not convinced of the guilt of Sacco and Vanzetti and suspected that this verdict had stemmed more from anti-immigrant sentiment than from having committed the crime for which they were charged. Among these doubters was Harvard law professor, and later Supreme Court justice, Felix Frankfurter. In the climate of fear of the early 1920s, however, such doubts were labeled un-American and subversive. Goodwin claimed that Frankfurter, moderate socialists, pacifists, women's colleges, and university professors, were part of an organization led by the American Civil Liberties Union (ACLU) to "make America safe for Red criminals, and to tear down our institutions, and ultimately build up a Soviet Commonwealth." "We must see to it," he continued, "that when Red criminals are convicted by our juries, and the verdicts upheld by our courts, that those decisions shall not be overturned by petitions or threats from irresponsible mobs."*

---

*Emma Goldman and Alexander Berkman, from Emma Goldman Papers, University of California, Berkeley, http://sunsite.berkeley.edu/Goldman/Writings/Essays/sacco.html and Frank A. Goodwin, "Sacco-Vanzetti and the Red Peril," speech to Lawrence Kiwanis Club, pamphlet distributed by Industrial Defense Association (June 1927), 9–10 and 14. Text can be found at http://digital.lib.msu.edu/collections/index.cfm?action=view&TitleID=188&Format=gif&PageNum=1. In 1977, Governor Michael Dukakis proclaimed that Sacco and Vanzetti had not received a fair trial.

CHAPTER 13

ﾷ

Into the Twenties
Roads Taken . . . and Not

> The day of indiscriminate acceptance of all races has definitely ended.
> —ALBERT JOHNSON, R-WA, 1924

> The last moment belongs to us—that agony is our triumph.
> —NICOLA SACCO, 1927

WOODROW WILSON DIED in 1924. Theodore Roosevelt had died in 1919. With these progressive presidents gone, a national progressive movement for ongoing reform would peter out. Neither political party wanted to pursue the cause any further nationally. In 1920, the Republicans nominated Warren G. Harding, a small-town Ohio newspaper editor and politician. The Democrats nominated an equally obscure candidate, James M. Cox, who was also an Ohio newspaper editor. Harding won in a landslide and died in office after a scandal-ridden three years. His conservative vice-president Calvin Coolidge assumed the office and then was elected in 1924. Under this conservative Republican leadership, businessmen flocked to Washington, some progressives abandoned the cause, while others, especially women, kept at it. But the profound changes brought into American society by progressivism could not be rolled back. What remained to be seen was how these changes would play out across the 1920s, which progressive agendas would emerge victorious, and how various groups of Americans would be treated by government and society.

CITIZENSHIP IN THE 1920S

The ruthless suppression of free speech and dissent, the surge of antialien and antiradical sentiment, the assignment of the word *un-American* to anyone who disagreed, and the Red hysteria of 1919 and 1920 all determined that the more capacious progressive ideas of citizenship and democracy would be limited in the coming years. Wilson must be held at least partially responsible for setting this in motion. He had clearly understood what he was about to unleash domestically by going to war. Once the people were led into war, he mused to his advisors, "they'll forget there ever was such a thing as tolerance. To fight you must be brutal and ruthless, and the spirit of ruthless brutality will enter into the very fibre of our national life . . . Conformity will be the only virtue."[1] To be fair, he thought of this as happening only during the time of war. Yet, it was his attorney general who rounded up aliens and radicals in 1919 and who had empowered a new federal agency, the Bureau of Investigation led by J. Edgar Hoover. And it was Wilson who had wondered whether there should also be a peacetime sedition act. Nor did Wilson use his presidential powers to pardon Eugene Debs or other socialists who were languishing in prison as a result of the Espionage and Sedition Acts. In fact, the only thing that seemed to interest Wilson once the fighting stopped was his plan for the peace treaty. When he failed to secure the kind of treaty that he had wanted, and when Congress refused to ratify the treaty as signed at Versailles, Wilson went into a physical decline for the brief remainder of his presidency, but the progressive impulses went ahead.

Defining Americanism

In the wartime hysteria Congress had finally enacted a literacy requirement for potential immigrants, overriding Wilson's veto in 1917. With Chinese and Japanese immigration already restricted, attention now turned to other groups. Many progressives who were national figures opposed various restriction proposals. Frances Kellor continued to advocate Americanization of immigrants rather than restriction. Randolph Bourne in 1916 had declared that the steady flow of immigration would produce a new generation of cosmopolitan, internationalists who would eschew continuing to define an "Americanism" in favor of seeing themselves as part of the world. Unfortunately, Bourne died in 1919 so he was not around to make his case. John Dewey lost heart in the immediate aftermath of the war and left the country to spend two years in Asia, although he still believed that education was the means for fostering democracy. For other progressives, immigration restriction was acceptable as part of the struggle to end laissez faire liberalism and create a more orderly society. As early as 1916, *The New Republic* had declared that "Freedom of migration from one country to another appears to be one of the elements of nineteenth-century liberalism that is fated to disappear." This was a trade-off, the journal editors thought, for increased "responsibility of the state for the welfare of its individual members. . . . The democracy of today . . . cannot permit . . . social ills to be aggravated by excessive immigration." Those progressives who believed that everyone could be "Americanized," including Howe, Wald, Scudder, and Garrison Villard, formed the National Committee for Constructive Immigration Legislation in 1918 hoping to minimize the extent of restriction.[2]

---

1. Arthur S. Link, *Wilson: Campaigns for Progressivism and Peace, 1916–1917* (Princeton, NJ: Princeton University Press, 1965), 399.

2. John Higham, *Strangers in the Land: Patterns of American Nativism, 1860–1925* (New Brunswick, NJ: Rutgers University Press, 2002 edition), 302–03 and Eric Foner, *The Story of American Freedom* (New York: W.W. Norton, 1998), 189–90.

The new "science" of eugenics, which insisted that humans possessed in-bred traits of racial superiority and inferiority that could be measured, had gained a strong enough following in the preceding years to influence ideas about immigration also. At the 1915 Panama Pacific Exposition, the American Eugenics Society had awarded medals in a "Fittest Families" Competition. The medals were inscribed with the saying "Yea, I have a goodly heritage" and de-picted a mother and father passing strength to an infant. The Exposition itself exhibited the evolution of life from "primitive man" through a Fountain of Psychology of Life that featured sculptures titled "The Dawn of Life," "Nat-ural Selection," and "Survival of the Fittest."[3]

Anthropologists such as Franz Boas and Ruth Benedict strongly contested eugenics, but its arguments were now used to justify restriction, exclusion, and discrimination. Calls for tighter restriction quickly gained momentum. Ordi-nary Americans now joined in the so-called 100 percent American frenzy. Ital-ian miners and their families were beaten and burned out of their homes in West Frankfort, Illinois. California—a supposedly progressive state—in a pop-ular initiative passed a law restricting alien ownership of agricultural lands. Henry Ford launched an anti-Semitic campaign in the Upper Midwest. Anti-Catholic movements sprang up in the South. Assistant Secretary of Labor Louis Post, a longtime progressive, decried the mass roundups of suspected alien radicals. Without search warrants, he wrote, "homes were invaded, trunks broken open, personal papers seized and personal privacies shamefully disturbed." The progressive wish to Americanize newcomers gave way to re-striction, deportation, and a move to make everyone who resided in the coun-try conform to an ideal of what a good American was.[4]

Across the 1920s, defining what might be a good American occupied the at-tention of many Americans. The Reed-Johnson National Origins Act, passed by Congress in 1924, officially legalized racial categories for who could be an American. This was a temporary measure authorizing quotas by nationality and setting a yearly limit for immigrants at 150,000. It immediately restricted immigration to 2 percent annually of the number of any nationality recorded in the 1890 census, effectively reserving 85 percent of immigration for people from northern and western Europe. A *Los Angeles Times* headline captured the essence of the new law: "Nordic Victory Is Seen in Drastic Restrictions." Fur-ther, the act specifically excluded "descendants of slave immigrants" from this census count—thereby eliminating black African immigrants. U.S. residents who were ineligible for citizenship—Asians—were now totally excluded.

A permanent system was to be in place by 1927, although it would take un-til 1929 to reach agreement on the quota allocation and then it was extrapo-lated from the 1920 census rather than 1890. As put into practice, the quota system bore strong resemblance to Theodore Roosevelt's ideas of racial de-scent. It favored certain Europeans and clearly distinguished Europeans from

3. See Matthew Frye Jacobson, *Barbarian Virtues: The United States Encounters Foreign Peoples at Home and Abroad, 1876–1917* (New York: Hill and Wang, 2000), esp. 150 for the Fountain.

4. Higham, *Strangers in the Land*, 265. Louis F. Post, *The Deportations Delirium of Nineteen-Twenty: A Personal Narrative of an Historical Official Experience* (New York: Charles H. Kerr, 1923; republished 1970), 96–98.

all other peoples in the world. Non-Asians, for instance, who lived in Asian countries were given a yearly quota (100 from Japan, 100 from India, etc.). In effect, white Europeans were eligible for immigration by country of origin (nationality), whereas the rest of the world was divided into "five colored races" (black, mulatto, Chinese, Japanese, Indian) who could not come to the United States legally. To be American meant to be white European, or the "Nordic" peoples as the *LA Times* had put it. When a Japanese American challenged California's alien land ownership laws as discriminatory against the Japanese—the law's real target—the Supreme Court upheld the California laws, ruling that because the law as written applied to all aliens ineligible for citizenship, it did not discriminate against Japanese Americans. The Court's majority ruling also implied that the law was just because anyone who was not a citizen could not be counted on to work productively for the whole society. The Court, in effect, used circular logic: Japanese immigrants could not become citizens; noncitizens could not own land; hence the Japanese immigrants could not become good Americans. Such logic reified and legalized racial categories for who was an American.[5]

The Sacco and Vanzetti case made it clear that certain groups of white European immigrants were now a threat to bring radical and un-American ideas into the country. Even the working class, who undoubtedly chafed at instructions from the middle class about how to be an American, had used progressive ideology to participate in defining and broadening the understanding of American, citizen, and democracy to encompass all "white" Americans before the war.[6] Now, the progressives' sympathetic ideal of bringing all immigrant groups into the mainstream of American society and citizenship was transformed into a coercive and restrictive movement. Once the meanings of American, citizen, and democracy were so explicitly racialized, politicized, and codified into law, the progressive ideal of an open society into which all could be fit was replaced in favor of creating an orderly society into which only certain people and groups could be welcomed. Below the surface of law, even uglier manifestation of these ideas appeared.

White, Protestant, Male Americanism

The Ku Klux Klan (KKK) had resurrected itself in 1915. Its rebirth came in the aftermath of the lynching in 1915 of Leo Frank, the Jewish superintendent of the National Pencil Factory in Atlanta. Frank had been convicted amid anti-Semitic

---

5. Higham, *Strangers in the Land*, 300, for headline from *Los Angeles Times*, April 13, 1924; Eric Rauchway, *Murdering McKinley: The Making of Theodore Roosevelt's America* (New York: Hill and Wang, 2003), 140–48; and Mae M. Ngai, "The Architecture of Race in American Immigration Law: A Reexamination of the Immigration Act of 1924," *The Journal of American History*, 86 (June 1999): 67–92, provides an excellent discussion of the law and the development of the quota system and its relationship to racial thinking. Congress had passed a law in 1917 creating a "barred Asiatic Zone," making all Asians ineligible for citizenship. In 1924, Congress also passed the Indian Citizenship law giving citizenship to all Native Americans. This equation of race, citizenship, and immigration would endure until 1952 when the immigration laws were finally changed.

6. See James Barrett, "Americanization from the Bottom Up: Immigration and the Re-Making of the Working Class in the United States, 1880–1930," *Journal of American History*, 86 (December 1999): 996–1020.

hysteria for the murder of Mary Phagan, a fourteen-year-old factory employee. When the outgoing governor of the state commuted Frank's death sentence to life imprisonment, an angry mob stormed the Georgia State Prison, hauled Frank out, and lynched him. This same mob, calling itself the Knights of Mary Phagan (the original Klan had been the Knights of the While Camellia) then re-organized the KKK. This time, the Klan directed its hatred at any group that its members believed did not look, think, or act like their definition of an American. Hatred of African Americans remained central to their white nativist ideals, but now they attacked Catholics, Jews, immigrants, Bolsheviks, and women whom they believed were not behaving according to "traditional" American values.

Klaverns emerged throughout the country across the 1920s. They emerged in the South, of course, but the Klan also moved into cities such as Portland, Chicago, and Buffalo. One of the largest organizations grew in the state of Indiana.[7] Ironically, the resurgent KKK benefited from the organizational techniques that progressives had developed to promote their causes. In a further irony, it was a woman's talent for organizing as well as her experience in progressive women's crusades for children's health that helped foster the national growth of the KKK. Elizabeth Tyler had been a volunteer infant hygiene worker earlier in the 1910s. By 1920, she and Edward Clark had formed the Southern Publicity Association to market the work of organizations such as the Anti-Saloon League. In 1920, they took on the KKK as a client and in the first six months of their operation, they enrolled 85,000 new members.[8]

From Portland Klan members to those in Athens, Georgia, socially oriented progressivism was perceived as a challenge to the kind of masculine identity that Theodore Roosevelt's progressivism had advocated. One Atlanta Klan minister, writing in the *Kourier*, echoed Roosevelt's 1899 speech when he declared that "God intended that every man should possess insofar as possible, his own home and rule his own household." Nevertheless, as Kathleen Blee pointed out, plenty of women wanted to join. Conservative women who had had little to do with the progressive social agendas of other women's organizations during the era had nonetheless done their own organizing. Now such groups as the Dixie Protestant Women's Political Equality League, the Grand League of Protestant Women (headquartered in Houston), and the White American Protestants (WAP) shared the racist and exclusionary ideas of the KKK. The WAP claimed 12,000 female members in the mid-South and they all swore an oath "never to vote for, or to place as teacher, governess, or instructor of children, any non-American-born, nonwhites, or non-Protestants."

---

7. Nancy MacLean, *Behind the Mask of Chivalry: The Making of the Second Ku Klux Klan* (New York: Oxford University Press, 1994); Kenneth Jackson, *The Ku Klux Klan in the City: 1915–1930* (New York: Oxford University Press, 1967; reprint, 1992); Shawn Lay, *Hooded Knights on the Niagara: The Ku Klux Klan in Buffalo, New York* (New York: New York University Press, 1995) and *War, Revolution and the Ku Klux Klan: A Study of Intolerance in a Border City* (El Paso: Texas Western University Press, 1985); and Robert Johnston, *The Radical Middle Class: Popular Democracy and the Question of Capitalism in Progressive Era Portland, Oregon* (Princeton, NJ: Princeton University Press, 2003).

8. MacLean, *Behind the Mask of Chivalry*, 5–6 and Kathleen Blee, *Women of the Klan: Gender and Racism of the 1920s* (Berkeley: University of California Press, 1991), 20–22, for Tyler.

Women of similar persuasion organized LOTIE (Ladies of the Invisible Empire) clubs throughout the country.[9]

The Klan's resurrection was in great measure a response to the social, economic, and political changes brought by progressivism. Members of the organization believed, as Andrew Carnegie had written forty years previously, that the United States was great because it was a white, Anglo-Saxon, Protestant country. They did not wish to embrace the progressive agenda of social justice based on the idea that there were social rights owed to all individuals, especially if those individuals were black, Mediterranean, Asian, Jewish, or Catholic. For all those Americans who embraced the changes promoted by economic progressivism, there were groups who felt threatened and harmed by them. White small farmers and businessmen in the South and in the West, for example, but also in rural areas throughout the country still wanted to dismantle corporate capitalism rather than regulate it. As historian Robert Johnston showed so well for the Portland "middling classes," the ideal of "property-owning equality" still lingered among groups of Americans. As this ideal seemed to be slipping away from them, the KKK found converts even among these Northwest urbanites.[10]

"Protestantism," declared Imperial Wizard Hiram Wesley Evans, was "more than a religion." It was the bedrock of Americanism and the Bible was the literal truth. Such thinking was being challenged by new ideas such as evolution that were based on scientific knowledge rather than religious belief and were being taught in schools. The John Scopes "monkey trial" of 1925 brought this issue into public debate. Scopes was found guilty of having violated the law against teaching Darwinian theories of evolution in Tennessee, but his defense lawyer Clarence Darrow had made the creationist position, argued by the old populist William Jennings Bryan, look foolish. With hard science replacing old religious verities, social science investigation of social problems taking precedence over older ideas about how to order society, and new groups such as the ACLU (which had backed Scopes' defense) defending the rights and liberties of all Americans to equality, numbers of Americans felt the firmament of old ideas cracking beneath their feet and reacted violently against this. The resurrection of the KKK was an ugly response to a changing society.[11]

As a national phenomenon with strength in numbers the KKK quickly faded. Some of its prominent leaders had quickly fallen from grace. Indiana Klan leader D.C. Stephenson was convicted of second-degree murder after the young girl who had accused him of sexual assault poisoned herself. Eliza-

9. Theodore Roosevelt, Speech of 1899 in Chicago, printed in Theodore Roosevelt, *The Strenuous Life: Essays and Addresses* (New York: The Century Company, 1903); MacLean, *Behind the Mask of Chivalry*, quote 114; and Blee, *Women of the Klan*, 25–26, for WAP oath.

10. MacLean, *Behind the Mask of Chivalry*, 130, and Johnston, *The Radical Middle Class*, 238–47.

11. For the Scopes trial, see Jeffrey P. Moran, *The Scopes Trial: A Brief History with Documents* (Boston: Bedford Books of St. Martin's Press, 2002) and Clarence Darrow, *The Famous Examination of Bryan at the Scopes Evolution Trial* (Gerard, KS: Haldeman–Julius Publications, 1929). See also, MacLean, *Behind the Mask of Chivalry*, 92–94, 92, for Evans.

beth Tyler and Edward Clark were caught in flagrante.[12] Once immigration restriction had been achieved and economic prosperity seemed to be returning to the country, the reactionary backlash receded, although the Klan never disappeared. But the ideas of cultural pluralism once expressed by progressives such as Horace Kallen, John Dewey, and Lillian Wald—what Marjorie Feld has called Wald's "ethnic Progressive universalism"—were seriously damaged by this backlash. Kallen believed that the very strength of American democracy came from its diversity. Dewey had celebrated the hyphenated American as connecting people, not separating them. One result of measures such as official immigration restriction and the resurgent KKK was that many American Catholics and Jews, feeling embattled, retreated further into their own organizations. The National Catholic Welfare Council (NCWC) and the League of Catholic Women, along with B'nai B'rith, the Anti-Defamation League, and the National Council of Jewish Women, gained supporters and centralized control over certain aspects of their coreligionists' lives during the 1920s.[13] Thus, instead of transcending religious and ethnic barriers, as had been the goal of many progressives, the backlash of the 1920s drove even groups of "white" Americans into a defensive posture of maintaining separate cultural identities.

African American Citizenship

There can be no doubt that the most tragic road not taken during the Progressive Era was that toward eradicating racial inequality. The history here is littered with ifs: if Jane Addams had made a greater fuss in 1912; if the progressive candidate Theodore Roosevelt had not developed his ideas of racial hierarchy; if the Democratic Party had not been so beholden to the South; if the labor movement had been open to organizing black workers; if the General Federation of Women's Club (GFWC) had welcomed black women's clubs; if there had been a united African American movement; if the Supreme Court had struck down racial segregation and disfranchisement—could the outcome have been different? Unfortunately, none of these was the case,[14] and it probably would have taken all these elements put together to have changed the course of race relations in the United States.

---

12. Higham, *Strangers in the Land*, 328–29.

13. Kallen's idea was that Jewish life was "national and secular" and that Zionism was compatible with an American identity. For Kallen and Wald, see Marjorie Feld, "'An Actual Working Out of Internationalism': Russian Politics, Zionism, and Ethnic Progressivism," *The Journal of the Gilded Age and Progressive Era*, 2 (April 2003): 119–49. For Dewey, see Alan Dawley, *Struggles for Justice: Social Responsibility and the Liberal State* (Cambridge, MA: Harvard University Press, 1991), 258. Deirdre M. Moloney, *American Catholic Lay Groups and Transatlantic Social Reform in the Progressive Era* (Chapel Hill: University of North Carolina Press, 2002).

14. It should be noted that in 1924, largely through the instigation of Florence Kelley, the National Association of Colored Women joined the Women's Joint Congressional Committee and that local women's clubs in the GFWC continued to try to maintain interracial ties. The GFWC co-sponsored in 1920 a Women's Interracial Conference in Memphis. Glenda Gilmore, *Gender and Jim Crow: Women and the Politics of White Supremacy in North Carolina, 1896–1920* (Chapel Hill: University of North Carolina Press, 1996) discusses white and black women in that state.

African American faith in the progressive spirit of inclusion was still strong
at the war's end. Local chapters of the NAACP in the South grew rapidly following the war, as African Americans demanded the equality of citizenship
they believed due them on the basis of their war participation. But southern
whites used mass terror to squash this initiative, as when a number of black
sharecroppers—many of whom had served in the military—in Arkansas attempted to form a union. Federal troops were sent to stop this effort. Two hundred and fifty sharecroppers were killed and another 1,000 were arrested, including women. Such violence and government collusion against African
Americans destroyed most NAACP chapters and halted attempts to form
unions in the South across the 1920s. Membership in the Texas chapters, for example, dropped from 7,700 to just a little over 1,000. Attacks on the NAACP
were so violent that when Texas NAACP leaders asked former NACW president Mary Burnett Talbert to help revive their efforts, she agreed to come only
as a member of the NACW. "*None* of us can afford to go to Texas as NAACP,"
she informed the national NAACP leadership. "Jim Crow travel is not only
hard but *hazardous* in that part of *Hell* where we should work." After southern
senators thwarted a second attempt to pass the Dyer antilynching bill (which
had passed the House) in 1922, Talbert followed Ida B. Wells-Barnett's path
and turned her attention to protecting African Americans from lynching. She
formed a new group, the Anti-Lynching Crusaders, whose membership soared
from sixteen women to more than 900 in just three months. The antilynching
crusaders did not secure a federal antilynching bill, but the women continued
agitating and gathering information to put before the public and the politicians. The women attempted to attract as much support as possible from white
women, without a lot of success. Florence Kelley had actively supported the
Dyer bill and was appalled in 1922 when her pleas to the National League of
Women Voters (NLWV) had not elicited strong action on its behalf. Antilynching crusaders especially sought support from southern women, but it was not
until 1930 that Jessie Ames Daniels formed the Association of Southern
Women for the Prevention of Lynching (ASWPL).[15]

In the face of such events, along with racial rioting in Chicago in 1919, Tulsa,
Oklahoma, in 1921, and so many other places, by the early 1920s African

15. Steven A. Reich, "Soldiers for Democracy: Black Texans and the Fight for Citizenship, 1917–
1921," *Journal of American History*, 82 (March 1996): 1478–1504, table 2 for membership totals, Talbert quoted on 1501. Leonidas Dyer (R-MO) had introduced his bill in 1918 and Wilson supported
it. When it failed, Dyer continued to promote it, including wording he applied to protecting aliens
as well as citizens to go beyond the citizenship guarantees of the 14th Amendment. One of the chief
legal counsels for the NAACP, Moorfield Storey, argued for the constitutionality of such a new law
by drawing upon Justice Brandeis' former opinions that it could be the responsibility of the federal
government to see that the rights guaranteed by the 1st and 14th Amendments were not merely impinged upon by government, but that these rights were not violated by "irresponsible" individuals. See William B. Hixson, Jr., "Moorfield Storey and the Defense of the Dyer Anti-Lynching Bill,"
The New England Quarterly, 42 (March 1969): 65–81, Storey quoted on 79. For Talbert and antilynching crusaders, see Jacqueline Jones Royster, ed., *Southern Horrors and Other Writings: The Anti-
Lynching Campaign of Ida B. Wells, 1892–1900* (Boston: Bedford Books of St. Martin's Press, 1997), introduction 26. For Kelley and her lifelong campaign for equal rights, see Louis L. Athey, "Florence
Kelley and the Quest for Negro Equality," *The Journal of Negro History* (October 1971): 249–61 and
257 for her correspondence with the NLWV.

American hopes that participation in the war effort would bring equal citizenship were dimmed. W.E.B. DuBois, who had gone to Europe in 1919 to plead for a treaty granting colonized peoples their independence, was deeply disappointed with the treaty's failure to do so. He and African and Caribbean internationalists then founded the Pan-African Congress. But the Versailles Treaty's failure to demand racial equality and the racialized categories of the National Origins Act demonstrated the truth of DuBois' declaration that there was an international dimension to the "problem of the color line." Moreover, although the migration of African Americans out of the South had indeed given northern African Americans political rights, including women after 1920, their competition for jobs, housing, and recreation was increasing racial intolerance in the northern cities.

It is hardly surprising in these circumstances that African Americans were attracted to the separateness movement headed by Marcus Garvey and his international organization, the Universal Negro Improvement Association (UNIA). Garvey believed that the United States would always be a "white man's country." As DuBois was putting together another Pan-African Conference in 1921 to call again for civil and political rights for people of Africa and of African descent around the world, Garvey offered a vision of racial separateness in which the "New Negro" man would stand strong and militant. When Chicago's African Americans fought back in July 1919 they had signaled their determination to resist racism. The UNIA gave African Americans across the country an organization that promised to help them do just that. Black poets such as Claude McKay celebrated the strength of the new black man:

**"Though far outnumbered let us show us brave,
and for their thousand blows deal one death blow!"[16]**

The UNIA also preached gender equality, although it never delivered on that promise. Instead, it offered black women the protections and admiration of strong black men. According to Deborah Gray White, "Contrary to the Association's woman-centered race-progress ideology, the proponents of New Negro ideology made race progress dependent on virile masculinity." The strong feminist presence of Garvey's second wife, Amy Jacques, may also have attracted African American women to the UNIA. Jacques demanded absolute equality for black women, writing to black men that "we are very sorry if it hurts your old-fashioned tyrannical feelings. We not only make the demand but we intend to enforce it."[17]

Although most assessments of Garveyism contend that it failed when Garvey was deported to his birthplace of Jamaica after spending a few years in

---

16. For the tension between Garvey and DuBois, see Alexandre Mboukou, "The Pan African Movement, 1900–1945: A Study in Leadership Conflicts Among the Disciples of Pan Africanism," *The Journal of Black Studies*, 13 (March 1983): 275–88. Claude McKay, "If We Must Die" (1919).

17. Deborah Gray White, *Too Heavy a Load: Black Women in Defense of Themselves, 1894–1994* (New York: W.W. Norton, 1999), 120–24, quote 124, 138–40 for Amy Jacques, quote 138. See also, Karen S. Adler, "'Always Leading Our Men in Service and Sacrifice': Amy Jacques Garvey, Black Feminist Nationalist," *Gender and Society*, 6 (September 1992): 346–75.

prison during the mid-1920s, new work on the movement is suggesting that this assessment must be reconsidered. Even without the leader, UNIA clubs carried on in the United States into the 1930s, providing essential community services for their members. DuBois, for his part, moved more centrally into Pan-Africanism and into defining a "new race consciousness" in which the older progressive transatlantic connections would ultimately be reconfigured as a black Atlantic and a white Atlantic. What DuBois and the Pan-Africanists most wanted in the 1920s was to free Africa politically and economically from white colonialism and exploitation.[18]

Yet throughout the country, African Americans continued their quest for racial justice as American citizens through the 1920s and beyond. The work of the African American community in St. Louis provides just one example. Building on a tradition of racial justice pursued by their churches, black St. Louis residents forged a "black civic ideology" that demanded "racial democracy," not the biracial democracy that some southern white progressives had wanted, and worked through a variety of organizations. Some of these were local branches of the NAACP and the National Urban League, for example, but others were more local, such as the Association of Colored Women. This latter group, beginning with protests over racist regulations at the 1904 Fair, continued to engage in "Progressive-era concerns . . . in parallel with the whites-only League of Women Voters." The failure of white progressivism to strongly advocate and then build a racially equal society paved the road for black nationalism, founded in the midst of the dashed hopes of many African Americans, to carry that ideal into the future.[19]

Women's Place, Women's Citizenship

By the 1920s, progressivism had profoundly changed the place of women in the United States. Suffrage was merely the next step in a process that had seen women throughout American society insert themselves so centrally into public life that they could never be removed and put back into the home, despite the efforts of the KKK and other reactionary groups.[20] Young women had decisively thrown off "male supervision" in public: they flocked to dance halls, saloons, amusement parks, and moving pictures on their own. Progressive women's campaigns to regulate dance halls and control vice had been motivated by a desire to protect women in public by regulating these new public spaces, not to reconfine them to the private world under male supervision. Progressive women's crusades against prostitution reflected their sense that girls and young women were being exploited by a male-privileged and property-oriented society, not

---

18. For DuBois and the new race consciousness, see Matthew Pratt Guterl, "The New Race Consciousness: Race, Nation, and Empire in American Culture, 1900–1925," *The Journal of World History*, 10 (Fall 1999): 350–51. See also, David Levering Lewis, *W.E.B. DuBois: The Fight for Equality in the American Century, 1919–1963* (New York: Henry Holt, 2000). I wish to acknowledge the work in progress on this subject by Daniel Dalrymple, graduate student at Michigan State University.

19. Joseph Heathcott, "Black Archipelago: Politics and Civic Life in the Jim Crow City," *Journal of Social History*, 38 (Spring 2005): 705–36, quotes 719 and 720.

20. MacLean, *Behind the Mask of Chivalry*, is the most thorough examination of the sexist ideas of the KKK.

that these were "immoral" women. "Certainly we are safe in predicting," Jane Addams had declared in her writing against prostitution, "that when the solidarity of human interest is actually realized, it will become unthinkable that one class of human beings should be sacrificed to the supposed needs of another; when the rights of human life have successfully asserted themselves in contrast to the rights of property." Nor can these types of progressive moral reforms merely be seen as middle-class women trying to control working-class women. Antiprostitution measures and safer public amusements for women, for example, were central issues in the campaigns of Los Angeles socialist women when they ran for office after receiving suffrage in 1911.[21]

Women had moved into the public arena in a variety of other ways beyond voting and public recreation. The number of young women attending universities rose, their path having been opened by many of the older generation of progressive women leaders. Women now carved out whole sectors of professionalism for themselves as teachers, social workers, and nurses. For African American women, nursing presented the opportunity to eschew the domestic work done by their mothers. Lillian Wald employed 25 black and 150 white nurses at the Henry Street Nurses Settlement. They were paid equal salaries and given the same professional courtesies and recognition as white nurses. In 1905, the white-led Chicago Visiting Nurses Association hired one of the first African American public health nurses, Tallahassee Smith, and had hired more by 1920. The black nurses, however, were not sent into white homes nor given supervisory positions, but they formed their own organizations to fight for equality within the profession. Science and social science had challenged older ideas of moral behavior based on religious belief and loosened other restrictions on women. There was an upsurge in divorce, and advocates of free love and of birth control, especially Margaret Sanger's American Birth Control League founded in 1921, sought to expand women's sexual freedom. Women activists set up private birth control clinics around the country despite political and legal attempts to thwart them. Socialist women in Los Angeles had been among the earliest supporters of birth control in that city.[22]

---

21. Elisabeth Israels Perry, *Belle Moskowitz: Feminine Politics and the Exercise of Power in the Age of Alfred E. Smith* (New York: Routledge, 1987); Jane Addams, *A New Conscience and an Ancient Evil* (New York: Macmillan, 1912), 217; and Sherry L. Katz, "Redefining the 'Political': Socialist Women and Party Politics in California, 1900–1920," in *We Have Come to Stay: American Women in Political Parties, 1880–1960*, Melanie Gustafson, Kristie Miller, and Elisabeth Israels Perry, eds. (Albuquerque: University of New Mexico Press, 1999), 28.

22. See MacLean, *Beneath the Mask of Chivalry*, for reactions against the "new woman"; Darlene Clark Hine, *Black Women in White: Racial Conflict and Cooperation in the Nursing Profession, 1890–1950* (Bloomington: Indiana University Press, 1989), 101 for Wald, but also the entire book for black nurses' fight against racism in the profession. For Chicago, see Maureen A. Flanagan, *Seeing with Their Hearts: Chicago Women and the Vision of the Good City, 1871–1933* (Princeton, NJ: Princeton University Press, 2002), 168. For socialist women and birth control see, Katz, "Redefining 'The Political,'" 28, and Mari Jo Buhle, *Women and American Socialism, 1870–1920* (Urbana: University of Illinois Press, 1981), 268–80. For history of the birth control movement, see David Kennedy, *Birth Control in America: The Career of Margaret Sanger* (New Haven, CT: Yale University Press, 1970); see also, Rosemarie Holz, "The Birth Control Clinic: Women, Planned Parenthood and the Birth Control Manufacturing Industry" (Ph.D. diss., University of Illinois at Urbana, 2002).

DEMOCRACY IN THE 1920s

Even progressives who were disappointed that they had not achieved more of their objectives believed that they had sufficiently eliminated laissez-faire economics and politics to make the United States more democratic. They had also reasoned that if citizenship was national rather than local, and if all Americans were to receive the same rights and protections from a stronger national state, then citizenship had to be national rather than local. Having accomplished both ends by the early 1920s, not all progressives would be happy with future developments. Those progressives who had wanted to see power flow from the bottom of a democratic society were surely disappointed that what resulted instead was a corporate, regulatory state; a well-ordered one to be sure, but one in which power flowed from the top.

1. The Corporate Regulatory State

How this expanded and empowered state would function became apparent in the war's aftermath. During the war, businessmen and efficiency experts, many of whom had participated in progressive organizations, had flocked to Washington, D.C., to organize the war effort. After the war, many of these men remained there, determined to replace laissez-faire and weak government with a corporatist (or associational) state. Future president Herbert Hoover, for example, was an administrative "expert" who believed that government and business cooperation (associationalism) could judiciously run the country to guarantee economic prosperity. Hoover had honed his ideas while heading the wartime Food and Fuel Administration and sharpened them in its aftermath when he helped direct the European recovery program. Hoover also believed that once the economy was well run, economic prosperity would "trickle down" and obviate the need for a welfare state. The private sector of capitalism could then supply what limited welfare was required. As secretary of commerce from 1921–1927, Hoover's policies were all directed to maintaining high production rates and good relations with business. He declared that "the dominating fact of this last century has been economic development. And it continues today as the force which dominates the whole spiritual, social and political life of our country and the world." Businessmen could hardly have been happier. They had a business expert in an important government office, and they quickly learned how to use the strong state to their benefit.[23]

---

23. Daniel Rodgers, *Atlantic Crossings: Social Politics in a Progressive Age* (Cambridge, MA: Harvard University Press, 1998), 378–79, and Ellis W. Hawley, *The Great War and the Search for a Modern Order: A History of the American People and Their Institutions, 1917–1933*, 2nd edition (New York: St. Martin's Press, 1992), 54–55 and 84–86. See also, Guy Alchon, *The Invisible Hand of Planning: Capitalism, Social Science, and the State in the 1920s* (Princeton, NJ: Princeton University Press, 1985). Dawley, *Changing the World*, 314, quotes Hoover. For extensive discussion of how businessmen adapted progressive ideas to their own advantage, see Gabriel Kolko, *The Triumph of Conservatism: A Reinterpretation of American History, 1900–1916* (Chicago: Free Press of Glencoe, 1963) and James Weinstein, *The Corporate Ideal in the Liberal State, 1900–1918* (Boston: Beacon Press, 1968).

Labor could not mount any realistic challenge to the corporatist state. The Red Scare decimated the IWW leadership, most of whom were indicted for conspiracy against the U.S. government. Emma Goldman was deported, "Big Bill" Haywood fled the country, and radicals such as Carlo Tresca were under Justice Department surveillance. Tresca's anti-Fascist paper, *Il Martello*, was confiscated in 1923 under the pretext that it published obscene matter—a birth control ad—and Tresca spent four months in jail. Gompers had hoped that the AFL would be an important player in a postwar cooperative business-labor government. His hopes vanished with the dismantling of the wartime agencies in which labor had had a voice and the denationalization of the railroads. While Gompers was relying on hope, loyalty, and faith in Wilson to strengthen labor's position once the war was won, businessmen were acting to ensure this would not happen. They drew up the "American Plan" to reassert their control over labor after the war. When the 1919 labor strikes hit the country, business was ready to strike them down. They were able to call on federal troops again in 1922 when 250,000 railway shop men struck across the country. The strike was the last of the great labor strikes of the period, and its failure began the decline of the organized labor movement until it rallied in the New Deal era.[24]

Progressives made a last try to stave off the corporatist state. They organized a Farmer-Labor party in 1919, backed mainly by local labor organizations such as the garment workers in New York and the Chicago Federation of Labor. The party had little success in the 1920 elections, but progressives kept going. Howe then organized a Conference for Progressive Political Action in 1922, and along with Addams, DuBois, Kelley, Dewey, and Rose Schneiderman, he attempted to revive the Progressive Party. The movement succeeded in electing a number of progressive candidates to Congress in that year's election. In 1924, they nominated Robert LaFollette for president. LaFollette tried valiantly to bring the "people" back in, reviving the old populist slogan of the people versus the interests. He attacked the Supreme Court for overturning child labor law, asking "which is supreme, the will of the people or the will of the few men who have been appointed to life positions?" Unfortunately for LaFollette, by 1924 the country looked and felt pretty prosperous to many Americans and labor, the "hardy working men and women" to whom his appeal was intended, gave him weak support. The AFL endorsed LaFollette, but the leaders of the United Mine Workers Union (UMW) ultimately backed Republican Calvin Coolidge, believing he would win and that in backing the victor the union would have a strong hand for negotiating after the election. When the Democrats chose a Wall Street lawyer, John Davis, Coolidge's election was all but assured. The Republicans took the opportunity after the election to deprive all progressive Republicans in Congress of their committee rank. They removed LaFollette from his powerful seat on the Interstate Commerce Committee and replaced him with a conservative. Other progressives drifted into the Democratic Party. Progressivism was essentially dead inside

---

24. For more on the "American Plan" and government actions against strikers, see Dawley, *Changing the World*, 262–63 and 324.

the Republican Party. In the meantime, the Democratic Party was focused on capturing the allegiance of the reactionary "solid South" with its determination to preserve racial segregation. In terms of party politics, progressives had little effect through the 1920s.[25]

Was the prosperity brought on by the corporatist regulatory state real enough that Americans should have given so much confidence to its Republican practitioners? On the surface it seemed to be the case in the 1920s. Ownership in consumer goods such as cars and radios soared; their production provided tens of thousands of jobs for unskilled factory workers at decent wages. National chain stores and mail-order catalogs brought a wide range of consumer and household goods to all Americans. The real estate market boomed and housing starts accelerated dramatically. Yet, appearances were deceiving. The cost of living was rising even faster. The best estimates are that only one-third of Americans could afford even the cheapest home. The wages of unskilled and even skilled laborers steadily fell behind that cost of living as the top 1 percent of Americans dramatically increased their share of the wealth and the bottom 93 percent lost. By 1929 an estimated 60 percent of American families did not earn the $2,000 yearly wage needed to provide basic necessities. Wealth and welfare trickled up as Hoover and other Republican experts gave business a virtual free hand by enacting almost no new regulatory legislation in the 1920s. President Calvin Coolidge, after all, was famous for propounding that "The chief business of the American people is business."[26] The UMW had been sadly wrong in betting that in supporting Coolidge it would receive consideration in return from his administration.

The emphasis on the "corporate" in the corporate regulatory state also allowed business to keep large areas of social need—such as housing, education, social welfare generally—in the private sector. The women of the Woman's City Club (WCC) of Chicago lamented that while the country "has spent large sums of money on the promotion of scientific farming, the care of cattle, sheep and bees, on the development of commerce and manufacturing . . . [it] has taken no cognizance of the problem of housing its citizens." The insurance industry, professional organizations, and the AFL stymied all attempts to expand social insurance and health insurance. Social justice progressivism fell victim to the law of unintended consequences: there was indeed a stronger state, but how it functioned depended on who was in charge of that state. At least for much of the 1920s, the majority of Americans were content to let those in power design the corporate state, rather than move toward the social welfare one that many progressives had desired.[27]

---

25. For accounts of the attempts to keep a progressive movement alive and of the 1924 Progressive Party, see Nancy Unger, *Fighting Bob LaFollette: The Righteous Reformer* (Chapel Hill: University of North Carolina Press, 2000), 288–307, quote from 289–90; Rodgers, *Atlantic Crossings*, 315–16; Dawley, *Changing the World*, 323–30.

26. Rodgers, *Atlantic Crossings*, 381–82.

27. WCC quoted in Flanagan, *Seeing with Their Hearts*, 166. See also, Morton Keller, *Regulating a New Society: Public Policy and Social Change in America, 1900–1933* (Cambridge, MA: Harvard University Press, 1994), 196–209.

2. Bureaucratic Democracy

Perhaps even more disappointing to many progressives was how their work to craft a strong state in order to secure a common welfare instead produced a state that could be used against some groups of Americans. Many historians have castigated the progressives for creating a strong state that would be able to impinge upon personal and group liberties. The Red Scare activities and the Sacco and Vanzetti case easily provide evidence for such criticism. The Department of Justice's new Bureau of Intelligence, soon renamed the Federal Bureau of Investigation, organized government surveillance of individuals. The bureau put spies into the prison cells next to Sacco and Vanzetti and began its practice of compiling dossiers on any suspected agitators across the remainder of the twentieth century. With more powerful federal bureaucracies it was easier to deport suspected radical aliens and to restrict entry into the country without having to answer to anyone outside of the bureaucracy. In the waning time of the Wilson presidency, Assistant Secretary of Labor Louis Post had been able to use his position to cancel many deportation orders. The Harding administration had more compliant appointees.[28]

If the progressives' hope that a strong state would craft a more democratic society was not always realized, it was less their fault than that of other groups who wanted to use the state for their own purposes. Although many progressives had optimistically believed that publicizing the problems of American society would create a groundswell for adopting a welfare agenda, they discovered that the people could not be counted on to make the decisions that the progressives had hoped for. Moreover, publicity was a double-edged sword, depending on who was wielding it. The wartime discovery of the weak physical and mental state of draftees had given women progressives a temporary opportunity to promote health care funded by government. But after the war, eugenicists and racists publicized the writings of authors such as Madison Grant to promote restriction, outlaw miscegenation, and call for sterilization of "lesser" peoples. The prohibition movement also gained strength from the findings on army conscripts. No one denied the truth of these findings, but they gave the Anti-Saloon League ammunition to argue that health standards would be raised by eliminating alcohol. The league tapped into the antiurban and anti-immigrant feelings of many rural and native-born people, as well as southern racism, to push the Prohibition Amendment through Congress in late 1917 and its ratification only a little more than a year later.[29]

28. See Federal Bureau of Investigation, Surveillance Files on Nicola Sacco and Bartolomeo Vanzetti (Microfilm, 2 reels, File No, 61–126, Scholarly Resources); and Lucy Sayler, *Laws Harsh as Tigers: Chinese Immigrants and the Shaping of Modern Immigration Law* (Chapel Hill: University of North Carolina Press, 1995), 121, 136, and 134. See also, Paul Avrich, *Sacco and Vanzetti: The Anarchist Background* (Princeton, NJ: Princeton University Press, 1991).

29. Madison Grant, *The Passing of the Great Race, or The Racial Basis of European History* (New York: Charles Scribner's Sons, 1916); Lisa Lindquist Door, "'Arm in Arm': Gender, Eugenics, and Virginia's Racial Integrity Acts of the 1920s," *Journal of Women's History*, 11 (Spring 1999): 143–66; MacLean, *Behind the Mask of Chivalry*; and Keller, *Regulating a New Society*, 135–39.

Eugenicists, prohibitionists, and businessmen thus converted to new uses the wartime publicity machine that George Creel had boasted had reached into every corner of American society and welded "the people of the United States into one white-hot mass instinct." Edward Bernays, for example, left the CPI convinced that public relations "experts" could shape citizens' ideas to benefit whomever was most powerful. He and other men of the "new public relations" profession built a strong publicity machine to make information flow down from the top rather than up from the bottom and to help create a new domestic homogeneity. Publicity, as with the strong state, could be used by those in power to thwart what other groups of Americans wanted.[30]

3. The Vigilant Citizenry

The progressive faith in democracy was challenged by rabid nativism, the Prohibition Amendment, the failure of the child labor amendment, the use of government to repress dissent, and other events. The progressive ideal of a collective welfare had always coexisted uneasily with the ideal of individual freedom. Now many progressives discovered just how thin and porous the membrane was between the voluntary social morality advocated by Jane Addams as early as 1902 and the power of the state to coerce social conformity that had developed during the war and the Red Scare. Yet, their idea that a democratic society had to defend the rights of all Americans did make some headway, even in the face of other repressive actions.

The Defense of Civil Liberties

Groups of Americans rallied in the 1920s to defend civil liberties. One group of pacifists and progressives founded the American Civil Liberties Union in 1919 as a national watchdog against government intrusion on freedoms guaranteed by the Bill of Rights. At the same time, the Supreme Court justices began to reconsider the relationship between the 1st Amendment right to free speech and the 14th Amendment definitions of national citizenship. In 1925, Judges Oliver Wendell Holmes and Louis Brandeis dissented from the majority opinion upholding the conviction of the newspaper editor Benjamin Gitlow under a New York criminal anarchy act. Holmes declared that "the only meaning of free speech" was that those expressing any opinions had the right to put them before the public. Louis Brandeis concurred, referring back to the 1874 Court rulings on the application of the 14th Amendment to property rights. "I cannot believe," he wrote, "that the liberty guaranteed by the Fourteenth Amendment includes only liberty to acquire and enjoy property." Even the majority justices in the *Gitlow* decision cautioned the state to refrain from unreasonable restraints on free speech and press. One of the enduring results of the Progressive Era, thus, was that "by the 1930s, the 1st Amendment had a

---

30. Kevin Mattson, *Creating a Democratic Public: Urban Participatory Democracy During the Progressive Era* (University Park: Pennsylvania State University Press, 1998), 117, for Bernays as well as Bernays, *Crystalizing Public Opinion* (New York: Boni and Liveright, 1923). See Chapter 11 for Creel and the CPI.

place in American law and public discourse" much different from that of the beginning of the twentieth century. Freedom of speech became protected under the "liberty" protection of the 14th Amendment.[31] Despite the repressions and nativist legislation of the 1920s, progressivism had pushed the Court to redefine free speech as a protected aspect of a national American citizenship, rather than a product of state citizenship.

Democratic Education

Almost all progressives had identified education as absolutely vital to a democratic society. From large cities to small towns and across rural areas, progressives had undertaken reforms of the public school system. On the local level, teachers (often with the support of women's organizations) had struggled for the right to organize, to receive better pay and pensions, and to have a stronger voice in educational matters as experts in their own right. How much success they had varied across the country, so by the 1920s many women's organizations argued that a federal Department of Education was the next essential step in securing a democratic public education that would provide all children the opportunity to advance in life. Through the common experience of the public school system, they believed, all children would learn to see themselves as part of a collective citizenry. Only federal law, direction, and some federal funding would secure a common educational system because individual states would always resist education reforms. But when the Smith-Towner Act, drafted by the National Education Association in 1920, proposed to create such a department, these progressives learned how little agreement there was among Americans that education should be a collective national enterprise. The American Federal of Labor supported this proposal as a means to enhance access to education for the working class. But the NCWC fought it, fearing that it would damage Catholic parochial schools and become a vehicle for inculcating 100-percent Americanism. The fact that the Masons supported the bill as an anti-Catholic measure certainly enhanced their suspicions. Florence Kelley, a staunch advocate of state power, could not support the measure because it did not go far enough. It promised no federal government interference in how the states or localities ran their schools, which she believed would give a federal imprimatur to southern racism and segregation. The NCWC also argued that it was anti-American for threatening states' and local rights and impinging upon individual freedom, and as such, potentially socialistic. In the end, the opposition was strong enough to thwart passage of the legislation.[32]

---

31. Jane Addams, *Democracy and Social Ethics* (Urbana: University of Illinois Press, reprint edition, 2002); Keller, *Regulating a New Society*, 106–07 and 108; and Foner, *The Story of American Freedom*, 184–85, 191–92, Holmes and Brandeis quoted 184.

32. The WJCC, GFWC, NWTUL, and NLWV supported the bill. See Keller, *Regulating a New Society*, 44–52, for discussion of progressive education reform through the 1920s; Lynn Dumenil, "'The Insatiable Maw of Democracy': Antistatism and Education Reform in the 1920s," *Journal of American History*, 77 (September 1990): 499–524, 520 for Kelley; Foner, *The Story of American Freedom*, 191–92; and Moloney, *American Lay Catholic Groups*.

Removed from the controversy of the public school system, however, other proposals for the democratization of education were more successful. The idea that education could be an ongoing experience for protecting democracy was put into practice by a group of progressive men—historian James Harvey Robinson, Herbert Croly, Charles Beard, and John Dewey—who founded the New School for Social Research in New York in 1919. The New School was for adults. The founding idea was a very progressive one: it would be staffed by "experts" who would transmit knowledge to adult students, who in turn would apply that knowledge to their actions and decisions as democratic citizens.[33] The New School was to be staffed by "experts," mainly men who would lecture on any number of issues. Many women's organizations also turned to adult education for citizenship. On the local levels, women's city clubs organized citizenship classes for women, training them to teach other women about politics and elections. The League of Women Voters (LWV), founded in 1920 to replace the NAWSA, proposed to educate Americans about politics and also declared that its intention was to work for "measures which it believed were in the public interest." The Illinois chapter of the league declared that it was founded on the "unshakeable conviction that self-government should include all the people; that citizens need training for their responsibilities; that certain social problems moving into the area of government had long been of particular concern to women and still should have their special attention." Democracy, according to the LWV, was a "cooperative" process.[34]

The struggles in the Progressive Era and the 1920s over education illuminate how Americans came to think of schools as the definitive venue for inculcating American values and not just the place for acquiring knowledge. Moreover, these struggles reveal how the purpose of education came to be defined as providing something useful. Ever since the Progressive Era, various groups of Americans have struggled with each other both about what values should be taught by public schools—a struggle that seems never-ending in American society—and about what constitutes a "useful" education.

4. Practicing Democratic Citizenship

When it came to political citizenship, women had been the only group excluded from equal rights on the basis of a social construct. With the exceptions of Native American men (until full citizenship had been conferred) and Asian-born immigrant men, it was assumed that citizenship gave equal political standing to men. Between 1907 and 1922, female citizens who married noncitizen males were even

33. Kevin Mattson, "The Challenges of Democracy: James Harvey Robinson, the New History, and Adult Education for Citizenship," *The Journal of the Gilded Age and Progressive Era*, 2 (July 2003): 48–79. See also his explanation of how Robinson and Croly came to differ over the relationship between experts and students.

34. For general information on the LWV, see Kristi Andersen, *After Suffrage: Women in Partisan and Electoral Politics Before the New Deal* (Chicago: University of Chicago Press, 1996), 36, for "cooperative" process. For the Illinois league, see Illinois League of Women Voters, "Forty Years of Faith and Works," pamphlet at Chicago Historical Society, Illinois League of Women Voters Ms. Collection.

stripped of their citizenship, the assumption being that citizenship came through men. Since men had put all women into the category of private citizenship, women's entry into and ideas about political participation developed differently from those of men. And during the Progressive Era, groups of women had debated precisely what their relationship to the political party system should be. Should women participate in partisan politics, following the lead of the men controlling the parties, or should they practice nonpartisanship and vote for candidates according to their stand on specific issues?[35] In fact, true nonpartisanship was never really a path pursued by most women; even before suffrage, most women had aligned with a political party. Nevertheless, with suffrage, women had to grapple with a fully formed system that had only grudgingly allowed them in, and they were not united in how to go about this task.

Women and Party Politics

In 1924, Chicago progressive Harriet Vittum told social workers at a national meeting that they should engage in "precinct work" if they wanted to encourage their neighbors to vote for social welfare. She quoted Jane Addams as saying that women had to work for specific candidates because "you do not vote for issues, you vote for men." But neither the Republican nor the Democratic Party welcomed women as equal partners in the party and most of these men hoped that with suffrage attained women would keep quiet. In 1920, feminist Crystal Eastman predicted that when the amendment passed men would say, "Thank God, this everlasting woman's fight is over!" Women instead would say, "Now at last we can begin!" It did not take long for her prediction to see fruition. Attending the Republican Party Convention in June 1920, New York suffragist Mary Garrett Hay was congratulated by one of the men. When she asked what for, he replied "For placing your sex on an equal footing." She stiffly responded: "I haven't. They aren't'"[36]

Women saw three roads they might possibly take: they could acknowledge that the male-controlled party system would never give women equality and join the NWP; they could adopt complete nonpartisanship and support whichever party was willing to support a women's agenda; or, they could acknowledge partisan allegiance while continuing to work through their female organizations. The first route was troubling for most progressive women because the NWP was single-mindedly focused on passing an Equal Rights Amendment (ERA). Florence Kelley, the NWTUL, the LWV, and the Women's

---

35. Southern state laws that effectively disfranchised African Americans were local inventions that did not affect African Americans elsewhere and that is the distinction here. No group of citizens other than women after 1870 were disfranchised because of a perpetual social distinction, i.e., gender, race, ethnicity. Asian Americans born in the United States were citizens.

36. For Vittum and the Addams' quote, see Harriet Vittum, "Politics from the Social Point of View," *Proceedings of the National Conference of Social Work* (June 25–July 2, 1924): 422–28, a copy of which can be found at http://www.uic.edu/jaddams/hull/urbanexp/contents.htm. For women and political parties after suffrage, see Andersen, *After Suffrage*; Flanagan, *Seeing with Their Hearts*; and various essays in Melanie Gustafson, Kristie Miller, and Elisabeth Israels Perry, *We Have Come to Stay: American Women and Political Parties, 1880–1960* (Albuquerque: University of New Mexico Press, 1999). Eastman and Hay quoted in Elisabeth I. Perry, "Defying the Party Whip: Mary Garrett Hay and the Republican Party, 1917–1920," in ibid., 97 and 99 respectively.

Bureau opposed the ERA, fearing it would negate the working-women reforms they had accomplished, and that it would divide activist women into
opposing camps.[37] The second route also had its problems. By the time the suffrage amendment passed, most women had already declared themselves
members of a party, but men categorically refused to accept women as equal
partners while simultaneously demanding that women faithfully support the
party platform and candidates. As suffragist turned political activist Mary
Garrett Hay discovered, men were not willing to give women any power inside the party while simultaneously demanding that women give strict obedi-
ence to the party. When Hay opposed a party nominee who refused to support
women's issues, despite her obvious party partisanship, she was quickly os-
tracized by the men of the party for not being loyal.[38]

Most women opted for the third route. The fierce male resistance to women
suffrage and refusal of either party to support a women's agenda was discour-
aging. With rare exceptions women found it very difficult to change men's
minds after suffrage. One of the few women elected to the Illinois legislature in
the 1920s reported that most of women's proposed legislation failed, she was
told by a fellow legislator, because "the women asked too much." As she informed the Woman's City Club of Chicago, women had advanced just twelve
to fourteen bills upon which they agreed; men had proposed 1,300 bills in the
same legislative sessions! Some states even refused to amend their state consti-
tutions that specifically banned women from holding state legislative offices.
By 1931 there would be only 146 women in state legislatures.[39]

So, while women joined the parties, they also organized the Women's Joint
Congressional Committee (WJCC) in 1920 to monitor national congressional activities, keep member organizations updated on the progress of desired legislation, and lobby for their legislation. Their efforts had results. New legislation
was passed further regulating packing houses and stockyards (1921), outlawing
using "fillers" in milk (1923), and a 1922 amendment to the Federal Water Power
Act prohibited private interests from acquiring water rights in national parks.
Women also fought to maintain the Women's and Children's Bureaus inside the
Department of Labor. They sensed correctly that without these bureaus their
social justice agenda could never be advanced, and that these bureaus could be a
source of political power for women. The leadership and staffing of these
bureaus in the 1920s show how they became a power base for progressive
women well into the New Deal era.[40]

Women's politics into the 1920s had mixed results for cross-race alliances.
As part of its campaign for full legal equality, the NWP did propose legislation

37. Nancy F. Cott, "Feminist Politics in the 1920s: The National Woman's Party," *Journal of American History,* 71 (June 1984): 43–68 and Wendy Sarvasy, "Beyond the Difference Versus Equality Policy Debate: Postsuffrage Feminism, Citizenship, and the Quest for a Feminist Welfare State," *Signs*
(Winter 1992).

38. Perry, "Defying the Party Whip."

39. Woman's City Club of Chicago, *Bulletin* (July–August 1923) and Andersen, *After Suffrage,*
16–17.

40. See Muncy, *Creating a Female Dominion;* Lindenmeyer, *"A Right to Childhood";* Andersen,
After Suffrage, 155, for successful legislative efforts; and Susan Ware, *Beyond Suffrage: Women in the
New Deal* (Cambridge, MA: Harvard University Press, 1981).

to punish those states that would not allow African American women to vote, but it left other kinds of racial discrimination off of its agenda. Ida B. Wells-Barnett had attended the founding convention of the LVW and local-level leagues of African American women flourished, although they were racially segregated. The NACW eventually became part of the WJCC. Their own Progressive Era experiences, however, gave African American women the power and confidence to claim a place in Republican Party politics across the 1920s. Despite that party's own racist stances, African American women demonstrated that they were "in politics to stay." Both white and black women agreed with socialist Estelle Lindsey's point that "suffrage without holding office [was] like apple pie with the apples left out." But women's desires to win public office had scant success across the 1920s as the men controlling the political parties refused them equal access to the system.[41]

Citizen Organization

The Progressive Era had taught all Americans to organize if they wanted a voice in an increasingly complex democratic society. One reason why citizen organizations are such a significant feature of American society and politics is the absence of enduring third parties. Most Western democracies through the twentieth century have sustained labor parties, social democratic parties, green parties, socialist parties, and religious-based parties. These parties are organized to pursue a specific political ideology, thereby giving European voters, for example, more options to work through a party that they believe stands for their interests. If the United States had had a parliamentary system of voting for the party rather than the man in presidential elections, with proportional voting, the Progressive Party's 27 percent of the vote in 1912 and 17 percent in 1924 could have established the party as a real presence in Congress. Eugene Debs' 6 percent of the vote in the 1912 election might have given the socialists a few more seats in Congress. As it was, the presidential system, the constitutional constraints of the electoral college system, and universal white male suffrage from the 1840s combined to stabilize the American two-party system.[42]

---

41. For the NWP, see Cott, "Feminist Politics in the 1920s"; see also, Rosalyn Terborg-Penn, "Discontented Black Feminists: Prelude and Postscript to Passage of the Nineteenth Amendment," in *Decades of Discontent: The Woman's Movement, 1920–1940*, Lois Scharf and Joan M. Jensen, eds. (Westport, CT: Greenwood Press, 1983), 261–78; and Evelyn Brooks Higginbotham, "In Politics to Stay: Black Women Leaders and Party Politics in the 1920s," in *Women, Politics, and Change*, Louise Tilly and Patricia Gurin, eds. (New York: Russell Sage Foundation, 1990), 199–220. For more on the political work of Wells-Barnett, see Patricia Schechter, *Ida B. Wells-Barnett and American Reform, 1880-1930* (Chapel Hill: University of North Carolina Press, 2001). For Lindsey, see Sherry Katz, "Redefining 'the Political': Socialist Women and Party Politics in California, 1900–1920," in Gustafson, et al., *We Have Come to Stay*, 23.

42. The winning candidate in the presidential election must secure over 50 percent of the votes in the electoral college, making it difficult for third parties to win. This also encourages one of the two parties to incorporate a third party into it, such as the Democrats did with the Populists in 1896. Parliamentary and proportional systems would have given the Progressive Party seats in Congress and quite possibly given them a role in a coalition government. The fact that most white men were already voters by the Progressive Era, meant that the United States never had a strong labor party to fight for working-class suffrage, as had been the case in Europe.

Because most progressive political reforms were not designed to change the political system, which would have required serious constitutional amendments, but to urge people to organize in order to control the politicians and their decisions, interest-group politics was the result. Early professional groups such as the AMA, the National Association of Manufacturers (NAM), the American Dairy Association, the AFL as a lobbying organization as well as a union group, civic organizations such as the National Municipal League, women's groups such as the NCL and NWTUL, and ethno-religious organizations such as the NCWC, NAACP, and the National Urban League were the Progressive Era manifestations of this interest-group politics. Moreover, by the Progressive Era the political party system itself was too entrenched to be changed and so many progressives chose the interest-group route to a better democracy. The People's Institute and the Social Centers Movement, the enormous variety of clubs and civic associations, were all the means by which Americans sought to insert themselves into the political system along with the parties. They hoped, and believed, that these organizations would enhance citizenship and civil society and make the democratic system itself more open to popular participation.[43]

---

43. Some sense of the extent of such organization can be found in Luther Gulick, "Voluntary Organizations that Promote Better Government and Citizenship," *Annals of the American Academy of Political and Social Science*, 105 (January 1923): 71–75. But this only lists major white male organizations. For African Americans, see Heathcott, "Black Archipelago," 705–36; Arvarh Strickland, *The History of the Chicago Urban League* (Urbana: University of Illinois, 1966; reprint, 2001); Laura Tuennerman-Kaplan, *Helping Others, Helping Ourselves: Power, Giving and Community Identity in Cleveland, Ohio, 1880–1930* (Kent, OH: Kent State University Press, 2001), which also contains information on Italian and Jewish organizing in the city; Richard Thomas, *Life for Us Is What We Make It: Building Black Community in Detroit, 1915–1945* (Bloomington: Indiana University Press, 1991); and Dolores Greenberg, "Reconstructing Race and Protest: Environmental Justice in New York City," *Environmental History*, 5 (April 2000): 223–50.

Conclusion
An Imperfect World

Injustice anywhere is a threat to justice everywhere.
—MARTIN LUTHER KING, 1963

MARTIN LUTHER KING wrote these words while sitting in jail in Birmingham, Alabama almost 100 years after the end of slavery. His call for universal justice and for direct action to overturn racism, as well as his expressed belief in democracy, could have been written during the Progressive Era. If racial segregation and discrimination still existed in 1963, as well as many other injustices that the progressives had fought to eliminate, how do we evaluate the Progressive Era? Was it a success or a failure? Did it end or was it just a beginning?

To begin this book in the 1890s and close it in the 1920s is to a great extent an arbitrary decision. No single event began progressivism, as no event ended it. Even designating these dates as an era, and labeling it as such, suggests a temporally limited historical period. Historians do always like to have beginning and ending dates, however, and without them a book would never finish. This book has aimed at exploring how across these four decades certain groups and their ideas came into public discussion and how by implementing them into public policy they reformed the social, political, and economic institutions of the United States in ways that were obvious by the mid-1920s. It has explored how these ideas were translated into actions, and which progressive reform proposals succeeded and others failed.

To answer one obvious question, yes, America was reformed in this time period. Federal government was strengthened and the presidency began to accumulate more power to determine the country's political and economic course. Citizenship was increasingly defined as national citizenship. Laissez faire liberal ideals of government, economics, and society gave way to a belief that democratic society had to work for everyone in it. Most Americans accepted that it was the government's job to help regulate the economy and to provide at least a modicum of protections for all people.

Progressive reforms resulted in no one group in the country any longer being allowed to control the destiny of everyone else. They put significant brakes
on rapacious capitalism and its exploitation of the country's natural resources.
Citizens adopted an activist and positive stance toward government. Special-
interest lobbying gave progressive groups entree into the political system that
they would otherwise not have had, and that structure characterizes American
politics today. Some of those groups, such as the NCL, the GFWC, the NAACP,
and the National Civic Federation, still exist and the contemporary urban landscape is prolific with city clubs and civic associations, housing associations, and
neighborhood groups, many of which survive from the Progressive Era.

Progressivism also made Americans aware that they were connected to one
another and that they had to accept at least a modicum of social responsibility
for other people. Individualism was thereafter balanced against a sense of social responsibility in public discourse and in policy-making.

Progressivism also thrust the United States into the world. The sense of internationalism promoted by groups of progressives meant that, even when
they objected to many foreign-policy initiatives, Americans had at least been
forced out of isolation and into seeing that they were connected. The women's
international peace movement, the Pan-African movement, and international
workers organizations became part of the global political landscape in which
Americans participated.

Yet, progressivism only went so far in reforming the country. Significant social problems were left unresolved. It took the massive depression begun in
1929 to push government and the American people to accept more government responsibility for social welfare. Only then did some progressive measures such as old-age pensions, no child labor, and minimum wage and maxi-
mum hours laws become reality. Without these issues having been raised
earlier, however, and without the women of the Children's and Women's Bureaus, the progress of the New Deal would have been undoubtedly different.
Even when such social protections were enacted, they never went nearly as far
as the social justice progressives had wanted. And private enterprise continued to resist government intrusion too far into welfare issues such as housing.

One of progressivism's most conspicuous failures was in not resolving the
problem of racism in American society. In some measure, progressives would
have faced formidable structural obstacles to attempt this. States' rights arguments, and the Supreme Court's upholding of these rights, made it virtually
impossible to attack legalized segregation and discrimination. But it is also
true that most white progressives failed black Americans by not mounting a
strong challenge to legalized segregation and not demanding their social and
economic integration into society. Most progressives simply could not get past
their own racism. They rejected theories of innate racial inferiority, but took
comfort in believing that equality would happen eventually, once African
Americans were better prepared for the responsibilities of citizenship. Many
progressives were also unable, or unwilling, to fight strenuously to bring all
people of color into equal citizenship or to confront an imperialistic foreign
policy based on ideas of racial superiority.

Progressives were also unable to counter other trends in American society.
They could not stop immigration restriction nor reactionary antiprogressive

movements such as 100 percent Americanism. Many Americans willingly accepted government regulation and some measure of social welfare, but they remained convinced that there were specific characteristics that defined who was an American. These were long-held ideas in the United States that many people were unwilling to surrender.

World War I probably harmed the course of a progressive movement more than anything else. Once the United States entered war, the idea of loyalty produced the corresponding reaction of dissent and repression. Progressives were caught in the middle. The best they believed they could hope for was that by remaining loyal to their country, even if they remained unconvinced about the righteousness of the war, international progressivism would result. Their hopes were dashed and repression of civil liberties remained a constant problem in the aftermath.

Progressives never set out to change the structure of American society. They were not revolutionaries but reformers and regulators. They did not object to capitalism per se as an economic system; they objected to how it was practiced and how it harmed large segments of American society. They also objected to the undemocratic idea that one or two groups could determine the fate of everyone else and they decried the political corruption that accompanied this process. The vast majority of Americans had agreed with them that change was needed. The enormity of change that would have been needed to create the socially just democratic society that many progressives wanted would have daunted even the most committed reformer. The fact is, the majority of Americans seemed satisfied by the 1920s that economic regulation had sufficiently reformed society to make it work better for more, if not all, Americans. They were willing to accept a certain level of injustice, most especially when they did not feel it touching themselves. They also remained convinced that the United States was the best democracy in the world and rejected any ongoing criticism of it.

As this book depicts, progressivism as both idea and ideal did not stop in the 1920s. The concept of social justice in a democratic society is still being debated. Although the majority of Americans agree that social justice should be part of democracy, not all Americans agree that it is the job of government to provide for it. The ideal of individualism has never faded from American society, so that some Americans remain suspicious that social welfare means "handouts" to the undeserving who have not tried hard enough to make it on their own. The debate continues as to whether the economic structure and prejudice against certain groups is the cause of poverty, homelessness, unemployment, etc., or whether it is individual failure to take advantage of the opportunities offered by capitalism. The early twenty-first century debate over whether to privatize social security is rooted in the idea that capitalism and private enterprise, not government, is the best means to provide for old-age security. The United States remains the only industrialized country without a national health care system.

But, the argument goes beyond that of how best to secure pensions or health care. It returns Americans to the disagreements of the Progressive Era over individualism versus social responsibility. That is the argument that the social justice progressives never quite won. They never successfully convinced

Americans that social responsibility had to come before individual needs in order to create a good democratic society. Since the Progressive Era, the United States has vacillated between periods that emphasize social responsibility and those that emphasize individualism.

The Progressive Era also inextricably linked democracy and capitalism in the minds of most Americans, although not all progressives intended that as an outcome of their internationalism. Since the Progressive Era all foreign-policy developments have been undertaken with those two ideas as one inseparable concept. When Colin Powell appeared before the U.S. Senate on January 17, 2001, for hearings on his nomination as secretary of state his opening remarks suggested just that. Among his declarations were the following statements: "I have seen more and more nations moving on to the path of democracy and the free enterprise system." "Democracy and free markets work, and the world knows it." In the United States, the ideas of social democracy or industrial democracy never gained a foothold as they did all across western Europe.

Finally, the Progressive Era did settle the question that citizenship was national, not local. By making citizenship national, the progressives opened the door for the federal government to make laws guaranteeing and protecting equal rights of citizenship. On the other hand, the debates over citizenship also produced the equation of American with certain ways of thinking and acting. The concept of "un-American" thinking, speech, and behavior entered into the national consciousness. It even appeared in government as the U.S. House of Representatives formed a House Committee on UnAmerican Activities (HUAC) in 1938, which was not disbanded until the 1970s.

Progressivism did not create a perfect world. Some of its results can seem dubious at best in terms of whether they were progress. But progressives believed that people possessed the intelligence and the will to continue to fashion a good democratic society. Despite its shortcomings, progressivism made the United States by the mid-1920s a far more orderly, well-regulated, and fairer society than it had been in the 1890s.

INDEX